D0076322

1/28/2020

The Crimean War: 1853–1856

MODERN WARS

Series editor: Hew Strachan, Chichele Professor of the History of War, All Souls College, University of Oxford (UK)

Advisory editor: Michael Howard, Emeritus Fellow of All Souls College, University of Oxford (UK)

Covering the period from 1792 to the present day, the *Modern Wars* series explores the global development of modern war. Military history is increasingly an integrated part of 'total history', and yet this is not always reflected in the literature. *Modern Wars* addresses this need, offering well-rounded and balanced synoptic accounts of the major conflicts of the modern period. Each volume recognizes not only the military but also the diplomatic, political, social, economic and ideological contexts of these wars. The result is a series that ensures a genuine integration of the military history with history as a whole.

Published:

The South African War, Bill Nasson (1999)

The Crimean War, Winfried Baumgart (1999)

Thunder in the East, Evan Mawdsley (2005)

Allies in War, Mark A. Stoler (2005)

The First World War (Second Edition), Holger Herwig (2014)

The Wars of German Unification (Second Edition), Dennis Showalter (2015)

Thunder in the East (Second Edition), Evan Mawdsley (2015)

New Order Diplomacy, Martin Folly (2015)

The Crimean War (Second Edition), Winfried Baumgart (2020)

Forthcoming:

The British Raj at War, Douglas Peers (2021)

The Crimean War: 1853–1856

2nd Edition

Winfried Baumgart

BLOOMSBURY ACADEMIC
LONDON • NEW YORK • OXFORD • NEW DELHI • SYDNEY

BLOOMSBURY ACADEMIC
Bloomsbury Publishing Plc
50 Bedford Square, London, WC1B 3DP, UK
1385 Broadway, New York, NY 10018, USA

BLOOMSBURY, BLOOMSBURY ACADEMIC and the Diana logo are trademarks
of Bloomsbury Publishing Plc

First published in Great Britain 2020

Copyright © Winfried Baumgart, 2020

Winfried Baumgart has asserted his right under the Copyright, Designs and Patents Act,
1988, to be identified as Author of this work.

Cover design by Tjaša Krivec
Cover image: Consultation about the state of Turkey
(© John Leech/Universitätsbibliothek Heidelberg)

All rights reserved. No part of this publication may be reproduced or transmitted
in any form or by any means, electronic or mechanical, including photocopying,
recording, or any information storage or retrieval system, without prior permission
in writing from the publishers.

Bloomsbury Publishing Plc does not have any control over, or responsibility for, any
third-party websites referred to in this book. All internet addresses given in this
book were correct at the time of going to press. The editor and publisher regret
any inconvenience caused if addresses have changed or sites have ceased to
exist, but can accept no responsibility for any such changes.

A catalogue record for this book is available from the British Library.

A catalog record for this book is available from the Library of Congress.

ISBN: PB: 978-1-3500-8343-1
       HB: 978-1-3500-8344-8
       ePDF: 978-1-3500-8345-5
       eBook: 978-1-3500-8346-2

Series: Modern Wars

Typeset by RefineCatch Limited, Bungay, Suffolk

Printed and bound in Great Britain

To find out more about our authors and books visit www.bloomsbury.com
and sign up for our newsletters.

CONTENTS

ILLUSTRATIONS

MAPS

GENERAL EDITOR'S PREFACE

The Crimean War is poorly named. The possession of the Black Sea peninsula was never at issue, nor was the war fought exclusively within it. Russia's bid for suzerainty over Turkey, which precipitated the conflict, was at first fought out on the Danube and later extended to the Caucasus. It was the French and British who decided to focus their land operations on the Crimea. The legacy to the English language – in William Howard Russell's despatches to *The Times* and Alfred, Lord Tennyson's poetry – is at least one reason why subsequent British perspectives have remained so narrowly focused. But the navy, not the army, was Britain's primary striking force in European warfare in 1854, and not least as a result of these maritime capabilities the war was extended into the Baltic, the White Sea and even the Pacific.

Winfried Baumgart's title cannot avoid the geographical confines, but the book's contents range over all the war's theatres. The wider implications lead him to conclude that, if the fighting had carried on during 1856, 'The First World War would then have taken place 60 years earlier.' Although Britain began the war with comparatively limited objectives, when Palmerston became Prime Minister in 1855 he saw 'the real object of the war' as being 'to curb the aggressive ambition of Russia'. He tried to create an alliance which would constitute 'a long line of circumvallation' so as to curb the westward expansion of the Tsarist Empire. In France, Napoleon III was anxious to exploit the opportunity to reshuffle most of the major issues of European politics, from Poland to Italy, and from Switzerland to Sweden. In doing so he introduced the vocabulary of nationalism to international relations, and gave voice to the secondary as well as the great powers of Europe. Moreover, London's discomfiture threatened to become Washington's opportunity. The great war which did not happen in the nineteenth century, that between Britain and the United States for control of North America and the Western hemisphere, could have merged with that between Britain and Russia for mastery in the Mediterranean and Asia.

All these factors strained the Concert of Europe to breaking point, but in the event the war was not fought on a broad European front; it remained confined to theatres on the peripheries only of two continents, Europe and Asia; and ultimately in 1856 the great powers sat down in congress to broker a peace that – even if short of the ambition of Vienna – still paid obeisance to the ideas of 1815. Thus diplomacy never lost its control over the use of war as an instrument in power politics. It was for this reason above all that the conflict remained limited, that the fighting never assumed (in the vocabulary of Clausewitz) its own logic as well as its own grammar. Professor Baumgart is a master of the diplomatic correspondence which the war generated. He shows above all how the power that stood to lose most from the breakdown of the Concert of Europe, Austria, proved particularly adroit in her pursuit of peace and in her resistance to revolution as an instrument of war. She mobilized her army not as a preliminary to war but as an adjunct to her foreign policy, and in the process levered Russia out of the Danubian Principalities.

These were the actions of a conservative, not a revisionist, power. Nonetheless, Professor Baumgart's study points forward more than it points backwards. If the Crimean War was in some respects a cabinet war, the cabinets were not always in control. In Britain in particular, opinion, especially as articulated by *The Times*, had a vital role in shaping and determining policy. In France, Napoleon's espousal of both nationalism and revolution had similarly populist undertones. Even states with more backward economies and less literate populations proved not insensitive to the pressures of street politics: the Ottoman Empire itself responded to the call for a Holy War.

The pointers to 1914 are not simply political, they are also military. The armies of 1854 saw the fighting on land as the tactical test of the rifle, newly issued in place of the smooth-bore musket, and possessed of a range and power of penetration which in due course would require infantry to use cover and to disperse into looser formations. Even in the Crimea itself, static, trench warfare prevailed. This was more a response to the siege of Sevastopol than to the rifle, but it meant that artillery dominated the conduct of the land war. The techniques of long, destructive bombardments, the reactions of the Russians in defence, and the counters of the allies in attack all prefigure the experiences of 1916.

In one very important respect, however, the fighting in the Crimea did not anticipate that of the First World War. It did not institutionalize the mass army. Professor Baumgart computes that Russia had 1.1 million men under arms in 1853, and by 1856 had called up a total of over two million. Britain and France put a maximum of only 400,000 soldiers into the field, and yet they won the war. Moreover, even on the battlefield itself, most notably at Inkerman, the big battalions did not always prevail. Russia failed, as Miliutin realized at the time, in part because her army had to be equipped with the latest weaponry and that in turn depended on industrialization. For the time being the already industrialized powers concluded that new technology could be a supplement to professional standards of training and (in the British case) antiquated methods of recruiting, rather than a force multiplier for a conscript army based on a large reserve. Moreover, the mass army required the conquest of cholera and typhus to ensure its health, and the advent of the railway to sustain its logistical support. In the Crimea, disease remained the biggest killer and maritime communications still prevailed over land routes.

Yet the diminishing utility of navies in affecting the course of continental warfare was only too evident. Maritime operations in the Baltic and elsewhere achieved little in military terms. In the Crimea itself, Russian coastal batteries prevailed over warships. Here too technology provided some solutions. Both steam and screw came of age in the Mediterranean and the Black Sea. As significant was their potential marriage to armour: at Kinburn in the Black Sea and at Sveaborg in the Baltic, ironclad floating batteries shattered shore defences. Ideas also played their part. The notion of blockade as an instrument of economic warfare between industrialized powers was enshrined in international law in 1856 in the Treaty of Paris. Much of its thrust presumed British neutrality, and was designed to preserve Britain's trading position in the event of a European war between other parties. However, the Royal Navy's actual conduct of coastal operations showed it was as willing to engage civilian targets as the ultimate logic of a blockading strategy implied.

To suggest a straight line from 1854 to 1914 would be grotesque in its oversimplification and use of hindsight, yet it remains remarkable that military historians, particularly in the English language, have been reluctant to look at the Crimean War in terms of modernity, preferring instead to refer to the American Civil War. The battlefield technologies of the latter were first deployed in the former. Not only for that reason but also for many others, as Professor Baumgart shows, it is inappropriate to approach the Crimean War with preconceptions derived from those of the Napoleonic Wars and thus of half a century earlier.

Hew Strachan

PREFACE TO THE FIRST EDITION

The Crimean War is the only general war of European dimensions in the 100 years between the Napoleonic Wars and the First World War. Not only were the five great European powers directly or indirectly (Austria, Prussia) involved in it; but all the secondary states of Europe that had stayed neutral – from Sweden to Greece and Sicily, from the German Confederation to Portugal – had to face the issue of joining in or sitting precariously on the fence. The war that was seemingly confined to the Crimea contained numerous germs of a worldwide conflict: from the point of view of military strategy, it was the first trench war of modern history; on the level of arms technology, it pushed on the development of new instruments of war: the Minié rifle, mines, armoured ships; in terms of war economy, it prefigured numerous methods of economic warfare of the wars of the twentieth century; geographically speaking, there were secondary theatres of war not only in northern Europe, in the Baltic and in the White Sea, but also in the Pacific; the political ramifications even extended to the American continent since it led to sharp altercations between Britain and the United States; it even reached the Australian continent which suffered for months from an invasion scare.

The most important question emanating from such a *tour d'horizon* is why did the Crimean War not evolve into a world war? Why was world peace maintained? In this respect the Crimean War must be regarded as an unfinished or unfought world war and as a stepping stone leading indirectly and directly to the First World War. Viewed in this light the most important question about the history of international relations between 1856 and 1914 is how was the outbreak of a world war prevented in those decades? In looking for an answer to this question, attention is naturally drawn to the way the European Concert of the great powers was able to maintain peace, to its crisis management by way of international congresses and conferences and to the many war-in-sight crises after 1856. The investigation of the devious road leading to the First World War can receive a fresh impulse not by putting the question of why did the First World War break out in 1914, but by asking why did it not break out sooner?

The intention of this small book is, first of all, to give a comprehensive and succinct picture of the more important aspects of the Crimean War, and, secondly, to strike the balance of 160 years of research on it. Although the series in which this book is published is primarily devoted to the history of warfare, the Crimean War is not only seen as a military contest between two warring factions, but is also set in its political context. In this respect, the author has the advantage of drawing from his experience of editing a multi-volume documentation of the Crimean War. The war is set in the framework of the most complicated international issue of the nineteenth century: the Eastern question. As it was not only fought on the battlefield, but also around the green table where representatives of the belligerents and non-belligerents were meeting throughout the war, a chapter is devoted to the diplomatic battle. All the belligerents had specific war aims. These are investigated, as are the attitudes of the two German great powers, Austria and Prussia, which were pressed hard by each war camp to join its side. Austria exerted great military pains to mobilize her army and to keep the two camps away from the Balkans. Austria's military efforts forced the two sides to meet each other on the periphery of Europe, on the Crimean peninsula.

Although all the secondary powers of Europe had, sooner or later, to make up their minds as to which of the two camps to join, limitations of space forbid an investigation of the situation of each of them. Therefore a selection is made of those nearest geographically to the actual theatres of war – Sweden, Greece, the minor German states – and of those which had a special military and political potential – Spain and the United States. Finally attention is paid to the military arsenal, the armies and navies, of the five belligerent powers, Russia on one side, France, Great Britain, Turkey and Sardinia on the other.

The major part of the book is devoted to the theatres of the war: the Danube front, the Crimea, the Baltic, the Caucasus and finally the White Sea and the Pacific – areas which clearly indicate the dimensions of the conflict and the aspects it would have assumed, if the Tsar had not made up his mind in January 1856 to give up the war for lost.

It is typical of many books on the military history of the Crimean War that they devote most or all of their attention to the Crimea only. It was certainly the most important theatre of war where the military decision was to be enforced. This book attempts to devote adequate space to all the other secondary and minor theatres which actually existed.

Another characteristic typical of virtually all books on the military history of the war is that they base their accounts primarily on the viewpoint of one of the major belligerents – Russia, France or Great Britain. It seems that authors drew their knowledge almost exclusively from one national source only – Totleben and Bogdanovič in the case of Russia, Bazancourt in the case of France, and Kinglake in that of Britain. Even modern accounts of one of the major battles and of the siege of Sevastopol create the impression that the authors must have described wholly different battles and subjects. The author of this book therefore attempts to give a bird's-eye view of the warfare, and to draw a balance sheet of more than one century and a half of historical research on the Crimean War.

PREFACE TO THE SECOND EDITION

The second edition has been revised in manifold ways: although the core of the book was retained, all chapters were brought up to date, especially in the footnotes and the annotated bibliography, in view of the stupendous amount of books and articles (more than fifty were used) that were published in the twenty years that have elapsed since the first edition. A completely new chapter (no. 19) was added about the medical services on both sides of the war fronts, Allied and Russian, in conformity with the multifaceted and multinational approach of the book. The final chapter (20), also new, offers a bird's-eye view of Crimean history from 1856 to the present. As the structure of the book was not changed, a chronological table was added that epitomizes the most important aspects of the diplomatic and military events month by month from 1853 to 1856. Another new addition to the book are the twenty-one cartoons and photographs which liven up the text in a condensed form. Two more geographical maps were added to the existing nine. The footnotes are numbered consecutively and placed at the end of the text. The bibliography (monographs, published documents, articles) has been completely revamped and made more user-friendly by being placed at the end of the book in strict alphabetical order.

The second edition now mirrors more than 160 years of unabated research about that most curious historical event – the Crimean War.

PART ONE

Origins and Diplomacy of the War

1

The real cause of the war –
the Eastern Question

The Crimean War is a direct outgrowth of the so-called Eastern Question. This international issue preoccupied the chancelleries of the European great powers for fully a century – from the Greek struggle for independence in the 1820s until the aftermath of the First World War. Although, as far as Turkey is concerned, it could be regarded as formally closed after that war, it survives until the present day in a number of related international problems in the Near East, for example in the struggle about Palestine and in today's Arab–Israeli and Syrian conflicts; in the tensions between Greece and Turkey about territorial waters and offshore islands; in the related conflict about Cyprus; in the various tensions in the Balkans, amongst them the break-up of Yugoslavia; in the Kurdish problem; and in the manifold disputes in the Caucasus. No other diplomatic question occupied international relations in the nineteenth century with such constancy and with so much inextricable tension as the Eastern Question. In terms of statistics it produced a Russo-Turkish war every twenty or twenty-five years in the period between Peter the Great and the Eastern crisis of 1875–8. In the nineteenth century there were such wars in 1806, 1828, 1853 and 1877. Almost twenty years later a war did not break out, in spite of the Armenian massacres of 1895–6, because Russia's attention was at that time focused on the Far East. Twenty years after that the two Balkan wars which led directly to the First World War broke out, pointing once more to the highly explosive character of the Eastern Question.

Each of these Russo-Turkish wars ended, with the exception of the Crimean War, with victory for Russia and a corresponding loss of territory by Turkey. At the beginning of the eighteenth century the Black Sea was a Turkish inland sea surrounded on all sides by Turkish-held territory. Turkey had to give up this area bit by bit until 200 years later she only retained the southern shores of the Black Sea, including, however, the strategic Straits – Russia's old dream.

What does the Eastern Question mean? Put in a nutshell, it is the aggregate of all the problems connected with the withdrawal and the rollback of the Ottoman Empire from the areas which it had conquered since 1354 in

Europe, Africa and Asia. In terms of geography it was a huge and imposing empire that the Ottoman sultans had hammered together on these three continents through war and conquest. The climax of their external power was reached in the seventeenth century. Their gradual retreat began with the defeat in 1683 at the siege of Vienna and with the Peace of Karlowitz in 1699, which for the first time forced the Turks to give up territory (Hungary and Transylvania) which they had conquered. During the course of the eighteenth and nineteenth centuries and as a consequence of the First World War the Ottoman Empire gave up the whole Balkan peninsula except a small stretch round Adrianople, the territories on the northern shore of the Black Sea with the Crimea in the centre, the Caucasus region, North Africa from Algeria to Egypt, the whole Arab peninsula and Mesopotamia up to the Persian Gulf.

The Eastern Question only became an international problem in the 1820s when all of the five European great powers became interested in it. In the preceding decades only the two neighbouring powers, Russia and Austria, profited from the withdrawal of the Ottoman Empire.

Looking into the causes of the Eastern Question, three main layers can be discerned: the internal decay of the Ottoman Empire; its weakening through the explosive nationalism which the Balkan peoples developed in the nineteenth century – followed by the peoples in the Near East and North Africa in the twentieth century – all of whom struggled to free themselves from Turkish dominion; and finally the intervention of the European great powers in this process of disintegration.

For the first two causes a few remarks must suffice. There is first of all the geographical overstraining which resulted from the Ottoman conquests: in the end it became more and more difficult to control the periphery from the centre. Next there is the heterogeneous ethnic and religious composition of the conquered peoples. Eventually the Turks as the master race made up only a third of the whole population. The economic structure of the empire was weak, the administration became more and more inefficient and venality and corruption were widespread at all levels. The system of collecting taxes was harsh and arbitrary and constantly led to unrest. At the top of the empire's administration the system of succession degenerated when the eldest member of the Sultan's family succeeded to the throne having waded through a welter of blood and murder. The army became increasingly unruly and unwieldy. The crack unit of janissaries developed as a state within the state. In the second half of the eighteenth century the Sultan and his government started reforms. In 1826 the rebellious janissaries, amounting to several thousands, were literally wiped out in one night. British and Prussian officers were engaged to reform the army. In 1839 the Sultan issued a *firman* decreeing legal equality of Muslims and non-Muslims (rayahs), but in practice this important edict existed only on paper and the other reforms did not go beneath the surface of the problems.

In addition to these symptoms of internal decay there was the disrupting force of nationalism, which permeated the Balkan peoples from the beginning of the nineteenth century. The Serbs were the first to wrest one piece of autonomy after another from the Turks until in 1878 they obtained their independence under the guarantee of Europe. The Greeks followed suit, and, after a prolonged war in which the European powers intervened, became independent in 1830 under the protection of Russia, France and Britain. The Rumanians, first with the help of the Russians, then after the Crimean War aided by France and exploiting dissension among the great powers, obtained self-government step by step until they, too, became independent in 1878.

The third main cause of the disruption of the Ottoman Empire, probably the decisive one, was the intervention of the European great powers. As already mentioned, the destiny of the Ottoman Empire, which was spread over three continents and held, along with the Turkish Straits, the strategic routes to Asia, possessing the isthmus of Suez, Mesopotamia and the Persian Gulf, became an object of general European interest in the 1820s. In those years the term 'Eastern Question' was coined, as was the phrase 'the sick man on the Bosphorus' who would not survive long and for whose death all should take precautions, in view of his huge inheritance.

CONSULTATION ABOUT THE STATE OF TURKEY.

FIGURE 1 *'Consultation about the State of Turkey'. Napoleon III and an English Minister brooding over the fate of 'the sick man'. Punch 25 (1853), p. 118. University Library of Heidelberg, CC-BY-SA 3.0.*

The interests of Russia as Turkey's direct neighbour consisted of a mixture of territorial, strategic, economic and religious motives. The Russians had tried to gain access to the 'warm seas' (the Sea of Azov, the Black Sea and the Mediterranean) since the time of Peter the Great. After each war with the Turks they made progress, until in 1783 they obtained the Crimea as a springboard to Constantinople and founded Sevastopol as the finest harbour in the world; in 1829, by virtue of the Peace of Adrianople, they occupied the mouths of the Danube and various positions on the eastern shores of the Black Sea. Odessa was founded as a commercial harbour for the exportation of grain from southern Russia and the Russian government became interested in untrammelled transit through the Straits. In the 1830s, during Mehemet Ali's struggle with the Sultan, the Holy Places in Palestine were opened up to Christians for the first time for centuries. Russia, her Orthodox Church and the Tsar as its head developed a special interest in the Holy Places, beginning with the Church of the Holy Sepulchre in Jerusalem. From the 1830s onward, Russian Orthodox pilgrims were foremost among the Europeans to visit Jerusalem and Bethlehem. A rivalry of all Christian churches developed in Palestine. This religious fervour caused the respective governments of the European powers to gain a political foothold in this area. Great Britain especially grew suspicious of Russia's religious activities, since they were harbingers of future political influence in an area that lay across one of the lifelines to Britain's Indian Empire.

Since the eighteenth century, Austria had watched Russia's forward push south into the Balkans with mounting apprehension. Under Metternich she pursued a policy of preserving the weak Ottoman Empire since it granted as much security as a sea, whereas the rising power of Russia would dwarf her own position in the area. Territorial gains in the Balkans would benefit Russia but not Austria, and nationalism spreading among the Turkish-held Balkan peoples might endanger peace and tranquillity in Austria's own multinational empire. Metternich's maxim of upholding the integrity of the Ottoman Empire was maintained by his successors in Vienna.

Great Britain had developed a massive interest in the destiny of the Ottoman Empire during the Greeks' struggle for independence in the 1820s. In the 1830s – since 1833, to be more precise, that is, after the Treaty of Unkiar Skelessi which gave Russia a protectorate over Turkey, then threatened by Mehemet Ali – Britain proclaimed the integrity of the Ottoman Empire to be of vital interest to her. This became a fundamental principle of British foreign policy for the rest of the century. The main reasons for this were strategic, political and commercial.

With the advent of steam shipping and railways, from the 1820s the old routes through the Levant to the Far East, and to India especially, which had fallen into disuse, were rediscovered because they saved time and money compared with the route around the Cape of Good Hope. In the 1830s, land-surveying companies bustled in Syria and Mesopotamia and bandied about proposals for building railways. Russia's forward thrust south to the

Turkish Straits was felt to be dangerous to the security of these lines of communication. In these years British public opinion, whipped up by the rabidly Russophobe David Urquhart, developed strong anti-Russian feelings.

Finally, the Ottoman Empire became important by leaps and bounds as a market for British industrial products, especially textiles, and also as a source of raw materials and foodstuffs, foremost among them grain from the Danubian Principalities. Freedom of passage on the lower Danube, the mouths of which – the arm of St Kilia – the Russians deliberately failed to dredge in order to favour the development of their own harbour of Odessa, became a capital British interest. Through the commercial Treaty of Balta Liman of 1838, the Turkish market was thrown open to British commercial enterprise. It has been calculated that British exports to Turkey rose by 800 per cent between 1825 and 1852, and British imports from Turkey rose almost twofold. Thus from the 1830s a deep-seated antagonism developed between Britain and Russia in the Levant and in the Balkans and lasted until the First World War. Further to the east it became simultaneously intertwined with the 'Great Game for Asia'.

France's interest in the Ottoman Empire is the oldest among the European great powers. It dates back to the sixteenth century when Francis I, 'the most Christian king', allied himself with the head of Islam against the Catholic Habsburgs. The Franco-Turkish treaty of 1535, renewed in 1740, formed the basis of close relations. It granted consular jurisdiction (extraterritoriality) to France over her nationals in the Ottoman Empire – a privilege which was eventually extended to other European countries. During Napoleon I's expedition to Egypt in 1798, which was directed against Britain's position in India, French interest in the Ottoman Empire was upgraded politically and strategically. After Nelson's victory at Abukir a strong rivalry developed in the Levant between France and Britain, but it was not as deep-seated as the corresponding Anglo-Russian competition and was interrupted by periods of cooperation. Still, it remained alive below the surface throughout the nineteenth century. After Napoleon III came to power, France's interest in the Ottoman Empire was once more outspoken. In his domestic policy the Prince President and Emperor chose to lean on the Catholic Church and therefore turned his attention to the Holy Places in Palestine which had, since the eighteenth century, fallen more and more under the influence of the Orthodox Church, the protector and head of which was the Russian Tsar.

The interest that Prussia took in the fate of the Ottoman Empire was marginal, but by no means negligible. In 1829 she mediated the Russo-Turkish Peace of Adrianople. In the 1840s the romantic and flamboyant King Frederick William IV took a personal interest in the Holy Places and even managed, by a remarkable cooperation with the British government and the Church of England, to establish a common Anglo-Prussian bishopric in Jerusalem in order to proselytize among the Muslim and Jewish population there. The fate of the Ottoman Empire, however, was a matter of indifference to him. During the Crimean War he, his government and court circles in

Berlin tried to exploit Austria's predicament in order to make gains on German territory, that is, to strengthen Prussia's standing in Germany and correspondingly weaken Austria's position. This was a maxim which Bismarck later took up under changed circumstances: he used and manipulated the strong interests of the other four powers in the Eastern Question to further Germany's interest in Central Europe. This was a very cunning and remunerative game until at the end of the century, Germany, to her eventual detriment, became directly involved in Balkan and Near Eastern affairs.

Annotated bibliography

The Eastern Question has been a favourite subject for historians of international relations for decades. Among older books, two classics should be mentioned: John A. R. Marriott, *The Eastern Question: An Historical Study in European Diplomacy* (Oxford, 1917, 4th edn 1940, repr. 1968), and Jacques Ancel, *Manuel historique de la question d'Orient, 1792–1923* (Paris, 1923, 3rd edn 1927). A superb modern handbook is Matthew S. Anderson, *The Eastern Question, 1774–1923: A Study in International Relations* (London, 1966, repr. Basingstoke, 1987). For the Balkan area the best guide is Leften S. Stavrianos, *The Balkans since 1453* (New York, 1958). It has a good bibliography, was long out of print and has fortunately been reprinted in 2000 and 2005.

For Turkey, a modern textbook is Stanford J. Shaw and Ezel Kural Shaw, *History of the Ottoman Empire and Modern Turkey*, vol. 2 (Cambridge, 1977). A masterful, compact paperback is Roderic H. Davison, *Turkey* (Englewood Cliffs, NJ, 1968); all following editions have the title *Turkey: A Short History* (Walkington and Beverley, 1981; an updated 3rd edn Huntingdon, 1998). For the period of Turkey's Westernization, a pioneering study is Bernard Lewis, *The Emergence of Modern Turkey* (London, 1961, 3rd edn 2002). The reform period in the second half of the nineteenth century is discussed by Roderic H. Davison, *Reform in the Ottoman Empire, 1856–1876* (Princeton, NJ, 1963, repr. New York, 1973).

There is no English language book on Russia's interest in the Eastern Question. One has to turn to a Russian study: *Vostočnyj vopros vo vnešnej politike Rossii konec XVIII – načalo XX v.*, ed. Nina S. Kinjapina et al. (Moscow, 1978). Russia's policy in the Balkans is dealt with by Barbara Jelavich, *Russia's Balkan Entanglements, 1806–1914* (Cambridge, 1991, repr. 1993). Europe's newly awakened interest in the Holy Land (Palestine and Syria) in the 1830s and 1840s is well covered: Yehoshua Ben-Arieh, *The Rediscovery of the Holy Land in the Nineteenth Century* (Jerusalem, 1979, 3rd edn 1983); Derek Hopwood, *The Russian Presence in Syria and Palestine 1843–1914: Church and Politics in the Near East* (London, 1969); Abdul Latif Tibawi, *British Interests in Palestine, 1800–1901: A Study of Religious and Educational Enterprise* (London, 1961); Alex Carmel, *Christen als*

Pioniere im Heiligen Land. Ein Beitrag zur Geschichte der Pilgermission und des Wiederaufbaus Palästinas im 19. Jahrhundert (Basel, 1981); Abdel-Raouf Sinno, *Deutsche Interessen in Syrien und Palästina 1841–1898. Aktivitäten religiöser Institutionen, wirtschaftliche und politische Einflüsse* (Berlin, 1982). A revisonist article on the importance of the Holy Land for Russia is Jack Fairey, 'Russia's Quest for the Holy Grail: Relics, Liturgies, and Great Power Politics in the Ottoman Empire', in *Russian-Ottoman Borderlands: The Eastern Question Reconsidered*, ed. in Lucien J. Frary and Mara Kozelsky, 131–64 (Madison, WI, and London, 2014). See also the same author's well-documented study: Jack Fairey, *The Great Powers and Orthodox Christendom: The Crisis over the Eastern Church in the Era of the Crimean War* (Basingstoke, 2015).

On Austria's interest in the Eastern Question there is only the antiquated study by Adolf Beer, *Die orientalische Politik Österreichs seit 1774* (Prague and Leipzig, 1883).

Britain's policy is much better covered: Gerald D. Clayton, *Britain and the Eastern Question: Missolonghi to Gallipoli* (London, 1971); Frank E. Bailey, *British Policy and the Turkish Reform Movement: A Study in Anglo-Turkish Relations, 1826–1853* (Cambridge, MA, 1942, repr. New York 1970); Harold Temperley, *England and the Near East: The Crimea* (London and Toronto, 1925, repr. Hamden, CT, 1964). The latter book does not go beyond the outbreak of the Crimean War. The importance of the Turkish Empire as a link in Britain's lines of communication with India is well covered by Halford L. Hoskins, *British Routes to India* (London, 1928, repr. 1966). There are at least two good studies on the importance of public opinion in Britain with regard to Russia's bid for Constantinople: John H. Gleason, *The Genesis of Russophobia in Great Britain: A Study of the Interaction of Policy and Opinion* (Cambridge, MA, 1950); Hans-Jobst Krautheim, *Öffentliche Meinung und imperiale Politik. Das britische Rußlandbild 1815–1854* (Berlin, 1977). Britain's economic penetration of the Ottoman Empire after the introduction of free trade in 1838 is analysed by Vernon J. Puryear, *International Economics and Diplomacy in the Near East: A Study of British Commercial Policy in the Levant, 1834–1853* (Stanford, CA, 1935, repr. Hamden, CT, 1968). A collection of relevant essays is J. A. Petrosjan (ed.), *Vnešneėkonomičeskie svjazi Osmanskoj imperii v novoe vremja (konec XVIII–načalo XX v.)* (Moscow, 1989). Puryear also stresses Anglo-Russian policy and commercial rivalry to explain the Crimean War in his book *England, Russia, and the Straits Question, 1844–1856* (Berkeley, CA, 1931, repr. Hamden, CT, 1965). A broader European approach is furnished by Şevket Pamuk, *The Ottoman Empire and European Capitalism, 1820–1913: Trade, Investment, and Production* (Cambridge, 1987).

France's role in the Eastern Question in the nineteenth century is dealt with in the book by Ancel mentioned above and by Alyce Edith Mange, *The Near Eastern Policy of the Emperor Napoleon III* (Urbana, IL, 1940, repr. Westport, CT, 1975).

2

Diplomacy during the war, 1853–6

Given these preliminary remarks on the Eastern Question, it is not difficult to fathom the real causes of the Crimean War – although they are complex enough. The purpose of this chapter is to offer a résumé of the diplomacy of the war from its outbreak until the beginning of the Paris peace congress.

The Crimean War took a long time to get started. The preliminary phase lasted from 1850 to the early months of 1853, and the hot phase of fragile peace took fully a year from the spring of 1853 to March 1854 to develop into an outright European war. In contrast to the great wars of the twentieth century, but in common with most European wars in modern history up to the nineteenth century, the outbreak of the Crimean War did not stop the frantic and continuous diplomatic activities of the belligerent powers. Although diplomatic relations were severed in February 1854, the three great belligerent powers – Russia on the one side, Great Britain and France on the other – kept up a close, though indirect, diplomatic contact through the two German powers, Austria and Prussia. In different ways the latter managed to stay out of the war, although at various moments they seemed to be or actually were on the brink of joining the fray. At one time, during the Vienna peace conference of March–June 1855, the three belligerents even unwillingly sat together round the peace table which was arranged for them by Austria. During these conferences there was no cessation of hostilities; the guns kept on roaring on the southernmost tip of the Crimean peninsula.

Another curious trait of the war is that it was mainly fought in a faraway peripheral theatre, the Crimea, where it could hardly be hoped that a final and decisive military solution would be brought about. The war thus never developed into a frontal war between the two sides, with the one side caving in militarily and the other then dictating peace terms. At the beginning of the war, that is during the preliminary Russo-Turkish war, there was the classical broad front, the lower Danube. When the Western armies eventually approached that front, the Russians evacuated it, not through the impending pressure of the Allied armies, but because a non-belligerent, Austria, had contrived to force the Russian troops out of the Danubian Principalities through diplomatic pressure backed by an army on the frontier intent on marching in if diplomacy did eventually fail. For a short time, everybody in Europe expected Austria to become involved in hostilities. The spectacle of a victorious army retreating before the weight of an army not officially at war but assembling on its flank was almost unbelievable.

Another curious fact about the Crimean War is the relative military strength of the two parties. In terms of numbers only, Russia, at the height of the war, had an army of two million on her soil whereas the Western Allies, at the peak of their military involvement (February 1856), mustered only a tenth of that strength, that is, roughly 200,000. The main reason Russia eventually gave in after the loss of part of the fortress of Sevastopol was the painful prospect of other European countries becoming involved on the opposite side: Austria first of all; then, against her will, Prussia; finally Sweden, who, after playing a long waiting game, finally made up her mind to enter the fray.

Thus at the turn of 1855–6 the Crimean War, fought on the tip of a peripheral peninsula, was on the verge of escalating into a full-scale European war with the prospect of becoming worldwide: in the Western hemisphere the United States was at loggerheads with Great Britain, severed her diplomatic relations with that country in the spring of 1856 and would very probably have entered the war on Russia's side in order to gobble up Britain's and Spain's possessions in North America (Canada), the Caribbean (Cuba) and Central America (Honduras).

Thus the Crimean War bore the germs of a world war. It would have become a struggle between the great powers for the redistribution of power in Europe and North America. The interesting question is therefore, why did it not evolve into a world war? Why did it end at the threshold of becoming universal? The answer is the force of diplomacy or, in other words, the functioning of the European Concert, though it had been badly shaken by the revolutions of 1848–9 and almost collapsed through Russia's bid for hegemony in the Near East in 1853.

To turn back to the Ottoman Empire, the prelude to the Crimean War was the so-called 'monks' dispute' in the Holy Places of Palestine. In itself this was a petty and absurd affair of only local relevance. However, because the claims of the Catholics there were now supported by France, and to a lesser degree also by Austria, and since the Orthodox claims were backed by Russia, the dispute quickly assumed international dimensions. It was about such questions as who was to be in possession of the keys to the Church and Grotto of Nativity in Bethlehem, who had the right to restore the Church of the Holy Sepulchre in Jerusalem, and so on. After two years of pressure from the French government, the Sultan in Constantinople granted wide-ranging rights to the Catholics in the Holy Land which were embodied in a firman of 9 February 1852. As they collided with concessions which he had simultaneously made to the Greek Orthodox monks, the local dispute was transported to Constantinople as well as to Paris and St Petersburg, and thus evolved into an international affair.

MAP 1 *European Russia, 1853–6.*

Although there was no such thing as public opinion in Russia in the Western European sense, a religious dispute of this sort was sure to whip up resentment and passions among the Russian people. Capping everything, there was a personal pique which the Russian Tsar harboured towards Napoleon III. Since the advent of the July Monarchy in 1830, Nicholas I had regarded France as the hotbed of revolution. When Louis Napoleon came to power through popular election in 1848 and usurped the title of emperor in December 1852, Nicholas's disgust knew no bounds. When all the other great powers of Europe, starting with Britain and ending with conservative Austria and Prussia, recognized the new form of government in France, the Tsar deliberately slighted Napoleon by addressing him as 'Cher ami' instead of 'Mon frère', the usual salutation among European sovereigns. The crisis soon died down, but it pushed the French emperor into an anti-Russian mood.

There were two other affairs originating on the Russian side which complicated the political situation in Europe during the first months of 1853 without their being founded on deliberate warmongering. At the end of December 1852 a new coalition government was formed in Britain. It consisted of Whigs and Peelites with the peaceful Aberdeen as Prime Minister. Nicholas had met Aberdeen in 1844 during a state visit to Britain and had come to a gentleman's agreement with him on the need to consult each other about the fate of Turkey. Seizing the opportunity of the new Aberdeen government, Nicholas had a number of conversations with the British envoy to his court, Sir George Hamilton Seymour, during January and February 1853. The gist of these perhaps somewhat unguarded comments was that the Tsar stated his belief that the 'sick man' was on the verge of dying and should be properly interred. His utterances culminated in the proposal to create the Danubian Principalities and Bulgaria as independent states under Russian protection, to give Serbia and the Herzegovina as a sop to Austria, and to offer Egypt and Crete to Britain. His offer to Austria was addressed a little later in a personal letter to the Austrian Emperor Francis Joseph. The Tsar's offer amounted to a grandiose plan for the partition of the Ottoman Empire, leaving Constantinople outside of the bargain by setting it up as a 'free city'. As for Austria, the Tsar trusted to the gratitude which he thought he was owed for Russia's aid in suppressing the Hungarian revolution of 1849.

Although Britain's reply was evasive, it held out, in the spirit of the agreement of 1844, the prospect of mutual consultations in case the Turkish Empire collapsed. Nicholas was, for the time being, quite happy with this general promise from London. The turn which events took, however, made him feel disappointed when he saw the promise was not being kept. One year later he felt personally cheated when the British government, in March 1854, published his intimate confessions in a blue book, which led to a public outcry in Britain. It was a gross error on the side of the Tsar to believe that foreign policy decisions in Britain were taken by the monarch and his government. He simply did not know how government worked in Britain: what the parliamentary system meant, that in matters of foreign policy there was a complicated system of checks and balances between Crown, Cabinet and Parliament, and that far-reaching promises for the future could never be made by a British government. The Tsar's ignorance had fateful consequences. Seymour's verdict on the Tsar in one of his reports published a year later, that he was a scheming hypocrite, did not do the Tsar justice, but hurt him deeply.

Nicholas made another foolish mistake at the same time that his conversations with Seymour took place: the famous Menshikov mission to Constantinople. It was induced by a similar action on Austria's side, the so-called Leiningen mission. At the beginning of February 1853 the latter resulted, after the delivery of an ultimatum, in a speedy removal of grievances which Austria complained of in Montenegro, among them the cessation of frontier disputes between Turks and Montenegrins. The Tsar thereupon sent Admiral Alexander S. Menshikov to Constantinople at the end of February. Ostensibly Menshikov was directed to conclude a convention with Turkey in which the privileges of the Orthodox Church in the Holy Places were to be renewed and guaranteed. In this way another scene in the protracted tug-of-war about the status of the Christian denominations was enacted in the Holy Land.

In reality the Menshikov mission inaugurated the first hot phase leading to the Crimean War. It lasted from Menshikov's arrival at Constantinople at the end of February until the beginning of July when Russia, after the failure of the mission, occupied the Danubian Principalities in order to enforce her demands upon Turkey. The next phase witnessed repeated attempts at mediation by the other four great powers of Europe and was ended by Turkey declaring war on Russia on 4 October 1853. A third phase followed in which still more attempts at solving the Russo-Turkish dispute were made in various conferences in Vienna, a phase in which both Russia and the two Western powers tried hard to win the two German powers over to their side. It ended with both powers declaring war on Russia: Britain on 27 March and France on 28 March 1854.

What were Menshikov's demands, which set in motion the chain of events which led to the outbreak of war?

Besides the open demand to re-establish the privileged status of the Orthodox religion, there was a far-reaching political instruction of which Menshikov was the bearer and which he was to put forward in strict secrecy: the demand to conclude a protective treaty along the lines of the Treaty of Unkiar Skelessi. This was a demand which was certain to leak out sooner or later and which the other great powers, Britain primarily, simply could not and would not accept. The Tsar's worst miscalculation was that he believed Britain would acquiesce in Russia's ascendancy in the Levant. When Menshikov realized that this political demand was refused – although the religious one was accepted – he departed from Constantinople. After another ultimatum from St Petersburg which the Turkish court and government (the Porte), by now sure of French and British support, disregarded, Russian troops crossed the Pruth on 2 July 1853 and occupied the Turkish Danubian Principalities as a gage to enforce the demands of the Tsar.

After Menshikov's spectacular departure from Constantinople, the British Cabinet made up its mind to send the Mediterranean fleet to Besika Bay at the entrance of the Dardanelles. Napoleon III had preceded Britain's step

FIGURE 2 *A French soldier explaining Constantinople to a Cossack. Cartoon by E. Bich. Courtesy of Archives du Ministère des Affaires étrangères, collection iconographique.*

and sent his fleet from Toulon to the island of Salamis in Greece to await further orders. Both fleets assembled in Besika Bay on 13 and 14 June. Thus the screws were further tightened towards war. During the rest of the year, eleven peace proposals were hammered out in Vienna, but were obstinately refused by either Turkey or Russia. The most important one was the Vienna note of 31 July 1853 in which the Ottoman government was to promise Russia that it would abide by the religious articles of the treaties of Kutchuk-Kainardji of 1774 and of Adrianople of 1829, and that it would not alter the religious status quo in Palestine without the previous understanding of both France and Russia.

In Constantinople, a war-like spirit arose among religious leaders, students of theology and the general population, who called for a 'holy war' against Russia. It was heightened when the Egyptian fleet arrived in the Bosphorus. In the end it was this outbreak of Turkish public opinion which led to the Turkish declaration of war on Russia on 4 October 1853. It was not, as many contemporaries, foremost among them the Tsar, and many historians to the present day maintain, the secret doings and the alleged warmongering of the British ambassador, Stratford de Redcliffe.

The local war on the Danube and in the Caucasus had now broken out, but it did not automatically lead to the European war, which took another six months to come about. The decisive turn of events in this phase was the so-called 'massacre of Sinope' of 30 November 1853. This is a misnomer for a 'normal' act of war. On that day a number of Turkish warships conveying supplies from Constantinople to the Caucasus front had taken refuge in the harbour of Sinope on the north-eastern coast of Turkey. They were attacked by superior Russian forces under Admiral Pavel S. Nakhimov and sunk within a few hours. The only remaining ship brought the news of the disaster to Constantinople whence it was forwarded to the European capitals, part of the distance by way of the telegraph. It reached London on 11 December and caused a storm of public indignation which swept away what resistance remained in the British Cabinet against military intervention on the side of Turkey. That a large part of the Turkish navy was annihilated by the Russians while the Royal Navy was riding at anchor in Besika Bay, within easy reach of Sinope, seemed almost unbearable. At the end of December 1853 the British and French squadrons were ordered to pass through the Straits and enter the Black Sea to force any Russian man-of-war to return to Sevastopol.

Again public opinion, rather than a political decision or non-decision, played a key role in the progression towards war. Since the 1830s and the days of Unkiar Skelessi, a strong Russophobia had built up in Britain, kindled by Russia's southward expansion towards the Turkish Straits and Persia, and fuelled by the Russian army steamrollering the struggle for freedom of the Poles (1831) and the Hungarians (1849). A crusading spirit was whipped up in Britain and among liberal public opinion elsewhere in Central and Western Europe against Russia as the seat of autocracy and tyranny. The Sultan, no less an autocrat in his empire than the Tsar, was eulogized as the paragon of tolerance and freedom and as the victim of the Russian bear.

The leading vehicle of this rabid Russophobia in Britain was the press, especially *The Times*. As Kingsley Martin has shown, this paper literally forced the Cabinet to close ranks and help Turkey, which was lying prostrate in front of the Russian bear. The official history of *The Times* may appear arrogant when it says, 'The paper might claim to have made the war ... it had been largely responsible for the Crimean campaign that had brought victory in the end; it had "saved the remnant of an army"; it had destroyed one Ministry and forced important changes in another; and it had caused the removal of a Commander-in-Chief.'[1] These assertions refer to the decision to enter the war; the transfer of the theatre of war from the Danube to the Crimea; the exposure of the utter breakdown of the supply and sanitary systems during the 'Crimean winter' of 1854–5; the collapse of the Aberdeen government in January 1855, and the replacement of the Commander-in-Chief Sir James Simpson by General Sir William Codrington in October 1855. But *The Times*' historian is not far off the mark:

"RIGHT AGAINST WRONG."

FIGURE 3 *'Right against wrong'. Punch 26 (1854), p. 143. University Library of Heidelberg, CC-BY-SA 3.0.*

Russophobia in Britain and the demands of public opinion are two major reasons for Britain's entry into and conduct in the war. To sum up, the outbreak of the Crimean War is a chain of many links: of mistakes, miscalculations, misunderstandings, of false charges and irrational phobias and passions, less of cool calculations and ill will. The British Foreign Secretary, Lord Clarendon, was right when he said 'that we [were] drifting towards war'.[2]

Sinope and the Franco-British decision to send warships into the Black Sea made war almost inevitable, yet it took another three months for the two maritime powers to declare war on Russia, on 27 and 28 March 1854. As is customary among partners fighting together in a war, the two Western powers and Turkey concluded a treaty of alliance on 10 April 1854. Besides the usual stipulations of restoring peace by common efforts and consultations, Britain and France proclaimed themselves to be fighting for the integrity of Turkey and the European balance of power. These two general war aims, harmless in themselves, point to the intention of the Western powers to oust Russia from the Principalities and to help Turkey oppose any further Russian advance southwards to Constantinople. It was therefore obvious that any Western armies sent to the east would assemble near the Turkish capital or at a port to the north. Another important aspect of the treaty is that the principle of the integrity of the Ottoman Empire was considered as part and parcel of the general balance of power in Europe. A third point is that other European powers not yet at war were invited to join Britain and France (art. 5).

This article was mainly directed towards the two German great powers, which, if they remained neutral, would shield Russia from any direct attack from the west. The early months of 1854 witnessed a frantic struggle between Russia and the maritime powers to win Prussia and Austria to their respective sides. Russia could justifiably hope for active sympathy and support from her two conservative allies, members of the Holy Alliance. The Tsar was mistaken in his expectation that Austria would be grateful for the decisive aid he had rendered her in 1849 in crushing the Hungarian revolution. Both German powers were, as we will see in a later chapter, averse to joining the fray on Nicholas's side because they regarded his occupation of the Danubian Principalities as a rash and ruthless act productive of revolutionary uprisings in the Balkans, in Poland and elsewhere. Thus there was some chance of the Western powers' invitation to join them being accepted by Prussia and Austria. The Prussian King, however, decided against the willingness of his government to close ranks with Britain and France, and on 27 February 1854 proclaimed his 'sovereign neutrality' and turned down the Western proposal.[3]

Austria, on the other hand, as the power more closely interested in the maintenance of the status quo in the Balkans, was all for joining the Western powers. The simple calculation was that the Tsar, confronted with the united resistance of four of the five great powers of Europe, would think twice before crossing the Danube and would even yield to the demand to evacuate the Principalities and restore the status quo ante in the East. With Prussia backing out, the Tsar's attitude stiffened, thus making a great-power struggle almost inevitable. As Frederick William felt that he was in a false and isolated position – only certain circles at court leaned towards Russia while public opinion was more or less in favour of the Western powers – he agreed on a treaty with Austria promising to defend her if she were attacked by Russia while the latter was being forced out of the Principalities. This 'defensive and offensive treaty' of 20 April 1854 between the two German powers was, however, a dead letter as soon as the ink was dry.

Austria decided to go it alone and on 3 June summoned the Russians to evacuate the Principalities or be compelled to do so by force of arms jointly with the Western powers. After many tergiversations the Russians gave in,

THE FOUR POINTS—(AND PLENTY MORE TO FOLLOW).

FIGURE 4 *'The Four Points'. Britain, Turkey, Austria and France trying to goad the Prussian King Frederick William IV into adopting their war aims against Russia.* Punch 28 (1855), p. 25. *University Library of Heidelberg, CC-BY-SA 3.0.*

and on 7 August 1854 declared that they would evacuate the Principalities for strategic reasons.

Only one day later, on 8 August, the two Western powers and Austria exchanged notes which contained their general war aims in the famous 'Four Points' in Vienna. Austria, which had mobilized her army and massed it on the frontiers of Galicia and Transylvania, in the flank of the Russian army of occupation, seemed to be on the brink of entering the war. Prussia had partly excluded herself from the talks in Vienna leading to the Four Points; in part she was excluded by the other three powers because of her constant hesitation and her only lukewarm support. The Four Points were the public war aims of France, Britain and Austria. By signing them, Austria, not yet at war with Russia, showed Europe unequivocally which side she was on. She made it clear to Russia that their political ties had been severed and that if the Four Points were not accepted by Russia, Austria would finally enter the war.

The first point stated that Russia should give up her protectorate over Wallachia, Moldavia and Serbia and that they should henceforth be placed under the guarantee of all the great powers. The second point stipulated that the mouths of the Danube should be free from all obstructions. The third point was of the utmost importance; it would later be the greatest obstacle on the road to peace. It was, as it were, the pivotal point of the Crimean War and was, in its vague wording, open to much interpretation: the treaty of 13 July 1841, which all the five great powers and Turkey had signed and which stipulated the closure of the Turkish Straits to warships in times of peace, should be revised 'in the interest of the European balance of power'. The fourth point related to the immediate cause of war: Russia was to relinquish her claim to protect the Orthodox population of the Ottoman Empire. The Christians of the Empire were to be placed under the protection of the great powers.[4]

It is obvious that points one and two were of primary importance to Austria. Point two was also of special interest to Great Britain because of her desire for free access to the Principalities as a grain-exporting region. Point three was of almost exclusive interest to Britain. France, apart from point four which was of instrumental relevance to Napoleon's internal policy, was thus the power with the least interest in the Four Points as such.

In order to step up her pressure on Russia, Austria had concluded a convention with the Turkish government on 14 June 1854 (at Boyadji-Köi), in which she obtained the right to drive the Russians out of the Principalities and to occupy them temporarily by force of arms. The exchange of notes of 8 August 1854 was originally meant to be a convention or even a treaty of alliance between the three powers. Such a treaty was in fact concluded after much diplomatic haggling on 2 December 1854. Russia had tried, although belatedly, to prevent Austria from closing ranks with the Western powers by proclaiming, on 28 November, that she would accept the Four Points as a basis for peace negotiations. The tripartite negotiations were conducted in strict secrecy. Russia's acceptance of the Four Points did not stop the treaty's conclusion, which burst on Europe like a bombshell. It marked the climax of Austrian cooperation with the Western powers and included a statement to the effect that more could be added to the four war aims, without explaining what this might mean in detail. Austria engaged to protect the Principalities against a return of Russian troops. If Austria found itself at war with Russia as a result of this engagement, the three powers promised to conclude a military alliance. The stipulation which proved to be the most controversial and the most illusory was article V, which said that unless peace was secure by the end of the year – that is, within four weeks! – the three powers would consult each other on new measures to obtain their common aims.

Count Buol, the Austrian Foreign Minister, managed to persuade the Russian government on 28 December 1854 to express its desire to begin peace talks on the basis of the Four Points. Thus the representatives of the three powers at war in the Crimea assembled round the green table in Vienna while their armies were entrenched at Sevastopol, the soldiers on both sides dying from cold and deprivation and wounds, with what fighting there was proving inconclusive, Austria trying hard to get general peace talks started. From documents published recently[5] it emerges that France and Britain frantically attempted to give more precision to the new fifth point in order to let the peace talks miscarry. Both governments congratulated themselves on making the fifth point so unacceptable to Russia that, in view of the stalemate in the Crimea, the armies would have the decisive word, not the negotiators round the peace table.

The fifth point, which was secretly arranged between Paris and London and which was really to specify the third point, said that Russia would have to give up her 'preponderance' ('faire cesser la prépotence') in the Black Sea by reducing her navy there to four ships of war, by demolishing Sevastopol and not re-establishing it as a great naval arsenal. The official peace talks which were soon to open thus seemed to be doomed to failure. They were given the knock-out blow by another secret arrangement, hitherto unknown to contemporaries and historians alike. In a private audience which the Austrian Emperor Francis Joseph granted to Prince Alexander M. Gorchakov, the Russian envoy to Vienna, at the beginning of January 1855, the former gave his word that Austria would not accept the third point, which impaired the honour and sovereignty of Russia in the Crimea and on her Black Sea coast. Thus any arrangement which would unilaterally be to the detriment of Russia would not have Austria's support.

This word of honour, given by the Austrian Emperor to Russia's representative, is the real reason why the Vienna peace conferences ended in failure. Their opening on 15 March 1855 was, however, a grand and promising affair. The British side was represented by Lord John Russell, former Prime Minister and Foreign Secretary. France's interests were, two weeks after the start of the conferences, in the hands of Foreign Minister Edouard Drouyn de Lhuys. Turkey sent her Grand Vizir, Ali Pasha, to Vienna, and Buol was president of the conferences.

The remarkable thing was that once the first two points had been speedily solved, after considerable haggling a formula was found for the third point and accepted both by Russell and Drouyn de Lhuys. This, in fact, ran counter to the determination of both the British and French governments to let the conferences fail. The formula was a complicated compromise between the far-reaching Western demands and Russia's resistance to any unilateral disarmament in the Black Sea. It stipulated that Russia should agree to limit her naval forces to the status of 1854 while Turkey and the Western powers were allowed to step up their maritime presence there to Russia's level. This was Buol's pet idea of 'equipoise', which was really an expression of Francis Joseph's word of honour given to Gorchakov. Both Russell and Drouyn de Lhuys were convinced of the viability of this solution.

At home both ministers were disavowed by their governments at the beginning of May. The final decision was made in Paris. The documents now published show that Napoleon was harassed by the British ambassador, Lord Cowley, to disavow his Foreign Minister.[6] Had Napoleon remained staunch, the British government would have backed down, although grudgingly. The newly found formula would have to be presented to the Russian government as an Austrian ultimatum. In case of rejection, Austria had promised to enter the war on the side of the Western powers. It is tragic to see from the newly published documents that Austria made up her mind seriously, for the first and only time, to join her allies and that at the same time the two Western governments broke up the bridge by which Austria would have crossed the Rubicon, that is, the River Pruth.

Drouyn resigned at once, Russell a few weeks later. The Austrian army was demobilized because the government could no longer bear the financial strain of mobilization. Russia, witnessing the disunion of her opponents, exulted at the spectacle played out in front of her. There were months of diplomatic estrangement between Austria and her December allies. It is almost certain that Russia would have had to accept the Austrian ultimatum had the three powers shown unity. The war would have ended in the summer of 1855. Buol managed to organize a closing session of the Vienna conferences on 4 June 1855, but the scission among the three powers was open to the world. The arms at Sevastopol had to speak the final word. After much bloodletting they did so on 8 September 1855, when the Allies at last occupied the south side of the city.

After the Russians had partly compensated for their defeat at Sevastopol by storming the Turkish fortress of Kars on 26 November 1855, the time was ripe for a fresh attempt at peace efforts. Buol, with French aid, formulated a new ultimatum to be presented to Russia. The third point was now no longer based on the principle of equipoise of naval forces in the Black Sea but on the principle of neutralization of the Black Sea, that is, of its demilitarization. Russia was to renounce, except for some vessels for police purposes, all her naval potential, men-of-war and naval installations in the Black Sea. The ultimatum, delivered on 28 December 1855, was accepted by the Russian government, after some heart-searching, on 16 January 1856. The door was now open for serious peace talks.

Annotated bibliography

The documents on the diplomacy of the Crimean War were published by the author of this book in four series and twelve volumes: Winfried Baumgart (ed.), *Akten zur Geschichte des Krimkriegs [AGKK]*, Serie I, *Österreichische Akten* ..., 3 vols (Munich and Vienna, 1979–80); Serie II, *Preußische Akten* ..., 2 vols (Munich, 1990–1); Serie III, *Englische Akten* ..., 4 vols (Munich, 1988–2006); Serie IV, *Französische Akten* ..., 3 vols (Munich, 1999–2003). Because of the difficulties in using the Russian documents, a Russian series is not projected. Official documents (such as treaties, protocols of conferences, open diplomatic despatches) published by the governments during the war in their official organs, in blue books or in the newspapers, are accessible in two useful collections, among others: Julius von Jasmund (ed.), *Aktenstücke zur orientalischen Frage. Nebst chronologischer Uebersicht*, 2 vols (Berlin, 1855–6); *British and Foreign State Papers*, vols 44 (1853–4), 45 (1854–5), 46 (1855–6) (London, 1865).

There are three useful research articles on the Crimean War with much bibliographical material included: Brison D. Gooch, 'A Century of Historiography on the Origins of the Crimean War', *American Historical Review* 62 (1956/7): 33–58; Edgar Hösch, 'Neuere Literatur (1940–1960) über den Krimkrieg', *Jahrbücher für Geschichte Osteuropas* 9 (1961): 399–434; Winfried Baumgart, 'Probleme der Krimkriegsforschung. Eine Studie über die Literatur des letzten Jahrzehnts (1961–1970)', *Jahrbücher für Geschichte Osteuropas* 19 (1971): 49–109, 243–64, 371–400.

For general treatments of the diplomacy of the war, three of the older studies are still of some use: F. Heinrich Geffcken, *Zur Geschichte des Orientalischen Krieges 1853–1856* (Berlin, 1881); Alexandre Jomini, *Étude sur la guerre de Crimée (1852 à 1856)*, 2 vols (St Petersburg, 1878) (Jomini writes from a Russian angle); Eugène vicomte de Guichen, *La guerre de Crimée (1854–1856) et l'attitude des puissances européennes* (Paris, 1936) (uses documents from the French Foreign Ministry archives).

The diplomatic background of the outbreak of the Crimean War has intrigued a host of historians. Long chapters in Temperley, *England*, more recently in Figes, *Crimea*, are devoted to that phase. A treatment from the Russian side, with an important, though unsystematic, collection of Russian documents (partly in the French original), which have been neglected by historians probably because they were published immediately before the outbreak of the First World War, is Andrej M. Zaiončkovskij, *Vostočnaja vojna 1853–1856 gg. v svjazi s sovremennoj ej političeskoj obstanovkoj*, 2 vols text, 2 vols *Priloženija* (Enclosures) (St Petersburg, 1908–13). For the personal relations between Napoleon III and Nicholas I, see Luc Monnier, *Étude sur les origines de la guerre de Crimée* (Geneva, 1977). For the role of Turkey and using Turkish documents, see Ann Pottinger Saab, *The Origins of the Crimean Alliance* (Charlottesville, VA, 1977). A new, though at times complicated, treatment is David Goldfrank, *The Origins of the Crimean War* (London and New York, 1994). From the French side there is Alain Gouttman, *La guerre de Crimée 1853–1856* (Paris, 1995, 2nd edn 2006). There are quite a number of recent comprehensive studies: Andrew D. Lambert, *The Crimean War: British Grand Strategy against Russia, 1853–1856* (Manchester, 1990, 2nd edn Farnham, 2011); Trevor Royle, *Crimea: The Great Crimean War, 1854–1856* (London 1999, repr. 2010); Clive Ponting, *The Crimean War: The Truth behind the Myth* (London, 2004); Orlando Figes, *Crimea: The Last Crusade* (London, 2010). All four rely on archival sources. Lambert stresses the fragile cooperation of British and French strategies and Britain's focus on maritime warfare. However, his claim that Russia gave in at the beginning of 1856 due to British plans in the Baltic overestimates the point (it was rather Austria's and Sweden's menace to join the fray and the knowledge in St Petersburg that Russia's internal resources would not stand another campaign in 1856). Figes stresses the religious, social and cultural aspects of the war. There is also a lengthy study of the Crimean War by two authors, one English and one Russian: Ian

Fletcher and Natilia Ishchenko, *The Crimean War: A Clash of Empires* (Staplehurst, 2004). Its geographical focus is on the Crimea only. A shorter new book, concentrating on the Crimea only, but lavishly illustrated is Hugh Small, *The Crimean War: Queen Victoria's War with the Russian Tsars* (Stroud, 2007, 2nd edn Stroud, 2018). A succinct new history of the war, with emphasis on the media side of the war (war correspondents, war artists, photographs): Trudi Tate, *Crimean War* (London/New York, 2019).

The special importance of *The Times* is well brought out by Kingsley Martin, *The Triumph of Lord Palmerston: A Study of Public Opinion in England before the Crimean War* (London, 1924, 2nd edn 1963).

PART TWO

The Belligerents and the Non-Belligerents

3

The war aims of the belligerents

Russia's war aims against Turkey in their most naked form are to be found in documents relating to the first half of 1853. This is when Tsar Nicholas had his intimate talks with Sir George Hamilton Seymour in St Petersburg and when he sent Prince Menshikov to Constantinople. He was at the height of his expectations with regard to a solution of the Eastern Question. His relations with France were strained because of French claims in the Holy Places question, he was angry about the Sultan's recalcitrance and thought that his relations with Britain were excellent. He was sure his two conservative allies, Prussia and Austria, would subscribe to anything he arranged with regard to the Eastern Question.

We have already seen how he opened his heart to Seymour and advocated the break-up of the Ottoman Empire. In his conversations he specified which parts of the Empire would accrue to Britain (and also to France). In a memorandum which he jotted down in his own hand in January 1853[1] he unfolded a large-scale plan for partitioning the Ottoman Empire after Russia had waged a successful war against it. This plan was even more specific than his utterances to Seymour. Russia, he wrote, would obtain the Danubian Principalities and the northern portion of Bulgaria down to Kustendje. Serbia and the rest of Bulgaria were to be granted independence. 'The coast of the Archipelago' – meaning probably the coastal areas of Epirus and the Gulf of Salonica – and 'the coast of the Adriatic' would fall to Austria. Britain should take Egypt, and 'perhaps Cyprus and Rhodes' as well. France would be granted Candia (Crete) and 'the islands of the Archipelago' (that is, in the Aegean). Constantinople should be made a free city; the Bosphorus should have a Russian garrison (thus rendering the neutral status of Constantinople a fiction) and the Dardanelles an Austrian one. Turkey proper should be relegated to Asia Minor.

Apart from a few vague references at the beginning of his memorandum, nothing is said about the religious issue. It therefore becomes obvious that the Tsar's harping on that question in his public and diplomatic declarations is a pure masquerade. Most books on the origin of the Crimean War fail to make that point clear enough and dwell on the religious question, which was a mere camouflage for Nicholas.

FIGURE 5 *Russia – the 'Colossus of the North'. Courtesy of the Archives du ministère des Affaires étrangères, collection iconographique.*

Another Russian document, again from January 1853 in Nicholas's own hand[2] and also hardly ever mentioned in the historiography, deals with the Tsar's plan of waging war on Turkey: a two-pronged lightning attack, starting from Sevastopol and Odessa with 16,000 troops, would aim at occupying the Bosphorus and Constantinople. The Dardanelles would also be occupied in case a French fleet approached.

This *Blitzkrieg* strategy remained valid when the Tsar sent Menshikov to Constantinople at the end of February 1853. Again it must be stressed that apart from the ostensible instructions dealing with the religious question, Menshikov had a secret instruction[3] which directed him to conclude a defensive alliance with the Sultan. Such an alliance would have been a second edition of Unkiar Skelessi of 1833. Besides trying to clarify his relations with Britain through Seymour, Nicholas also attempted to make

Austria the accomplice of his grand design. When Menshikov's mission failed, Nicholas was resolved to pounce upon Turkey and he offered Austria the occupation (and eventual acquisition) of Serbia and Herzegovina. If both powers would act in common, the Balkan populations would rise against the Turkish yoke and the 'the last hour' of the empire would sound.[4]

Francis Joseph was horrified at this idea and warned Nicholas not to go ahead with his plans.[5] They would mean revolution in the Balkans and elsewhere, and also war with the Western powers. Although the Tsar was not much impressed with such pleadings, they resulted in his being more careful in crossing the Danube after his troops had occupied the Principalities (2 July 1853) for fear of antagonizing Austria. The reticence and stubborn resistance of Austria created a strong impression on Field Marshal Paskevich, the Commander-in-Chief of the occupation forces, and it was he, eventually, who damped the Tsar's offensive spirit.

Paskevich, though, was mainly responsible for instilling in Nicholas the idea that the Balkan Christians would rise as a man against their oppressor once war had broken out between Russia and Turkey. He even expected to be able to form auxiliary troops from among them, consisting of 40,000–50,000 men who could be used to shake the foundations of the Ottoman Empire.[6] Nicholas became more cautious when his Foreign Minister, Karl Nesselrode, warned him not to use such revolutionary means because they would militate against the conservative doctrines of Russian policy. The Tsar therefore played a waiting game, and only harked back to his revolutionary plans when the first Russian troops crossed the Danube in March 1854 to lay siege to the fortress of Silistria. But the Christians did not budge, and it was Paskevich who now became pessimistic and told Nicholas that the Bulgarians would not rise and that the Serbians would send no more than 2,000–3,000 volunteers.[7] In the end it was only the Greeks who used the strained relations between Russia and Turkey to provoke insurrections in Thessaly and in Epirus, which were, however, easily put down by Turkey.

In January 1854, Nicholas made a final attempt to lure Austria into cooperating with him in revolutionizing the Balkans. He sent Count Aleksej F. Orlov, one of his intimate counsellors, to Vienna to ask for a promise of armed neutrality in the coming war with the Western powers. Prussia, too, was invited to join in. Orlov was quite frank in telling the Austrians that Russia might cross the Danube and that she would then support the Balkan Christians to rise against Turkey and would recognize their 'complete political emancipation', that is, independence under Russian tutelage.[8] He invited Austria to take a share in dividing up the Balkans, suggesting she might put Serbia under her protection.

Nicholas was being naive. The effect of his proposal in Vienna was disastrous. Francis Joseph and his government for the first time learnt for certain that Nicholas's scheming would mean revolution – a dangerous prospect for the Habsburg Empire. The proposal for armed neutrality was turned down flatly (as it was in Berlin). In a conference with his ministers, the Emperor decided to concentrate troops on the border with Serbia and in the last resort to invade the province, not to annex it ultimately, as Nicholas had offered, but in order to put down any anti-Turkish risings. Orlov's mission to Vienna was the turning-point in Austria's relations with Russia: she now made up her mind to join hands with the Western powers and force Russia to desist from her revolution-mongering policy in the Balkans. The Orlov mission also had the effect of making Nicholas, and even more Paskevich, think twice about crossing the Danube to precipitate the breakdown of the Ottoman Empire.

Although Nicholas continued to make further attempts to win over Austria and Prussia to his side, the negative reaction of both countries to his sweeping proposals of January 1854 was really the end of his plans for the downfall of Turkey. The immediate result of Orlov's mission was not a closer anti-Russian diplomatic union of the other four great powers, as Britain and France had proposed and as Austria had wished, but the defensive and offensive treaty of 20 April 1854 between Austria and Prussia, a treaty which for the time being brought about Russia's isolation in her dispute with Turkey. From that time onwards there is, understandably, no trace of any more wild Russian schemes against Turkey. Russia now had to prepare a defensive stand along the Danube and anywhere else on her frontiers. The siege of Silistria south of the Danube (March–June 1854) was more like beating a retreat than preparing an advance towards Constantinople.

Britain's aims during the Crimean War were merely the reflection of Russia's objectives at the beginning of the war. In the context of the Eastern Question, their essential ingredient is the maintenance of the integrity and viability of the Ottoman Empire, which was endangered by Russian encroachments. In the wider context of Britain's standing as a world power, they relate to Russia's tendency to grow in almost all directions to the detriment of her neighbours. Britain was, after the Napoleonic Wars, the real and only world power. Russia was on the road to becoming her rival. Based on her huge land mass she had the urge to be master of the adjacent seas: the Baltic, the White Sea, the Black Sea, the Caspian, the Persian Gulf. As has been said earlier, British public opinion became aware of Russia's growing expansionism in the 1820s and 1830s. Palmerston was the spokesman and symbol of that anti-Russian feeling. By the time of the Crimean War, all his colleagues, Whigs and Peelites, shared his general feeling of the growing danger from Russia's dynamic policy. Even a man like Gladstone recognized the justice of Britain's going to war in order to halt Russia's aggressiveness. He did not, however, share either the wide scope or certain details of Palmerston's war aims.

The more general war aims of Britain are, of course, embedded in the Four Points, of which the third was Britain's essential point: the revision of the Straits settlement of 1841 'in the interest of the European balance of power' or, in less diplomatic language, the reduction of Russia's power in the Black Sea. Palmerston's intentions, however, transcended this maritime objective. He wanted to curb Russia's expansionism on her European and Asian frontiers, by detaching from her tracts of land which she had acquired from north to south since the time of Peter the Great. In a memorandum that Palmerston circulated among his Cabinet colleagues on 19 March 1854, a few days before Britain's declaration of war, he drew up a plan of partitioning Russia which would have resulted in a Napoleonic 'remaniement de la carte de l'Europe'.[9] Finland and the Åland Islands were to be restored to Sweden; the Baltic provinces would be ceded to Prussia; Poland would be transformed into an independent 'substantive kingdom'; Austria would give up her possessions in northern Italy and be compensated for their loss by the acquisition of the Danubian Principalities; the Crimea and Georgia would return to Turkey. Lansdowne and Russell, two of Palmerston's Cabinet colleagues, dismissed these schemes as daydreams.

Although Palmerston himself at that time described his plan as his 'beau idéal', he kept harking back to it, with some variations, during the course of the war. He was naturally aware that its realization presupposed Russia's thorough military defeat, but he also discovered that there was a general congruity between his war aims and those of Napoleon III of France.

When, after the fall of Sevastopol on 8 September 1855, the Western powers tried to win over Sweden to their alliance, Palmerston once more put the Crimean War into the wider perspective of future Anglo-Russian relations. He wrote to Clarendon:

> The main and real object of the War is to curb the aggressive ambition of Russia. We went to war, not so much to keep the Sultan and his Musselmen in Turkey, as to keep the Russians out of Turkey; but we have a strong interest also in keeping the Russians out of Norway and Sweden ... The Treaty we propose would be a part of a long line of circumvallation to confine the future extension of Russia.[10]

If the Crimean War had continued in a third campaign in 1856 and been successful for the Allied powers, there is no reason to doubt that Russia would have had to pay the price Palmerston demanded. The documents show that in 1856 Palmerston would have used the same revolutionary means to undermine Russian power as Nicholas had planned with regard to Turkey in 1853–4. He would have tried to wage 'a war of nationalities' against Russia by staging insurrections among the non-Russian peoples of the Russian Empire, from Finland down to the Caucasus. Preparations were already advanced in 1855: there was a Finnish legion awaiting action in Sweden; an Anglo-Polish and an Anglo-Turkish legion were formed to be used in the Caucasus.[11]

Since the Crimean War ended, in Palmerston's eyes, prematurely, his 'beau idéal' shrank to minor proportions. They consisted of the Four Points plus a fifth point added at the instigation of the British government at the end of 1855. In addition to the demilitarization of the Åland Islands and some specifications of the third point, it referred to the Caucasus region. Britain had tried hard during the war to use the potential of the various tribes there, with Shamil as their most important leader, against Russia, to goad them into insurrection and to put at the disposal of the Allies cavalry troops for use in the Crimea. Clarendon dreamt of 10,000 such troops and was resolved to win over the Circassians, who inhabited the eastern shores of the Black Sea, by dangling before them recognition of their independence from Russia. Several missions to the Caucasus by consul Longworth, and the former Secretary of War, the Duke of Newcastle, in 1855 produced only meagre prospects of obtaining the expected aid from the Caucasian tribes. Britain's interest in that area was of course due to fear of Russia's advance south to Persia and east to the shores of the Caspian Sea and thence into Central Asia, thus threatening the Indian Empire.

Despite faint prospects, Clarendon had the cheek to propose the independence of Circassia during the Paris peace congress in March 1856. It was an embarrassing scene. The Russian delegate was angry about Clarendon's unilateral action, and the Turkish delegate was helpless to express his support since the question of right was obviously on Russia's side.[12] The only result of this British proposal was Russia's promise not to rebuild the forts on the coast and the decision of the congress to form a commission to draw more precisely the line of demarcation between Russia and Turkey in the Caucasus, which had been left vague after the treaties of Adrianople of 1829 and of St Petersburg of 1834.

Thus Britain's war aims did not really materialize. Although Russia was beaten militarily, her real and potential power remained unimpaired. She ceded a slice of Bessarabian territory to Moldavia and agreed to the demilitarization of the Black Sea – concessions which were humiliating but did not add up to any substantial curtailment of her power. This humiliation on Russia's side and disappointment on Britain's had important consequences. Russia strove hard, in the coming years, to undo these clauses and succeeded within less than 20 years (in 1871 and 1878). Britain's political interest in the Levant in general and in the integrity of the Ottoman Empire in particular cooled down markedly. The two world powers developed frictions in other areas – in Central Asia, in Afghanistan and in the Far East. Public interest in Britain in the fate of the Turkish Empire received a substantial blow.

France's war aims, which are to all intents and purposes Napoleon's aims, have little to do with the Eastern Question and appear to be complicated, but are in reality quite simple. Napoleon III wanted to use the crisis in the Near East for ulterior motives. First, he was interested in gaining the support of the Catholic Church in his country in order to prop up his uncertain domestic position; thus his attempt to gain as many privileges as possible in the Holy Places in favour of the Catholics is easily explained. Since Napoleon could expect Britain to follow his lead in the Levant because of her vital interests in that area, he curried favour with Britain in order to overcome

France's isolated international position in the wake of his revolutionary assumption of power in France. This aim was quickly achieved.

A more general war aim was to use the Eastern crisis of 1853 and the Crimean War as a means to revise the European order of 1815, which had been created to the detriment of France. Napoleon tried to realize this objective throughout his reign. His entry into the war and especially his alignment with Austria, which was also a favourite idea of his Foreign Minister, Drouyn de Lhuys, was to drive a wedge into the Holy Alliance – or what was left of it after 1848–49 – and finally to crush it, thus destroying the guardian of the order of 1815. This objective was achieved through the treaty of 2 December 1854 with Austria.

Turning to more specific and immediate war aims evolving from the general ones, Napoleon wanted to bring about the restoration of Poland and change on the Apennine peninsula in favour of Sardinia. These aims presupposed, of course, an extension of the theatre of war in the Crimea to Central Europe. The fall of Sevastopol on 8 September 1855 seemed to be a propitious moment to convince Britain to change the character of the war. When Britain turned down the Polish proposal, Napoleon hastened to finish the war altogether.

The restoration of Poland would have entailed a new order of things in Central Europe, the Balkans and Italy. There are sufficient documents to show how Napoleon proposed to bring about such a 'remaniement de la carte de l'Europe'.[13] It would have been similar to Palmerston's 'beau idéal'. In fact, both knew of each other's secret plans. Prussia, according to Napoleon, would be compensated for the loss of her Polish provinces by acquisitions in northern Germany. The German Confederation would, in the process, have to disappear. Austria would give up her hold over northern Italy and receive compensation in the Danubian Principalities (thus Napoleon made light of the officially proclaimed war aim of the integrity of the Ottoman Empire). Sardinia in Italy would be enlarged by the Austrian provinces of Lombardy and Venetia and perhaps also by Parma and Modena. Through this redrawing of the map of Europe, Napoleon could pose as the man favouring the wishes of the peoples, who would formally confirm these changes in plebiscites. He would thus be the champion of the principles of popular sovereignty and nationalities. Use of these principles was an important component of Napoleon's ideology.

What profits would Napoleon reap from this regrouping of the map of Europe? He gave the answer in a conversation with the German Count Ernest of Saxe-Coburg: 'By God, as to France I don't mind if I get compensations on the Rhine or in Italy.'[14] Thus the various objectives which Napoleon tried to pursue in the following decade and a half can already be traced back to the Crimean War. As with Palmerston's 'beau idéal', their realization would have meant a continuation of the war with Russia into 1856 or beyond. A world war might well have been the result.

The war aims of the other two belligerent powers, Turkey and Sardinia, are of minor importance. Turkey, in fact, almost played the role of a cipher. Turkish reactions towards Russian demands during 1853 were the result of developments on the spot in Constantinople to a greater extent than is evident from most books on that period. Ann Pottinger Saab has shown that there was a strong 'war-party' which was not only anti-Russian, but anti-European. It consisted of men at the top and of members of religious circles: the Minister of War, Mehmet Ali; the Minister of the Guards, Mehmet Rüştü Pasha; the Sheikh ul Islam, the religious leader and the softas, students of religious schools. They staged riots in the capital during the summer and autumn of 1853 that were directed against the government's and the Sultan's policy of improving the lot of the Christians in the empire. Saab has shown that the Allied fleets were called up to the Bosphorus not for fear of a Russian offensive, but for fear of further riots in Constantinople.[15]

Characteristically, the Turkish government during the war took no part in formulating the Four Points of 8 August 1854 or the Austrian ultimatum of 16 December 1855, which included the fifth point (Circassia, etc.). Turkish war ideas can, however, be deduced from some of the Western documents. Any arrangement on the lot of the Christians (the fourth point), whether of Russian or Western origin, was anathema to the Turks. With regard to the Principalities, the Turkish government did not wish Austria, or Europe as a whole, to become their protector in lieu of Russia. They wanted the strengthening of Turkey's hold on the provinces. Further to the east they dreamt of the independence of the Crimea and of Circassia and Georgia under the suzerainty of the Sultan. But their opinion was of no relevance at any time.

Almost the same can be said of Sardinia's war aims. When the country joined the Western Alliance in January 1855, there were of course high hopes of bringing the Italian Question, especially Austria's presence in northern Italy, and the Roman Question before the peace conference. Austria had already made it clear that she would not conclude the December treaty of 1854 unless she was assured of the strict observance of the status quo in Italy. As Austrian cooperation was more important to the Western powers than Sardinia's, the Turin government joined the alliance – after sharp internal dissensions – unconditionally. Cavour, however, was invited to take part in the final peace congress. After the Eastern Question had been settled, the Italian Question was put on the table, with angry discussions ensuing between Austria on the one side, the Western powers and Sardinia on the other. No result was reached. Cavour left Paris an utterly disappointed man, but imbued with the notion that only the cannon would solve the Italian Question, that is, quench his thirst for Sardinia's expansion. In a general sense, however, Sardinia's participation in the war and in the peace talks pointed to the fact that the situation in Italy was of common concern for the great powers: the Italian Question was Europeanized or, as Di Nolfo has put it, was 'diplomatized'.[16]

Annotated bibliography

Of great importance for describing Russia's war aims is the documentary evidence published for 1853 and 1854 by Zaiončkovskij, *Priloženija* (quoted in the preceding chapter). The most important study of Russia's position in the Crimean War, both for the political and for the military side, is Evgenij V. Tarle, *Krymskaja vojna*, 2 vols (Moscow and Leningrad, 1941–3, 4th edn in Tarle's collected works, Moscow, 1959; all quotations from the 4th edn. Written during the Second World War, it has a nationalistic slant; Tarle quotes lavishly from published and unpublished documents. A more recent treatment of both the political and military aspects is John Shelton Curtiss, *Russia's Crimean War* (Durham, NC, 1979). Cf. also Igor V. Bestužev, *Krymskaja vojna 1853–1856 gg* (Moscow, 1956) (succinct, but also with a nationalistic bias).

Britain's war aims may be culled from a number of studies: James B. Conacher, *The Aberdeen Coalition, 1852–1855: A Study in Mid-Nineteenth-Century Party Politics* (Cambridge, 1968); James B. Conacher, *Britain and the Crimea, 1855–56: Problems of War and Peace* (Basingstoke and London, 1972) (Conacher's first book is rich in details on domestic policy and parliamentary affairs); Paul W. Schroeder, *Austria, Great Britain, and the Crimean War: The Destruction of the European Concert* (Ithaca, NY, and London, 1972) (sometimes unfairly critical of Britain's role, but with many sensible suggestions on Austrian policy); Hermann Wentker, *Zerstörung der Großmacht Rußland? Die britischen Kriegsziele im Krimkrieg* (Göttingen and Zürich, 1993) (focuses on the role of the Cabinet, the Crown and a few of the more important ambassadors).

For France's war aims, see the book by Mange, *Near Eastern Policy* (mentioned above in Chapter 1); Martin Stauch, *Im Schatten der Heiligen Allianz. Frankreichs Preußenpolitik von 1848 bis 1857* (Frankfurt, 1996).

At long last there is a well-researched general book on Turkey during the Crimean War: Candan Badem, *The Ottoman Crimean War (1853–1856)* (Leiden and Boston, 2010); Saab's book (cf. Chapter 2) is relevant for the years 1853–4 until the outbreak of the European war. Lengthy portions on the military structure of the Ottoman Empire and also a long chapter on the Crimean War are in James J. Reid, *Crisis of the Ottoman Empire: Prelude to Collapse 1839–1878* (Stuttgart, 2000).

Sardinia's role is well documented and well treated. The more important documentary collections are Federico Curato (ed.), *Le relazioni diplomatiche fra la Gran Bretagna e il Regno di Sardegna*, III serie: 1848–60, vols 4–5 (Rome, 1968–9); Federico Curato (ed.), *Le relazioni diplomatiche tra la Gran Bretagna e il Regno di Sardegna dal 1852 al 1856. Il carteggio diplomatico di Sir James Hudson*, vol. 2 (Turin, 1956); Franco Valsecchi (ed.), *Le relazioni diplomatiche fra l'Austria e il Regno di Sardegna*, III serie: 1848–60, vol. 4 (Rome, 1963); Carlo Pischedda (ed.), *Camillo Cavour, Epistolario*, vols 10–13 (1853–6) (Florence, 1985–92); Camillo Cavour,

Carteggi, vol. 7, *Cavour e l'Inghilterra. Carteggio con V.E. d'Azeglio*, vol. 1, *Il Congresso di Parigi* (Bologna, 1961). Monographic studies include Franco Valsecchi, *L'Europa e il Risorgimento. L'alleanza di Crimea* (Florence, 1968); Ennio Di Nolfo, *Europa e Italia nel 1855–56* (Rome, 1967); Peter Klemensberger, *Die Westmächte und Sardinien während des Krimkrieges. Der Beitritt des Königreichs Sardinien zur britisch-französischen Allianz im Rahmen der europäischen Politik* (Zurich, 1972).

4

The non-belligerent German powers: Austria and Prussia

Austria's policy and attitude during 1853 and 1854 are responsible for the theatre of the Russo-Turkish war being moved from the Danube to the Crimean peninsula. When the two Western powers declared war on Russia on 27 and 28 March 1854, they assembled their troops along the Turkish Straits in order to protect Constantinople from a Russian onslaught from the Danube. When it became obvious that the Turkish troops were holding out in the fortress of Silistria just south of the Danube, the Commanders-in-Chief of the Western troops decided to move their men to Varna to assist the Turks at Silistria and to warn the Russians not to move further south.

However, this was not the main reason for the Russian evacuation of the Principalities in August 1854; this was due to the threatening attitude adopted by Austria. She had mobilized her troops and massed them on the right flank of the Russian occupation forces, in the Banat, in Transylvania and in Galicia. On 3 June 1854 the Vienna government summoned St Petersburg to demand evacuation of the Principalities; otherwise, Austrian troops would move in and evict the Russians by force of arms. With this unexpected prospect of four enemies fighting Russia in that corner of Europe, the Tsar, pressed by Paskevich, his Commander-in-Chief, did the only sensible thing and after some hesitation, feigning strategic reasons, evacuated the Principalities. Austrian troops moved in to the same extent as the Russians had moved out; troops from the two countries never came into contact with each other. The Austrians stayed there during the rest of the war and until March 1857.

What was the aim of this remarkable Austrian action which did not mean open war, but was at the least an open threat towards a power with which Austria had been in a close conservative alliance and which had helped her out of dire straits during the Hungarian revolution of 1849? The answer is not easily found. Contemporaries and historians have made numerous misleading statements and written many half-truths about this issue. Only recently have newly published Austrian documents allowed us to get nearer to the truth.[1]

Austrian policy, although threatening military intervention and leading to the occupation of the Principalities by Austrian (and Turkish) troops, was never of an offensive or expansionist character; it was strictly defensive. There were, it is true, voices in Austria among the military leaders and among diplomats that wanted to seize the opportunity to make gains for Austria in the Balkans: in the Danubian Principalities, in Bosnia and Herzegovina. At times even the Tsar or the French Emperor urged Austria to be the accomplice of their expansionist or revisionist policy. But Austria acted on the maxim *Si vis pacem, bellum para*. Austria was the only one of the five great powers that needed peace in order to survive. Buol, the Foreign Minister, and the young Emperor Francis Joseph acted according to Metternich's defensive and conservative principles.

It was Austria that attempted, during the whole of 1853 and the first months of 1854, to get together great-power conferences in Vienna in order to preserve peace. After the war had broken out, she kept on trying to bring the belligerents back to the conference table. Each war party tried hard to win Austria over to its side, sometimes luring her, sometimes threatening her. She steadfastly resisted offers to annex adjacent territories, whereupon she was told that other means could be applied to bring her to reason. Tsar Nicholas threatened the Vienna government: he would revolutionize the Balkan peoples; Napoleon warned 'J'insurgerai l'Italie.'[2]

The feeling of being threatened by revolution is the key to understanding Austria's attitude during the years 1853–6. The revolution of 1848–9 had almost resulted in the ruin of the Habsburg monarchy. The Emperor and his counsellors were deeply aware of the danger of revolution raising its head again. Martial law, proclaimed during the revolution, was still in force in many regions of the empire during 1853–4. The war that broke out between Turkey and Russia on Austria's frontier in October 1853 conjured up the threat of new insurrections within the empire. If Austria – and Prussia – had joined the war on either side, such a European war would have kindled new revolutions in Hungary, northern Italy and Bohemia, and would have dealt the final death-blow to the Habsburg monarchy.

At the beginning of the crisis, Austria tried to sit on the fence and on 10 November 1853 declared her armed neutrality, an attitude which could not be maintained for long because the torch of revolution could as easily be hurled into the empire from without. Therefore, Austrian policy moved step by step to the side of the Western powers in order to be safe from revolutionary plans from their side. The most important stages of this policy were the attempt in the spring of 1854 to conclude a four-power convention with France, Britain and Prussia (it failed because of Prussian resistance); the formulation of the Four Points on 8 August 1854 together with France and Britain; the alliance of 2 December 1854 with the Western powers which held out the prospect of Austria's entering the war in case the peace talks that were to be convened before the end of the year failed; and finally the Austrian ultimatum of 16 December 1855 in which Russia was told either to accept the war aims of the three powers (the Four Points plus the new fifth point) or see Austria enter the war on the side of the Western powers.

These steps seem to point to an offensive, warlike policy. Contemporaries saw them in this light; historians have misunderstood them in this way. Austria's preparedness for war was, however, mere pretence. Buol cunningly and wittingly built up this smokescreen in order to effect two things: on the one hand to coerce Russia, in the face of a three-power or four-power coalition (since Prussia could not stand aside in the long run), to give in; on the other hand to delude the Western powers with the false hope that Austria would enter the war and thus to make them desist from stoking the fire of revolution, prevailing upon them to formulate war aims that were not too exorbitant. This explanation also holds good with regard to the Austrian occupation of the Danubian Principalities in August 1854. It was an act of war only in outward appearance; in truth, it was an act of peace aimed at removing the dangerous theatre of war on her own flank and making the question of the Danubian Principalities, which was hitherto shaped by Russia alone, a European concern. Moreover, the occupation of the Principalities was not intended (this is another common misinterpretation) to be the first step towards their annexation by Austria.

Thus Austria's behaviour during the Crimean War shows a warlike policy on the surface only; at the root of the matter it was a defensive calculation, forced upon her leaders because they had to fight for the very existence of the empire, which needed law and order inside and peace outside. Buol's policy was dangerous brinkmanship, but everybody was deceived: the Western powers in believing that Austria would soon enter the war on their side; Russia in being frightened that Austria would soon be entrenched on the opposite side. Francis Joseph once said that the sword of Damocles must hover over the Russian leaders; and Buol at the end of the war asked friend and foe alike, 'Did you really believe that Austria could have risked joining the war without risking universal war and revolution and thus the final ruin of her Empire?'[3] Decades later, it was to be the World War and revolution at its end that sounded the last hour of the Habsburg monarchy.

The same yardstick must also be applied to Austria's relations with Prussia and her policy at the Federal Diet at Frankfurt. Austria tried over and over again to line up Prussia and the states of the German Confederation behind her; these attempts were supposed to increase her own political and military weight, thus enabling her to work, with greater emphasis, for peace east and west. It is wrong to blame Austria for having followed a seesaw policy between the two camps, for having forfeited the sympathies of all the other powers, for being responsible for her isolation in Europe after 1856 and for having had to pay for this in 1859. According to the laws of her fragile existence, Austria could not have helped acting as she did during the Crimean War unless she was willing to invite her own ruin.

Prussia, too, was subject to the fear of revolution almost to the same extent as Austria. But there are additional factors to explain her policy. To begin with, the structure of foreign policy in Berlin at that time did not permit of any homogeneous action. Prussian foreign policy was managed by King Frederick William IV, by the Foreign Ministry under Otto von Manteuffel, by the pro-Russian camarilla at court, and at times by Prince William and the Party of the *Wochenblatt* (a liberal weekly leaning towards the West).

Viewed from the outside, all these influences negated each other, with the result that Prussian foreign policy seemed to be a non-policy. The documents[4] show that there was a hidden guiding hand in this inactivity and chaos: that of the King, who managed to build up for himself the image of a romantic, theatrical, volatile and incompetent sovereign. At the end of 1853 and in the spring of 1854 the pro-Western tendencies in Berlin, favoured by Manteuffel and Prince William, seemed to have gained the upper hand in the tug of war with the Russophile party.

Prince William's political ideas were simple and straightforward. He once wrote to his brother, the King, 'A great power cannot look on, it must act

MONSIEUR CLICQUOT THINKS IT SAFER TO TAKE SHELTER TILL THE SHOWER PASSES OVER.

FIGURE 6 *The Prussian King Frederick William IV declaring his neutrality. He is shown as a tipsy man with a bottle of champagne in his hand.* Punch 26 (1854), p. 182. *University Library of Heidelberg, CC-BY-SA 3.0.*

unless it wants to abdicate from this status and wants to retreat to the position of Belgium, Holland, Denmark, Sweden, the opinions of which do not matter in questions of high policy and which therefore are not asked to express any.'[5] William reasoned that the Tsar, by ordering his troops to occupy the Danubian Principalities, had committed a blatant injustice and violated the rules of the Concert of Europe. He must be coerced to return to this European Areopagus by being made to realize his injustice and repent. The safest way to bring this about was to align Prussia with the Western powers and Austrian policy, to take part in their diplomatic offensive and by common threats to force the Tsar to give up his false position in the Principalities. The simple reasoning behind such demands was that the Tsar would, in view of the imposing union of the four great powers, give in and not dare begin a great war.

His brother, the King, sharply dissented. After much hesitation he refused to subscribe to a convention which the other three powers had proposed to him in February 1854. On 27 February he made up his mind by stating in a memorandum:

> Prussia must remain in a status of neutrality; not in a vacillating and indecisive neutrality, but in a sovereign neutrality ... She must lean to neither side ... On both sides the war that is on the point of breaking out is unjust. And I do not permit of an unjust war being forced upon Prussia.[6]

The real cause for this decision was the reasoning that Prussia could never profit from this war and that her vital interests, at least until the end of 1855, were in no way endangered. Lining up with Russia was out of the question, for the simple reason that the main theatre of war would then be transferred from the Danube (later on from the Crimea) to the Rhine, where Prussia would serve as Russia's battering ram and experience a second Jena and Auerstedt. Although the Tsar, at the turn of 1853–4, offered Prussia Russian auxiliary troops, her unfavourable strategical situation would not have changed. Most of the German secondary states would, by an instinct of self-preservation, have allied themselves with France as they had done fifty years before. Revolution, barely suppressed, would have resurfaced, at least in the western half of the kingdom, and the Rhenish provinces would thus have been lost. The British Navy would have effectively blockaded Prussia's Baltic coast, thus cutting off her overseas trade. Austria, in the event of her joining the West, would have taken back Silesia, which she had lost to Frederick the Great.

In the opposite case of Prussia joining the Western powers (in which case Austria would certainly have been on the same side), the main theatre of war would have been moved from the Danube to the Vistula. A victory of the four allied powers over Russia would then have been a matter of course. But for Prussia it would have been a Pyrrhic victory: she would have been under the thumb of France which would have taken the Rhenish provinces from her as a trophy; Poland would have been restored and Silesia lost; Prussia would have been compensated for this loss by territories in northern Germany, probably in Saxony. The most dangerous prospect besides this territorial reshuffling would have been the proximity of an overwhelming France on her western frontier and a revengeful Russia on her eastern frontier.

The Prussian King, having made up his mind to remain neutral, at once felt the acute danger of his isolation. In order to soften it he offered an offensive and defensive alliance to Austria. No sooner was it concluded, on 20 April 1854, than the King, goaded by the camarilla under Leopold von Gerlach, tried to extricate himself from the far-reaching obligations to which he had subscribed. These demanded he support Austria, if need be by force of arms, in her impending summons to Russia to evacuate the Principalities.

This conduct was henceforth typical of the Prussian King: as soon as he had taken a step in favour of one side of the Crimean War protagonists (in this case in favour of Austria and indirectly of the Western powers), he retracted in part or in full in order to appease the other side. Thus, at the end of July 1854 he ordered his representative at the Vienna Conference not to sign the Four Points. From this time onwards he was regarded by the Western powers and by Austria as having excluded himself from the Concert of Europe. Feeling the pinch of his isolation he offered Austria, after the Russians had evacuated the Principalities, an additional article to the April treaty, promising Prussia's aid in case of a future Russian attack on the Danubian Principalities. This again was a pro-Western initiative. It became a dead letter at once when Austria concluded her December alliance with Britain and France behind Prussia's back. The Prussian King then reverted to a pro-Russian attitude.

During 1855, Prussia and her King were no longer taken seriously by the other great powers. Russia was at least content that she remained neutral. Prussia was not admitted to the Vienna peace conference early in 1855, and after the fall of Sevastopol the King again became acutely aware of the danger of his isolation. When Austria delivered her ultimatum to Russia at the end of December and Prussia was invited to endorse it, the King hesitated again. He received threats from Paris and London: when the French guards, having left the Crimea, were received in Paris on 31 December 1855, the Emperor asked them 'to be prepared for new and greater tasks'.[7] On 1 January 1856 an article in the London *Morning Post* warned Prussia of the consequences of staying out of the war.

A week later Clarendon drafted a despatch to Bloomfield, the British envoy in Berlin, in which he warned the Prussian government 'that the neutrality which Prussia for a time maintained is now considered by Her Majesty's Government to be at an end'.[8] Although the despatch was delivered in a mitigated form, the language of the Western powers was well understood in Berlin. The King was aware that the new campaign in 1856 would be waged in the Baltic and that Prussia's neutrality would then be terminated

FIGURE 7 *The Prussian King trying to get into the Vienna conference, 1855. Punch 28 (1855), p. 125. University Library of Heidelberg, CC-BY-SA 3.0.*

by force. He thereupon sent letters and telegrams to St Petersburg imploring the Tsar to accept the Austrian ultimatum. In case of refusal he let it be known that there was 'the possibility' of Prussia 'drawing nearer to the attitude of Austria', in other words, of breaking off relations with St Petersburg.[9]

Relations between Prussia and the Western powers had become especially strained because of the continued passage of arms, ammunition and war matériel across Prussian territory to Russia. The problem is to be seen in the wider context of Russia's foreign trade during the war years.[10] In 1852, a normal peace year, the value of Russia's exports amounted to 100.1 million rubles, of which roughly half (48.1 million rubles) passed through the Baltic, and a large amount (35.1 million rubles) through the Black Sea, while just

over 11 per cent (11.3 million rubles) took the land route and the smallest
fraction arrived through the White Sea (5.6 million rubles). In 1855, a full-
length war year, Russian exports sank to just over a quarter (27.5 million
rubles) of the figure of 1852, of which the bulk (23.7 million rubles) was
transported overland. Russia's imports in 1852 amounted to goods worth
83.1 million rubles, of which the bulk (59.5 million rubles) passed through
the Baltic, and 14.4 via the land route. In 1855 the Allied blockade of
Russia's coast was quite effective, so that goods amounting to the value of
only 3.7 million rubles used the sea route whereas goods worth 52.5 million
rubles were transported overland. Russian imports in 1855, therefore, did
not shrink to the same proportion (56.2 million rubles as compared to 83.1
million rubles in 1852) as her exports.

Prussia was the transit country for this overland trade. The ports of
Danzig, Königsberg and Memel were much busier during the war than in
times of peace. Prussia's economy (and also that of the Hanse towns) thus
profited markedly from the war. The interesting thing about Prussia's transit
monopoly (only a very small fraction seems to have passed through Austria)
is that through it British goods found their way to Russia and vice versa.

Russia's imports of war matériel were not interrupted altogether in spite
of the Allied coastal blockade and Prussia's interdiction of their transit.
Russia's war industry in the 1850s was underdeveloped compared to that of
France or Britain. To carry on a war with the foremost industrialized powers
of the world for any length of time (more than two years), Russia was
dependent on imports for her war machinery. The Prussian King issued a
decree under pressure from the Western powers on 18 March 1854, that is,
ten days before the outbreak of the war, prohibiting the transit of arms
through his territory. In the eyes of the Allies this was supposed to stop the
arms trade between Belgium and Russia.

On 1 June 1854 another royal decree prohibited the transit of all kinds
of ammunition, including raw materials like lead, sulphur and saltpetre. But
the effect of these decrees was evaded because arms and war matériel were
legally imported into Prussia – the traders paid considerable import duties
for them – and the goods then found their way into free circulation, and
from there across the Prussian border into Russia. In view of fresh Allied
protests and pressure – the threat of blockading the Prussian coast was most
effective – a third decree, issued by the King on 8 March 1855, forbade the
export of the aforementioned goods unless they originated from members of
the German Customs Union. Allied protests still continued after this because
the British and French consuls were aware of the uninterrupted clandestine
exports of non-German arms to Russia. This caused much irritation until
the very end of the war.

Neither Russian nor Prussian statistics are available to calculate the
volume of this trade with Russia. The Prussian Foreign Ministry set up a
special file on this matter, consisting of four volumes; but they were seized
by the Red Army in 1945, have not yet been returned and thus remain

inaccessible to historians. From other Prussian sources it becomes obvious that the British government acted hypocritically because the Prussian decrees were to the detriment of Russia only, not the Allied powers.[11] They were still able to procure foreign arms from other countries, especially Belgium, whereas Russia could not. Furthermore, large quantities of the contraband of war which reached Prussia, such as sulphur and saltpetre, originated in Britain, and the British government took no effective measures to stop this trade.

Annotated bibliography

The literature on Austria's role during the Crimean War is ample, but controversial. The first serious treatment is Heinrich Friedjung, *Der Krimkrieg und die österreichische Politik* (Stuttgart and Berlin, 1907, 2nd edn 1911). Friedjung is of the opinion that Austria, or at least Foreign Minister Buol, wanted to join the war on the side of the Western powers and that Austria's occupation of the Danubian Principalities was meant to be a preliminary step on the road to their annexation. A revision was begun, but not pushed very far, by Bernhard Unckel, *Österreich und der Krimkrieg. Studien zur Politik der Donaumonarchie in den Jahren 1852–1856* (Lübeck and Hamburg, 1969). With Schroeder, *Austria* (cf. Chapter 3), the wheel finally swung round. Through a fresh interpretation he was able to state that Austria's policy was peaceful from beginning to end, that Buol and the Emperor Francis Joseph never had the idea of annexing the Principalities. This view is also held by the author of this book. Besides the articles cited in note 25, see Winfried Baumgart, *The Peace of Paris 1856: Studies in War, Diplomacy, and Peacemaking* (Santa Barbara and Oxford, 1981).

Prussia's role during the war is covered by Kurt Borries, *Preußen im Krimkrieg (1853–1856)* (Stuttgart, 1930). Both Prussian and Austrian diplomacy is now copiously documented in the relevant series *AGKK* I and II (over 4,300 pages).

5

The neutral powers

Sweden

Next in strategic and military importance to the Allied war effort against Russia after Austria and Prussia was Sweden, Russia's neighbour in the north. In view of the Allied war aim to reduce Russian power in European affairs, not just to solve the Eastern Question in the south-east, Sweden's role in the war obviously seemed essential to Allied war-planners.

Since the Napoleonic Wars, Sweden had pursued a friendly policy towards her powerful neighbour, but the Crimean War marked a change of front in favour of the Allied powers. In 1854 the first alliance feelers were thrown out by France and Britain and the political alliance of 21 November 1855 was, on both sides, meant to open the door to Sweden's entry into the war if it continued in 1856.

At the beginning of the Eastern crisis, on 20 December 1853, Sweden, together with Denmark, declared her neutrality. At the outbreak of the European war at the end of March 1854 it was Napoleon III who took the initiative to invite Sweden's cooperation on the side of the Allies. The Swedish King Oscar I was aware of the strategic importance of his country and therefore set his demands at a very high level. Britain put the brakes on the negotiations with Sweden in this phase because, being the junior partner militarily in the alliance with France, she felt that Sweden would lower her weight even more by joining as a French satellite. In 1855 the roles were reversed. The new vigorous Palmerston government reopened the initiative to entice Sweden into an alliance, with Napoleon, particularly after the fall of Sevastopol on 8 September 1855, acting as the brakeman.

Here then are the more important details. On 25 March 1854, just before the declaration of war on Russia and when the Allied squadrons were sailing and steaming towards the Baltic, the French Foreign Minister instructed his envoy in Stockholm, Charles-Victor Lobstein, to begin overtures to the King of Sweden. During the ensuing months the King realized that he was in a position to raise his demands, in order to receive as much military aid as possible from the Allies during the war and as many gains and guarantees for the future as possible, to guard against Russian revenge in peacetime. He saw that the Allies could not muster powerful navies in the Baltic, and would only deliver pinpricks on Russia's coast. The 10,000 French troops that were transported to the Baltic were simply not enough to venture a landing on Russian soil; when they destroyed and occupied the fortress of Bomarsund on the Åland Islands on 16 August 1854, this was not enough to goad the Swedish King into either lowering his demands or entering the war.

What were the King's demands and what did he offer in return? During the months of May to August 1854 it became clear what he wanted: the return of Finland, which Sweden had lost in 1807; the guarantee of this retrocession and of the whole Kingdom of Sweden-Norway; subsidies for the duration of the war amounting to 5 million francs per month; 60,000 auxiliary troops from France to fight alongside the Swedish troops against Russia; Swedish participation in the peace negotiations; and the guarantee of Austria's entry into the war and of her sanction of the Swedish war gains. In return, Sweden promised to put at the disposal of the Allies 60,000 ground troops and 10,000 naval troops, including four ships of the line, two frigates, a dozen other vessels and 192 gunboats. The latter were especially valuable for manoeuvring in the shallow coastal waters of the Baltic.[1]

It is remarkable that the French government was in favour of negotiating on this basis, but the Aberdeen government poured water into the French wine. It did not want to have Finland in the programme and did not expect Austria – and the rest of Germany – to subscribe to such a drastic weakening of Russian power. From the documents it also appears that Clarendon felt some pique at the French going it alone in Stockholm, sending special emissaries there without properly coordinating their diplomacy with the British government. In any case, by August 1854, even after the conquest of the Åland Islands, it was much too late to hope for Sweden's entry in the campaign for that year.

The negotiations slumbered for almost ten months and the attention of the Allies was fixed on the Crimean theatre of war. With the advent of the Palmerston government, British policy towards Sweden changed radically. Palmerston's interest in the northern theatre of war increased substantially when he read a long despatch which the British consul at Christiania, John Crowe, had sent to London on 23 May 1855.[2] In it he dealt with Russia's interest in and claims to Finmark, the northernmost province of Norway. Although Russia demanded rights of pasturage for the reindeer herds of the Lapps of northern Finland, Crowe wrote that it was access to an ice-free harbour that Russia really wanted. Crowe linked Russia's wish to seize Finmark with her simultaneous attempts to gain a foothold on the mouth of the Amur river in China.

Such a global viewpoint was much to Palmerston's liking. He had Clarendon draft a despatch to Stockholm asking the King of Sweden to grant Russia no concession in Finmark, and promising British naval support in 'repelling any aggressive act on the part of Russia'. King Oscar concurred with the British demand, but asked for a guarantee of the whole territory of the monarchy, not only of northern Norway. By 30 August 1855 both London and Paris had accepted the extended guarantee and the Swedish King had stepped down his demands by no longer insisting on the retrocession of Finland. At this point, too, there was no longer any discussion of Sweden's immediate entry into the war, the siege of Sevastopol dragging on, Austria having distanced herself from the Western powers, and the Baltic campaign of the Allies of 1855 having effected nothing tangible.

After the fall of Sevastopol it was now Napoleon III who became sceptical of the extension of the war to northern Europe, especially after Britain had rebuffed him in his wish to broach the Polish question and thus to open a land front in Central Europe. This is the origin of Palmerston's emphatic 'circumvallation' letter of 25 September 1855, mentioned above, in which he argued passionately for a treaty of guarantee with Sweden.[3] There were further delays, but finally a treaty was concluded between the Western powers and Sweden on 21 November 1855. In it Sweden promised not to grant any rights of pasturage, fishery or territory to Russia. The Western powers in return promised Sweden that they would repel any such Russian demands by the use of force. The treaty, which was made known to Russia on 17 December 1855, looked innocuous, but it was meant to be the first step towards Sweden's entry into the war. Its greatest effect was, however, psychological. The prospect of multiplying her enemies induced Russia to accept the Austrian ultimatum in January 1856 and thus open the door to peace. Both Britain and King Oscar regretted the Russian decision, and on 12 January he proposed an offensive alliance to the Western powers. He toned down his war aims substantially: besides a subsidy for his army, he was content with the cession of the Åland Islands.[4] But by now it was too late.

Spain

The participation of Spain in the Crimean War was never so imminent as that of Sweden. The situation of the two countries is not really comparable, but that of Spain and Sardinia is. Both countries had no vital interest in the Eastern Question, but both had ulterior motives in joining the fray. Sardinia wanted to further her expansionism in Italy; Spain was on the lookout for a great-power guarantee for her overseas possessions, especially for Cuba, which the United States coveted.

On 12 April 1854 Spain declared her neutrality. It was benevolent towards the Western powers since Spain was, at least on paper, a constitutional monarchy favouring the crusading spirit of the West against autocratic Russia and, of course, the Catholic cause in the Holy Places issue. Diplomatic relations with Russia had been broken since the death of Ferdinand VII in 1833; in other words, since the beginning of the Carlist Wars. The international standing of Spain was low, and the internal political situation was more unstable than that of any other country in Europe. Since the defeat of the conservative Carlists in 1839, government power had shifted to and fro between the two liberal factions of the *Moderados* and *Progresistas*. The danger of either a revolution or a military dictatorship was always hanging in the air. There was such a revolution on 28 June 1854, which brought the *Progresistas* to power, but produced a rift within the army.

In the *Progresista* government there were sympathies for the cause of the Western allies that led to the first feelers promising Spanish intervention being thrown out to Paris and London. At the beginning of 1855 British commissioners bought up horses for the Crimea at Algeciras and San Roque. On 30 January the Spanish steamer *Trento* left Alicante with 200 mules – much more serviceable than horses in the Crimea – for Balaklava. On the same day the Spanish chargé d'affaires in Paris had a conversation with the French Foreign Minister in which the latter asked whether Spain would not follow Sardinia's example in joining the Western alliance. He even hinted at guaranteeing Spain's overseas possessions.[5]

Meanwhile, on the battlefield, there were concrete signs of Spanish interest in the war. After the outbreak of war on the Danube, a Spanish military mission under Field Marshal Juan Prim was sent to join the Turkish army. It produced a lengthy report on the war on the Danube which was published in Madrid in 1855. After the revolution of 28 June 1854 it was replaced by another mission, headed by Colonel Tomás O'Ryan, who was with the Allied siege army at Sevastopol. Another sign of Spanish presence was a number of Spaniards serving in the French Foreign Legion – O'Ryan estimated them at 900 – but they were mostly refugees of Carlist background.

After the accession of Sardinia to the Western alliance in January 1855 and the despatch of Sardinian troops to the Crimea, the Spanish government earnestly considered the idea of following suit. On the Allies' side it was the French government and Napoleon who tried to persuade the Spanish government to accede to the treaty of 10 April 1854; the British were more reticent. When General Juan de Zabala became Foreign Minister in June 1855, he took matters in hand energetically. On 22 June the British minister at Madrid reported Zabala's offer to send a contingent of up to 20,000 men to the Crimea. The reaction in London was unenthusiastic because it was obvious that all the cost for its transport and upkeep would fall on Britain, and that Parliament would be unlikely to grant the money. The Spaniards were told to declare war on their own account against Russia and send an army as a separate body to the seat of war.[6]

The Spanish offer was renewed a month later and Napoleon left the decision to the British, knowing that they would have to defray the cost in the end. Eventually the Spanish government enumerated the conditions under which they were ready to take part in the war, one of which was the guarantee of the Spanish overseas possessions. Spanish historians are not correct in saying that the fall of Sevastopol on 8 September 1855 made all further discussions superfluous.[7] On 17 September, Clarendon wrote in a letter to his minister at Madrid that the Spanish offer should be unconditional, that is, not be mixed up with territorial or financial guarantees. Three weeks later most of the conditions were scrapped by the Spanish government, except the demand that the Allies find means to transport a Spanish force, which had now been increased to 30,000 men.

By now, however, relations between Britain and Spain had become so soured over the affair of Mr Boylan, an Irish iron-manufacturer at Santiago de Cuba who was at loggerheads with the Spanish local authorities there, that the British government took no further note of the Spanish offer. Spanish pride and the nationalist spirit in Britain at that time could not, it seems, meet halfway.

The United States

The United States played a much more decisive role in the conduct of the Crimean War than did Spain. Anglo-American relations were severely strained after the American War of Independence and during the first half of the nineteenth century. Areas of friction during the 1850s were widespread and all had a common root: rivalry in the Western hemisphere, in the Pacific and in the Far East. Britain, on the whole, was already on the defensive at that time, whereas the United States was in the throes of expansion. The Pierce administration (1853–7) was in the tight grip of 'manifest destiny' and 'spread-eagleism'.

On the other hand, relations between the United States and Russia had traditionally been friendly and reached a high pitch during the Crimean War. The astonishing fact that the most democratic and freedom-loving nation and the most autocratic and repressive great power in the world were holding each other in high esteem and acting cordially together in international affairs is to be explained by their having Great Britain as their common enemy. During the war there were growing signs of cooperation, which were regarded on both sides of the Atlantic as a prelude to America's entry into the war. Thus, Secretary of State William Marcy confided to Eduard von Stoeckl, the Russian minister to Washington, on 20 April 1854, that the United States wanted to remain neutral, 'but God knows if this is possible', and that Britain's attitude 'has considerably Russified us'.[8] On the other hand, British Cabinet ministers feared the prospect of the United States using the golden opportunity of Britain being hamstrung by the war in Europe to undermine Britain's position in Central America, the Caribbean and the Pacific. Thus the First Lord of the Admiralty, Sir James Graham, commented in October 1854, 'We are fast "drifting" into war with the United States.'[9]

Common antagonism towards Britain brought the United States and Russia together in many respects. At the beginning of July 1854, when the belligerents were not yet facing each other in the Crimea, President Pierce voiced the idea of offering his mediation to both camps. Both sides replied negatively to the idea, and the plan failed. On 22 July 1854 in Washington Marcy and Stoeckl signed a convention on the rights of neutrals at sea, which contained the principle of 'free ships make free goods' and was clearly directed at Britain's traditional practice of privateering. At the beginning of the war, furthermore, the Russian government let it be known in Washington that it would not oppose the United States seizing the Sandwich Islands (Hawaii). The calculation behind this was that such an act would raise tension between Britain and the United States. In fact, the American agent in Honolulu, David L. Gregg, was given full power to arrange for the transfer of the islands to the United States as quickly as possible. Vigorous protests in Washington were the result, and it was only King Kamehameha's staunch resolution to remain independent that made the Americans more discreet.[10] The same object, to sow the seeds of dissension between Britain and Russia, lay at the bottom of the attempt to send a ship ordered by Russia and built at New York round Cape Horn into the Pacific, to launch privateering raids on British ships there.

Public opinion in the United States was definitely in favour of the Russian cause. One of the more bizarre expressions of this was that 300 riflemen from Kentucky volunteered to fight on Russia's side in the Crimea. However, they were never shipped to Europe. On the other hand, about thirty-five American doctors came to Russia of whom about two dozen nursed wounded Russian soldiers and performed surgery in the Crimea. Eleven of them died of various causes, mostly typhoid fever. There was also an American military delegation in Russia in the spring of 1855 headed by Majors Richard Delafield and Alfred Mordecai and Captain George B. McLellan (afterwards a general in the Civil War). In June they were received by Nesselrode and Tsar Alexander II, but were unable to proceed to the Russian front in the Crimea. On their return journey via Berlin, Vienna and Trieste they managed to visit the British camps at Sevastopol. Like the two Spaniards Prim and O'Ryan, Delafield wrote an interesting *Report on the Art of War in Europe in 1854, 1855, and 1856*, published by the US Congress in Washington in 1860.

Two problems in Anglo-American relations, the origins of which had nothing to do with the war in the East, but the dimensions of which were clearly enlarged by it, were the questions of the Mosquito Coast in Central America and of Cuba. During the 1840s, rivalry between Britain and the United States was building up because plans to construct an interoceanic canal, either through the Isthmus of Panama or through Nicaragua, were under discussion. The United States acquired rights of transit through Panama, and Britain renewed claims to the eastern part of Nicaragua, the so-called Mosquito Coast. The Clayton–Bulwer Treaty of 19 April 1850 marked a temporary easing of tensions between the two sides, both parties pledging themselves to recognize the neutralization of the potential canal areas (Panama, Nicaragua, Tehuantepec). Many of the articles were deliberately ambiguous in their wording, and bickering about the strategic areas continued in the following years.

The American government seems to have tried to force the issue during the Crimean War. With its tacit connivance, or at least without trying to stop them, several American freebooters made their appearance at Greytown (formerly San Juan), the most important harbour of the Mosquito Coast, and in the interior. On 13 July 1854 Captain George Hollins bombarded Greytown; in June 1855 Captain William Walker landed on the coast and occupied Granada, the capital of the area; at the same time Colonel Henry Kinney installed himself at Greytown proclaiming himself governor. In reaction the British government publicly announced the reinforcement of its West Indian squadron. This news created alarm about an impending war, but also had a calming effect on the language of the American government.

Cuba, 'the pearl of the Antilles', had attracted the covetous eyes of many adherents of 'manifest destiny'. American presidents kept trying to purchase it from Spain, and American freebooters endeavoured to provoke Spain into war by various incidents. During the Crimean War the diplomatic offensive for the acquisition of Cuba was stepped up considerably. On 16 August 1854, Marcy directed his representative at Madrid, Pierre Soulé, to meet his colleagues from Paris and London, John Y. Mason and James Buchanan, to consult on the Cuban question and submit proposals to Washington. The trio met at Ostend in October. Their meeting attracted much public attention, whereupon they withdrew to the quiet resort of Aix-la-Chapelle. In a memorandum, the so-called 'Ostend manifesto' of 18 October 1854, they recommended immediate action to their government.[11] Spain should be offered up to US$120 million for Cuba. If Madrid refused, 'then, by every law, human and divine, we shall be justified in wresting it from Spain if we possess the power'. The costs of a war and diplomatic entanglements with the other European powers would not matter. The Ostend manifesto was stillborn because public opinion in the United States was against a war with Spain. Marcy did not take up the suggestions of his agents. Nonetheless the whole affair shows the inclination of the American government to exploit the distraction of Britain and France in the East.

Much more serious, in terms of the danger of involving the United States in the Crimean War, was the so-called recruitment controversy which was directly connected with the war.

After the debacle of the Battle of Inkerman in November 1854, the British government was frantically struggling to get reinforcements into the Crimea. On 23 December 1854 Parliament passed the Foreign Enlistment Act, which was the basis for recruiting mercenaries abroad, a time-honoured practice in British history. As early as December, the British envoy in Washington, John F. Crampton, and various consuls in the United States responded positively to Clarendon's enquiry whether sufficient recruits might be found in the United States. On 16 February 1855, Crampton was officially instructed to begin recruiting, but to take care not to infringe the neutrality laws of the

United States. He engaged a number of agents who began their business in various American cities.

The main difficulty lay in conducting the activity in secrecy. Would-be mercenaries had to be given money with which to be ferried to the central recruiting depot at Halifax in Nova Scotia. By the middle of May only 135 mercenaries had found their way to that location, although the promises made by the recruiting agents had given the fantastic figure of 30,000 to be recruited in a matter of months, principally Germans, among them officers of the Schleswig-Holstein army of 1848–50. Because of the watchful eye of the American authorities, the ineptitude of the recruiting agents, among whom there were some adventurers, and the anti-British feeling among the American public, the whole campaign was doomed to failure. On 22 June 1855 Clarendon therefore directed Crampton to abandon the project. To make matters worse, some of the recruiting agents were arrested and put on trial and on 7 July the British consul in Cincinnati was arrested. On 16 July Clarendon told the American minister in London in an official note that all recruiting measures had been stopped. In fact none of the few recruits that had found their way to Halifax ever boarded a ship bound for Europe and the Crimea.

But by now enough china had been smashed. Feelings ran high on both sides of the Atlantic and, prompted by public indignation, Marcy demanded the recall of Crampton. As this proved ineffective, the British envoy was finally dismissed by the American government on 28 May 1856.

At the turn of 1855–6, tensions between Britain and the United States had risen so high that they might well have ended in war, with the United States fighting side by side with Russia against the other European powers, had the Crimean War continued into 1856.

Greece

The position of Greece was of special strategic importance during the mounting Eastern crisis throughout the year of 1853 and during the first five months of 1854. In Russia's plans a pro-Russian Greece was of use in order to create trouble for the Ottoman Empire on its western flank. When the two Western powers made up their minds to grant military support to Turkey after Sinope, the assembly of French and British troops along the banks of the Straits necessitated a quiet Greece on their left flank. To the Greek government and the Greek nation, the Eastern crisis of 1853 was a golden opportunity to improve the unfavourable territorial situation of the new state as it had been formed under the aegis of the three European powers – Russia, Britain and France – in 1830, the year of birth of modern Greece. Her northern frontier had been drawn from the Gulf of Arta in the west to the Gulf of Volos in the east. All the areas north of that line remained Turkish provinces, although in Epirus and Thessaly the population was

Greek and in Thrace and Macedonia it was predominantly Greek. Thus, the new state was bedevilled by the problem of irredentism and developed the Megale Idea – the Great Idea – the restoration of such areas as had, in former times, belonged to Greece.

The first opportunity to realize this nationalist idea was the tension between Russia and the Ottoman Empire at the beginning of 1853. A member of Menshikov's mission, Admiral Vladimir A. Kornilov, later the hero of Sevastopol, visited Athens, creating a sensation and generating considerable speculation. Although his ostensible object was mediation about two villages on the Graeco-Turkish frontier, it was generally believed that he stiffened the opposition of Greece and held out hopes of Russian assistance. However, under pressure from the French and British representatives, to whom Menshikov himself gave a helping hand, the villages were finally awarded to the Ottoman Empire.

The tension between Greece and Constantinople did not die down and was fanned by the outbreak of the Russo-Turkish war in October 1853. In January 1854, open revolts broke out first in Epirus, then in Thessaly, and both attracted a great deal of assistance, in men and money, from Greece. King Otho and his government did not conceal their efforts to encourage the Greeks beyond the frontiers. Officers and soldiers left the army and went as volunteers to the areas in revolt. Soon Yanina, the administrative centre in Epirus, was in danger of being taken by the rebels. The Turks despatched reinforcements and launched a counteroffensive. This development was obviously what the rebel leaders and the government in Athens expected: that Russian troops would soon cross the Danube and the Balkan Mountains and would finally join hands with the Greeks for the final onslaught on Constantinople. In this, however, they were mistaken.

What was the extent of Russian support for the Greek cause and what was the reaction of the Western powers and of Austria?

Although Russian propaganda throughout 1853 and during the first months of 1854 emphasized Russian support for the oppressed Christian brethren in the Sultan's Empire and encouraged revolts among the Balkan peoples, and although, in the case of Greece, the insurgents received Russian money, the attitude of the Tsar and his government was ambivalent. In one of his conversations with Seymour in which he developed his ideas for partitioning Turkey (on 22 February 1853), Nicholas I made it clear that he would never allow the reconstruction of the Byzantine Empire nor of 'such an extension of Greece as would render her a powerful State',[12] but that he favoured the addition of Epirus and Thessaly to Greece. As late as March 1854, Nesselrode let it be known in Athens that this was Russia's official policy. The Greek government would have acted against the interests of the country had it not taken this promise at face value. Yet events in the Aegean and the Adriatic in the crucial months of January–April 1854 worked against Greek expectations; the Russian government had always been careful not to give pledges to Athens, and at the beginning of May the Tsar had written off Greece. Public opinion in Athens, furthermore, was provoked by the publication in London at the end of March of the Seymour conversations, which contained unflattering remarks about Greece.

On the opposite side it was France that acted with promptitude against the threat emanating from the Greek insurrection to the strategic plans of the Western Allies. Early in April in Vienna, Buol suggested the idea of forming a *cordon sanitaire* along Greece's northern frontier. As Austria was doing the same on Serbia's northern frontier in order to force Belgrade to remain quiet while the Russians were on the point of crossing the Danube, Drouyn eagerly took up this idea and invited Austria to send troops to northern Greece. In fact the Austrians sent a warship into the Gulf of Arta and on 4 May 1854 Francis Joseph ordered his governor of Dalmatia, General Lazarus von Mamula, to be ready to send a brigade in order to occupy the district of Scutari in Albania.[13] This plan did not materialize, however, not so much because of Russian warnings – as Monika Ritter suggests – but because Mamula advised against such a step and because the Ottoman government were not happy about this sort of Austrian support.

One day before the Austrian Emperor's order, Napoleon III had made up his mind in a ministerial council in Paris to force the hand of the Greek government and occupy Piraeus with French troops. The British government followed suit on 4 May. The military occupation was preceded by political demands: on 10 May King Otho was confronted with an ultimatum to declare his neutrality and recall his volunteers from the border regions. Ten days later, when French troops were already disembarking in Piraeus, he yielded unconditionally. His pro-Russian Cabinet was replaced by a pro-Western one, which in fact was mainly pro-British. The King, in consequence, lost much prestige among his Greek subjects. In June the insurrection in Epirus and Thessaly, deprived of support from Greece, was quashed.

The French troops that disembarked in Piraeus on 25 May were the division of General Élie Frédéric Forey, which was originally scheduled for the Turkish Straits. On 11 June they were replaced by troops (2,000 men) under General Joseph Mayran, having been joined two days earlier by a British contingent of 1,000 men. The Allied troops remained at Piraeus throughout the war and were not stationed in Athens proper. Their presence ensured that the Allies could feel safe along their vital line of communication from the western Mediterranean to the Turkish Straits. The troops remained on Greek soil well after peace was concluded on 30 March 1856. Britain and France used their presence to force a commission which was to control Greece's state finances on the Greek government, since the government was in arrears in paying back the credit which the two powers, together with Russia, had granted in 1832. When the commission was finally set up in February 1857, the troops were ordered to leave – the *Megale Idea* had to wait for another opportunity to be partially fulfilled.

The minor German powers (the German Confederation)

One of the German kingdoms, Bavaria, had a direct stake in the Eastern Question because King Otho was of Bavarian origin and brother to the Bavarian King, Maximilian II. Otherwise the German states of the second and third order had no direct interests in the Crimean War. Their indirect interests were, however, of considerable magnitude and weight. Geographically, these states formed, together with the two German great powers, the huge land barrier which kept the two belligerent camps apart and forced them to meet in peripheral areas like the Black Sea and the Baltic.

From the point of view of military potential, the minor German states were by no means of negligible importance: Bavaria, for example, had, in 1855, a standing army of 71,500 men, and Saxony had 26,600 men under arms. The army of the German Confederation, to which the member states had to contribute contingents, had a strength of 300,000 active men, including about 175,000 that came from Austria and Prussia. Politically speaking, the minor German states could assume importance if they spoke with one voice and if they were capable of acting in unison. There lies the problem which explains the utter impotence of the third Germany. A complementary explanation is the fact that the two leading powers of the German Confederation, Austria and Prussia, fought a bitter duel during the Crimean War, each trying to marshal the potential of the minor states for its own purposes: Prussia for her pro-Russian policy and Austria for her pro-Western policy.

Beneath this tug of war was the struggle for hegemony in Germany, the so-called German Question or German dualism, which had its origin in the wars between Frederick the Great and Maria Theresa in the eighteenth century. The issue lay dormant in the Metternichian era, but had surfaced in the revolution of 1848–50 and was taken up with fierce resolution from 1854 to 1856, by Buol as Austria's Foreign Minister and by Bismarck as the Prussian representative at the German Confederation at Frankfurt.

The German Confederation was a remarkable creation of Metternich's fertile mind, as a means to balance the disparate and centrifugal forces in Germany after the Napoleonic Wars. It was a confederation of thirty-five sovereign princes and four free cities. The two great powers, Prussia and Austria, also belonged to it, although not with their whole territory. Its only organ was the Federal Diet at Frankfurt, to which each member state sent a representative who wielded, depending on the importance of his state, between one and five votes. The Diet had the right to receive diplomatic representatives from abroad, but not to send one abroad. According to article 35 of its act of constitution of 1820, the Confederation could not wage an offensive war, but was only allowed to defend itself.

It is principally this idea of the innate defensive character of the Confederation that attracted the attention of those German historians who after 1945 were in search of the 'real' and harmless Germany of the past, to which they could point as a model after two terrible world wars of which the united German Reich of 1871 was the main instigator. In the process, the 'good old' German Confederation became mythologized and had to justify the division of Germany after 1945. In fact, there was no such model Germany in the past; the Confederation was rather a motley collection of egotistical states – some of operetta-like status – incapable of even the most basic unified policy and action, and incapable of reforming its complicated static constitution. The Crimean War is, in fact, the best illustration of its impotence and of the political danger emanating from the Confederation.

It must suffice to sketch in a few words the policy of the more important member states of the Confederation outside Austria and Prussia during the Crimean War; that is, of Bavaria, Saxony, Württemberg and Hanover.

The Bavarian Prime Minister Ludwig von der Pfordten was, in October 1854, in utter despair at the Confederation being unable to do anything to solve the crisis created by Russia's actions. As he saw no chance of Austria and Prussia uniting their efforts, he regarded the Confederation as being on the point of dissolution. He did not regret its destruction because

> ... it had produced nothing but trouble and restrictions to Bavaria's power. A state like Bavaria could as well exist as an independent state like Portugal, Belgium and Sardinia which, to be true, are not consulted in European questions, but which, at a given moment, are not asked to provide money and men and the neutrality of which remains unimpaired.[14]

Without the shackles of the Confederation's constitution, von der Pfordten expected to be able to lean more freely on one or two of the great powers, Austria and France for example, and to reap some tangible fruits in such an alliance, such as a territorial link between Bavaria and her enclave in the west of Germany, the Palatinate.

In contrast to von der Pfordten, his Saxon counterpart, Friedrich von Beust, was a staunch supporter of the Russian cause throughout the Eastern crisis. He thought that the Holy Alliance under Russian leadership provided the best security for Saxony against the powerful Prussian neighbour (who in 1814–15 had wished to swallow all of Saxony). Another reason for his support for Russia was that Beust believed in the possibility of creating a union of the German states of the second order which would constitute a third political force (the so-called 'trias') alongside the two German great powers. This was, of course, an impracticable idea in view of the petty jealousy of the princes and governments concerned, and also in view of Beust's reputation as a notorious troublemaker. Beust maintained his unconditional Russophile sympathies well into 1855, pleading incessantly for a restoration of the Holy Alliance and for Germany as a whole – the two great powers and the German Confederation – to enter the war on Russia's side. Beust may have speculated on territorial gains in the adjacent Saxon duchies after a Russian victory to compensate for Saxony's losses at the Congress of Vienna. Only after the fall of Sevastopol did Beust try a reorientation towards the Western powers.

In Württemberg, foreign policy was in the hands of King William. Uppermost in his mind was the wish to maintain absolute quietude in domestic and foreign policy. Dynastic ties with Russia were numerous. Like Beust, he believed Russia to be the best guarantor of the sovereignty of the middle-sized German states, and maintained that they were completely uninterested in the Eastern Question: 'Whether Russia or Britain is master of Constantinople is completely indifferent to us.'[15] In the event of the German states having to take part in the war against their will, he was ready to ally himself with the victorious coalition, hoping for territorial gains in Hohenzollern and Baden. All of the territorial aspirations of the German princes clearly show that the German Confederation was, in the last resort, completely irrelevant to them.

Hanover's policy during the Crimean War is of a different complexion. There were still numerous ties with Britain dating back to the personal union before 1837. In the army there were a number of officers who had served in the British army under Wellington (in the 'King's German Legion'). Colonel Harry Leonhart, for example, set up the German Legion in British service at the beginning of 1855. Another is the Hanoverian Minister of War, Lieutenant-General Bernhard von Brandis, who had served in the British army in Portugal. In April 1854 he told the French envoy at Hanover:

> We shall go with Austria through thick and thin, come what may, even if a Prussian detachment will again occupy the province of Hildesheim. The King will return to England, if need be, and we will set up a new Anglo-German legion on the Danube.[16]

Just as Saxony leaned towards Russia, Hanover leaned with equal absoluteness towards Austria and Britain. She, as much as Saxony, feared the heavy weight of her mighty Prussian neighbour.

During the Crimean War there was only one attempt by the German Confederation, or by its most important members, to intervene in a united fashion in the Eastern affair. The attempt was a complete failure.

After Austria and Prussia had concluded their alliance of 20 April 1854, they invited the Confederation to accede to it. As had been usual in the past, they expected it to join immediately and unconditionally – but they were mistaken. King Maximilian of Bavaria, in view of his dynastic ties with the Greek throne, took the initiative for a meeting of representatives of the German minor states where conditions that should be attached to their accession to the April alliance were to be worked out. This meeting took place at Bamberg between 25 and 30 May 1854. The leading politicians of eight German secondary states (Bavaria, Saxony, Hanover, Württemberg, Baden, the Grand Duchy of Hesse, the Electorate of Hesse and the Duchy of Nassau) were present. The outcome was an identical note, dated 3 June, which was to be delivered collectively to the two German great powers. Several conditions for the accession of the Confederation were listed, among them the demand that the belligerents should simultaneously stop hostilities by sea and land (this was favourable to Russia as it went against the Austrian demand that Russia evacuate the Principalities unconditionally); the demand that the Confederation be represented in the future peace negotiations; and a guarantee of the integrity of Greece. (The latter was clearly of Bavarian origin.)

The reaction of the great powers dashed all hopes of the secondary German states having any say in international affairs. Austria and Prussia voiced their indignation at the claim that a European question of such magnitude be subject to the paralyzing vagaries of the Confederation's cumbersome machinery. Buol, in his reply, made an interesting remark about the role which the Confederation was to play in his policy: 'Let us hope that a speedy accession to a treaty, which is to serve us as long as possible as a weapon of peace ... will terminate the miserable role which Germany plays at this moment in the eyes of Europe.'[17] Thus the April treaty was to put pressure on Russia to get off her high horse and accept the conditions of the other great European powers in the Eastern Question.

In Paris, Foreign Minister Drouyn de Lhuys reacted with hilarity, accusing the German ministers of an 'absence d'esprit politique' and calling them Russian barnstormers. In London, Clarendon described the Bamberg demands as 'ill-advised interference'.

After this excursion into high politics, the Bambergers gave in and acceded to the April treaty on 24 July without any strings attached. Buol, tired of these German delays, had by then made up his mind to go it alone, and on 8 August he signed the Four Points with the two Western powers. But like Sisyphus he tried again a few months later and knocked at the door of the Diet. After the treaty with the Western powers of 2 December 1854, he hoped once more to be able to add Germany's (and Prussia's) weight to the scales of Austrian policy. His representative at Frankfurt tabled the motion to mobilize half of the federal army. After weeks of haggling, this anti-Russian move was transformed into a motion to prepare mobilization (the technical term was to introduce 'war-preparedness' or *Kriegsbereitschaft*) 'in all directions', that is, towards east and west, so that the anti-Russian sting was completely taken out of the resolution.

Without going into further details, the Federal Assembly at Frankfurt was the scene of various attempts by Austria to combine the power of the rest of Germany and attach it to her own political and military weight, not in order to create more favourable conditions to enter the war against Russia, but to bring Russia to her senses and force her to the peace table, and at the same time to demonstrate to the Western powers the weight of Central Europe and thus force them not to overstrain their peace demands on Russia. These attempts, however, failed completely. A French observer was right in saying that the policy of the German secondary states 'never had any other motives than the fear of feebleness and the instincts of egotism'.[18] It may well be argued that the Crimean War would not have broken out if Germany – and Prussia – had stood as a man behind Austria. The Tsar would then have had second thoughts and evacuated the Principalities without any further ado. As it was, Central Europe had paralyzed itself and had thus encouraged Russia to pounce on Turkey and destroy the European balance of power.

Annotated bibliography

A general study on neutrality in the nineteenth century is Maatje M. Abbenhuis, *An Age of Neutrals: Great Power Politics, 1815–1914* (Cambridge, 2014).

The attitude of each of the secondary powers of Europe during the Crimean War, from Sweden to the Kingdom of the Two Sicilies, from Finland and Poland to Portugal, is investigated either in monographs or in articles. The sole exception is Holland.

Sweden's role is well covered, on the basis of the Swedish documents, by Albin Cullberg, *La politique du Roi Oscar I pendant la Guerre de Crimée. Études diplomatiques sur les négociations secrètes entre les cabinets de Stockholm, Paris, St. Pétersbourg et Londres les années 1853–1856*, 2 vols (Stockholm, 1912–26); Carl Hallendorff, *Oscar I, Napoleon och Nikolaus. Ur diplomaternas privatbrev under Krimkriget* (Stockholm, 1918). There are two useful articles: Edgar Anderson, 'The Role of the Crimean War in Northern Europe', *Jahrbücher für Geschichte Osteuropas* 20 (1972): 42–59; Axel E. Jonasson, 'The Crimean War, the Beginning of Strict Swedish Neutrality, and the Myth of Swedish Intervention in the Baltic', *Journal of Baltic Studies* 4 (1973): 244–53.

For Spain there is only one relevant article, based on newspaper material: Luis Mariñas Otero, 'España ante la guerra di Crimea', *Hispania. Revista española de historia* 26 (1966): 410–46.

United States policy is covered by Alan Dowty, *The Limits of American Isolation: the United States and the Crimean War* (New York, 1971). Dowty deals with all the major issues: Cuba, Central America, the recruitment controversy. On the latter, cf. the relevant documents in *AGKK* III/3–4. The British government published several blue books on the issue (cf. the bibliographical references, p. 1039, also in *AGKK* III/3, 890–1). For Cuba, cf. Amos A. Ettinger, *The Mission to Spain of Pierre Soulé 1853–1856: A Study in the Cuban Diplomacy of the United States* (New Haven, CT, 1932).

Greek policy during the Crimean War is analysed in three studies: Eugenia Voyiatzis Nomikos, *The International Position of Greece during the Crimean War* (Stanford, CA, 1962); Monika Ritter, *Frankreichs Griechenland-Politik während des Krimkrieges. (Im Spiegel der französischen und bayerischen Gesandtschaftsberichte 1853–1857)* (Munich, 1966); Jon F. Kofas, *International and Domestic Politics in Greece during the Crimean War* (New York, 1980). On the Greek legion which fought on Russia's side, see Maria N. Todorova, 'The Greek Volunteers in the Crimean War', *Balkan Studies* 25 (1984): 539–63.

For Serbia's neutrality during the war, based on reports from the British consul general to London, see Čedomir Antić, *Neutrality as Independence: Great Britain, Serbia and the Crimean War* (Belgrade, 2007).

There are numerous books on the German secondary states during the Crimean War. For a general treatment, including Austria and Prussia and based on archival material from Vienna and Berlin, see Franz Eckhart, *Die deutsche Frage und der Krimkrieg* (Berlin and Königsberg, 1931). A fresh look in the light of new material is provided by Winfried Baumgart, 'Die deutschen Mittelstaaten und der Krimkrieg 1853–1856', in *Landesgeschichte und Reichsgeschichte. Festschrift für Alois Gerlich zum 70. Geburtstag*, ed. Winfried Dotzauer, 357–89 (Stuttgart, 1995). For each of the secondary German states there exists at least one monograph. This clearly points to the significance which the war on the periphery of Europe had for the German Question (rivalry between Austria and Prussia and the standing of the 'third Germany'). Here is a selection confined to the important secondary states: Siegmund Meiboom, *Studien zur deutschen Politik Bayerns in den Jahren 1851–1859* (Munich, 1931); Peter Hoffmann, *Die diplomatischen Beziehungen zwischen Württemberg und Bayern im Krimkrieg und bis zum Beginn der Italienischen Krise (1853–1858)* (Stuttgart, 1963); Götz Krusemarck, *Württemberg und der Krimkrieg* (Halle (Saale), 1932); Harald Straube, *Sachsens Rolle im Krimkrieg*, PhD thesis, unpublished (Erlangen, 1952); Werner Husen, *Hannovers Politik während des Krimkrieges* (Emsdetten, 1936). The military organization of the German Confederation for the years 1853–6 is investigated in Jürgen Angelow, *Von Wien nach Königgrätz. Die Sicherheitspolitik des Deutschen Bundes im europäischen Gleichgewicht (1815–1866)*, pp. 165–90 (Munich, 1996). The article by John R. Davis, 'The Bamberg Conference of 1854: A Re-Evaluation', *European History Quarterly* 28 (1998): 81–107, is useful, but lacks a new hypothesis in spite of its subtitle.

PART THREE

The Armies of the Belligerents

6

Russia

The Russian army in the nineteenth century was by far the largest in the world. Before and after the Crimean War its peace strength was 800,000 to 900,000 men. This formidable number is directly related to Russia's antiquated social structure which was, up to 1860, dominated by serfdom. Landlords had to send between three and six men from every thousand serfs to enrol in the army. This meant an annual levy of 60,000 to 80,000 men. When the next levy was due, the recruits from the preceding year were incorporated in the standing army and had to serve for 25 years. After that they were free men, that is, they were not required to return to serfdom. Very few, however, were pleased by the exchange. The result of this military system was that no reserve army which could fill up the peace army in time of war existed.

From 1853 to 1855 there were five levies which together added 878,000 men to the Russian army, a formidable figure which almost doubled the military force, but the new men were raw recruits of poor fighting quality. The three levies of 1854 meant a quota of 31 serfs per 1,000, a drain of labourers which the Russian social system could not endure for any length of time. Indeed, the frequent levies inspired rumours that the recruits would be free men and would not have to return to their landlords after the war, so creating unforeseen problems of internal security. There was mounting unrest among the serfs eager to be registered. In many parts of the country there were even open revolts that had to be put down by the regular army, with the loss of many lives. There was a special section of the peace army, called the 'corps of interior fighting', whose task was to deal with such events.

It is difficult to give a reliable number for the strength of the Russian army at the beginning of the Crimean War. According to official figures the regular army amounted to 971,000 men, including officers, at the beginning of 1853. There was a small reserve force of 160,000 men, plus an irregular army (of Cossacks) of 246,000, so that the total strength would make up an army of almost one and a half million men.[1] However, the actual force that could be used against an external enemy was only half that figure; the interior forces had to be increased to more than half a million men and

150,000 troops were earmarked for fighting in the Caucasus against the mountaineers under their leader Shamil.

Russia, with her vast landmass, is almost impossible to attack, as Napoleon had learned in 1812. The reverse of this is that due to the uncertain political outlook in Europe during the Crimean War, Russia had to deploy her army along her frontier from the Gulf of Bothnia down to the Black Sea. As the most vital area, St Petersburg had to be defended against Allied landing troops and also against a Swedish attack, and therefore had an army of 270,000 men during the war. The army of Poland, too, was of vital importance as it was to put down a possible Polish uprising and oppose an army from any European country. In April 1854 its strength was 200,000. The rest of the regular army was deployed in the south-west and the south. In the Crimean peninsula at the beginning of the war there were only 50,000–60,000 troops.

Besides the internal security aspect and the uncertainty as to which of the powers of Northern or Central Europe might join the Western allies, the mobility of the Russian army was hamstrung by the huge expanse of the Russian country and the complete lack of modern means of transport. The only railway line that existed at the time of the war in Russia was that between Moscow and St Petersburg. Draught animals needed months in order to overcome the long distances and in winter had to carry their forage with them, which in itself was next to impossible. Thus they reached their destination very late or not at all. In contrast, the troops of the Western powers, using a good system of rail transport in Britain and France and with efficient navies, could reach the Crimea much more quickly than Russian troops could move south from Moscow.

In their equipment the Russian army was in many respects inferior to its Western counterparts. The infantry had smooth-bore muzzle-loading muskets with bullets that could rarely range beyond 200 to 250 metres. They had a maximum rate of fire of two rounds per minute. The infantry therefore had to rely more on the use of the bayonet. Only a tiny fraction had the modern Minié rifle. Russian artillery, on the other hand, was hardly inferior to its Western counterparts and used heavy guns that could cover a distance of 3–4 kilometres.

The Russian foot soldiers marched and attacked in the old-fashioned oblong column, which was awe-inspiring and easy to control but offered an easy target to the enemy. Only the first two ranks were able to engage their counterparts. The whole army was well drilled and functioned admirably on the parade ground, but in the field it acted like a machine incapable of adapting itself to circumstances. The same applied to the officer corps, which completely lacked initiative. Each subaltern officer waited for orders from his superior and was punished if he acted otherwise. In the last resort it was the Tsar in whom absolute command was vested. Thus the Russian army was like an automaton which only moved and acted according to the commands inserted into it. It also had no general staff comparable to that possessed by the Prussian army: in other words, there was little or no systematic training in war planning, command structure, topography, history of war and the like.

None of the commanding generals of the Crimean War were of outstanding quality, although in this respect the Russian army very much resembled the Western armies. The Commander-in-Chief of the Russian army in Europe was Field Marshal Ivan Fedorovich Paskevich. In 1854 he was seventy-two years old. He was a veteran of the Napoleonic Wars and had earned his laurels in wars against inferior enemies: in 1826–7 against the Persians, in 1828 against the Turks, in 1831 against the Poles and in 1849 against the Hungarians. Probably because of these successes he had a curious relationship with Tsar Nicholas, who revered his old Field Marshal and addressed him as 'father-commander'. At the beginning of the Crimean War, however, Paskevich developed qualities which exasperated the Tsar, although in the end he always heeded his advice. The Commander-in-Chief was slow to reach a decision. Although he had advised that the Danubian Principalities be occupied, he feared a confrontation with the German powers as much as with the Western allies. The Danubian campaign, especially the months of January to June 1854, was characterized by hesitation and indecision, the Tsar in St Petersburg constantly goading his 'father-commander' into action with innumerable letters, Paskevich in return always expressing doubts and especially fear of Austrian intervention, more or less openly sabotaging the commands or rather the pleas of Nicholas. It may safely be said that the Russian army would, without Paskevich, have crossed the Danube more quickly, besieged the Turkish fortresses south of the river, swept down the Balkans towards Constantinople and there dictated peace terms. As it was, he was responsible for raising the siege of Silistria and, probably pretending to have received a wound, left his army and returned to Warsaw.[2]

When the theatre of war shifted from the Danube to the Crimea, the Commander-in-Chief of the Russian troops there was Prince Alexander Sergeevich Menshikov, the same man who had led the ill-starred special mission to Constantinople in the spring of 1853. He was a careerist who was distrustful of those around him, tried to do everything himself and rarely discussed his plans and manoeuvres with his subordinates. His leadership in the Crimean campaign, during the battles of the Alma and of Inkerman and during the siege of Sevastopol, proved very poor. In February 1855 he was replaced by Prince Michael Dimitrievich Gorchakov, who had commanded the Russian troops on the Danube, after Paskevich had quitted the scene. Gorchakov was an even worse choice than Menshikov. He was irresolute and pessimistic, and wanted to give up the defence of Sevastopol after the second bombardment in March 1855.

The two Commanders-in-Chief of the Crimean army usually stayed outside the fortress of Sevastopol. The troops inside were commanded by an exceptionally able leader: Admiral Vladimir Alekseevich Kornilov. He was energetic and full of genuine patriotism which he was able to transmit to all around him. The rank and file revered him. In an extraordinarily short time Kornilov was able to put up the lines of defence around Sevastopol, strengthening them with the guns and crews of the ships of the Black Sea fleet. On 17 October 1854 he died during the first bombardment of the town. His successor was his close collaborator, Admiral Pavel Stepanovich Nakhimov, who wielded the same authority with the defenders of the fortress and organized its defence with the same energy and ability. Like Kornilov, he received a fatal wound on the Malakhov hill and died on 7 July 1855.

Both Kornilov and Nakhimov were navy men. The Russian navy was, at the beginning of the war, of considerable strength. There were two large fleets, one in the Baltic and one in the Black Sea, consisting of thirty-one and sixteen ships of the line and twenty and fifteen frigates respectively, with a host of smaller men-of-war and auxiliary ships. The total number for the Baltic fleet was 218 ships and 181 for the Black Sea fleet. A small proportion of the ships were screw-driven. Together with the flotillas of the White Sea, the Caspian Sea and Kamchatka, the Russian fleet was manned by 90,000 men and officers. The Baltic fleet was of poor quality, although Sir Charles Napier regarded it highly when he set out with his squadron for the Baltic in March 1854. The Black Sea fleet, by contrast, was better, and its fighting spirit was high.[3]

However, this big fleet played no role whatsoever during the war. The only battle was in the Bay of Sinope on 30 November 1853 against a Turkish squadron. When the Allied armies marched towards Sevastopol after the Battle of the Alma, some of the Russian ships were scuttled at the entrance of the Bay of Sevastopol in order to obstruct the incursion of Allied ships. The rest were used for the defence of the town towards the land side. In the Baltic the fleet took shelter behind the formidable fortress of Kronstadt and never dared to engage the Allied fleets.

Russian war plans and plans of operations varied, naturally, according to circumstances. However, two phases can be clearly distinguished. As long as Turkey was Russia's potential enemy, that is, during 1853, the war plans were offensive. From the turn of the year 1853–4, when Russia had to reckon with the intervention of France and Britain, they were clearly defensive. There is a revealing document in the Tsar's own handwriting dated 19 January 1853.[4] This was the time when Nicholas began his conversations with Seymour. His diplomatic offensive was accompanied by plans to bring about the downfall of Turkey by waging war on that country. Nicholas planned a lightning attack on Constantinople and the Straits: he earmarked the 13th Division at Sevastopol and the 14th Division at Odessa, altogether 16,000 men, for a descent on the Bosphorus and on Constantinople. Unless Turkey surrendered unconditionally, the capital would have to be bombarded. Nicholas did not rule out the intervention of France, in which case the Dardanelles would also have to be occupied. As the Tsar was at that time discussing plans for partitioning Turkey with Britain, clearly he did not expect intervention from that side.

The existence of this document clearly shows the aggressive nature of Nicholas's thoughts and plans. This is underlined by the fact that Menshikov's presence at Constantinople from March to May 1853 was also a mission of military reconnaissance. On 28 March, Menshikov sent a report to Grand Duke Constantine Nikolaevich in which he described the weakness of the Turkish fleet and of the fortifications of the Straits, and also named two points (Buyukdere and Kilios) as the most suitable places for landing Russian troops.[5]

After the occupation of the Danubian Principalities, Nicholas became more cautious because of the anti-Russian reaction of the two Western powers, particularly that of Austria. However, he still planned to cross the Danube and take the Turkish fortresses of Vidin and Silistria. He hoped that during that phase the Balkan Christians would rise; Russia would promise them liberation from the Turkish yoke. On the Asiatic side, in the Caucasus, Russian troops would begin the offensive, take the fortresses of Batum, Kars, Ardahan and Bayezid and encourage Persia to wage war on Turkey.[6]

After Britain's and France's entry into the war, Nicholas finally gave up all offensive plans in the European theatre of war. Instead he drafted a plan for the defence of the Russian Empire in which he divided Russia's defence into three sections. The first comprised Finland, St Petersburg and the Baltic provinces. The second, which consisted of Poland, was the most vulnerable one in his view because it protruded far into Central Europe and was exposed to attacks from Prussia and particularly from Austria. The southern section consisted of Volhynia, Podolia, Bessarabia and the Black Sea coast. It had to be defended against an Austrian attack and against landings by the Western allies.

Annotated bibliography

Details about Russia's army are to be culled from L. G. Beskrovny, *The Russian Army and Fleet in the Nineteenth Century: Handbook of Armaments, Personnel and Policy* (Gulf Breeze, FL, 1996), pp. 300–1. Cf. also John Shelton Curtiss, *The Russian Army under Nicholas I, 1825–1855* (Durham, NC, 1965). His use of Russian material is invaluable, but it is often presented unsystematically, which is also true of his book mentioned in Chapter 3. Useful remarks are also made by Albert Seaton, *The Crimean War: A Russian Chronicle* (London, 1977), pp. 21–34.

Recent books on the Crimean campaign in Russian include Nikolaj Vladimirovič Skrickij, *Krymskaja vojna 1853–1856 gg* (Moscow, 2006); Sergej Viktorovič Čennyk, *Krymskaja kampanija 1854–1856 gg. vostočnoj vojnyj 1853–1856 gg. Voenno-istoričeskij očerk*, Č. 1–5 (Sevastopol, 2010–14). The latter book is a very detailed account (about 1,600 pages) of the Crimean campaign starting with the Danube front, going on to the battles of the Alma (pt. 2), Balaklava and Inkerman (pt. 4) and the last bombardment (pt. 5).

7

France

In the nineteenth century (after the Napoleonic Wars) the French army was the second largest army in Europe. In 1850 its official strength was 439,000 men and officers.[1] At the height of the Crimean War in 1855 it was brought up to 645,000. Although conscription existed on paper, under the laws of 1818 and 1832, it was basically a professional army. In contrast to Prussia, where military service was regarded as a civic right, conscription in France was felt to be an irksome burden which should be evaded if possible. On the other hand, the Chamber of Deputies had wrested the right to fix the annual intake of recruits, whose term of service was up to six years, from King Louis Philippe. It remained in force after 1848, but those liable to military service could legally buy themselves off by sending a proxy (a *remplaçant*) in their stead and there were specialized agencies which looked after such *remplaçants*. Thus young men who could afford it were exempt from military service and only the poor were drafted into the army. This was a fundamental weakness of the French army system and the situation was not improved by the way the officer corps was recruited. At least half the officers were taken from the other ranks; the complaint that many could not properly speak their mother tongue and could not write was well justified. In addition, theoretical training – the use of maps, topography, strategy and so on – was as much scorned as in the Russian army.

Against all these drawbacks, which did not militate in favour of the professionalism and efficiency of the French army, there was one great advantage: a high proportion of the men and officers had seen service in Algeria, where the ordinary rules of military exercises and any formalism in waging war were not applicable. Those who returned were battle-tested and seasoned. Most of the French generals in the Crimea had served in Algeria, including Bourbaki, Canrobert, MacMahon and Pélissier. There were even special units that were proud of their Algerian service, the Zouaves. Originally, in 1830, the Zouaves were soldiers taken from local tribes and serving under French officers. In January 1852, Napoleon III created three Zouave regiments; their members were now mostly of French origin. With their picturesque uniform they were clearly distinguishable from the rest of

FIGURE 8 *La Vivandière: a French canteen-keeper in full dress. Photo by Roger Fenton.*

the army. They established their international fame during the Crimean War. During the Battle of the Alma, the 2nd Regiment took Telegraph Hill, where General Menshikov had his headquarters. They were also among the troops that stormed the Malakhov on 8 September 1855. By decree of the Emperor, a fourth regiment of Zouaves, which belonged to the Imperial Guard, was formed in December 1854.

The equipment of the French army in the Crimean War was on the whole better than that of the Russian army. Many of the units, though, were still armed with old muzzle-loading percussion rifles, although one-third were equipped with modern rifles of the Minié type. French artillery was basically of the same type and quality as that of the Russian army. The administration of the French army proved to be far superior to that of the Russian or British army, with supply arrangements and the medical service functioning superbly compared with the chaos in the British army.

As with the Russian army, only part of the French army was used in the Crimea. Other units remained stationed in France: in the north, where they were kept ready for expeditions to the Baltic (in the summer of 1854, 18,000 men were actually used to occupy the Åland Islands); in eastern France, whence they might be moved through Germany to join with Austrian troops on Austria's north-eastern and eastern borders; and in the south, in order to replenish the losses in the Crimea and to strengthen the army there numerically.

The French expeditionary force, which was first shipped to the Turkish Straits from March 1854 onwards, thence to Varna and in August 1854 to the Crimea, was called the *Armée d'Orient*. Originally, when it was planned by a joint Anglo-French commission in January 1854, it was to be of modest dimensions, only 6,000 men. Month after month, however, its strength was raised by leaps and bounds until it reached its peak of 120,000 in the summer of 1855. When war was declared on Russia at the end of March 1854, 34,700 men were on their way to the East. In December of that year, official figures put its strength at 70,000. Through a rotating system, some of the troops in the Crimea were relieved by fresh units so that the grand total of those having seen action in the Crimea (and on the minor fronts elsewhere) was just over 309,000. This figure shows, on the one hand, the great effort that France carried out and, on the other hand, the advantage the Allies possessed in being able to concentrate their war effort on one point of Russia's territory, whereas the Tsar had to deploy his army on a long frontier line, not knowing where his opponents might strike next.

The three generals commanding the *Armée d'Orient* were not much better than their Russian counterparts. Two of them were daring and energetic, one timorous and lacking in self-confidence. All three were close followers of Emperor Napoleon and had in one way or another helped to bring the latter to power; he was not slow in repaying them for their allegiance. The first was Marshal Achille Le Roy de Saint-Arnaud, a flamboyant and adventurous man. In the 1820s he joined the Greek insurgents as a volunteer in their war of independence, and after his return home spent some time in a French prison because he was involved in a case concerning debt. From 1837 onwards he served for many years in Algeria, took part in Napoleon's coup d'état of 1851, and was made Minister of War. He left this post on 11 March 1854 in order to take over the command of the *Armée d'Orient*. Already an ailing man, Saint-Arnaud won the Battle of the Alma together with the British. Nine days later, on 29 September 1854, he died of cholera.

Saint-Arnaud was replaced by François Certain Canrobert, another veteran of the army in Algeria and participant in the coup d'état of 2 December 1851. He sailed to the East as commander of the 1st Infantry Division and became Saint-Arnaud's successor two days before the latter's death. He was thus Commander-in-Chief during the Crimean winter, when the siege of Sevastopol made no progress, depleting the French as well as the British forces. He did not dare develop ideas of his own for changing Allied strategy and was soon at odds with his English colleague, Lord Raglan, and with General Niel, who had been sent to the Crimea by Napoleon in January 1855 in order to goad him into greater activity. On 16 May 1855, weary of his burdensome task, Canrobert handed in his resignation.

He was replaced by General Aimable Pélissier, who had ended his service in Algeria at the beginning of 1855 and been placed at the head of the 1st Army Corps in the Crimea. He at once instilled a different spirit into the French officer corps in the Crimea, being ruthless with critics and even flouting the telegraphic commands of the Emperor from Paris, who wanted to bring more mobility into the war in the Crimea by launching diversionary attacks on Simferopol, the Russian supply base in the centre of the peninsula. Pélissier took it into his head to put more and more men against the Russian defenders of Sevastopol in a Verdun-like war of attrition. The result was appalling loss at first, but a resounding success in the end, when the crucial Malakhov bastion was stormed by French troops on 8 September 1855. After this success, Pélissier sat still and ignored Napoleon's advice to follow up his success by marching into the interior.

The real Commander-in-Chief of the French forces was of course Napoleon himself, just as Tsar Nicholas was the head of the Russian army. Napoleon's ideas for beginning and waging the war against Russia were quite simple and straightforward. Besides a diversionary attack against Russia in the Baltic in the spring of 1854, the main effort of the Western Allies should be concentrated against the Russian army marching southwards across the Balkans. On 12 April 1854, a fortnight after the declaration of war against Russia, he wrote to Marshal Saint-Arnaud, 'Either march and meet the Russians on the Balkans, or take possession of the Crimea or, again, disembark at Odessa or at any other point on the Russian coast of the Black Sea.'[2] This outline left much freedom of action to the commander on the spot; it also shows that the idea of landing in the Crimea goes back to the very outbreak of the war.

There were two moments during the siege of Sevastopol when Napoleon tried to change the course of the war. The first followed on the prospect of Austria joining the war on the side of the Western Allies after the conclusion of their alliance of 2 December 1854, and the second was his visit to London and Windsor in April 1855, when a common war plan was hammered out by the two governments.

The December treaty had provided for consultations between the three allied partners. For this purpose, the Austrian government sent a military commissioner, General Franz Count Crenneville, to Paris. In several interviews with Emperor Napoleon in February and March 1855, Crenneville delivered two memoranda drawn up by the Austrian Commander-in-Chief, General Heinrich von Hess. They did not contain a plan of campaign against

Russia, but rather statistical tables of the Russian, Austrian and Western armed forces. Hess gave a precise figure for the Russian forces: 848,271 men. For an offensive war against them, he deemed an Allied army of 1,230,000 men necessary. Of these, Austria could furnish an army of 300,000 men within thirty to forty days, with a reserve army of 150,000. The other two-thirds of the proposed force had to be provided by Prussia (200,000) and the rest of Germany (100,000), by France (375,000), Britain (30,000), Turkey (80,000) and Sardinia (15,000). These fantastic figures, with which Crenneville had to operate in Paris, make it obvious that Austria was not in earnest. Crenneville's mission seems to tally with Buol's diplomatic tactics.[3]

Oddly enough, Napoleon took up the Austrian ball, reacting with figures and a virtual plan of campaign of his own. He accepted that the total number of Russian forces might well be 848,000, but that they were lined up on the long frontier from Finland to the Caucasus. His own plan to deal with them was not to invade Russia and march to Moscow, but to deliver additional blows to Russia in the same manner as the Crimean campaign: to attack her in the north with a Swedish army and an Anglo-French fleet, and in the centre with an Austrian army of only 200,000 (and a reserve army of 100,000). One wing of the latter would have to seize the fortress of Brest-Litovsk, thus obliging the Russian army to evacuate Poland, and the other wing would march on to Kiev, thus cutting the Russian forces in two. France's contribution would be to keep Prussia in check with 200,000 men on the Rhine. When Napoleon later pressed Crenneville to conclude a military alliance on the basis of Hess's second statistical table, which deemed an Allied central army of 500,000 (plus a reserve army of 400,000) necessary, the Austrian general evaded any obligation by pointing out that such a treaty would have to wait until the Vienna peace conference was terminated. The failure of the peace talks at the beginning of May made all further military consultations illusory. Crenneville therefore left Paris for Vienna by mid-July.

The military talks with Austria having proved a soap bubble, Napoleon tried to close the ranks more tightly with his British ally. He paid a state visit to Britain in mid-April 1855 in connection with the pressure the British government put on him to give up his planned visit to the Crimea (which will be dealt with in a later chapter). One of the results of his consultations was a plan of campaign signed by both sides on 20 April. It was designed to bring mobility into the deadlocked siege warfare round Sevastopol. The gist of the plan, which was essentially Napoleon's long-cherished personal idea, was to maintain the siege with 60,000 troops at the most; to act offensively with the rest of the Allied armies against the Russian army outside Sevastopol, beat it and thus cut the supply route with the beleaguered army in Sevastopol, and then turn against the latter in full force. The offensive army was to consist of three parts: a Turkish army of 30,000 men would occupy Eupatoria to threaten the Russian right flank; an Allied army of 55,000 men, mostly British under Lord Raglan, would turn north and take the Mackenzie heights, a Russian strongpoint on the route to Simferopol; and a second army, consisting of French troops drawn partly from the army of Sevastopol and partly from the reserve at Constantinople, would move by sea to Alushta on the eastern shore of the Crimea, land there and move on to Simferopol in order to meet the Russians there in a pincer movement with Raglan's army.[4]

It was one thing, however, to hammer out such a plan at the green table at Windsor, quite another to put it into execution on the spot. When the plan was in Canrobert's hands on 8 May, the French general discussed it with his English colleague. They differed sharply on the merits of the plan, and the choice which confronted Canrobert, either to carry out the plan without the concurrence of the British or to disobey his Emperor, made the French general hand in his resignation on 16 May. His successor, Pélissier, was strong willed enough to ignore the orders received from Paris and try his luck with increased vigour in the trenches round Sevastopol.

The contribution of the French navy to the war effort was second only to that of the British. In some respects the French navy was even better than the Royal Navy. In terms of numbers of ships and men it was, of course, inferior to its British counterpart. According to the Navy List of 1854, Britain possessed 385 armed ships with over 13,000 guns and another 100 unarmed brigs. The French navy at the same time disposed of 300 warships, of which one-third were steam-powered, the same proportion as in the British navy. Since his advent to power, Napoleon III had devoted much attention to modernizing the French navy. A symbol of the progressive spirit and of the high technological standard was the *Napoléon*, the first modern screw-driven ship of the line, built in 1852 by the gifted naval engineer Stanislas Dupuy de Lôme.

The French navy was also ahead of the British: in the construction of the first ironclad ships, which were at that time called 'floating batteries'. Under the personal supervision of the Emperor, five of these ships were built in France within a matter of months. The ships were made of two casings; a wooden structure 42 cm thick covered with an additional iron layer of 11 cm which was impenetrable by all cannon shot of the time. Originally built for taking part in the siege of Sevastopol, three of them arrived just after the fall of the fortress, but saw action in mid-October during the bombardment of Kinburn. They decided the fate of this Russian fortress. The British followed suit in constructing ironclads of their own; two of them were actually towed to the Crimea but arrived too late to take part in any operations. Although the engineering feat of the floating batteries should not be exaggerated, it paved the way for the construction of the armoured ships of later days.

The quality of the crews of the French navy was high, and the reinforcements that were necessary during the war were of higher quality than the British equivalent in the Royal Navy, as most of them were taken from the merchant marine and fishing vessels, often by force.

Annotated bibliography

On the French army, especially on its leadership, cf. Brison D. Gooch, *The New Bonapartist Generals in the Crimean War* (The Hague, 1959). On Marshal Saint-Arnaud, see Maurice Quatrelles L'Épine, *Le Maréchal de Saint-Arnaud*, vol. 2, 1850–1854 (Paris, 1929), pp. 289–455. There is a voluminous biography of Canrobert based on interviews with him in his later life: Germain Bapst, *Le Maréchal Canrobert. Souvenirs d'un siècle*, vols 2–3 (Paris, 1902–4). On Pélissier, see Victor B. Derrécagaix, *Le Maréchal Pélissier, Duc de Malakoff* (Paris, 1911). On the French navy during the Crimean War, see Michèle Battesti, *La marine de Napoléon III. Une politique navale*, vols 1–2. (Houilles, 1997); Claude Farrère, *Histoire de la marine française* (Paris, 1934).

8

Great Britain

The British army system was the most antiquated, the most complicated and the most curious in comparison with the corresponding organizations of the continental great powers in the nineteenth century. To begin with, there was no compulsory service in Britain. Soldiers were hired mercenaries, as soldiers on the continent had been in former centuries. Their status was the lowest in the social scale. Their term of service was twenty-one years, that is, practically for life. The body of officers was organized, again compared to continental standards, along feudalistic lines. Service in the cavalry and guards was a comfortable sinecure for the younger sons of the aristocracy and formal standards of professional education were low. Commissions could still be acquired by purchase. In 1856 the commission of a lieutenant colonel was fixed at £7,000; for the ranks of a lieutenant in the line infantry and a major in the guards it ranged between £1,000 and £6,000.

Another characteristic of the British army in the nineteenth century is that it was a 'parliamentary', not a 'royal army'. This meant that Parliament fixed army estimates annually and discussed all sorts of questions from the overall strength of the army to minute details of armament and equipment. One result of the army being dependent on Parliament was its bewildering lack of organization at the highest levels. As the Prince Consort wrote in a memorandum on army reform on 14 January 1855, at the height of the Crimean winter:

> We have … no general staff or staff corps; – No field commissariat, no field army department; no ambulance corps, no baggage train, no corps of drivers, no corps of artisans; no practice, or possibility of acquiring it, in the combined use of the three arms, cavalry, infantry, and artillery; – No general qualified to handle more than one of these arms, and the artillery kept as distinct from the army as if it were a separate profession.[1]

This description is by no means exaggerated. Without going into excessive detail, it can be said that there was not one minister responsible for the army as a whole – as in the countries on the continent – but several. There was a Secretary of State for 'War and the Colonies', indicating that the empire and its military control belonged together. The Home Secretary was responsible for the reserve forces and the regular forces within the British Isles. Military finance was the domain of both the Secretary of War and the Treasury. The responsibility for supplies rested with two institutions: the Commissariat and the Ordnance Department. There was a Commander-in-Chief at the Horse Guards who was responsible for the preparedness of the army within the United Kingdom, but once an expeditionary force operated overseas he was almost powerless.

Due to the chaos which this system produced in the British army in the Crimea, some minor reforms were introduced. The post of Secretary of State for War and the Colonies was separated into two departments in June 1854; the Secretary of War was given a wider range of responsibilities; the post of Secretary at War was scrapped altogether under the Palmerston government. On the spot in the Crimea the Land Transport Corps was formed (later called the Military Train) – thus relieving the Commissariat of responsibility for provision of land transport – but it was raised too late to have any great effect.

The commanding general of the British expeditionary force sent to the Crimea was Lord Fitzroy Somerset, first Lord Raglan. He was a typical office general who had become Master-General of the Ordnance in 1852. Britain had not been involved in any major European war since the time of Napoleon, and colonial warfare was the only experience a British general could look back on. Raglan himself was conscious of this when he described his expeditionary force as capable of waging a colonial war, but not a war against a European power. In contrast to his French counterparts, Raglan was cultivated and gentle, and an able administrator who was devoid of strategic ideas and any sense of initiative. He scrupulously executed the commands he received from the Cabinet in London, in constant fear of being reprimanded or called before a parliamentary committee of investigation. True to his Whitehall experience as a desk warrior, he was content to be immersed in minute administrative details.

Cabinet ministers in London, themselves dreading unpalatable questions in Parliament, despaired of Raglan's lack of ideas for solving the deadlock before Sevastopol. Thus the Foreign Secretary, Lord Clarendon, sighed in a letter which he sent to Stratford de Redcliffe in Constantinople on 15 January 1855, 'Ld Raglan writes about individuals & regimental changes & Morning States just as if he was again Mil. Secy at the H Gds but with respect to what he is doing or meditating nil, nil, nil.'[2] Raglan died of cholera on 28 June 1855. He was succeeded by General Sir James Simpson who laboured hard under his new burden, was recalled after only four months and replaced by General Sir William Codrington.

Thus, with the possible exception of Pélissier, none of the commanding generals in the Crimea – Russian, French or English – was of outstanding quality.

The numerical strength which the British army contributed to the Allied war effort was clearly subordinate to the French army. The aggregate total of the British army in 1854 was, according to the parliamentary Army Estimates for that year, 153,000. To this can be added 30,000 troops stationed in India who were paid by the East India Company. Most of the troops were scattered throughout the colonies and could not be spared for a war on the Continent. In the summer of 1854 the British army of the East numbered 21,500 men; the French army was about treble that size. This proportion did not vary much in the ensuing months; if it did change, it was to the detriment of the British.

In spite of reinforcements, the British army dwindled during the coming months, mostly due to deaths from sickness. In December 1854, Sidney Herbert estimated British strength at 20,000, and at the end of January the effective strength had fallen to 13,000 due to the extraordinary rigours of the winter. In May 1855, after great efforts had been made to replenish the troops, the British could muster 32,000, the French 120,000 troops. According to unpublished official figures, almost 98,000 British soldiers had landed in the Crimea during the whole war. To solve the problems of manpower, the militia in Britain was tapped, which provided 33,000 men altogether.[3]

The numerical inferiority of the British army is the main reason that the two Allied armies were never put under one single command, although Napoleon III tried hard to bring about this sensible solution. On 22 January 1855 he addressed a private letter to the British ambassador in Paris, Lord Cowley, in which he urged that each should concentrate on its proper task, that is, Britain should provide four-fifths of the sea power and France four-fifths of the ground troops; Paris should be in command of the two armies and London of the two navies. But there was too much sensitivity on both sides, which had of course its historical background. At one point the British even stopped sending their troops by rail through France because they were manhandled by inhabitants in southern France. Palmerston's reaction to the Emperor's idea was negative: his reply was *suum cuique*.[4]

Almost the same sensitiveness reigned at the front round Sevastopol. Both armies had their separate supply bases, the British at Balaklava and the French at Kamiesh; each had its section of the besieging front, the British the right hand side, the French the centre and the left. Only when the British wing was on the point of breaking down, because of the length and difficulty of the supply route from Balaklava harbour, did they accept French reinforcements for their supply system and for their siege troops.

In terms of equipment the British army was up to the standard of Britain's industrial power, and thus on a par with the French and superior to the Russians as far as the infantry was concerned. The Enfield rifle, an improved version of the Minié rifle, had been introduced in the British army in 1853. The pride of the artillery was the Lancaster gun, which could fire a 68-pound shell over a distance of up to 2.2 kilometres, that is, double the range of other guns of the same calibre. It was much feared by the Russian defenders of Sevastopol, but the British did not have enough pieces available. A peculiar aspect of the British army was the use of linear tactics in its infantry, which appeared outdated by the middle of the nineteenth century. As the Battle of the Alma showed, it took a long time to prepare the 'thin red line' in rugged and hilly country and it was tantalizingly difficult to manoeuvre with the long line. Despite this, the firing power of the line was devastating, as the Russians at the Alma and at Inkerman experienced.

After the inconclusive Battle of Inkerman and the November storm of 1854, which played havoc with the British supply base at Balaklava, the British government was acutely aware of the need for reinforcements. The troops dispersed in the colonies could not be called upon; a reserve army was not available because there was no conscription. The thriving economy of the early 1850s produced a high demand for labour, which meant that young men saw no attraction in enlisting in the army. Thus the government fell back on the ancient practice of hiring mercenaries abroad. It was the last time in British military history that this practice was revived; indeed it was thought to have disappeared with the end of the Napoleonic Wars. The Aberdeen government tabled a Foreign Enlistment Bill in early December 1854 which passed both Houses by an unimpressive majority. The greatest difficulty in implementing the Act was that international law by then regarded official toleration of recruiting activities in foreign countries as a breach of neutrality, quite apart from the fact that the nationalism of the time was averse to such an outmoded practice.

After Clarendon had sounded out his representatives in Europe and in the United States, it soon emerged that success was only to be expected in the United States, the German states, Switzerland and Sardinia. Apart from Sardinia, recruiting activities had to be conducted clandestinely, and were conducive to diplomatic friction. This was especially true in the case of the United States and Prussia, as already noted in earlier chapters. The efforts had to be ignominiously abandoned in the United States – no recruit ever leaving the American continent for Europe – with several British consuls detained and charged with breaching American neutrality laws, and diplomatic relations broken off as a result in May 1856. Recruitment in Prussia ended almost as badly. The British consul at Cologne, John Robert Curtis, was condemned to imprisonment, but subsequently pardoned by the Prussian King.

Young Germans from Prussia and from other German states were, however, recruited in their thousands. They found their way clandestinely in fishing vessels and by night to the British island of Heligoland, and thence to Britain. This success was mainly due to the efficient work of Baron Richard von Stutterheim, a man of Prussian origin who had served in the British Legion in Spain in the 1830s and in the Schleswig-Holstein army against Denmark in 1848. On British soil a 'British-German Legion' was formed consisting of three regiments, which, having been trained and equipped at Aldershot and Shorncliffe, were transported to Scutari and Constantinople between November 1855 and January 1856. The war being almost at its

FIGURE 9 *Recruitment of German soldiers on the island of Heligoland in the North Sea*. Kladderadatsch 32, 8 July 1855, p. 128.

end, the Legion was soon disbanded. The men, having transgressed the law of their country of origin, could not return and were offered emigration to various British colonies; most of them went to South Africa. The strength of the German Legion was almost 10,000 men.

Recruitment in Switzerland, a traditional foreign recruiting ground throughout modern history, was another successful venture, although the Swiss Constitution of 1848 forbade such activities. The authorities, however, turned a blind eye to the practice, which was also carried out by French officers for their *Seconde légion étrangère*. This produced competition between the two countries. The main British recruiting depot was at Schlettstadt in Alsace. Colonel Charles Sheffield Dickson, a British soldier, was the main organizer and the eventual commander of the 'British–Swiss Legion'. Its strength was brought to just over 3,000 men and its first regiment was transported to Smyrna early in December 1855. The disbandment of the Swiss Legion was less difficult than that of the German Legion as most of the men were able to return to Switzerland.

The third foreign legion to be successfully formed was recruited in Sardinia. Many of its members were political exiles or deserters from the nearby Austrian vice-kingdom of Lombardy-Venetia, a fact which produced some diplomatic friction with the government in Vienna, so much the more as the main recruiting depot was at Novara near the Austrian border. The 'British–Italian Legion' had an eventual strength of 3,500 men. It was an unruly band which left Sardinian soil as late as April 1856 for Malta. After disbandment the majority returned to Sardinia, but about 1,200 were allowed to emigrate to the Argentine Confederation to settle there as military colonists.

Distinct from these foreign legions, the British took in pay two peculiar military organizations: the so-called 'Turkish Contingent' and the 'Polish Legion'.

The 'Turkish Contingent' was the hobby horse of the British ambassador at Constantinople, Stratford de Redcliffe. On 3 February 1855 he signed a convention with the Turkish government which provided for the employment of a body of Turkish troops in the British service. Parliament passed the convention, which meant that money had to be raised for a contingent of 20,000 Turks. The officers were to be British, on the lines of the army in India. Besides the idea of strengthening the British effort during the war, de Redcliffe had the ulterior motive of opening the Contingent to Christian subjects of the Sultan (the corps was originally to consist of Muslims only) and thus of contributing to the realization of his notion of equality among all subjects of the Sultan. The Turkish Contingent was set up in the ensuing months and was commanded by the British general, Robert John Vivian. A year later, by February 1856, it seems to have reached its nominal strength of at least 20,000.

When the common plan of campaign for 1856 was drafted between London and Paris, the British had the satisfaction of contributing slightly more than half the 200,000 troops earmarked for the campaign in the East. For the first time during the war, the British were equal to the French: their army was to consist of 104,000 troops, leaving the French to bring only 96,000 into the field. The British contribution was made up of 61,000 British troops, 10,000 of the Foreign Legion (German and Swiss), 18,000 of the Anglo-Turkish Legion (of which 15,000 were from the Turkish Contingent and 3,000 'Osmanli Cavalry', that is, irregulars) and 15,000 Sardinians. On paper the British army was about two-fifths non-British.[5]

An integral part of the Turkish Contingent was the 'Turkish Cossacks' or 'Polish Legion'. This body already existed before the formation of the Turkish Contingent and originally served in the Turkish army under Omer Pasha. It consisted of two regiments, one being commanded by Michael Czajkowski, the other by Władisław Zamoyski. Both commanders were of Polish origin. The former served in the Turkish army during the war as a general (his Turkish name was Sadik Pasha). When the Turks occupied Wallachia together with the Austrians in the summer of 1854, Czajkowski became governor of Bucharest and his Legion was stationed in the city. Some of the soldiers under his command were deserters from the Austrian army, which created endless friction between the two occupation forces until the Turkish authorities withdrew the Legion from the town. It took part in the Battle of Tulchea on 7 January 1855 against the Russians, but after repeated remonstrances from the Austrian government it was removed, in the summer of 1855, to the Caucasian front.

In September 1855 the 'Turkish Cossacks' were reorganized. The second regiment under Major General Zamoyski was placed under British control. Whereas the first regiment consisted of a hotchpotch of Polish and Hungarian emigrés and of various other Slavs (among them Zaporogian Cossacks whose forebears had fled from the Ukraine to Turkey in 1775), the members of the second regiment were of Polish origin only. Besides emigrés and deserters, it was augmented by Polish prisoners of war from the Russian army in the Crimea. During the winter of 1855–6 it had its headquarters at Baltchik, north of Varna and a depot of organization at Scutari. At the end of the war it reached a strength of 1,500 men and officers and was returned to the Turkish army.

The formation of these various foreign legions clearly demonstrates Britain's frantic efforts to make up for the deficiencies of her army and to draw even numerically with the French army in the East.

British war planning at the beginning of the war was either non-existent or hazy. After Russia's evacuation of the Danubian Principalities, it concentrated on the southern tip of the Crimean peninsula and remained fixed on Sevastopol until the latter's fall in September 1855; it then moved to the Caucasian front in order to avoid the trammels of the sterile cooperation with the French army, but was brought back to reality when a war council in Paris in January 1856 clearly showed that the whole Crimean peninsula had first to be cleared of Russian troops before opening up other theatres of war. Efforts in the Baltic with the final aim of attacking the formidable fortress of Kronstadt, which protected the capital St Petersburg, were in fact restricted to naval raids on the Baltic and Finnish coasts and the Åland Islands. Because of the lack of troops, an invasion on that front on any large scale was never seriously entertained.

The first phase of Britain's war planning was dominated by the navy and its First Lord of the Admiralty, Sir James Graham, and was also subservient to the war plans of France, which provided the stronger land army. At the beginning of 1854 the greatest problem was how to protect Turkey from a recurrence of Sinope, and the Straits and Constantinople from a Russian march from the Principalities through the Balkans. The idea of invading the Crimea was already present at that early stage in strategic thinking, as it was understood that Austria would hold back the Russian army from crossing the Danube. On 1 March 1854, Graham explained his strategy in a letter to Clarendon. He took it for granted that the Dardanelles had to be secured and a position in front of Constantinople fortified:

> But *the* operation which will be ever memorable and decisive, is the capture and destruction of Sevastopol. On this my Heart is set: the Eye Tooth of the Bear must be drawn: and 'til his Fleet and Naval Arsenal in the Black Sea are destroyed there is no safety for Constantinople, no Security for the Peace of Europe.[6]

This was the plan that was finally carried out when the Allied troops assembled at Varna and found that the Russians had raised the siege of Silistria and evacuated the Principalities. The invasion of the Crimea in September 1854 boiled down to an unexpectedly long siege of Sevastopol. Both the British and the French governments became worried about the stalemate which developed in front of Sevastopol. Napoleon wanted to cut the Gordian knot by going to the Crimea in person, thus instilling more mobility into the Allied troops there and enforcing a military solution. His own ministers and also the British and Austrian governments left no stone unturned to dissuade him from this dangerous plan. A way out was found when Queen Victoria invited the Emperor to come to London and Windsor in April 1855. Both governments decided on a pincer movement, already mentioned, that was supposed to wrest Simferopol, in the centre of the Crimea, from the Russians and thereby cut the vital supply line to the beleaguered fortress. An army under Canrobert was to be left in the trenches round Sevastopol; a second under Raglan was to turn north, cross the Tchernaya and occupy the Mackenzie heights on the Russian supply line between Simferopol and Sevastopol; a third under Omer Pasha was to march east from Eupatoria; a fourth on the east coast of the Crimea was to march west into the interior. Thus, it was hoped, the Russians would seek a battle in the open field.

The Allied generals on the spot cared not a jot for this plan and tried one assault after another on the Russian fortress of Sevastopol. When it finally fell on 8 September 1855, Napoleon became weary of the dreadful drain of men and money and withdrew part of his troops to France either to end the war or open up new fronts elsewhere in Europe, preferably on the Rhine. Palmerston's plan of campaign for 1856 was to hold the positions in the Crimea that were in Allied hands (Sevastopol, Eupatoria, Kertch); send an Anglo-Turkish army with a French contingent to drive the Russians out of Georgia and Circassia; despatch a French army with a British contingent to conquer Kherson and Nikolaev; and launch a combined fleet with 10,000 ground troops to attack and destroy Kronstadt.

These divergent views were the reason for the convocation of an Anglo-French council of war in Paris which discussed various plans between 10 and 20 January 1856. As the Russians had decided on 16 January to accept the Austrian ultimatum and end the war, the decisions of the council almost became a dead letter, but from a military point of view it was expedient to have a plan for 1856 for all contingencies. The British gave up their plan for a simultaneous campaign in Asia Minor. Instead, both governments fell back on the basic idea of their original plan of 20 April 1855. The Crimea was to be cleared of Russian troops by concentrating an Allied army of 120,000 at Eupatoria under French command; another army of 65,000 under a British general was to move northwards from Sevastopol, and the Turkish Contingent of 15,000 was to occupy Kertch and Yenikaleh. As mentioned above, the British army, including all non-British parts (foreign legions, Turkish Contingent, etc.), numbered 104,000 and was thus slightly superior to the French army.[7]

The impending peace conferences in Paris ensured that this plan of campaign for 1856, the first and only one during the war hammered out conjointly and sanctioned by both governments, remained confined to paper.

The backbone of the British war effort during the Crimean War was the Royal Navy. As the huge but obsolete Russian navy withdrew to its harbours, the Royal Navy never had a chance to meet its enemy in an open battle. It was thus reduced to an inconspicuous role, but this was by no means unimportant. It provided mobility to the British army without which the latter could not have been used in the East. The new screwdriven ships were especially invaluable. These vessels could ply the Mediterranean – from Marseilles to the Straits – within twelve to sixteen days, whereas sailing ships needed fifty, sixty or seventy days. The fleet was the lifeline of the army before Sevastopol and was in command of the entire Black Sea.

In the Baltic its main task was to ensure the blockade of the Russian coast. This was difficult because it lacked flat-bottomed coastal vessels, thus the Russian coastal trade could never be stopped completely. The situation in this respect improved somewhat in 1855. In 1854 the main feat of the Allies in the Baltic was the occupation and destruction of Bomarsund on the Åland Islands in August 1854, but this was mainly due to a French expeditionary corps of 18,000 men. Public opinion in Britain was therefore impatient of the relative impotence of the British fleet in the Baltic. In 1855 it did not fare much better. The main action was the bombardment of Sveaborg on the Finnish coast in August 1855, which was, however, of minimal strategic importance. Plans for 1856 were therefore stepped up on a grand scale, the main object being the destruction of Kronstadt.

Whereas in 1854 the Royal Navy, according to the Navy list, consisted of 385 armed vessels with slightly over 13,000 guns, the majority of which (301) were in European waters, the squadron earmarked for the Baltic campaign of 1856 alone consisted of a total of 336 vessels. Besides twenty-five ships of the line it numbered 164 gunboats and 100 mortar vessels and floats which were vital for operations in the Bay of Kronstadt. It also included eight floating batteries which had proved their worth in the bombardment of the fortress of Kinburn in October 1855. This force, together with a smaller French squadron, would have sealed the fate of Kronstadt in 1856. Although a large expeditionary force was not to be sent to the Baltic, it was to be expected that Sweden would enter the war according to her treaty with the Western powers of 21 November 1855, which was to be widened to an offensive treaty in January 1856. According to a secret memorandum drawn up by King Oscar at that time, Sweden was to provide an army of 165,000 men to drive the Russians out of Finland. Russia's suing for peace in January 1856 stopped all these plans.

Annotated bibliography

For general remarks on the British army (and also on those of the other European great powers), see the various studies by Hew Strachan, *European Armies and the Conduct of War* (London and New York, 1983, repr. 2004 and 2010); *Wellington's Legacy: The Reform of the British Army, 1830–54* (Manchester, 1984); *From Waterloo to Balaclava: Tactics, Technology, and the British Army, 1815–1854* (Cambridge, 1985). On the organization of the British army, cf. also John Sweetman, *War and Administration: The Significance of the Crimean War for the British Army* (Edinburgh, 1984). Much material on numerous aspects of the British army during the Crimean War is in the life-and-letters biography of Sidney Herbert, Secretary at War from 1852 to February 1855: A. H. Gordon, Baron Stanmore, *Sidney Herbert, Lord Herbert of Lea*, 2 vols (London, 1906). Also of importance is Sir George Douglas and Sir George Dalhousie Ramsay (eds), *The Panmure Papers: Being a Selection from the Correspondence of Fox Maule, Second Baron Panmure, afterwards, Earl of Dalhousie*, 2 vols (London 1908). There are two studies on Lord Raglan: Christopher Hibbert, *The Destruction of Lord Raglan* (London, 1961); John Sweetman, *Raglan: From the Peninsula to the Crimea* (London, 1993, 2nd edn Barnsley, 2010). The latter tries to rehabilitate Raglan. On the introduction of modern firearms, see C. H. Roads, *The British Soldier's Firearm 1850–1864* (London, 1964). The best monograph on the foreign legions is C. C. Bayley, *Mercenaries for the*

Crimea: The German, Swiss, and Italian Legions in British Service, 1854–1856 (Montreal and London, 1977). On the Swiss legion, cf. also Peter Gugolz, *Die Schweiz und der Krimkrieg 1853–1856* (Basel and Stuttgart, 1965). There is no study on the Turkish Contingent. Cf. the relevant documents (also on the Polish legion) in *AGKK* III/3–4. On the Polish Legion, see Marja Pawlicowa, 'O formacjach Kozackich w czasie wojny krymskiej', *Kwartalnik Historyczny* 60 (1936): 3–50, 622–55; Ion I. Nistor, 'Die Polenlegion im Krimkriege', *Codrul Cosminului* 9 (1935): 69–102. On British war planning, see Hew Strachan, 'Soldiers, Strategy and Sebastopol', *Historical Journal* 21 (1978): 303–25; Andrew D. Lambert, *The Crimean War: British Grand Strategy, 1853–56* (Manchester and New York, 1990, 2nd edn Farnham, 2011). General questions concerning the Royal Navy are discussed by Wilhelm Treue, *Der Krimkrieg und seine Bedeutung für die Entstehung der modernen Flotten* (Herford, 1980), pp. 26–31. British naval campaigns in all theatres of the war are discussed by Peter Deckers, *The Crimean War at Sea: The Naval Campaigns against Russia, 1854–1856* (Barnsley, 2011); Andrew Rath, *The Crimean War in Imperial Context, 1854–1856* (New York, 2015).

9

Turkey

Very little research has been done until recently on the Turkish army during the Crimean War. But a few basic facts can be given here.

Since the 1830s the Turkish army had been reorganized on European lines. Soldiers had to serve for five years, which meant that there were enough trained soldiers to fall back on in times of war. The strength of the army could then be doubled. It is difficult, however, to give any approximate idea of its actual strength during the Crimean War. Figures vary between just over 200,000 and 400,000. Turkish authorities themselves would probably not have known how many heads its army counted at any given time. A figure provided by the Turkish Minister of Finance at the turn of 1855–6 puts the army of the line, the *nizam*, at 105,325 men, including 2,259 in British service, and the reserve army, the *redif*, at 103,827 men, including 7,741 men of the Turkish Contingent.[1]

Added to these must be the troops of the vassal provinces, such as Tunisia and Egypt. They were of poor quality and were raised like indentured labour. Thus the Egyptian contingent which arrived at Constantinople in August 1853 was a motley of 14,000 men, mostly veterans who had been seized and brought in chains to Alexandria where they were shipped off to Constantinople. According to contemporary sources, 60,000 of these troops were sent to the Danubian front and another 30,000 to the Caucasian front. In action, as in the Caucasus, they would desert in their hundreds and thousands.

A further addition to the Turkish Army were three special units, the largest – at least on paper – of which was the so-called 'Turkish Contingent'. The idea for its formation came from the British government and from its ambassador at Constantinople, Stratford de Redcliffe. They were desperately looking for troops that would prop up their own army which was so much inferior to the French *Armée d'Orient*. On 3 February 1855, a convention was signed at Constantinople 'for the Employment of a Body of Turkish Troops in the British Service'. The Contingent was to consist of 20,000 soldiers, whom the Porte had to supply, and who were to be led by British officers. The commander was Lieutenant-General Robert Vivian. As the Turkish government was unable to furnish the recruits, the British government hit upon the idea to induce the Porte to recruit Christians from the empire who were normally exempt from militäry service. But the idea soon fell to the ground. Anyhow, the build-up of the Contingent was a novelty in Ottoman history since the higher-ranking British officers were Christians and the ranks were Muslims.

Another special unit was the 'Turkish Cossacks' ('Corps des Cosaques Ottomans'). It was founded at the instigation of Count Adam Czartoryski, leader of the Poles in exile in Paris. It consisted of Polish prisoners of war and deserters from the Russian army. At the end of 1855 it was earmarkd to form part of the 'Turkish Contingent' and serve as an occupation unit at Kertch; it was to be brought to a strength of 4,000 men, but never reached that number.[2]

Finally, there were the Bashi-Bazouks, irregular troops that were mostly recruited in Albania and Asia Minor. They received arms and ammunition from the Turkish army, but no pay and no uniforms. They fought on their own, their main concern being booty and the killing or mutilating of the enemy.[3]

The Turkish regular army was well drilled, well armed and good on the defensive. About a quarter was equipped with modern percussion rifles bought in Britain. The Turkish artillery was as good as any at the time, the guns being of French and British origin.

The most able leader of the Turkish army was Omer Pasha. He was a Croatian by birth, who had deserted from the Austrian army and held various posts in the Turkish army and administration. In 1853 he commanded the Turkish army on the Danubian front. He was fêted in the European press for his successes against the Russians at Kalafat and Oltenitsa and for the stubborn resistance of his troops at Silistria. After much friction with the Austrian occupation army in the Principalities, Omer left with part of his army for the Crimea in January 1855 and entrenched himself at Eupatoria to threaten the Russian right flank there. As he did not like cooperating with the Allied commanders there and at Sevastopol, he took his troops to the Caucasus in September 1855 in order to relieve the beleaguered fortress of Kars, but arrived there too late.

In all, the Turkish army cut a fairly decent figure on the Danube, but in order to win the war Turkey was wholly dependent on the Allied war effort.

Annotated bibliography

Until recently no research had been done on the Turkish army during the Crimean War. Some useful information could be gained from Adolphus Slade, *Turkey and the Crimean War* (London, 1867). But now, at long last, two recent books shed light on the matter: James J. Reid, *Crisis of the Ottoman Empire: Prelude to the Collapse, 1839–1878* (Stuttgart, 2000); Candan Badem, *The Ottoman Crimean War (1853–1856)* (Leiden, 2010).

Not surprisingly, Badem devotes more space to the Danubian and Caucasian fronts than to the Crimea. Note also his remarks on Turkish military history, pp. 19–22, and on the special units of the army, pp. 257–68. See also M. E. S. Laws, 'Beatson's Bashi Bazooks', *Army Quarterly and Defense Journal* 71 (1955): 80–5.

10

Sardinia

The fifth army which served in the Crimea was that of Sardinia. It participated in the war at the instigation of the British, not of the French government. Initially, however, it was the Sardinian government itself that wanted to join the Western powers against Russia for political and ideological reasons. There was a strong current within the government and in public opinion in Sardinia that the war was a crusade of the liberal and progressive West against the conservative and reactionary Russia. It was even hoped that the war in the East might develop into a general war of liberation of oppressed nationalities in Europe.

For the British and French governments the participation of Austria was of far greater importance than that of Sardinia, so the hopes of the latter were damped down for the time being. They were certainly not raised by the treaty of 2 December 1854 between Austria and the Western powers, which opened up the prospect of French troops marching through southern Germany and northern Italy to bolster up the Austrian army, once the Viennese government had declared war on Russia. Might not the Western powers treat Sardinia as they had treated Greece in May 1854, and force her to remain quiet and not provoke Austria in her rear? There was much discussion about how to deal with this untoward situation. King Victor Emanuel and Prime Minister Cavour were both in favour of taking the bull by the horns and offering assistance to the Allies, whereas the Foreign Minister, Dabormida, was strongly against any unconditional participation.

On the other hand the British government was searching Europe for troops after the inconclusive Battle of Inkerman and the terrible hurricane of 14 November 1854, particularly in view of its numerical inferiority in relation to the French. As early as 15 November, Palmerston had asked Russell, 'Might we not get six thousand men from Portugal, ten thousand from Spain, and ten thousand from Piedmont?'[1] On 29 November, Clarendon asked Hudson to sound out Turin about providing 10,000 troops. The Sardinian government responded positively, promising as many as 15,000 men, but with strings attached. Sardinia was to take part in the future peace negotiations on an equal status and the Allies were to pledge themselves to put the question of Italy on the agenda of the peace conference and were to ask Vienna to raise the sequestration of the property of emigrants from

Lombardy and Venetia. London and Paris were adamant in rejecting these conditions. On 7 January 1855 the British and French ministers at Turin presented a virtual ultimatum to the Sardinian government: either adhere to the Allied treaty of 10 April 1854 unconditionally or give up any idea of an alliance. Cavour accepted the ultimatum, whereupon Dabormida, the Foreign Minister, resigned. Cavour took the risk of the new alliance becoming a conservative one.

On 10 January 1855 a treaty of accession was signed between Sardinia and the two Western powers. It was completed by a tripartite military convention on 26 January by which Sardinia pledged herself to furnish 15,000 men. On the same day a financial convention was signed between Sardinia and Britain only, by which the latter pledged herself to grant a loan (not a subsidy, which the Sardinians regarded as dishonourable) of £2 million.

When the Sardinian troops under their commanding general Alfonso La Marmora prepared to embark for the East in March and April, an altercation developed between Paris and London about how to employ them and who should do so. Napoleon planned to use them as a portion of his army of reserve at Constantinople, whereupon the British government maintained its right to use them at Sevastopol because it bore the financial burden of their upkeep. When Napoleon was on his state visit to London, he gave in to the British demand.

When the Sardinians eventually landed at Balaklava on 8 May 1855, they were in fact placed under joint Allied command and stationed well outside the siege perimeter, with Gasfort Hill (near the Valley of Death) as their centre. They were at once afflicted by cholera: 3,000 fell ill and 1,300 died. On 16 August they became involved in the battle on the Tchernaya and lost fourteen dead and 170 wounded.

Did Sardinia reap any fruits from her participation in the war in the East? Cavour and his King managed to ingratiate themselves with Napoleon, Queen Victoria and the British government on their state visits to Paris and London in December 1855. Cavour was allowed to take part in the Paris peace congress, thus fulfilling one of the three conditions he had originally raised for Sardinia's accession to the Western alliance. In the official sessions the Italian Question was not broached at all because of the stiff resistance of the Austrian delegation. Backstage, Cavour tried hard to further the cause of Italy, but to no avail. In the end he was highly disappointed: 'Peace is signed. The drama is finished and the curtain has fallen without having brought about a solution which would have been materially favourable to us. This is a sad result.'[2]

Even so, there were intangible results. After the congress had ended its meetings on the war results, it discussed, without coming to a decision, various questions of European interest, among them the Roman Question and the situation in the Kingdom of the Two Sicilies. Thus the Italian Question, in two of its particular aspects, was brought before the European

Areopagus. Cavour had managed, as an Italian historian has put it, to 'diplomatize' the Italian Question.[3] He himself drew the conclusion from his vain efforts at the congress that the only efficient solution to that question would be 'the cannon'. And it was Napoleon who three years later helped him to load the cannon.

Annotated bibliography

For Sardinia's intervention in the war, see the titles listed above in Chapter 3. See also Harry Hearder, 'Clarendon, Cavour, and the Intervention of Sardinia in the Crimean War, 1853–1855', *International History Review* 18 (1996): 819–36. The military side is treated in Cristoforo Manfredi, *La spedizione sarda in Crimea nel 1855–5* (Rome, 1896).

PART FOUR

The War

11

The Danube front, 1853–4

The Allied fleets in the Levant and the Russian occupation of the Danubian Principalities

The first open act of hostility leading to war was Napoleon III's decision of 19 March 1853 to send a squadron from Toulon to the island of Salamis off the eastern coast of Greece near Athens. The decision was published in the *Moniteur* on the following day, and the squadron, under Admiral Aaron L. F. Regnault de La Susse, reached its destination on 23 April. The dispatch of the fleet in the midst of the Menshikov mission was meant to be a political demonstration in the tug of war between France and Russia in their fight for a dominant influence at Constantinople. It was also aimed at forcing the hand of Britain, which at that time was still sitting on the fence, in the Holy Places dispute.

Napoleon's calculation was correct. After some hesitation the British followed suit and on 2 June 1853 Admiral Sir James Dundas at Malta was ordered to sail to Besika Bay, 12 kilometres south of the entrance to the Dardanelles. He was there to wait for orders from Stratford de Redcliffe at Constantinople; de Redcliffe was given full powers to call up the fleet in case of danger. The British fleet arrived at Besika Bay on 13 June, to be followed a day later by the French squadron from Salamis. The junction of the two fleets underlined the resolution of the two governments to help the Sultan in resisting any further exorbitant demands from Russia.

Menshikov had just ended his mission to Constantinople unsuccessfully. Russia's final ultimatum, delivered from St Petersburg on 31 May 1853, was to be propped up by a military threat: the invasion of the Danubian Principalities. It must be stressed that this action was a concomitant of the Menshikov mission, and not a response to France's and Britain's sending of their Mediterranean fleets to the Levant. Nicholas had already made up his mind, as is evidenced by a letter of 28 May 1853 which he sent to Paskevich: after Menshikov's failure he would occupy the Danubian Principalities and wait for the Sultan's response. If the latter proved obstinate, he would block the Bosphorus, clear the Black Sea of Turkish ships and propose that the Austrians occupy Herzegovina and Serbia. If that was to no avail, their independence and that of the Principalities should be proclaimed.[1]

The date on which Nicholas resolved to occupy the Principalities was 28 May 1854. On 7 June, Prince Michael Dimitrievich Gorchakov was nominated commander of the occupation forces. They were to consist of the 4th Corps and of part of the 5th Corps stationed in south-west Russia. They began concentrating along the border of the Principalities from 5 June onwards. On 3 July the first Russian troops crossed the Pruth. Bucharest, where Gorchakov set up his headquarters, was reached on 15 July. He was ordered not to cross the Danube and not to occupy Little Wallachia on the border with Serbia, in order to placate the Austrians. The total number of the occupation forces was just over 80,000 men.

Nesselrode, the Russian Foreign Minister, stressed in public that the occupation of the Principalities was not an act of war, but a political demonstration, 'a gage' to bring the Sultan to his senses.[2] Oddly enough, the governments of the other great powers accepted this interpretation and did not regard Russia's occupation as an act of war. Diplomacy was still in full swing in order to bring about a peaceful solution, but in September 1853 feelings at Constantinople were running high. A grand council was convened by the Sultan and unanimously resolved to declare war on Russia. The official declaration of war was issued on 4 October in the form of a manifesto which Omer Pasha sent to Gorchakov two days later, demanding that he evacuate the Principalities; in the case of non-compliance, hostilities would commence a fortnight later.

The local Turkish–Russian war was now declared. Nicholas was still in high spirits, although he expected the Allied fleet to enter the Bosphorus soon and even the Black Sea. On 21 October 1853 he wrote to Menshikov, now commander of Russia's naval forces, that the Russian troops would not cross the Danube in order to pursue the Turks, but that in the Caucasus Prince Michael S. Voroncov, Commander-in-Chief of the Russian troops there, should begin the offensive and try to occupy the Turkish fortresses of Kars and Ardahan and possibly Bayezid. On the Black Sea, Kustendje and Varna should be bombarded to sever the Turkish lines of communication on the western coast, and the Turkish fleet should be annihilated if it ventured out of the Bosphorus ('give them another Chesmé', as he put it, alluding to Russia's burning of the Turkish fleet in 1770). The French and British ships should be ignored, but if they acted in conjunction with the Turkish ships, they should be treated as enemy vessels.[3]

Almost simultaneously the British Cabinet reached a momentous decision, thereby giving the lie to Nicholas's exuberant optimism. On 7 and 8 October 1853 the Cabinet decided to allow the British fleet to enter the Turkish Straits and even the Black Sea, if the protection of Turkey warranted its appearance there. As a result, the fleet, together with the French squadron,

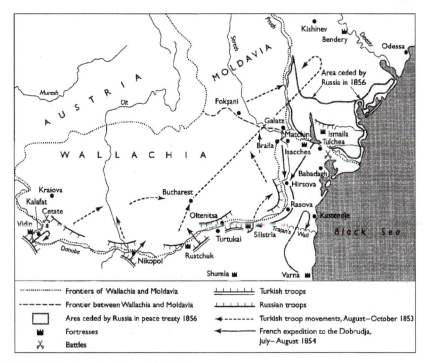

MAP 2 *The Danube front, 1853–4.*

began its movement through the Dardanelles on 22 October, the advance ships reaching the Bosphorus on 1 November.[4]

On the Danube, Omer Pasha sensed the importance of his westernmost fortress, Vidin, which the Russians might target to bring them as near as possible to the Serbian frontier. Between 28 and 30 October, 10,000 Turkish troops crossed the Danube from Vidin to the opposite bank, occupied the small town of Kalafat and fortified it as their first bridgehead on the left bank.

In the centre of the long front along the Danube, Omer Pasha planned another crossing of the river, and, in case of success, a march on to nearby Bucharest. On 2 November he despatched 10,000 troops across the river and occupied the quarantine house at Oltenitsa. Two days later the Russians decided on a counter-attack to throw the Turks back. They came under heavy fire, whereupon General Pëtr A. Dannenberg, their commanding general, gave the signal to retreat. According to official sources, the Russians lost 236 dead and 734 wounded. Although the Turkish detachment had stood the test, Omer Pasha decided to give up Oltenitsa and recross the Danube – this was achieved on 15 November. He may have feared Russian reinforcements and a long winter campaign. In fact, the occupation of

Bucharest without advancing from the Danube on a broader front would have left him in an exposed position that would have soon become untenable. Although from a military point of view Oltenitsa was but a skirmish, its importance was inflated by the European press as a Turkish success, and it certainly damaged the pride of the Russians.

There were a few more minor skirmishes along the Danube throughout the rest of 1853. A more important one occurred on 6 January 1854 and closed the winter campaign of 1853–4 on that front. The Turkish bridgehead at Kalafat was fortified and the troops there were augmented. The local Turkish commander, Ahmed Pasha, therefore left Kalafat on 31 December 1853 with a few thousand horsemen and some infantry and attacked the village to the north – Cetate – which was held by a Russian detachment under Colonel Alexander K. Baumgarten. The attack was repulsed, but renewed with superior forces (about 18,000 men) on 6 January 1854, the orthodox Christmas Day. Baumgarten's detachment, several times inferior in number, gave up the village with heavy losses, but during the day reinforcements came in from two directions, whereupon the Turks preferred to break off the battle and retreat to Kalafat. Cetate was the most bloody encounter on the Danube front: official Russian sources put the losses at 831 dead and 1,190 wounded. From the strategic point of view it was indecisive, but the Turks firmly held their bridgehead at Kalafat, thus protecting their fortress of Vidin and preventing the Russians from reaching the Serbian frontier.

The naval engagement at Sinope, 30 November 1853

Six weeks before the bloody encounter at Cetate, the general aspect of the war had changed dramatically with the opening of the door to a general European war. This was due to the naval engagement at Sinope on 30 November 1853.

During October and November the Turks were endeavouring to send supplies and men to Batum, on the eastern coast of the Black Sea, destined for the mountaineers of the Caucasus in their struggle against the Russians and for their own troops on that front. A flotilla of seven frigates, three corvettes, one steam frigate, one small steamer and four transports had sought shelter from bad weather in the harbour of Sinope on the Anatolian coast. This was a dangerous move as Sinope was little more than 300 kilometres away from Sevastopol, but almost double that distance from Constantinople. The Russian Admiral Nakhimov, who had been reconnoitring the Black Sea in spite of the inclement weather, had spotted the Turkish ships.

The Tsar's order of 21 October 1853, quoted above, to sink Turkish ships wherever they were found, was clear enough. Nakhimov asked for reinforcements from Sevastopol. When they arrived, he had at his disposal six ships of the line and two frigates. Although the Turks had no counterpart to the Russian ships of the line, they had more guns (about 500 as against 359 Russian guns) because there were a number of batteries on the shore. The commander of the Turkish flotilla, Osman Pasha, and his English adviser, Captain Adolphus Slade, felt relatively safe because of their superiority in firepower.

However, on 30 November, Nakhimov's ships entered the harbour, opened fire and within two hours the Turkish flotilla was annihilated. Only Slade's ship, the small steamer *Taif*, was ordered to leave; it slipped through the Russian lines and steamed to Constantinople to deliver the news of the disaster. The Turkish losses were heavy; the number of dead and drowned and of those who died at the batteries is estimated at about 3,000. Russian losses, in contrast, were light: the damage done to their ships was insignificant and they lost thirty-eight men dead and 235 wounded.

The *Taif* arrived at Constantinople on 2 December. From there the news was relayed to Europe, partly by telegraph: in Paris it was known on 10 December, in London a day later. Napoleon reacted with fury. He let it be known in London that if the British government kept refusing to send its fleet into the Black Sea, he would go in alone. The Cabinet was in the midst of a crisis: Palmerston, the Home Secretary, left it in protest because of an issue of domestic policy. Public opinion was in uproar. Newspapers clamoured for revenge for the 'massacre of Sinope', as this legitimate act of war now came to be called. National humiliation was deep because the navy had stood idly by while a Turkish fleet which the British ships had been sent to protect was reduced to nothing. Any qualms which still existed among Cabinet members were simply swept away by the public outcry. Vacillation in the government would have meant its downfall after the Christmas recess. On 20 December 1853, Stratford de Redcliffe was authorized to send the British fleet into the Black Sea in order to obtain complete control of it and to inform the Russian admiral at Sevastopol of the British intention. Palmerston, the symbol of the anti-Russian spirit in Britain, returned to the Cabinet on 24 December. On 4 January 1854 the combined Anglo-French fleet entered the Black Sea. War between the two Western powers and Russia, though still formally undeclared, was now almost inevitable. Sinope, unexpected by the Russian leaders who felt elated by their triumph, had brought this about. It had also produced almost complete harmony between France and Britain.

The siege of Silistria, March–June 1854

The two winter months of January and February 1854 brought about no change on the Danube front. Diplomatic activity, on the other hand, reached a high pitch during that period when both Russia (through the Orlov mission) and the Western powers (through a four-power convention) tried to win the two German powers over to their side. The outcome was that Austria took on a more anti-Russian stance after the Tsar had invited Francis Joseph to make common cause with him against Turkey and to liberate the Balkan peoples from Turkish yoke, thus revealing the revolutionary character of his designs on Turkey.

Nicholas, however, went ahead with his plans to destroy Turkey even without Austria as his accomplice. He knew that France and Britain would soon declare war and that they were fitting out expeditionary corps. He obviously thought, given his vastly superior military forces and the favourable geographic position of Russia, that his country was impregnable and that he could still deal with Turkey as he liked. He continued to harbour the illusion that the Balkan peoples, especially the Serbians and the Bulgarians, would rise as one against the Turkish yoke. The anti-Turkish risings in Thessaly and Epirus fortified this illusion, and Nicholas hoped that they would spread into Herzegovina so that the whole Balkan peninsula would be in flames.

The military plans for the opening of the spring campaign were laid down by the Tsar in a letter, which he sent to Gorchakov on 13 February, and in an undated memorandum, which he obviously drafted a few weeks later.[5] He ordered the crossing of the Danube on the whole length between Vidin in the west and Silistria in the east, the siege of these Turkish fortresses and also of those of Rustchuk in between and of Galatz and Braila on the northern section. Taking Silistria was necessary in order to have a stronghold from which to attack the Allied expeditionary force, which the Tsar expected to land at Varna. He thus either sensed the Allied plans correctly or had received intelligence from his ambassadors in Paris and London. The conquest of Vidin was important in his eyes in order to cooperate with the Serbs and Bulgarians. By the time of his memorandum he had second thoughts about the prospects of a Serbian rising, since Austria was already concentrating troops on the Serbian frontier. In considering Austria's political attitude he estimated – quite correctly as it turned out – that by July she would have made up her mind either to stay neutral or be hostile towards Russia.

In accordance with the Tsar's orders, Russian troops started crossing the Danube on the north-eastern section around Galatz and Ismaila on 23 March 1854 and occupied strongholds in the Dobrudja. Tulchea and Isacchea were reached almost without fighting on 24 March, Matchin on the 25th, and Hirsova on the 26th. Babadagh was in Russian hands on the 29th. At the beginning of April the whole length of Trajan's wall between Rasova and Kustendje was occupied. The Russian army across the Danube numbered 45,000 men under General Alexander N. Lüders and the entire operation had cost them 201 dead and 510 wounded men.

It is characteristic of the attitude of the Russian army on the Danube that during the following three months it did not exploit its position in the Dobrudja and did not concentrate all its efforts on the conquest of Silistria and Rustchuk, but went about this task at a leisurely pace. The reason was that Field Marshal Paskevich in Warsaw had meanwhile ordered Gorchakov not to cross the Danube, or, if he had already done so, not to go beyond Matchin. The order was received by Gorchakov on the evening of 24 March in the midst of the troop movements. What made Paskevich, who had goaded his master into occupying the Principalities and awaiting the uprisings of the Balkan peoples, think of retreat? The main explanation is not the arrival of the Allied troops at Gallipoli but the concentration of Austrian troops on the frontiers of Moldavia and Wallachia. He had received news that the Austrian army had reached a strength of 280,000 men. They posed a real threat in the flank and rear of the occupying army, so much the more as the Vienna government had several times warned St Petersburg not to cross the Danube and had even urged Russia to evacuate the Principalities.[6]

In order to be nearer the centre of events, Paskevich went to the Principalities in person and took command of the troops there. He arrived at Bucharest on 22 April. It was obviously due to his anxiety and vacillation that the siege of Silistria was undertaken without energy. One of his letters to the Tsar at this time is especially revealing of his despondency and pessimism, and of his desire to evacuate the Principalities. He said he could not pin his hopes on the Bulgarians; they had no desire for emancipation. As to the Serbs, nothing could be expected from them under their present Prince. At the most 2,000 or 3,000 volunteers could be recruited, but their use by Russia would only provoke Austria. He bluntly told the Tsar that Austria's wrath could only be placated by a voluntary evacuation of the Principalities. Russia would thus gain time, and by the autumn the Allied fleets would be paralysed by bad weather. Meanwhile the army in southern Russia could be brought up to 200,000 men and that of Poland to 250,000 men. 'In the course of the year we can expect: risings in Italy, risings in France or a downfall of the ministry in England.'[7] Paskevich's pleadings with the Tsar were to no avail. The siege of Silistria had to be continued and there was no question of the Russian troops quitting the Principalities.

Silistria, on the right bank of the Danube, was an important Turkish fortress. In the Russo-Turkish war of 1828–9 it had taken six months for the Russians to capture it. It had by now been fortified by a number of outer forts, ten altogether. The Russian siege works were begun on 5 April by General Karl A. Schilder, a talented engineer whose closest aide was Lieutenant-Colonel Eduard I. Totleben, who was to acquire fame during the siege of Sevastopol. After reinforcements had begun to arrive from the army of General Lüders from the Dobrudja, the bombardment was started on 10 May. The Turks had a force of 12,000 men in the fortress and were able to bring in supplies and reinforcements since Paskevich thought it impossible to encircle it completely. On 28 May the Russians launched an assault on the strategic outwork of Arab Tabia, but were repulsed, losing 317 men dead and 623 wounded. According to Russian sources, on average eight out of ten wounded later died.[8] On 9 June, Paskevich believed he had been injured after a projectile had exploded near him. He complained of pain in his shoulder and left the area of operations. There was much speculation at the time, and there still is in Russian historiography, as to whether he had actually suffered a contusion or not. In any event, it was typical of his wariness and anxiety that he left the field for good and returned to Warsaw. Gorchakov took command of the siege operations in his stead. On 13 June, General Schilder was severely wounded and died shortly afterwards. Seven days later, Arab Tabia was taken by the Russians, so that the storming of the main fortress was fixed for 4 am on 21 June. At 2 am, Gorchakov received an order from Paskevich to raise the siege and recross the Danube. The order was obeyed instantly and on 24 June the last Russian soldiers left the right bank and destroyed the bridge across the Danube. The fruitless siege of Silistria had cost the Russians 419 dead and 1,783 wounded.

What made Paskevich give this remarkable order? On 3 June, Austria had summoned Russia to evacuate the Principalities – a summons that had been announced weeks ahead and was now delivered. A few days later, the Austrian Emperor met the King of Prussia at Tetschen in Bohemia. In Russian eyes this must have seemed to be a strengthening of the ties which the two German powers had made in their treaty of 20 April. On 14 June, Austria and the Porte signed the convention of Boyadji-Köi in which the Sultan granted Austria the right to occupy the Principalities. All these political developments seemed highly dangerous to Paskevich in Warsaw, and also to Nicholas in St Petersburg. The military situation further to the south was equally menacing. On 19 May there was a war council between Omer Pasha and the Allied commanders at which the French and British agreed to rush troops as quickly as possible from the Straits to Varna. Saint-Arnaud promised to concentrate 55,000 Allied troops there to reinforce the Turkish troops south of the Danube. They numbered 104,000 men, of whom 45,000 were massed at Shumla and 20,000 at Vidin and Kalafat; 20,000 troops had been sent to Silistria and the Allies particularly wanted to relieve them.[9]

Confronted with so much threatening news, Paskevich was fully justified in countermanding the siege of Silistria. Continuing it would have meant sending the Russian troops into a trap set by the Austrians and the Allied armies. There is no foundation, therefore, for laying all of the responsibility for the Russians' retreat at Paskevich's door. The Tsar himself was highly alarmed at the sombre military prospects. On 13 June he wrote to the Field Marshal, 'The siege of Silistria must be raised if it [the fortress] is not yet taken at the receipt of this letter.'[10] Six days later he reiterated his opinion. The only difference between the two was that Paskevich was pessimistic about the siege from the outset, whereas the Tsar had always entertained false hopes and wavered for a long time; but by 13 June he was resigned to retreat. On 1 July he even praised his Field Marshal for having done what to both had seemed inevitable: 'I'm afraid I must agree with Paskevich if I take a look at the map in order to be convinced of the impending danger.'[11]

The lifting of the siege of Silistria was the signal for the general retreat of the Russians from the Principalities. This, too, was mainly due to the threatening military and political attitude of Austria. On 29 June, Nesselrode gave an affirmative, although conditional, reply to Austria's summons of 3 June. After leaving Silistria, the Russians began to evacuate the Dobrudja. At Giurgevo, between 5 and 7 July, there were major clashes between them and the Turks, with heavy losses on both sides. Apart from this the Russians retreated in orderly fashion without being molested by the Turks. On 24 July the Tsar's order for the total evacuation reached Gorchakov's headquarters. The retreat was called a strategic withdrawal in order that it would not appear a defeat in the eyes of the Russian soldier or be perceived as such in European public opinion. On 1 August the Russians evacuated Bucharest. Six weeks later, on 7 September, the whole Russian occupying army had retreated beyond the Pruth, that is, to the starting point of their invasion of 3 July 1853. Only a few regiments remained in the northernmost part of the Dobrudja on the right bank of the Danube, occupying the strategic fortresses of Tulchea, Isacchea and Matchin. They stayed there until the end of October 1854.

Russian military policy now took on a purely defensive attitude and Russia now regarded herself a vast beleaguered fortress.

The Austrian occupation of the Danubian Principalities

As we have seen, the Russian retreat from the Danubian Principalities was mainly due to the hostile attitude of Austria and to the massing of her troops in Galicia, the Bukovina and Transylvania in the Russian rear and right flank. It is thus appropriate at this point to look at Austria's military dispositions during the Crimean War.

At the beginning of the war, in 1854, Austria's military behaviour appeared to be offensive towards Russia, but was in reality defensive. The government in Vienna took great pains to leave the Russians in the dark in order to make them yield by a show of force. This was a tricky game, but it worked and served its purpose, especially in ousting the Russians from the Principalities.

As discussed in an earlier chapter, Buol's main concern was to keep Austria's border regions and the neighbouring countries quiet for fear of a new outbreak of the revolution. As soon as he learned of Nicholas's plans to revolutionize the Balkan peoples, he and his Emperor took precautionary measures. When the Russians occupied the Principalities in July 1853,

Francis Joseph ordered troop concentrations at Peterwardein in Slavonia, not in order to occupy Serbia as the Tsar had suggested to him in the Russian effort to involve Austria in the attempt to overthrow Turkey, but to keep Serbia quiet and prevent her from rising in favour of Russia.

The commander of the troops, Johann Count Coronini, was ordered to march into Belgrade as soon as the Turkish troops in the fortress there were threatened by a Serbian coup de main or if Prince Alexander Karageorgevich, who was leaning towards Austria, were overthrown. When in January 1854 pro-Russian riots broke out in Thessaly and Epirus, Coronini was ordered to move a brigade to Semlin just opposite Belgrade. In this way the Russians were persuaded not to change the status quo in Serbia and the latter was forced to remain neutral. It was due to this concentration of Austrian troops near Belgrade that the Russians delayed crossing the Danube until March 1854.[12]

The same reasons which caused the Austrians to be on tenterhooks on the Serbian frontier put them on the lookout on the border with Wallachia. When the Orlov mission to Vienna had finally opened the Emperor's eyes to Nicholas's real intentions, Francis Joseph also ordered troop concentrations in other parts of southern Hungary. On 31 January 1854, General Hess, the Commander-in-Chief, told a ministerial conference in Vienna that 15,000 troops would suffice for a local occupation of Serbia, but that a special army corps of 50,000 was necessary for other purposes; it would have to be brought up to a strength of 150,000 in case the Russians crossed the Danube. Accordingly, on 2 February the Emperor ordered the build-up of a mobile army corps in southern Hungary (this came to be called the Serbian-Banat corps) under Fieldmarshal-Lieutenant Coronini, the governor of the Banat.[13]

Orlov's mission was thus the turning point in Austrian military planning. On 28 March the Emperor put all troops in Hungary on a war footing. This applied to the 3rd Army. As the Russians reinforced their troops in Poland and Volhynia with their reserve divisions, Francis Joseph ordered, on 15 May, the full mobilization of the 4th Army in Galicia. Also in May, when unrest in Thessaly and Epirus reached its highest pitch, Austria made preparations to occupy the port of Scutari on the Montenegrin coast with a brigade of 4,000 men, in order to warn the Montenegrins and Albanians not to rise against the Sultan or join hands with the rebellious Greeks. On 29 May a ministerial conference in Vienna adopted the plan of summoning the Russians to evacuate the Principalities unconditionally. This summons went out to St Petersburg on 3 June. When the Russian government hesitated to reply, but raised the siege of Silistria, Buol advised the Western governments and Berlin of the Austrian intention to occupy the Principalities, if need be by force of arms.[14]

Hess, who had been nominated Commander-in-Chief of the 3rd and 4th armies on 21 June, drafted a plan of campaign which envisaged a greater concentration of troops in Galicia and the transfer of Coronini's army corps to the north to occupy the passes through the Carpathians. This is clearly the moment when Austria, for the first and only time during the war, was resolved to use force against Russia, and in the last resort also to invade the country. A plan of campaign drafted by Hess's deputy in the summer of 1854 testifies to the same spirit: a smaller army was to invade Podolia, but the main force was to be directed to Poland where it was to advance between the Vistula and the Bug with Bialystok as its first target.[15]

Such an offensive of course was not envisaged as an isolated move, but presupposed the cooperation of the Western Allies and the Turks moving northwards from the western Balkans, and of the Prussian army keeping itself ready on the eastern border of Poland. For both purposes liaison officers were sent to the relevant headquarters: Lieutenant-Colonel Anton Kalik to Varna and Major-General Ferdinand Mayerhofer to Berlin. Both missions proved, however, completely abortive. When Kalik met Marshal Saint-Arnaud and Lord Raglan, he found them actively preparing to transfer their troops to the Crimea. Mayerhofer, who was to remind the Prussians of their promise to mobilize 200,000 troops in the east (the promise, the Austrians thought, was to be derived from the treaty of 20 April 1854), was not only talking to the winds in Berlin, but also, to the utter dismay of Buol and the Emperor, developed strong pro-Prussian (which also meant pro-Russian) sentiments when in the Prussian capital. This led to his speedy recall in September 1854.[16]

In any event, Austria's military build-up on her borders with Russia in the summer of 1854 was formidable enough. On 22 August, Hess could write to his Emperor that the troops under his command in the east amounted to 205,000 men, to whom another 125,000 men were to be added as non-combatant troops. In February 1855 the corresponding figures were 327,000, plus 80,000 to 100,000 men.[17]

Despite this massive build-up of troops – or because of it – the Austrians never met their Russian counterparts in action. When the Russian troops left Bucharest, it was the Turks who, because of the location of their troops, moved in first, not the Austrians. On 8 August a Turkish detachment of 2,000 men under Halim Pasha arrived at Bucharest, and on 22 August Omer Pasha himself celebrated the arrival of a whole division.

Francis Joseph's order to occupy Wallachia had already been issued on 5 July, but was cancelled on 8 July because of the slow retrograde movement of the Russians. The definitive order was given on 17 August, and five days later the first column of Austrian troops crossed the frontier into Wallachia. The Austrians were careful not to meet the retreating Russians, as they now knew that the Western Allies were leaving the Balkans for good. On 6 September they entered Bucharest, its population watching for the second time within a few days the entry of a foreign army.[18]

Considerable friction developed during the following weeks between the two occupying forces for both political and military reasons. Coronini, the

Commander-in-Chief of the Austrian forces, issued a proclamation calling on the inhabitants to obey the orders of the Austrian military administration. A corresponding order was promulgated by the Turkish authorities. On the military level each army tried to occupy as much of Wallachia as possible in order to get ahead of its rival. At Ibraila and Galatz on the left bank of the Danube a veritable scramble developed. The Turks were the first to occupy Ibraila (on 17 September). On 22 and 23 September, small Austrian cavalry detachments arrived at Ibraila and Galatz. This unworthy competition was ended by a fiat from Vienna. Buol pressed his Emperor on 3 October to issue an order to Hess that the military movements of the Allies (including the Turks) must not be impeded as this would be contrary to the pro-Western policy of Austria and also to the Austro-Turkish convention of 14 June.[19]

The occupation of Moldavia was mainly effected by Austrian troops moving in, in the wake of the retreating Russians, from Transylvania and Bukovina. On 2 October, Iași, the capital, was occupied, but at the beginning of November Omer Pasha took measures to assemble two armies, one at Fokşani and the other at Ibraila, each 18,000 men strong, in order to cross the Pruth and invade Bessarabia. The object of this move was to prevent Russian reinforcements from this area marching to the Crimea. These Turkish preparations jeopardized Austria's position, given her determination not to become involved in military clashes with Russia now that the Allies had left the Balkans and the Prussians were showing themselves intractable. But they proved harmless. On 7 December, Omer Pasha received an order from Constantinople to move 35,000 of his best troops to the Crimea in order to reinforce the Allied troops there, who were by now in dire straits.[20]

The peaceful occupation of the Danubian Principalities and the transfer of the Anglo-French troops to the Crimea removed the danger of war in south-eastern Europe and between Austria and Russia. Thus Francis Joseph's order for total mobilization, issued on 22 October, was retracted on 21 November. Besides the clarification of the military situation in the Principalities, this was mainly due to the mounting cost of military preparations. In fact, Austria's financial situation was becoming more and more desperate. The Minister of Finance, Baron Andreas Baumgartner, resigned in January 1855 because his warnings about the hopeless state of Austria's indebtedness were not heeded. On 11 June 1855, after the failure of the Vienna peace conference, which also led to a cooling off of Austria's relations with the Western powers, a ministerial conference in Vienna decided to reduce the standing army by 62,500 troops.[21]

The sanitary state of the Austrian army in the east also made a reduction imperative. The army in Galicia had spent most of its time strengthening the fortresses there and building railways between Cracow and Lemberg and other places. As was usual in the armies of the time, epidemics played havoc, especially with the troops in Galicia. Between August 1854 and the end of May 1855 over 7,200 men died in the 4th Army.

The occupation troops in the Principalities amounted to almost 57,000 men, half of whom were billeted in Wallachia and half in Moldavia. In Moldavia, all Turkish troops had left by December 1854, and in Wallachia only a symbolic force remained quartered in Bucharest. To the south, however, in Bulgaria, the strength of the Turkish troops in April still amounted to 40,000 men, of whom about half were concentrated in the fortress of Shumla.[22]

The Austrian occupation forces managed to make themselves singularly unpopular in the Principalities. In May 1855, Coronini introduced martial law, mainly to check refugees from Poland and Hungary in their attempts to persuade Austrian soldiers to desert. This produced friction, as has already been noted, with the Turkish authorities, the Western consuls in Bucharest and Iaşi and with the British government. A case in point is the arrest in Bucharest of the deserter Stephan Türr on 1 November 1855.

On the political level the Austrian generals, Coronini in the forefront, behaved as if the Principalities belonged to Austria for good. This was diametrically opposed to Buol's policy in Vienna. When peace was concluded in Paris on 30 March 1856, Buol complained bitterly to his Emperor about the constant meddling of the generals in political matters in the Principalities. He therefore pleaded with Francis Joseph to evacuate the Principalities as quickly as possible. The belief, which is expressed in many older books on Austria's role in the Principalities, that Buol worked with the military for a future satellite status for the Principalities is utterly wrong. When the last Austrian troops evacuated the Principalities in March 1857, the army left behind 1,780 men who had died during the occupation.[23]

It may safely be said from an overall point of view that Austria's pressure on Russia to evacuate the Principalities and their subsequent occupation by Austrian troops not only removed the danger of war in south-eastern Europe, but also of an Austro-Russian war, which would almost automatically have entailed the entry of Prussia and the rest of Germany into the conflict, and probably that of other countries in Europe like Sweden. Thus Austria's stand prevented the Crimean War from developing into a European and even a world war.

The Allied military build-up at Constantinople and Varna

Also present on the Danube front in the summer of 1854, but at some distance from the Russian lines, were the first Allied armies to arrive in the East. They first assembled at Gallipoli and Scutari on the Turkish Straits, then Varna on the western coast of the Black Sea.

After Sinope (30 November 1853) and the entry of the first Allied ships into the Black Sea in the early days of January of 1854, war between

Russia and the Western powers was almost certain, although still undeclared. The official object of the war being to protect the integrity of Turkey, the military plans of France and Britain were obvious: besides mastery of the Black Sea, the Turkish capital had to be protected from a Russian coup de main launched simultaneously from the stronghold of Sevastopol and from the Danubian Principalities occupied by Russian troops.

Thus, in the beginning, Allied military planning was by necessity defensive on this front. On the second front in the north, in the Baltic, it assumed an offensive character, the aim being in the last resort a descent on Russia's fortified places like Helsingfors, Reval, Kronstadt and Bomarsund. The naval expedition to the Baltic which set out on 11 March was also aimed at blockading the Russian coasts and preventing the Baltic fleet from entering the open seas and threatening the British coast. Whereas in 1853 it was Napoleon III who was practising a forward policy by sending his fleet to Salamis and urging, after Sinope, entry to the Black Sea, now, in the first months of the new year, it was the British who urged quick military action in order to satisfy public opinion at home, which was enraged by the 'massacre of Sinope'.

As Andrew Lambert has shown, it was the First Lord of the Admiralty, Sir James Graham, who had the most coherent ideas in London for dealing with the military threat posed by Russia. He urged the defence of Constantinople by fortifying Adrianople in order to cover the Turkish capital, or landing a force at Varna to be ready to attack the flank of the Russians if they crossed the Danube. Conjointly he was in favour of attacking and destroying Sevastopol to prevent a Russian amphibious assault on Constantinople.[24]

On 29 January 1854, the English Inspector-General of Fortifications, Sir John Burgoyne, arrived in Paris, en route for an inspection of the Turkish Straits, and had several discussions with the Emperor about Graham's plans which had by then been adopted by his Cabinet colleagues and also by Napoleon himself. Initially, it had been suggested in Paris that 6,000 French and 3,000 British troops be sent to help the Turks in covering Constantinople. After the fact-finding mission of Burgoyne and two French colonels, Charles-Prosper Dieu and Paul-Joseph Ardant, had yielded its first results, the Anglo-French expeditionary force was gradually increased to 30,000 French and 18,000 British troops in early March, and to 60,000 and 30,000 respectively a month later.

At the beginning of April the first French troops arrived at Gallipoli. The British followed suit from Malta and established their main rallying point at Scutari. By 20 May more than 30,000 French and 20,000 British soldiers had arrived on both shores of the Straits. On 9 May, Napoleon briefly outlined his plan to his Commander-in-Chief of the *Armée d'Orient*, Marshal Saint-Arnaud: '1. If the Russians advance, let them do so until an advantageous point is found and chosen to give battle. 2. If they don't advance, take the Crimea.'[25] These ideas dovetailed well with those of Graham in London.

The first military engagement with Russia, after the official declarations of war on 27 and 28 March by Britain and France, did not take place on land but at sea, off Odessa.

The details about the encounter are conflicting, as the accounts of the two sides differ widely.[26] But certain facts are clear. On 9 April the British frigate *Furious* arrived at Odessa with the instruction to take the British consul there on board. A sloop was dispatched from the *Furious* with a white flag to contact the port authorities. The officer of the sloop was told – according to Russian sources – that the consul had already left, whereupon the sloop returned to the frigate. On its way back the Russian port battery fired some rounds of shot – it was not clear whether they were aimed at the sloop or at the frigate, which was in any case out of reach of the batteries. No damage was done, but Admirals Dundas and Hamelin decided that the attack on the sloop, flying a flag of truce, was a breach of international law.

The Admirals sent a division of war steamers back to Odessa to demand the extradition of all British, French and Russian ships at anchor in the port as an act of reparation. The governor, of course, refused the demand. On the following morning, 22 April, the Allied ships opened fire on the harbour and its facilities trying, according to Allied sources, to avoid damage to civilian buildings. The bombardment lasted all day long and did considerable damage to the harbour, the storehouses and the batteries. On both sides there were a few dead and wounded, and some of the Allied ships were also hit.

Apart from the occasion that gave rise to the bombardment, the Allied ships made an impression on the Russians who now feared a repetition of such cannonades on other points of their coast. The Allied navies made their presence felt on the eastern shores of the Black Sea immediately afterwards, thus forcing the Russians to be on their guard against a probable Allied descent there, or even to abandon one or the other stronghold.

When the first French and British troops arrived at Gallipoli, it was already known that the Russians were crossing the Danube and that their first target was Silistria, where the siege works had begun on 5 April. When the two Allied Commanders-in-Chief arrived on the scene, at Gallipoli and Constantinople, they had to react to the Russian danger brewing north of the Balkans. On 19 May, Saint-Arnaud, Lord Raglan and the Turkish Minister of War, Riza Pasha, held a conference at Varna with Omer Pasha, who had come over from his nearby headquarters at Shumla. Omer painted a grim picture of the situation along the Danube. Silistria, he said, might hold six weeks or it might be taken within a fortnight. The Russians would then advance to Shumla, where he had concentrated 45,000 of his Turkish troops.

Saint-Arnaud and Raglan at once decided to send one division each of the troops which had just disembarked at Gallipoli. When two days later the two commanders went in person to Shumla, they heard the latest news from Silistria – that 70,000 Russians were pressing the attack on the fortress and that the bombardment continued without interruption. They decided on the spot to send all available forces from Gallipoli and Scutari to Shumla. The plan was to be ready in force at Varna on the left flank of the Russians should they advance south after the fall of Silistria.[27]

By the beginning of June the first Allied troops were arriving at Varna. Most were transported by sea, and two incomplete French divisions marched overland via Adrianople because of lack of sea transport. On 11 June, Saint-Arnaud officially transferred his headquarters from Gallipoli to Varna. Gallipoli, Scutari and later on Constantinople itself remained transit depots for incoming reinforcements and for all kinds of matériel and supplies. At the beginning of July the operation had practically ended. On the 10th the Allies could muster 50,000 French, 20,000 British and 60,000 Turks in or around Varna. On the coast, the Allied fleets were concentrated at Baltchik, north of Varna, unless some of the ships were on duty in other parts of the Black Sea. It was a formidable force which the Russians would have to meet if they decided to sweep down south. There was no plan among the Allies to march into the interior, to come to the relief of Silistria, to meet the Russians at other points along the Danube or to march into the Principalities and thence into Bessarabia. It was expected that the Austrians would do their part of the common job by ousting the Russians from the Principalities.

Great was the astonishment when news reached the Allies at Varna that the Russians had unexpectedly lifted their siege of Silistria during the night of 22 to 23 June. The Allied troops were now condemned to utter inaction. On the surface, the war with Russia could have ended at that moment. The main object of the Western Allies and of Austria was on the point of being fulfilled: the evacuation of the Danubian Principalities. The three powers were now brooding over the broader war aims which they had solemnly sanctioned on 8 August 1854 in the Four Points: replacement of the Russian protectorate over the Principalities by a European one; free navigation on the Danube; revision of the Straits Treaty of 1841 in the interest of the European balance of power; and renunciation by Russia of her protectorate over the Christians in Turkey. Russia was not yet ready to subscribe to such demands. The war therefore had to continue.

The French expedition to the Dobrudja, August 1854

On 23 June, Napoleon ordered Saint-Arnaud 'to do something' and vaguely hinted at two objectives: Anapa on the eastern shores of the Black Sea, and the Crimea. In London, Graham had persuaded his colleagues that the destruction of Sevastopol was a British as well as a European necessity. On 28 June the Cabinet met and decided to press upon Lord

Raglan 'the necessity of a prompt attack upon Sebastopol and the Russian Fleet'.[28]

Raglan received these orders from London on 17 July at Varna. On the following day the Allies convened a council of war. The two Commanders-in-Chief took part as well as the admirals of the fleets and their deputies, Ferdinand A. Hamelin, Armand J. Bruat, Dundas and Sir Edmund Lyons. Saint-Arnaud was optimistic, and relieved to have a definite aim before him. Raglan, too, was in favour of an expedition to the Crimea as were Bruat and Lyons. Hamelin and Dundas, who had seen the formidable fortifications of Sevastopol at close quarters during an earlier inspection tour, were against an attack, fearing the loss of their ships. The majority being in favour, the decision was taken to send the armies to the Crimea, but before embarking, a reconnaissance was to be undertaken for the most suitable landing place. This mission, which was headed by General Canrobert, Brigadier-General Louis-Jules Trochu, General Sir George Brown and Lyons, weighed anchor early on 20 July for the Crimean coast.[29]

One of the reasons why Saint-Arnaud was pressing for action in July 1854 was that his army was hit by an enemy almost beyond human control – cholera. The disease was fairly new in Europe at the time. It had its origin in the Ganges region in India, and was brought to Europe during the 1820s via Central Asia and Russia. The first wave of cholera swept across Europe between 1830 and 1837; a second wave started in 1847 and only died down ten years later. Its causes were unknown at the time, thus the measures taken against it proved useless. But it was striking that it infested densely populated port and city areas, whereas the thinly populated rural regions remained almost unscathed. There was an outbreak of cholera in London during the summer months of 1854 with a loss of 11,777 lives. It was also in 1854 that the English doctor, John Snow, detected a connection between the outbreak of cholera of that year and the use of the water pump in London's Soho – the drinking water had been contaminated by sewage water. As is usual in such cases, his discovery was not yet accepted and effective countermeasures were not taken.[30]

In the French Army of the Orient at Varna the first cases of cholera were reported at the beginning of July 1854. A short time later, the British camp was affected as well. The disease spread quickly in highly favourable conditions – an overcrowded place with bad hygiene and sanitation. By the end of July, 100 cases per day were being reported in the French army. Gallipoli was affected too, 234 fatal cases being counted in seventeen days. At Piraeus the French brigade of occupation suffered 105 dead in ten days. On 20 August the French army lost 5,000 victims. The British fared better, and lost only 350 men. The origin of the epidemic could be traced to southern France at Avignon, Arles and Marseilles, places where the troops were assembled for embarkation to the east.

In order to rid himself of the scourge, Saint-Arnaud hit upon the not unreasonable idea of dispersing his troops. Even military reasons could be adduced for this measure. Why not chase the rearguard of the retreating Russians north of Varna in the Dobrudja? Why not let the Russians surmise that this was a prelude to a massive military action and to a more substantive cooperation with the Austrian army? His army, having been shuffled across half of Europe, never having seen the enemy and now being plagued by a worse than human enemy, was certainly thirsting for action.

On 20 July, Saint-Arnaud decided to launch an expedition to the Dobrudja. Most of his troops were to take part in it. The spearhead was to be formed by a new special cavalry unit, the *spahis d'Orient*, under the legendary General Yussuf. The *spahis* consisted of Bashi-Bazouks – bands of irregular Ottoman soldiers – 2,500 of whom had by now been taken into the corps. Yussuf was given a fortnight to stage his raid into the Dobrudja and then to return in order to be embarked to the Crimea; 700 regular Ottoman cavalry were to accompany him. He was to be followed by the 1st Division under Canrobert (temporarily replaced by General Esprit C. M. Espinasse), ready to help him in case of need. The 2nd (General Pierre F. J. Bosquet) and the 3rd Division (Prince Napoleon) were to march in echelons behind them. The British took no part in the expedition.[31]

The troops had hardly left Varna on 21, 22 and 23 July when cholera made its first appearance among the *Bashis*. The unhealthy climate of the Dobrudja in summertime favoured an explosion of the disease which played havoc first among the *spahis* and then among the 1st Division. During the night of 30 July, 150 men died. The rate of deaths increased until only 300 of the 2,500 *spahis* returned to Varna; the unit was practically annihilated. The 2nd and 3rd Divisions returned on 4 and 9 August respectively, with 389 cholera victims. The 1st Division, which returned on 18 August, lost 1,886 men. The expedition thus ended in complete failure.

Saint-Arnaud had sent his troops on a death march. The question is, had not worse been avoided by sending 30,000 men away from the overcrowded camps at Varna? True, French and British troops who remained were not spared. The crews on board suffered too. It was after the first troops had moved away from Varna that the cholera in the camp began to die down. So, from a military point of view the Dobrudja expedition was a disaster, but in the fight against cholera it was not an unreasonable undertaking.

To make matters worse a fire broke out in the evening of 10 August in the bazaars of Varna, threatening the powder magazines, ammunition stocks and supply depots of the Allied camps. Luckily, the wind changed during the night and did not come near the powder kegs, but the supply stocks were completely lost. After all these disasters, the armies, from the commanders down to the privates, were eager to leave such a pestilential and overcrowded place. Luckily, the reconnaissance mission had already returned on 28 July with the news that a suitable landing place on the western coast of the Crimea had been found, at the mouth of the River Katcha, some five to six kilometres north of Sevastopol. Feverish preparations for departure were now in hand.

On 22 and 26 August the military and naval commanders met for two final councils. Admirals Dundas and Hamelin were still sceptical about the expedition. They were all for meeting the Russian fleet in open battle, but not for cruising along the coast, let alone appearing in front of the strongly fortified coast off Sevastopol, for fear of being routed by the impregnable land forts. Among divisional commanders there were warnings about the lateness of the season, the lack of information about the Russian forces, about the terrain, the lack of suitable ports for the Allies, and so on.[32] The Commanders-in-Chief prevailed. They had precise orders from their governments: there was nothing more to be done in the Balkans, and other landing places, such as Anapa on the Circassian coast, did not promise the same success as the Crimea with Sevastopol.

It must be stressed here that the invasion of the Crimea was, in the last resort, a political and not a military decision. The Cabinet in London was resolved to seize the opportunity of reducing the naval threat posed by Russia in the Near East, with the Crimea and Sevastopol being its symbol. This was the real meaning behind the third of the Four Points agreed upon with France and Austria on 8 August ('revision of the Straits convention of 1841'). For Napoleon the Crimea in itself mattered little, although he was all in favour of the expedition. What counted, especially after the fruitless sojourn in European Turkey and the dreadful experience in the Dobrudja, was some telling success over Russia, and the Crimea happened to be the best means of achieving this.

Thus Napoleon wrote to Saint-Arnaud on 23 June 1854, 'I don't see anything else to be done than taking the Crimea ... To all intents and purposes, means must be found to land a great stroke [*frapper un grand coup*] before the bad season begins.'[33] It is interesting to note that Napoleon at this time was also in favour of carrying the war into Asia if the expedition to the Crimea should prove impossible from a military point of view. His Minister of War, Marshal Jean-Baptiste Vaillant, favoured a diversionary movement to the Circassian coast in order to underpin the resistance of Shamil's mountain warriors against the Russians and thus to divide the Russian forces.

At the last meeting of the Allied commanders at Varna on 26 August, the departure for the Crimea was finally fixed for 2 September. It was delayed by the slow preparation of the British fleet and army. The armada, consisting of some 350 ships carrying 30,000 French, 25,000 British and 6,000 Turks, set out on 7 September. Another 11,000 French troops were to follow later, depending on the transport facilities available. Of the French army, over 58,000 had by now been transported to the East, some 5,000 had died in the Balkans, and others were hospitalized at Gallipoli, Constantinople or Varna.

Annotated bibliography

Before dealing with the war on the Danube, general studies of the whole war must be considered. The most detailed and authoritative accounts by contemporaries are César L. de Bazancourt, *L'expédition de Crimée jusqu' à la prise de Sébastopol. Chroniques de la guerre d'Orient*, 2 vols (Paris 1856, 5th edn 1857; German trans., 2 vols, Pest, 1856; English trans., 2 vols, London 1856; editions after the 5th have the title *L'expédition de Crimée. L'armée française à Gallipoli, Varna et Sébastopol. Chroniques militaires*, 2 vols, Paris, 1858; last edn 1863–4); César L. de Bazancourt, *L'expédition de Crimée. La marine française dans la Mer Noire et la Baltique. Chroniques de la guerre d'Orient*, 2 vols (Paris, 1858); Modest I. Bogdanovič, *Vostočnaja vojna 1853–1856 gg.*, 4 vols (St. Petersburg, 1876); Arthur William Kinglake, *The Invasion of the Crimea: Its Origin, and an Account of its Progress down to the Death of Lord Raglan*, 8 vols (Edinburgh and London, 1863–87; 6th edn in 9 vols, Edinburgh, 1877–8; a French translation, incomplete, in 6 vols, Brussels, 1864–70). A later account, from a French point of view, is Camille Rousset, *Histoire de la guerre de Crimée*, 2 vols (Paris 1877, 2nd edn 1878). The more important accounts of the twentieth century are Tarle, *Krymskaja vojna* I–II (cf. above, Chapter 3). René Guillemin, *La guerre de Crimée. Le Tsar de toutes les Russies face à l'Europe* (Paris, 1981), is a very good account on the military and especially the naval side; the passages on diplomacy are faulty. The viewpoint is French, but it takes into account the British and Russian side as well. It covers most theatres of war; the chapters on the White Sea and the Pacific are somewhat out of proportion compared with those on the Crimea and the Baltic; and there is no chapter on the Caucasus. Alain Gouttman, *La guerre de Crimée 1853–1856* (Paris, 1995), is the newest account by a French historian, based almost exclusively on French published sources and concentrating on the Crimean theatre of war. A. J. Barker, *The Vainglorious War, 1854–56* (London, 1970), is the British equivalent of Gouttman; it is sound but does not go beyond the Crimea. Another solid account, based on archival research but again restricted to the Crimean theatre of war, is W. Baring Pemberton, *Battles of the Crimean War* (London, 1962). R. L. V. ffrench Blake, *The Crimean War* (London, 1971, repr. 1993), has some short chapters on the theatres of war besides the Crimea. See also German Werth, *Der Krimkrieg. Geburtsstunde der Weltmacht Rußland* (Erlangen, 1989; paperback edn Frankfurt and Berlin, 1992). As to the newest Russian studies, cf. the voluminous book by Čennyk, *Krymskaja kampanija*, and the shorter one by Skrickij, *Krymskaja kampanija*, listed above in Chapter 6.

For the war on the Danube in 1853 and 1854, the most detailed account is A. N. Petrow, *Der Russische Donaufeldzug im Jahre 1853/54*, ed. A. Regenauer (Berlin, 1891). This is a slightly shortened version of the Russian original, published in 1890 and based on Russian archival material. There is no equivalent for the Turkish side, but cf. now the short chapters in Badem,

The Ottoman Crimean War, pp. 101–9 (for 1853), pp. 177–90 (for 1854), and also in Reid, *Crisis of the Ottoman Empire*, pp. 242–7 (1853), pp. 254–68 (1854). On the naval engagement at Sinope there is a long chapter in Tarle, *Krymskaja vojna*, I, pp. 346–83. Cf. also Boris I. Zverev, *Sinopskoe sraženie* (Moscow, 1953). The significance of Sinope for Britain's entry into the war is stressed by Martin, *Triumph*, pp. 148–53, 170–8. On the siege of Silistria there are detailed accounts in Petrow, *Donaufeldzug*, and in Tarle, *Krymskaja vojna*, I, pp. 452–500.

12

The Black Sea theatre

The invasion of the Crimea and the Battle of the Alma, 20 September 1854

Sevastopol, the target of the Allied invasion, was a formidable fortress, impregnable from the sea. It was founded after the annexation of the Crimea from Turkey in 1783, as a military port and fortress to be used as a stepping stone for a future Russian naval descent on Constantinople. The name given to the place was derived from the Greek and means 'exalted city' or 'city of fame'. In 1804 it was designated the main naval port of Russia's Black Sea fleet. Admiral Michail Petrovich Lazarev, who was Commander-in-Chief of the fleet from 1833 to 1851, played the major role in its construction and development. His construction plan of 1834, imposing in its dimensions, provided for the building of eight forts or batteries, three on the north side of the main bay and five on its southern side – three more were added at the beginning of 1854. Altogether they contained 571 guns.

The fortress of Sevastopol had, however, an Achilles' heel: this was its almost open side towards the land. In the 1830s eight bastions were projected that were to protect the city along an arc of 7.5 kilometres. At the opening of hostilities in October 1853, only bastion eight was near completion. In the spring of 1854 the construction of the other bastions was hastened, but in September three-quarters of the defence line was still open. The main northern fort, which was to protect the city from the Allied army marching down from Eupatoria, was, according to Totleben, in a pitiful state.

Prince Menshikov, the Russian Commander-in-Chief and commander of the Black Sea fleet, exhibited an optimistic air throughout the summer of 1854. According to Totleben's testimony – the famous engineer had been sent by Prince Gorchakov from the Principalities to assist in the construction work at Sevastopol – Menshikov did not expect an Allied invasion of the Crimea in 1854 because he thought the season was too late, and did not deem it possible for the enemy to land a sufficient number of troops anywhere on the coast. The Tsar in St Petersburg was in the same haughty mood, and gleefully received the news about the poor state of the Allied armies at Varna. Menshikov had, however, requested and been granted

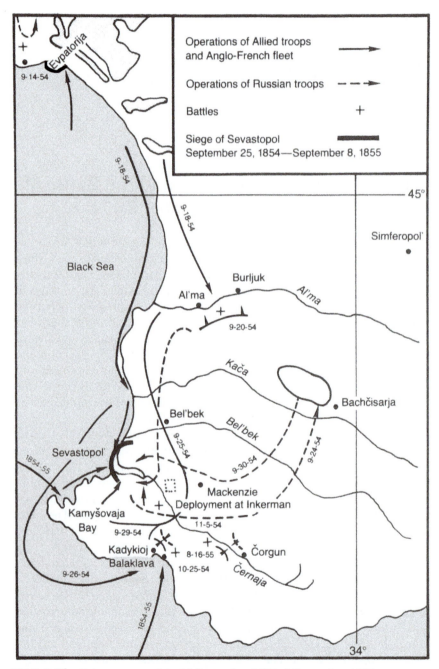

MAP 3 *The Crimean campaign, 14 September 1854–8 September 1855.*

reinforcements. The 16th and 17th Infantry Divisions based in Yaroslavl and Moscow were ordered south. It took them several months to reach the Crimea. They arrived in time, however, in September 1854. The forces at Menshikov's disposal in those fateful days were 38,000 troops and 18,000 seamen, who had already partly left their ships, lying idly at anchor in the bay, in order to help in the defence works. There were another 12,000 troops in the eastern part of the Crimea who guarded the areas of Feodosia and Kertch.[1]

Menshikov made no attempt to oppose the enemy when the latter finally landed on 14 September at Eupatoria and he has been much criticized for his failure to do so. It must be remembered that his reconnaissance facilities were very poor; he could not know that the Allies would land in force at that point. The enemy might use the landing there as a feint and then rush the bulk of his troops on board the ships to Sevastopol, or another point near to it, and land them there. At Eupatoria, furthermore, any Russian defenders rushed to the scene were the target of the powerful guns of the enemy ships. So his decision to wait for the enemy to assemble and then meet him in open battle on the banks of the River Alma was not an unreasonable one. What turned out to be at fault was his decision to meet the invading army frontally on high ground at the mouth of the river, instead of waiting further inland, so threatening the enemy's flanks and trying to throw him back into the sea.

While the Allied armada was en route from the Bulgarian coast to the Crimea, it was decided to send out another reconnaissance party to search for a new landing place – it had by now been established that the mouths of the Katcha and Alma rivers were occupied by an estimated 30,000 Russian troops. This mission, in which Lord Raglan took part in person, singled out the large and long beach of Eupatoria further to the north, where no Russian troops could be spotted and where the countryside was less rugged than further to the south, thus granting good observation for the ships' guns.[2]

After a leisurely seven days' cruise the armada finally arrived at Eupatoria on 14 September. The troops disembarked in fine weather, without being molested in any way from the coast. The disembarkation of the French troops took only two days; that of the British took double that time. Saint-Arnaud was dismayed: he wanted to give battle to the Russians as soon as possible and not grant them time to bring fresh forces into play. Menshikov, still full of optimism about the chances of an encounter, did not budge. On 19 September the Allied armies were at last ready to move south. The north side of Sevastopol was 46 kilometres away, and on the Alma Menshikov's army was waiting for them.

Saint-Arnaud's plan seems to have been this: to beat the Russian army and thus open the way to the north side of Sevastopol; occupy the north fort there overlooking the bay, overrun the rest of the northern batteries from behind, and then bombard, in concert with the fleet, the Russian fleet and the southern defences of the city.

The Allied armies marched south, their right wing formed by the four French divisions and the Turkish contingent, their left by the British army. On the coastline they were covered by the Allied fleet which was progressing south at the same speed. At noon the Bulganak river was crossed, the first of the four small rivers on the way to Sevastopol. Five kilometres to the south the Allied armies could clearly make out the heights beyond the Alma river where the enemy was waiting for them. As the British divisions were still incomplete, some of their troops not yet having left Eupatoria, it was decided to stop and wait until the next day to give battle to the Russians. Thus, on the evening of 19 September, the two armies camped within sight of each other.

Menshikov had local geography on his side. His troops were posted on the heights beyond the south bank of the Alma, overlooking the undulating plain to the north. He allowed his left wing, on the seaward side, to remain very weak with only one battalion being posted there. This proved to be the decisive mistake in his deployment. There are two possible reasons for the weakness of his left wing: first, massing troops within the range of the ships' guns would be suicidal; secondly, the coast on his side of the Alma was so steep and rugged that it seemed impossible for the enemy to climb up the escarpments.

Saint-Arnaud's plan of action did not neglect these steep coastal hills, because the ships had observed at least one narrow footpath leading uphill. Saint-Arnaud hoped to outflank the Russians on both wings. Bosquet's division with the Turks was posted on his right. The other French divisions formed the centre, two in front and one in reserve; the British army stayed on the left as they had brought part of their cavalry with them from Bulgaria (whereas the French cavalry had been left behind to hasten the embarkation and disembarkation). Raglan seems to have taken note of the plan of his colleague, but did not act accordingly on the following day; his men never tried to outflank the Russians as they were supposed to do. It was agreed that the troops should line up on the following morning between 6 and 7 o'clock.

The figures given in the sources for the strength of the two enemy armies vary. What is clear, however, is that the Allies had a substantial numerical advantage. Figures for the Russian army are given as between 33,600 and 40,000, those for the Allied armies vary as much; but 61,000 had landed at Eupatoria, so this must have been the total that opposed the Russians on 20 September.[3]

Early in the morning of that day, Bosquet's division was the first to move into position at the appointed time. The signal for the opening of the battle could not be given because the British were not ready, the formation of their thin long lines took hours, the officers insisting on a meticulous execution of what their men had learned on the parade ground. (Later on during the battle the British marched through the Alma river still trying to keep their formations. If someone drowned, the line closed up or the gap was filled by the man in the second rank.)

At last, after hours had passed, the signal for beginning the battle could be given. Bosquet had by then discovered that the ground uphill across the river was weakly manned. So he hastened his men, the famous Zouaves of Africa, to climb up the ravines – a considerable risk. If the Russians had discovered the danger on their left flank, they could easily have rushed reinforcements thither from the plateau. However, Menshikov did not allow his subordinate commanders to act on their own initiative and did not take seriously the news that the first French had appeared on the heights. Only later were five battalions sent as a relief, but by then Bosquet's men, to the amazement of the Russians, had even managed to find a path along which to drag their guns and bring them into position.

The success of Bosquet's audacity was greater than even Saint-Arnaud had expected. Without waiting for the British to do their outflanking manoeuvre on the opposite wing – which, in fact, they never intended to perform – Saint-Arnaud made his two divisions in the centre cross the river and climb up the heights and even brought up his reserve division from the rear. Although the French were received with cannonballs and shrapnel from the Russian guns, and although hand-to-hand fighting developed, the French had the advantage of the precision and long range of their Minié rifles. The crews of the Russian guns had not protected themselves by earthworks or other means and were therefore an easy target for French sharpshooters. Many Russian gunners, unless they were hit, simply deserted their guns.

On the left wing, which at its far end was 8 kilometres away from the coast, things did not go so well as on the right and in the centre. The British lines, many of them still in meticulous order, advanced and retreated several times. They, too, had the advantage of the Minié rifle, whose bullets, to the amazement of the Russians, penetrated several ranks of the enemy at close range. When French troops finally came to the relief of the British, the Russians on that wing had to fall back as well. Late in the afternoon the Russians were in full, but orderly retreat.

The Allies have often been criticized for not pursuing the shattered Russian army, and rightly so. There were of course enough reasons to halt and lick the wounds which the Allies had themselves received. The ground was covered with hundreds of their dead and of wounded who had to be looked after. The French, as was their custom in battle, had left their knapsacks behind and of course wanted to retrieve them. The commanders did not possess any information about possible Russian reserve forces further south or in the interior, and had no knowledge of the topography of the country on the way to Sevastopol. Therefore they never thought of pursuing the enemy. But did not Saint-Arnaud himself plan to march south after the battle and occupy the northern forts of the city? Already a dying man, the Marshal could not stand the physical strain of staying in the saddle and of crossing two more rivers and a terrain that became more rugged as one approached Sevastopol. Raglan, the one-armed office-general,

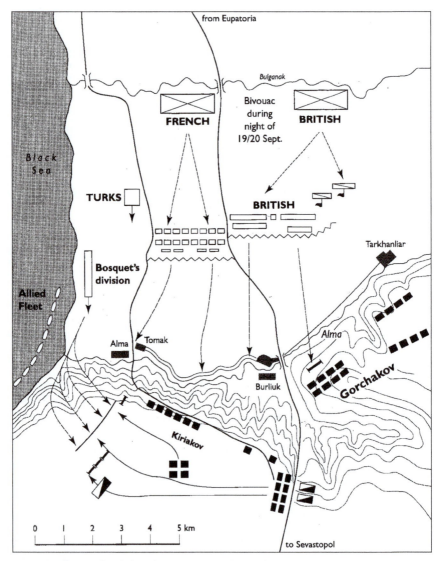

MAP 4 *The Battle of the Alma, 20 September 1854.*

was too old and feeble himself, and too gentle, to overtax the morale of his tired army.

However, the Russians feared that the Allies would pursue and enter Sevastopol from the north. A Russian eyewitness later wrote that the Russians wondered at the time why they were not being followed: 'This mistake saved our army from the final knock-out and it saved Sevastopol from being taken by the enemy.'[4]

For losses in dead and wounded at the Battle of the Alma, the statistics given later on by Totleben for the Russian side look fairly reliable: about 1,800 men and officers killed and 3,900 wounded, including 728 men missing. The British casualties are given as 2,000, of whom 362 were killed. Later figures published by the French *Moniteur* say that there were 2,060 wounded British soldiers in the French hospitals on the Bosphorus. The French losses are put at 1,200 to 1,400 wounded and 140 to 250 killed.

VICTORY OF THE ALMA.

FIGURE 10 *Victory of the Alma.* Punch *27 (1854), p. 148. University Library of Heidelberg, CC-BY-SA 3.0.*

The Alma produced a profound impression everywhere in Europe. A year and a half had passed since the Eastern crisis had begun and now the armies of three great powers had clashed for the first time. Menshikov reaped what he had sown in Constantinople. Tsar Nicholas and high society in St Petersburg and Moscow were dumbfounded, but continued to invoke the spirit of 1812. From a military point of view, the importance of the Alma must not be overrated. True, if the Russians had won the battle, this might well have been the turning-point of the war, for the Allies could hardly have stayed on in the Crimea. On the other hand, the Allies did not follow up their success; had they done so, this might have been the end of the war. When they had recovered and marched down to Sevastopol, they did not knock at its gates, which were defended by a mere handful of naval infantry from the ships (4,000 to 5,000 men). Menshikov with his defeated army had not dared go inside the fortress for fear of receiving the final blow, but made his way into the interior of the Crimea.

The siege of Sevastopol: the beginning

The behaviour of the Allied armies in the days immediately after the Battle of the Alma was of the utmost importance for the further conduct of the war. They spent fully two days on the battlefield resting, replenishing their supplies, burying the dead, collecting the wounded and bringing them on board the ships which in turn ferried them to the hospitals in and around Constantinople. At last, on 23 September, they began their march south across the Katcha and Belbek rivers to the north side of Sevastopol.

At the bivouac on the Belbek, on the evening of 24 September, the commanders took the fateful decision not to attack Sevastopol from the north. This was exactly contrary to Saint-Arnaud's original intention, but the Marshal had by now lost his power of decision: he was a dying man, cholera having attacked his body, which had long been in the grip of intestinal cancer. It was Sir John Burgoyne, the Chief Engineer of the British army, who had persuaded first Lord Raglan and then Saint-Arnaud to abandon the plan of attacking the north side. His main argument was that it was safer to invade the city from the south side, the defences of which would be almost non-existent, whereas the Russians would have used the time to strengthen their northern defences. Furthermore, the south side had a natural hinterland, the Chersonese peninsula, which had a number of good natural bays and harbours that could be used as supply bases for the Allied armies. Balaklava harbour, to the east of the peninsula, should be the first goal of the Allied movement round Sevastopol. On top of this the Russians had, on 23 September, blocked the entrance to the Northern Bay, the main bay of the city, by scuttling seven of their older warships. This made the cooperation of the Allied fleets in bombarding the north side impossible. Saint-Arnaud accepted these arguments, which were not opposed by any of the other British or French generals.

Thus, on 25 September, the Allies left their bivouac on the Belbek, the British still guarding the left flank as they were the only ones who had some cavalry to protect their march, the French and Turks keeping to the right. None of the opposing armies made any reconnaissance, so neither side knew anything of the whereabouts of the other. The Russians inside Sevastopol, who were daily and hourly expecting the invasion from the north, did not at once learn of the miraculous decision of the Allies, although it saved them from being quickly overrun.

What was the state of affairs of the Russian army and of Menshikov's plans in these fateful days after the Battle of the Alma?

Menshikov with his battered army had left the battlefield and moved south to Sevastopol. He made his army bivouac on the outskirts of the city and went inside to make his decision known to the local commanders: he would neither hold the Katcha or Belbek lines nor the north side of the city; the local forces, largely made up of sailors from the fleet, should take care of themselves. The entrance of the harbour should be blocked by scuttling some of the ships; the remaining ships should point their guns at the north side where the enemy was expected soon. He himself would march his army to the north-east on the road through Mackenzie's Farm to Bakchisarai, in order to save the vital link to Simferopol and from there to Perekop and southern Russia. Of course the local commanders felt betrayed by their chief, but could not argue with him and were obliged to accept this high-handed decision.

On 24 September, Menshikov's forces left the outskirts of the city and marched out to Bakchisarai. Menshikov was widely criticized then and later for his decision both to scuttle part of the ships and leave the local garrison to its fate. From a military point of view it made some sense: the sunken ships did effectively block the entrance to the main bay to the powerful Allied ships; Menshikov probably saved his army from a second defeat by not allowing it to be trapped in Sevastopol; and he could well use it to return to the city and either encircle the Allies after they had overrun the city or at least threaten their flank. The latter is what actually happened. It led to the curious situation that the Allied armies were besieging the city and were at the same time themselves being besieged in their rear.

It was a huge blunder on the part of the Allies not to attack the north side of Sevastopol, even after the scuttling of the Russian ships. The city on that side had poor fortifications and had 4,000–5,000 troops and sailors to defend it. The total strength of the garrison, when Menshikov left the city on the night of 23–24 September, amounted to no more than 17,800 men. General Dimitrij E. von der Osten-Sacken, who was later commander of the garrison, wrote in a letter at the beginning of October 1854:

If the enemy had acted energetically, then the whole army [of the Crimea] would not have been sufficient for the defence of Sevastopol which is completely unprepared to withstand a siege. The hope of Sevastopol lies first of all in God's help and then – in the intrepid Kornilov.[5]

And Kornilov himself wrote at that time in his diary, 'Maybe, God has not yet abandoned Russia. If, after all, the enemy, after the Battle of the Alma, had directly marched into Sevastopol, he would have easily conquered it.' It is interesting to note that both the Russians and the Allies had no proper reconnaissance service and were therefore moving and marching in the dark – a situation which is characteristic of the whole Crimean War.

This fact is thrown into full relief by another curious occurrence at this time: on 25 September a British advance guard inadvertently ran into the rear guard of Menshikov's army marching north-east near Mackenzie's Farm and took some of the Russians prisoner. Oddly, they were not properly interrogated, so the British marching south did not realize that they had just missed Menshikov's army marching north-east.

On the following day, Saint-Arnaud, feeling his death approaching, formally handed over command of the French army to General Canrobert. Saint-Arnaud died on 29 September on board the ship that was to bring him to Constantinople.

On arrival at Balaklava the Allies decided that the port was much too narrow for the two navies to remain there. The French navy had discovered that Kamiesh Bay, south-west of Sevastopol city, was a good and large base for the French army. It was another mistake for Raglan to accept this division of bases. It meant that the British army, facing Sevastopol during the coming siege operations on the right-hand (north-eastern) side, had a line of communication from Balaklava harbour that was far too extended. Supplies had to be brought uphill from the harbour to the Inkerman plateau over a distance of up to 14 kilometres. The disadvantage became painfully obvious during the coming winter months. Another drawback was that the British sector did not, because of lack of men, reach Inkerman Bay, the easternmost part of the main bay, thus leaving the Russians a vital opening to the road north to Bakchisarai and Simferopol. Finally, Balaklava harbour, even for the British army alone, was too small to be able to handle the transfer of supplies from the ships to the front line. The choice of Balaklava proved to be a fatal decision which was to be responsible for the bulk of British casualties during the months to come.

The two Allied commanders were far too timid to risk an immediate attack on the almost defenceless city. First they wanted to establish themselves at their bases and await reinforcements from Varna and Constantinople, only then venturing an attack. In fact, during the first days of October the British received 4,000 more men, bringing their total to 22,000; at the same time the French 5th Division and other detachments arrived so that Canrobert disposed of 42,000 troops, plus the 5,000 Turkish reserve troops. The Allies had to face two fronts, one visible, the other invisible as far as the Russian enemy was concerned: they formed a 'corps of observation' which had to face east and north-east and be on its guard against a possible attack by Menshikov's army; and a 'corps of siege', which was to form a semicircle on the heights surrounding the city of Sevastopol and the Korabelnaya suburb on both sides of the main bay, and prepare an attack downhill through the amphitheatre-like outskirts towards the centre of the city.

While the Allied armies were settling down, grouping their forces and leisurely preparing their siege, digging their first trenches (to the relief of the Russians who had by then realized that the Allies had no intention of storming the city immediately), the Russian defenders of the city used the invaluable time left to them to strengthen their incomplete defences. Their efforts approached a miracle which has gone into Russia's history as one of its greatest feats. It was supervised by Admiral Kornilov, who was ably assisted by Admiral Nakhimov and Colonel Totleben. Many guns were taken from the remaining ships and put into position. The defence works were carried out day and night. Not only were the sailors involved, but the whole population including women and children. Their frantic activity could at times be watched by the enemy soldiers only 2 kilometres away. Within a couple of days the line of defence round the city was visibly strengthened; ships were moored, their guns pointing to the Allied lines. By the middle of October, 341 guns were in position, 118 of which were of heavy calibre and able to reach the enemy siege lines, the rest being able to deliver grapeshot in case the enemy should storm the city.

The lines of communication within the city were also improved. As early as April 1854 a sapper battalion had begun the construction of a road from the Korabelnaya suburb to the Inkerman bridge, which for the most part ran near the coast and thus avoided the Sapun plateau which was now in the hands of the Allies. This road was the main lifeline from the city to the rest of the Crimea. Another improvement was the construction of a pontoon bridge across the Southern Bay, which shortened the distance between the city centre and the Korabelnaya suburb. From 3 October some of Menshikov's troops made their appearance on the Tchernaya river, and a few days later the defenders of the city received their first real reinforcements from Menshikov's army, bringing their total to 25,000 men. Menshikov's main force remained posted on the open north side, whence it could easily escape.

On the evening of 16 October an Allied council of war fixed the first bombardment of Sevastopol for the following morning. Should it succeed, an assault should be tried. The bombardment from both wings of the besiegers was to be reinforced by the cooperation of the Allied fleets. Both naval commanders were sceptical about the success of a ranged battery of wooden ships against well-protected, casemated forts on land. It must be remembered that Sevastopol had very strong coastal forts to meet an attack from the sea, whereas the defences on the land side had been neglected. The Allied naval commanders also knew that the very existence of the expeditionary corps depended on reliable sea communications, which the fleets were expected to provide. Risking them in a battle with coastal defences therefore posed a real problem. The reservations of both Dundas and Hamelin in granting naval support were therefore logical, but the commanders on land were their superiors, and they had to give in. Ideally the ships would have to open their broadsides simultaneously with the land batteries. Lack of proper coordination – and perhaps their clandestine opposition – made Hamelin and Dundas decide not to open the ships' fire before 10–11 o'clock.

The number of guns facing each other on land was about equal. The French had six batteries mounted with fifty-three guns on their left wing, the British eleven batteries with seventy-three pieces on the right. On the opposite side the Russians disposed of 118 guns (out of about double that number) capable of being used against the Allied batteries.

The Allied preparations on the heights surrounding the city were easily visible, so the Allies could not count on surprise when they opened fire on 17 October at 6.30 am. They were greeted by counter-fire almost simultaneously. Thus the bombardment was a veritable duel between the two sides. After 9.30 a Russian bomb hit a French powder magazine, producing havoc and resulting in fifty-five fatal casualties. When shortly afterwards a second, although smaller, explosion put another battery out of action, the order to cease fire was given to the remaining French batteries at 10.30.

On the right wing the British fared better. Their guns were superior in number and calibre to the Russians' and they had been properly dispersed, so they managed to maintain fire throughout the day. They were able to inflict heavy damage on the opposite batteries and bastions, especially to the Malakhov and to Bastion No. 3 (the Great Redan). In the latter a powder magazine exploded and battered the defences to pieces. Had Raglan been an abler and more audacious general, and known the extent of damage done, he would have realized that this was the moment to venture the assault and occupy one of the most important bastions inside Sevastopol. Totleben later admitted that this was another golden opportunity which Raglan let slip.

On the sea the Allies had met a near disaster. Their fleets had formed a line from north to south outside the entrance to the main bay, facing, among others, the formidable forts Constantine and Alexander. They were not ready to open fire before 1 pm, that is, hours after the French batteries had been silenced. Fire was exchanged for five hours, after which not one of the thirty major ships had escaped more or less serious damage. None of them had sunk, however. The casualties were high: seventy-four Allied sailors were dead, 446 wounded. This was a heavy toll compared with the slight losses in men and damage done to the Russian forts. The Allied naval commanders were justified in their doubts about leading a battle fleet of wooden ships, even though they had superior armament, against well-built and properly defended stone forts on land. Worse than the damage inflicted on the Allied fleets was their loss of prestige. They never again during the war lined up in a ranged formation in front of the coastal batteries of the Black Sea. The lesson the Western powers drew from this experience was to try out a new type of vessel, the ironclad ship, which could better withstand the impact of cannon fire.

The bombardment on land was also a dismal failure. It was resumed and continued during the following days at a diminishing rate until 25 October, but achieved nothing. The Russians managed to repair the damage done to their defences each night. They, too, had suffered a great loss: Kornilov had been in the Malakhov and died on the first day of the bombardment due to a severe wound. The hero was dead, but lived on in the defenders of the city, military or civilian. In his hour of death he is reputed to have said, 'May God bless Russia and the Tsar, and save Sevastopol and the fleet.' These are the words engraved on the monument later erected on the Malakhov in his honour. He was replaced as naval Commander-in-Chief by Admiral Nakhimov.

The Battle of Balaklava, 25 October 1854

The first and inconclusive bombardment of Sevastopol was the real beginning of more than 300 days of trench warfare between the two sides. The French and British were digging themselves in, opening a network of parallels and approaches and multiplying their batteries. The Russians were doing likewise, constructing new batteries such as the Gervais battery to protect the strategic Malakhov, and linking all their earthworks round the city centre and the Korabelnaya suburb with a deep trench. Both sides had also replenished their forces from the outside: the Allies could dispose, at the end of October 1854, of some 70,000 men, made up of 42,000 French, 23,000 British and 5,000 Turks. Menshikov's force at that time stood at about 65,000; it had just been strengthened by the 12th Infantry Division under Lieutenant-General Pavel P. Liprandi who had arrived by forced marches from Bessarabia. If Menshikov had waited a few days more before launching a diversionary movement, he would have had at his disposal, with the arrival of the two remaining infantry divisions from the 4th Corps in Bessarabia (10th and 11th), a total of 85,000 men.

But Menshikov gave in prematurely to the constant goading and prodding from St Petersburg that urged him not to give up Sevastopol, but to try a relief movement in favour of the beleaguered city. Thus he adopted General Liprandi's plan of an attack on the right south-easterly flank of the British line of observation, with Balaklava being the ultimate target. The plan was a sound one; if successful it would have evicted the British from their sole base of supply and might well have inaugurated a turning-point in the war.

The defences of Balaklava harbour, or rather of the entrance to the small valley of Balaklava, were weak. They consisted of an outer and an inner line.

The former was made up of four redoubts strewn along the Voroncov road, built on elevated ground between the North and South Valley and facing the Fedukhin heights in the north. Each of the lightly constructed redoubts was manned by about 250 Turkish troops who were mostly poorly trained Tunisians – Omer Pasha, still with the bulk of his forces at Eupatoria, had taken care not to give away first-line troops. The inner defence line consisted of a number of batteries forming a semicircle about a kilometre outside the entrance of the gorge to Balaklava. Towards the northern end of the circle was the village of Kadikioi, where a British field battery and an infantry battalion were stationed. Further outside was Lord Lucan's cavalry division, which was encamped at the foot of the Sapun heights.

It is again typical of the conduct of the Allied headquarters that they did not bother to carry out a systematic reconnaissance of the outer defence line of Balaklava or, for that matter, along the whole line of their corps of observation. Raglan even scorned the use of spies; otherwise he would have taken seriously a report that the Russians were assembling troops along the Tchernaya river between the Traktir bridge and the mouth of the Baidar river.

In fact, Liprandi was assembling a force of 25,000 men there. They were to advance in an extended line parallel to the outer defence line of Balaklava and then to overrun the four redoubts, with part of the force staying on the Fedukhin heights in order to protect the other part marching towards the gorge of Balaklava. The harbour installations and ships, being practically undefended, would then be destroyed. The troops would, according to circumstances, either install themselves inside Balaklava or leave it after carrying out the work of destruction.

Before dawn on 25 October the Russian troops deployed according to plan. The four redoubts were quickly overrun, most of the Turks having fled beforehand, in view of the vastly superior numbers of the enemy, and headed towards the inner defence line of Balaklava. The Fedukhin heights were also duly occupied, with Russian guns overlooking the North Valley firmly installed. The surprise achieved by the Russians was complete. Had Liprandi shown more dash and self-assurance he could have followed up his first performance by a second raid towards the inner defence line. Lucan's cavalry and a small force of infantry to the right flank of the Russians would not have been a match for the attackers. Instead, only part of his cavalry and some Cossack regiments advanced. What now developed during the morning hours of 25 October was more or less a duel of cavalry forces, on the lines of the artillery duel of 17 October, rather than a full-fledged attack by a superior force against a vastly inferior enemy.

Lord Raglan and, later on, General Bosquet had by then posted themselves on a vantage point on the Sapun hills overlooking the movements to the east of them. Raglan ordered two divisions of the corps of observation to march in the direction of the scene of action. Bosquet in his turn had some of his *chasseurs d'Afrique* march down into the plain. All these relief movements would take hours to perform.

In the meantime the Russian cavalry force was charged and driven back by the Heavy Brigade of Lucan's cavalry under Brigadier General James Scarlett. It smashed into the Russian ranks and within minutes returned with remarkably light losses, but with good effect as the Russian hussars and Cossacks retreated in disorder. This was a golden moment for the Light Brigade under its commander, Lord Cardigan, which was posted to the left of the Heavy Brigade, to take up the pursuit of the fleeing Russians. But Cardigan, being on bad terms with Lord Lucan, his chief and brother-in-law, kept to the letter of an order issued by Lucan and did not move, although some of his officers implored him to seize the opportunity.

What now followed has gone down in British military mythology and British national consciousness, immortalized by countless tales and by Alfred, Lord Tennyson's poem *The Charge of the Light Brigade*. Only the bare facts need be retold here.

The first stage of the famous 'charge of the Light Brigade' was a vague order given by Lord Raglan from his elevated vantage point on the Sapun mountains. To him the Russians seemed to be retreating. Through his telescope he was able to see that they were removing the British guns from the captured redoubts. In order to prevent this he issued the following order, scribbled down by the Quartermaster-General, General Richard Airey, on a paper to be passed on to Lord Lucan and then to Lord Cardigan:

> Lord Raglan wishes the cavalry to advance rapidly to the front, follow the enemy and try to prevent the enemy carrying away the guns. Troop of Horse Artillery may accompany. French cavalry is on your left. Immediate, R. Airey.[6]

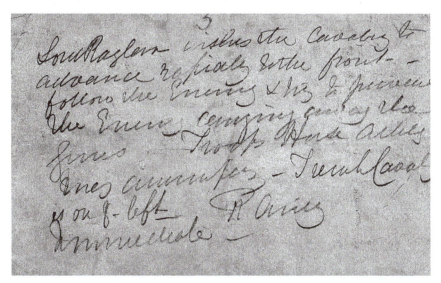

FIGURE 11 *Lord Raglan's order to the Light Brigade in his own handwriting. Courtesy of Inge and Dieter Wernet.*

Both Lucan and Cardigan could not make much sense of the order, since what Raglan was able to see from his elevated point was not visible in the plain where the cavalry stood. So they were completely in the dark about their real target. They both knew that if they obeyed the order to the letter the attack would not only be pointless but also suicidal. When Lucan remonstrated with the messenger, asking him to explain the order orally, he was angrily told with a contemptuous gesture: 'There, my Lord, is your enemy; there are your guns.' The gesture pointed to the east of the Voroncov road. The transmission of the order to Cardigan was marked with similar unhelpfulness and contempt. The delivery of the fateful message down the chain of command was thus marred by incompetence, personal pique, snobbishness and, in the end, by what would later come to be called *Kadavergehorsam* in the German army, that is, slavish obedience to a command.

To cap its pointlessness, the order was executed by Cardigan and his officers with the punctiliousness of barrack yard drill: when in the heat of the attack, a rider was being shot down from his horse, the cry 'Close the ranks!' was to be heard again and again. When Cardigan rode out with his 658 men into the open North Valley, which was surrounded on all three sides, left, right and ahead, by hills studded with Russian artillery, he did so as if he was on the parade ground. The three lines had to be formed meticulously. Then the orders were given to start and hasten the speed. The Russian gunners were for a moment seized with incredulous amazement before they started to pour their fire into the line. Everyone else looking on, including Raglan, was dumbfounded. Bosquet, stricken with horror, shouted, 'C'est magnifique, mais ce n'est pas la guerre. C'est de la folie.'[7] Liprandi, on later hearing of the rashness of the British cavalry, insisted that they were drunk.

Stolidly advancing and being showered with cannonballs, canister and bullets, the Light Brigade, or what was left of it, even reached the Russian guns and sabred some of the gunners. The retreat of the remnants was covered by a relief attack of the French *chasseurs d'Afrique*. Of the men who had ridden to the attack, slightly less than 200 returned; 134 were killed, many more wounded. Cardigan escaped the havoc in the 'Valley of Death'.

With the disastrous attack of the Light Brigade over, there was no further action between the Russians and the Allies. The affair of 25 October near Balaklava can hardly be called a battle. Losses on both sides were slight: the Russians put their casualties at 550 in all, of whom 238 were fatal; Allied losses were about the same.

The result of the 'battle' was relatively unimportant. The Russians had not reached their goal, the occupation or destruction of the British supply base. They kept, however, two of the four redoubts, those lying to the east, and also the Fedukhin heights. They could regard the 'battle' as at least a tactical success. On the Allied side, the spine of the British cavalry was broken for the rest of the war, though its role was unduly magnified by the contemporary world and by posterity. As a result of the experience of

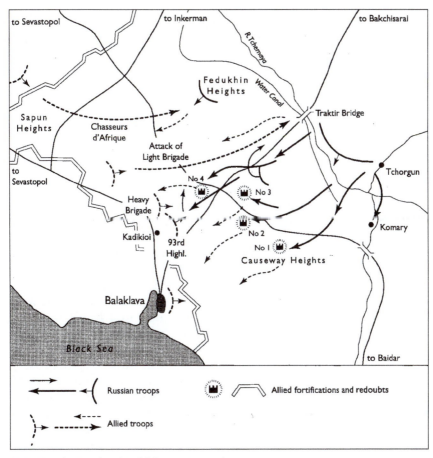

MAP 5 *The Battle of Balaklava, 25 October 1854.*

25 October, the right flank of Balaklava was strengthened in order to ward off another Russian attack. The Allied supreme command in the Crimea realized that after the failure of the first bombardment a long siege was in train. In London and Paris the governments and public opinion were beginning to realize that the invasion of the Crimea was not just a formality, and that the Western powers were not well prepared for an all-out war. But worse was to come in the following three weeks.

The Battle of Inkerman, 5 November 1854

With winter approaching, the Allies had decided on a new assault on the city of Sevastopol for 6 November, with the intention of making this a turning-point in the campaign – but the Russians thwarted their plan.

After the indecisive Battle of Balaklava and under mounting pressure from the Tsar in St Petersburg, Menshikov, although reluctantly and not believing in ultimate success, had made up his mind to act. Two of the Tsar's sons, Grand Dukes Nicholas and Michael, had just arrived as harbingers of the Tsar's impatience. At the same time, in the first days of November, the two remaining infantry divisions from the 4th Corps, the 10th and the 11th, had arrived from Bessarabia under General Dannenberg. The Russians now had a clear superiority in numbers: there were about 107,000 men outside and inside Sevastopol (not counting the sailors). The Allied forces could be estimated at 71,000 men, roughly half the Russian number.[8]

Besides the area north-east of Balaklava, which had just been probed, there was another even weaker point in the Allied line: the extreme easterly end of the observation line, the Inkerman ridge or Cossack mountain. It rises south of the butt-end of the main bay and bounds the Tchernaya at its mouth towards the east. To the west it is separated from the adjoining ridge, the Victoria ridge covering the Korabelnaya, by the Careening ravine (*Kilen-balka* in Russian) and is indented towards the bay and river by a number of smaller ravines. The Inkerman ridge, not to be confused with the Inkerman heights beyond the Tchernaya, rises to a height of about 130 metres. The ground is rocky and covered with brushwood. In October 1854 it was no man's land. At the northern end towards the coast of the bay ran Sappers' Road, which was in Russian hands. At the southern end on the heights was the easternmost end of the British line of observation, thinly manned by the 2nd Division under General Sir George de Lacy Evans. Their camp was poorly fortified. The 2nd Division stood at 3,500 men; to their left was posted the Guards Brigade with 1,600 men; adjoining them was the Light Division under Sir George Brown with another 3,500 men. Taken together they formed the British wing of the line of observation. Their strength – 8,600 men – was a third of the whole British force, the other two-thirds forming the siege line. Thus, because of its weakness and the exposed position, this sector was an easy and obvious target for Menshikov's army or part of it, the only difficulty being that the enemy was on elevated ground and access was not simple. From a topographical point of view the roles were reversed compared to the situation at the Battle of the Alma: there the Russians were on high ground and the Allies had to force their way up.

Menshikov's plan of campaign looked simple and logical on paper, and, if properly executed and if all imponderable factors – for example the weather – turned out well, it had every chance of success. The overall intention was to deliver a crippling blow to the British army, to destroy it or roll it back, occupy the Inkerman ridge and gain control of the Careening ravine and thus open the way to the strategic Sapun heights and the Chersonese plateau, easing the pressure from the north-eastern corner of the siege of the city. For the whole operation, Menshikov earmarked an imposing force of 57,000 men, almost treble the strength used against Balaklava on 25 October.

The main thrust of the attack, fixed for 5 November, was to be directed against Inkerman ridge. Menshikov assigned 35,000 troops, a force more than four times superior in number to the British defensive line. It was to approach the mountain in two columns. The right wing, under Lieutenant-General Fedor I. Soimonov, commander of the 10th Infantry Division, newly arrived, would move with 19,000 men from Sevastopol on Sappers' Road, cross the Careening ravine and then climb up Inkerman ridge on the right hand side. The left wing, under Lieutenant-General Prokofij Ia. Pavlov, would start off with 16,000 men from Inkerman village, cross the Tchernaya at its mouth on Inkerman bridge, which was under repair at the time (this was one of the snags in the plan!), then fan out into the various smaller ravines giving access to Inkerman ridge and join with Soimonov's column at the top.

Strangely, Menshikov would not accompany either of the columns; he would stay behind and let General Dannenberg, commander of the 4th Corps, newly arrived with his two divisions, accompany Pavlov's force and on joining with Soimonov's force assume overall command. Why Dannenberg, who knew nothing of the difficult terrain and was held in low esteem by all the other generals? Why did Menshikov himself virtually renounce leadership of the battle? Did he want to avoid a possible defeat like that on the Alma? Was he, the courtier and admiral, conscious that he lacked the capacity to lead a great army into battle? Perhaps so. As to his choice of Dannenberg, he later excused it by saying that it would not have mattered who of his generals had commanded.[9] Such strange behaviour is indicative of the utter distrust Menshikov felt towards the generals surrounding him. It is also typical that he worked out his plan in secret, without discussing it with, or even showing it to, his fellow generals.

A third sizeable force, made up of 22,000 men under General Piotr D. Gorchakov, brother of M. D. Gorchakov, Commander-in-Chief of the army of the Danube, was to be posted at Tchorgun village, upstream on the Tchernaya, to effect a diversionary movement: it was to distract the enemy forces at the centre of its observation line on the Sapun mountains, attack it and if possible occupy the heights. This was a clever move, since it would engage the French forces under General Bosquet nearest to those British who would bear the brunt of the main attack and deprive the British of the help which they would certainly need in view of their numerical inferiority.

A second diversionary movement, though of much smaller dimensions, was to be effected on the left wing of the French siege line by a force inside Sevastopol. General Nikolaj D. Timofeev was to make a sally from bastion No. 6 (Quarantine Bastion) with 3,000 men to immobilize the French forces in that sector. It was probably a flaw in this otherwise excellent plan of campaign that 3,000 men was not a strong enough force to achieve anything decisive.

In addition to the two intrinsic flaws in Menshikov's plan – the choice of Dannenberg as commander of the main force and the insufficiency of Timofeev's sallying party – there were more to come in the preparatory and main stages of its execution. First, the weather was inauspicious. During 4 November it was raining all day, and the rain continued throughout the night. On the following morning, when the attack was to start, it changed into a drizzle; the area was enwrapped in thick fog which reduced visibility to a few metres. This was both an advantage and a disadvantage: the marching columns could not be seen by the enemy but commands were difficult to execute; fighting was haphazard and invariably ended in utter confusion; the junction of the two main forces could hardly be effected; and many of the muskets and rifles could not fire because of the damp. During the morning, however, the fog partially lifted, so that the officers could more properly direct their men. Despite this, because of the fog there was no real battle between the forces involved, but a continuous series of uncoordinated small attacks and counter-attacks. The two sides intermingled with each other, with much hand-to-hand fighting, the Russians sometimes shooting or clubbing to death their own men, and the natural fright of the individual soldier degenerated into an animal-like frenzy, the men wrestling with each other and strangling the enemy with their bare hands.

Another flaw that quickly became apparent in the execution of Menshikov's plan of campaign, due this time to human incapacity, was that Dannenberg unilaterally changed parts of Menshikov's order after it had been issued to Pavlov and Soimonov. There were changes in the exact movement of Soimonov's troops, in the use of his reserves and, most important of all, in the timing of his march: instead of beginning it at 6 am, he was to start at 5 am. These changes were due in part to the vague wording of some of Menshikov's phrases, but may also have reflected the tense relations between the two commanders. In any event, the result was more confusion on the part of Soimonov and Pavlov – a repetition of what had occurred in the British command structure leading to the dreadful charge of the Light Brigade. Dannenberg's changes led to the two columns missing each other on the heights of Inkerman ridge the following morning.

The vagueness and confusion in the Russian order of battle is partly attributable to the fact that there were no maps available of the local terrain, while Dannenberg, having recently arrived from Bessarabia, had no personal knowledge of the ground on which he was to operate. Menshikov had been conscious of the lack of maps and had asked St Petersburg to send him one. First it was refused him with the excuse that it was the only one available; then it was sent to him and arrived – the day after the battle had taken place. This lack of theoretical preparation was typical of warfare in the middle of the nineteenth century, and especially typical of the Russian military establishment. A look at a good map would have shown Dannenberg and Menshikov – the latter at least must have had some knowledge of the terrain on and around Inkerman Ridge – that the ridge was too small an area on which to deploy so large a force (35,000 men), even taking into account that they would arrive there in echelons and that reserves would have to be held back.

A final, inexcusable mistake in Menshikov's plan of battle is the fact that on 4 November Inkerman Bridge, which Pavlov's 16,000 men were to cross, was still unusable and that Menshikov ordered it to be repaired during the night. Of course, it was not ready in the early hours of next morning, so that Pavlov's column was halted for some time and arrived late on Inkerman Ridge when Soimonov's troops were already engaged with the British.

The Russian preparations were bound to go wrong the following morning. It is most confusing for a latter-day historian to read and make sense of the accounts, Russian or English, of the Battle of Inkerman, which are mostly provided by 'eyewitnesses' pretending to give details which they could hardly have seen in view of the bad weather conditions on 5 November. At least the more important and decisive facts are known, as is, of course, the result.

In the early morning of 5 November, Soimonov's forces climbed up the western side of Inkerman Ridge in their grey columns, unseen by the British sentinels. Soimonov left his reserve behind and soon arrived at the crest without seeing or hearing anything of Pavlov's men who were to join him. His troops were soon involved in fierce fighting with the British. Soimonov was one of the first to be killed, and his second in command was immediately wounded. The Russians fell back on their reserve battalions. Their commander dared not move them forward without receiving an order from above. As Soimonov was dead, his deputy put out of action and Dannenberg still with Pavlov's forces, he stayed put.

Pavlov's 16,000 men, who were supposed to arrive simultaneously on Inkerman Ridge, were in the meantime halted at Inkerman Bridge and had to wait there until 7 o'clock. After crossing it, they fanned out on three different routes and by 8 o'clock began to climb up the mountain with their guns. Two of their regiments were soon involved in fighting with the British. They even took No. 1 redoubt on the British far right, the so-called Sandbag Battery. They had to retreat, however, when the British moved in reserves. After the mist began to rise slowly, the Russians could make use of their powerful artillery which they had massed in their rear; two frigates in the main bay were able to take part in the attack. With more Russian columns being able to press upon the British lines, the latter showed signs of giving in. Raglan, who had appeared on the scene, decided to send for French aid.

Bosquet's forces on the Sapun heights had in the meantime been tackled by Gorchakov's Tchorgun force of 22,000 men. But in what a way!

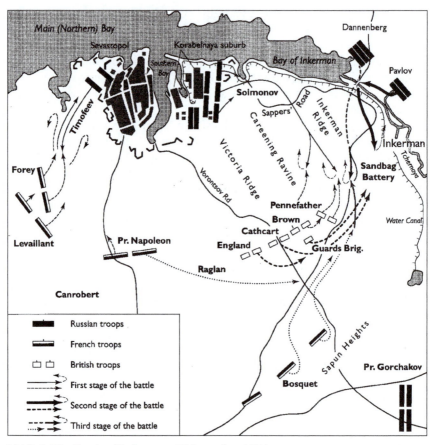

MAP 6 *The Battle of Inkerman, 5 November 1854.*

Gorchakov, who had obviously misinterpreted the word 'diversion', restricted himself to a cannonade that failed to do any damage as it was launched from too great a distance. His behaviour is only surpassed by the conduct of Menshikov, the nominal Commander-in-Chief who excelled in utter passivity, having retreated to a telegraph hill from which he thought he could oversee and direct the battle. Bosquet soon convinced himself that Gorchakov's pinpricks were a harmless 'distraction', and he therefore sent the relief demanded. At first, only a few units arrived, but then Bosquet committed the bulk of his troops. Their arrival was psychologically important, comparable to the appearance of the Prussians during the Battle of Waterloo. The British, on the verge of defeat, were crying, 'Hurrah for the French.' To the Russians the arrival of the fresh French troops, mostly Zouaves, struck terror into their hearts. Fierce fighting continued for a while; at the Sandbag Battery it was especially stubborn, the position changing hands several times. When Bosquet had the opportunity to inspect it after it had been retaken, he is reputed to have exclaimed, 'Quel abattoir [What a slaughterhouse].'[10] Later, this name was given to the Battery.

Dannenberg, who had arrived with Pavlov's troops, decided to give up the battle between 12 and 1 o'clock. There was no pursuit by the British or French, so the Russians made an orderly retreat down the ridge and across the Tchernaya.

The only Russian operation which went according to plan was the sortie by Timofeev's men from the Quarantine Bastion to the far left of the French siege line on Mount Rodolphe. By 9.30, covered by the mist, they started out unseen, suddenly appeared among the French batteries, put many of the French gunners to death and spiked a number of guns. However, they were soon repulsed by relief troops who furiously pursued them back to the Russian bastion. The French losses there were appalling, higher even than on Inkerman Ridge: 950 men dead and wounded. The Russian casualties are put at 1,100.

Timofeev's sortie completely achieved its aim of keeping the French busy in that sector. It is therefore safe to say that, if Gorchakov had acted in the prescribed sense and had not remained inactive with his large force, he might well have overrun Bosquet's position in the centre. Bosquet would then have been prevented from coming to the relief of the British and the whole outcome of the Battle of Inkerman would have been different.

The balance sheet in terms of human losses was appalling.[11] Russian casualties on Inkerman Ridge are given as almost 11,000 men dead and wounded; taking Timofeev's operation into account, the figure rises to about 12,000; the fifteen men lost in the Tchorgun force are negligible. It may therefore be said that of the 35,000 men involved on Inkerman Ridge, a third were annihilated, an extraordinarily high proportion for not more than six hours' fighting. The corresponding figures for the British and French are more difficult to assess. Official statistics for the British give 632 officers and men killed and 1,873 men wounded, of whom many probably died on their way to Skutari (Constantinople), or at that hospital. French figures released in Paris, and therefore most probably 'rectified', detail a loss of 1,726 men, including those at Mount Rodolphe (950 men).

What was the overall strategic result of Inkerman? The outcome revealed several points about the Russian army: first of all the incompetent leadership and the almost non-existent staff work at headquarters. It is strange that at the beginning of the battle, Menshikov transferred its direction to Dannenberg, who had already cut a poor figure on the Danube at Oltenitsa against the Turks. He had no knowledge of the terrain and could not acquire it on paper, as no maps were available. When he appeared on the scene he gave contradictory orders. The whole coordination of the troop movements to Inkerman Ridge and of the diversionary actions was flawed.

Menshikov must of course bear the brunt of the blame. His secretiveness, his envy of his rivals and the vagueness of many of the details in an otherwise good plan of campaign spoilt the chances of success right from the start. He was not able to use the substantial superiority in numbers of men and in artillery to strike a decisive blow at the enemy. Only a part of his force became actively involved in the battle; many of the guns remained unused down in the valleys and on Sappers' Road. During the engagement, the attack in columns proved deadly in view of the superior firepower of the British. The old smooth-bore muskets were no match for the long-range Minié rifles. Massed bayonet attacks for which the Russian soldiers were well trained proved obsolete against the modern rifles that kept the Russian columns at a distance of a hundred or more metres. In general, after Inkerman the Russians had to give up all hope of driving the Allies into the sea. But at least, through the bare fact of their attack, they forced the Allies to postpone the renewal of their bombardment of the city.

Inkerman was a victory for the Allies; for the British, though, it was a Pyrrhic one. It put their small army out of action for some time to come. The British in the Crimea and at home became acutely aware of the insufficiency of their army, of its inability to fulfil the threefold obligation of protecting Balaklava, covering their overextended lines from the harbour to their extreme right and simultaneously providing enough forces for the siege. The Allies had finally to resign themselves to a long siege. First of all they had to overcome the rigours of the oncoming winter, which soon proved to be especially hard and dreadful.

The November storm of 1854 and the Crimean winter of 1854–5

On 14 November 1854, a week after the bloody Battle of Inkerman, the belligerents were hit by a terrible storm that swept over the southern parts of the Crimea. It was accompanied by torrential rain that filled the trenches round Sevastopol with water and transformed the ground into a quagmire. The hardship it produced for men and animals, especially in the exposed British camp, the losses it entailed in supplies in Balaklava harbour, and the consequences, which were aggravated by a severe winter, have gone down in English historical consciousness as one of the great dramas of the Crimean War. The French in their trenches were of course as badly hit as their British comrades, but conditions at their supply base proved to be better after the storm, due to an old jetty dating back to Greek times which protected the ships at anchor in Kamiesh Bay. The Russians in the city of Sevastopol felt the rigour of the hurricane, too, but they had stone houses which provided better shelter, although many were unroofed by the storm.

On land, tents were torn down and barracks destroyed. The most pitiful creatures were the sick and wounded in the makeshift hospitals which often collapsed or were blown away. The chaos in the village and harbour of Balaklava was indescribable.

At sea the damage done to the Allied fleets and the supply ships was much greater. Balaklava and Kamiesh were two of the busiest harbours in Europe at that time, with numerous ships arriving and leaving daily. Balaklava was always so cramped that many ships had to wait outside. The warships were posted along the coast, most of them at the mouth of the Katcha and off Eupatoria. Both places had no harbours to offer shelter to ships in distress. At Eupatoria, one of the most modern vessels, the screw-propelled *Henri IV*, as well as the corvette *Pluton*, went aground. For the British the most grievous loss was the steamer *Prince*, which was riding at anchor outside Balaklava. It was laden with the major part of the winter equipment for the British army, with hospital material and other stores. The *Resolute* went to the bottom of the sea filled with ammunition. The total losses for the British side were five avisos or steam corvettes and fifteen transports; for the French, the losses comprised three transports, besides the *Henri IV* and the *Pluton*. The Turks lost two steam frigates. Human casualties, mostly on board the ships, are put at 500. Thus, on the Allied side, the November hurricane caused as many dead as the Battle of the Alma. As to the material losses, the figures which Sidney Herbert, the Secretary at War in London later published, obviously on the basis of the freight lists of the ships lost, give an idea of the extent of the disaster: 25,000 fur caps, 8,000 sealskin boots, 15,000 pairs of leather boots, 40,000 fur coats, 40,000 leggings, 10,000 gloves.[12]

The Battle of Inkerman and the November storm were the overture to a disastrous winter, in which all three armies in and around Sevastopol suffered. The British army was by far the worst affected. There were two reasons for this: the length of the line of communication from Balaklava harbour to the British camp on the heights and the British siege sector; and the incompetence of the British supply system. The November storm had aggravated a situation which was inherent in the army's lack of preparation and foresight for a siege operation. Up to the first bombardment of 17 October, Raglan had not envisaged a prolonged stay in the Crimea for his army; therefore he did not press for the necessary preparations to be made on a large scale. Responsibility for the supply of the army was in the hands of the Commissariat, a civilian organization that was under the direct control of the Treasury in London. As it turned out to be unable, during the ensuing months, to collect the necessary number of horses and mules in the Black Sea and Mediterranean areas, and as it was totally incapable of tackling the problem of properly distributing the large amounts of supplies at Balaklava up to the village of Kadikioi and thence to the British lines, it was dissolved in the spring of 1855 and superseded by a new military organization, the Land Transport Corps.

To people outside the Crimea it must have indeed looked unbelievable that supplies of every kind, which had been transported over 5,000 kilometres from Britain to the Black Sea, were rotting near the jetties at Balaklava, and that animals and men almost within sight of these necessities were starving and dying. Animals did not get enough hay and became too weak to haul their carts and carry their loads; there were cases of horses eating each other's manes and tails. As a consequence, the bulk of them died, their carcasses littering the roads to the front line. Cavalry horses had to take over their duties, but they, too, disappeared for want of forage. What was left of Lucan's cavalry practically vanished during the winter and as they were in charge of the guard duty on the far right of the British lines they had to be replaced by French troops.

The British soldiers had a miserable lot. Their rations were inadequate and their winter equipment was non-existent until the arrival of new supplies by ship at the end of the year. The effective strength of the troops was dwindling daily. On 12 December 1854 it could still be put at 20,000 (compared to the 70,000 French troops). Five weeks later it was down to 13,000, with over 5,000 men hospitalized, the rest having died in the meantime not because of enemy bullets, but because of the rigours of the winter.[13]

The communication lines from Balaklava harbour to the siege and observation lines were periodically impassable during the winter. No proper preparations had been made to metal them and in rainy periods they were transformed into mud tracks. After many of the draught- and pack-animals had died, men had to carry provisions and ammunition to the front. As the British soldiers were not used to such hard work or were too weak to do it, the Turks had to be used for the purpose. In the end, in order to prevent the British lines from collapsing, several hundred French soldiers had to assist them.

The situation improved somewhat when the British firm of Peto, Brassey and Betts arrived on the scene, with navvies and engineers to build a railway from Balaklava harbour to the British camp. The first section to Kadikioi village, begun on 8 February 1855, was opened on 23 February. A month later the final section to the camp was finished. For the second bombardment of Sevastopol, in April 1855, ample ammunition had been hauled up, especially of the heavier types which had hitherto been impossible to move to the front.

Although all kinds of supplies had arrived by sea at Balaklava harbour, the whole site was in utter chaos, as is evidenced by the accounts of eyewitnesses or by the photographs taken by Roger Fenton and James Robertson, the first war photographers in history. Here the incompetence of the Commissariat was especially glaring. After the *Prince* had gone down in the November hurricane, fresh orders had been placed in Britain for new winter equipment. When it arrived it turned out that all the boots were too small for the men to wear. As an eyewitness wrote at the time:

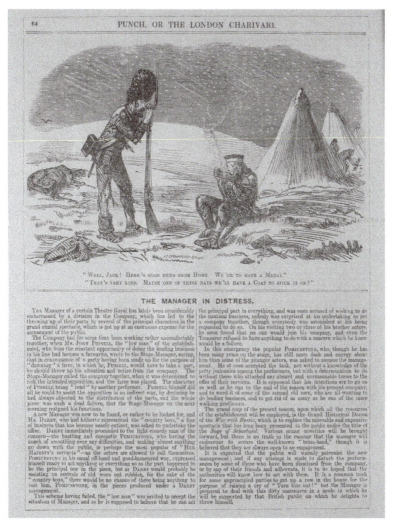

FIGURE 12 *The winter of 1854–5: the funny aspect.* Punch *28 (1855), p. 64.* *University Library of Heidelberg, CC-BY-SA 3.0.*

The men lie down in their tents, and to give ease to their feet take off their boots. The frosts, however, are sharp, and in the morning the boots are as hard as iron; there is no getting them on, nor is there a way to thaw or soften them.[14]

Sometimes ships arriving at Balaklava with vital necessities, like forage for the draught animals, were sent back to the Bosphorus because there was no space in the overcrowded harbour to unload them or – the most glaring example of red tape – the ships' papers were not in order. In another case, iron beds arrived in one ship at Scutari and were held there for some time, whereas the legs had long been sent to Balaklava.

The utter helplessness of the British army was soon highlighted by the British press. *The Times* opened a series of articles on 19 December by sharply criticizing the government and its agencies for the abject situation in which the British army in the Crimea found itself. The paper had an on-the-spot correspondent, William Howard Russell, who delivered, in minute detail, reports on the misery of the army. Until that time *The Times* had supported the government in its efforts to show teeth to the Russian bear; at the beginning, in fact, it had goaded the government on in its opposition to Russian pretensions. Once the war had begun, the paper had sent a bevy of correspondents to the war theatre on the Danube, to Constantinople, to Scutari and then to the Crimea. Their reports were avidly read by a public eager for news from the Orient. When the Allies landed at Eupatoria on 4 September 1854 and drove the Russians away from the Alma, it was expected that the war would soon be over.

But the confidence of the public was shaken, when, at the end of September, the news arrived in Western Europe that Sevastopol had fallen, only for those reports to be quickly proven false. The spirit of the public was again rising when the bad news of the murderous Battle of Inkerman and of the havoc the hurricane had wreaked arrived. Then Russell's articles about the disorganization of the army before Sevastopol led to a paroxysm of national hysteria. This in turn prompted a search for a scapegoat or scapegoats, which were found in Lord Raglan; his Adjutant-General, Major-General James Estcourt; the Quartermaster-General, Richard Airey; the various offices and departments responsible for the supply system; the government itself; and ultimately the outworn aristocratic leadership of the army and the state. On 23 January 1855 the radical Member of Parliament, James Arthur Roebuck, tabled a motion of inquiry into the conduct of the war in the Crimea, which a few days later swept away the government of Lord Aberdeen and brought a new administration, under the vigorous Palmerston, to power.

In comparison with the British army, the French *Armée d'Orient* was in much better shape during the winter of 1854–5, although it, too, had to cope with much hardship. First of all, its supply bases, Kamiesh Bay and the neighbouring Kazatch Bay, were much better suited for providing the army with the necessities of daily life and of occasional fighting. The bases were much more spacious and they were nearer the front. Then, most important of all, their whole administrative system was properly organized. Algeria had provided a perennial battleground where the army had acquired a system by which its most important asset, the individual soldier, was properly cared for. There were well-stocked warehouses on the quays of the bays in the Crimea, there were well-paved roads from both bays to the siege lines, the rations for the soldiers were sufficient and balanced and the clothing was appropriate for the winter season.

The French could even spare several hundred men for repair work on the road to Balaklava and for carrying ammunition on their backs to the front line. They assisted the British with various equipment, including the ingenious *cacolets*, a double-seat placed on the back of a mule which was often the only means of carrying a wounded soldier from the trenches down to the hospital. In sum, the French soldiers were generally well fed, well clad, well treated by their officers and well fitted for the murderous trench warfare. In contrast their British counterparts were, as one of their own veterans described them at the time, 'the careworn, threadbare, ragged men, who form the staple of the English forces in the Crimea'.[15]

The situation of the Russian army in the winter of 1854–5 was better than that of the British, but worse than that of the French army. Although the war was fought on Russian soil, the supply of the Russian army was more difficult than that of the Allies. As there were no railways south of Moscow, all supplies and reinforcements had to be transported on wagons. In winter the transport system came almost to a standstill, as the animals that drew the carts depended on hay which they could not carry with them. It was the southern provinces of Russia which had to provide the bulk of the provisions besides the Crimea itself, which, however, did not produce much beyond grapes in the southern parts and cattle in the northern parts.

In the long run the Russian supply problem remained chronic and insoluble. When the Russian army in the Crimea received 6,000 ox-carts in November 1854, this number melted away, until a few weeks later only 1,000 of them remained. When at the beginning of December the Tarutinsky Regiment, part of the 17th Division, left Nizhnyj Novgorod, it took five months to reach the Crimea.[16] Besides reinforcements in men, the problem of military supplies – ammunition, weapons and gunpowder – soon turned out to be unmanageable. During the first bombardment the defenders of Sevastopol made lavish use of the stocks within the city, but thereafter shortages forced Nakhimov to introduce rationing. During 1855 the relatively free supply of war materials on the side of the Allies and the dwindling resources in that sector on the Russian side became more and more decisive for the final outcome of the war in the Crimea.

Another distressing factor in the daily care for the armies in the Crimea was the hospital situation. Throughout the Allies' stay in the Crimea there were always tens of thousands of soldiers hospitalized. The majority of the patients were in hospital due to sickness; mostly cholera, scurvy and typhus. Those wounded in battle were in the minority. It may be said that roughly half of the patients died in hospitals on all sides, a high proportion of which was due to the low standards of hygiene and due to the medical service. About 80 per cent of the deaths during the Crimean War occurred in hospital, the balance on the battlefield.

During the first Crimean winter the British army was the worst stricken of the three armies. In the following winter the situation changed radically, and it was the French army that now suffered awful losses.[17]

FIGURE 13 *The winter of 1854–5: the tragedy.* Punch *28 (1855), p. 95. University Library of Heidelberg, CC-BY-SA 3.0.*

The siege of Sevastopol – the second stage, February–May 1855

The only military event of importance in the early months of 1855 was the Russian attempt to dislodge the Allies from Eupatoria. After the landing of the Allied armies on 4 September 1854 and their march south to Sevastopol, this seaside town had been garrisoned by only 300 French troops. Several

Allied warships were moored along the coast and after the November storm the *Henri IV* and the *Pluton*, which had been destroyed by the hurricane, were still used as sea-batteries, some of the guns pointing towards the town and others being transferred to the defences of the town.

From the beginning of 1855 the bulk of Omer Pasha's army of the Danube was being transported from Varna to Eupatoria. By the middle of February some 35,000 to 40,000 troops had disembarked there, with more to come. Naturally, the Russians became alarmed at such a concentration of enemy troops, the more so as the Turks were seen reconnoitring the road from Simferopol to Perekop. It was feared that they might cut this vital lifeline for the army of the Crimea. Menshikov, spurred on by the Tsar, decided to attack the Turks and drive them out of the place. The task was entrusted to General Stepan A. Khrulev. After reinforcements had arrived, bringing the Russian troops in the region to a total of 19,000 men, Eupatoria was attacked on the morning of 17 February 1855. Although preceded by a bombardment, the attack was repulsed. The Russians lost about 700 men, 109 of them dead, and retreated into the interior.

The defeat at Eupatoria created a bad impression in St Petersburg. It became more and more obvious that the balance of forces was changing in favour of the Western powers. One of the immediate results was that Emperor Nicholas recalled Menshikov from the post of Commander-in-Chief in the Crimea and put M. D. Gorchakov, just arriving on the scene from Bessarabia, in his place. Nicholas, who died shortly afterwards (on 2 March 1855), expressed his gloomy misgivings about the prospects of the Russian situation in his last letter to Gorchakov. Hearing of the rumours which were then prevalent in Europe, that French troops might march through Germany and attack Russia in Poland, so inciting the Poles to revolution, he was even ready to let the Austrians occupy southern Russia in order to strengthen his own position in Poland if they entered the war.[18]

Just as Nicholas had become more and more impatient with his Commander-in-Chief in the Crimea, Napoleon III in Paris was growing nervous about the prospects of the war. At the end of January 1855 he sent General Adolphe Niel, a siege expert and one of his close aides, to the Crimea. Niel had no precise orders, but his general mission was to spur Canrobert on to greater activity and to report home on the situation before Sevastopol. The French were to receive more reinforcements, and the depot at Constantinople was to be transformed into a camp where a substantial army of reserve was to be built up.

At the end of February, Napoleon surprised the world with the announcement that he intended to go to the Crimea in person in order to instil more fire into the French generals and bring the campaign to a successful close by meeting the Russian army in an open battle, preferably at Simferopol. This news created much unrest in the diplomatic and military world. Napoleon was, however, successfully talked out of this lunatic idea during his state visit to Britain in the middle of April, although officially he gave up his plan only a fortnight later.

In the Crimea itself the two commanding generals, Canrobert and Raglan, saw no other way out of the deadlock than energetically pushing on the siege until the final assault could be made on the city of Sevastopol. At the beginning of February 1855 the general plan of siege operations was changed. This corresponded to the wishes of Lord Raglan and also to the order which Niel had brought with him from Paris – the French, in view of their numerical superiority, were to take over the right sector of the siege ring, notably in front of the Malakhov and the Little Redan, the British concentrating their efforts in the centre on the Great Redan. This meant a deterioration in the French lines of communication and supply.

Canrobert grudgingly accepted the change. He also had to swallow a reorganization of his own troops, by now 80,000 strong. They were to be divided into two army corps: one in charge of the left sector of the siege against the city of Sevastopol, with General Pélissier, just arrived from Algeria, as the commander; the other forming the corps of observation with the additional charge of occupying the right sector of the siege, with General Bosquet in command. Bosquet had by now, prompted by many of his generals and also by Niel, accepted a change in the target of the main attack: instead of concentrating the main effort and the final assault on the left sector towards the city, they should be directed on the right and centre towards the Korabelnaya suburb and the Malakhov.

This reorientation of the 'old siege' was now called the 'new siege'. The Malakhov bastion was clearly the centrepiece of the whole Russian fortification system around Sevastopol, and Totleben had by now strongly fortified it. If the Allies could take it, they would achieve several aims: threaten both the suburb and the city itself, as well as a large section of the main bay and the ships' bridge which the Russians had by now built to connect the city with the northern side; and from the Malakhov the adjacent bastions, the Little Redan and the Great Redan, could be attacked in the flanks or in the rear.

Some 600 metres in front of the Malakhov, as seen from the Russian side, is a small hill which the French called *Mamelon vert* and which was, at the beginning of February 1855, in no man's land between the two sides. Bosquet decided to take it as a preliminary step to an attack on the Malakhov. To prepare for its occupation, work for the construction of two flanking batteries was commenced. Great was the surprise when the French saw that the Russians had overnight built a redoubt – the Selenghinsky redoubt – on the northern slope of the Inkerman Ridge which covered both the Malakhov and the *Mamelon*. Canrobert immediately reacted and had the redoubt attacked, but the French were driven off with heavy losses. The Russians had a second surprise up their sleeves when they built another redoubt close to first during the night of 28 February–1 March; this came to be called the Volhynian redoubt. The *Mamelon* was thus protected by two new earthworks. To top everything, Totleben's men erected, during the night of 10–11 March, a third redoubt, the Kamchatka lunette (in contrast to a redoubt, a lunette is open towards the defenders) right on top of the *Mamelon*. The Russians had thus outdistanced the French. During the following weeks sorties and counter-attacks were launched, each time with much bloodletting and no result.

At a council of war on 2 April 1855 the Allied generals decided to launch another all-out bombardment, the second according to the Russians who counted that of 17 October 1854 as the first. If successful, an attack would ensue. The army of observation was strengthened by the arrival of 20,000 Turks from Eupatoria. For the bombardment the Allies disposed of about 500 guns, roughly four times the strength they had had during the first bombardment. The Russians could use almost 1,000 guns for their defence this time. Both sides had improved their means of attack and defence in other respects. At the Mast bastion (No. 4 according to the Russian counting) the French had driven their trenches to within 130 metres of the salients, but the Russians had everywhere perfected their fortifications.

On the morning of 9 April the Allies started their bombardment. The Russians replied, although it became obvious that they had to economize with their projectiles which they hurled into the enemy trenches. On the following day the bombardment was continued. To the great amazement of the Allies, the Russians had set to work furiously during the night to repair the damage. So it went on day after day and night after night until the bombardment was stopped with the tenth bout on 18 April. The Allies had showered 168,700 rounds on the Russians and the defenders had replied with half that number. The strategical result of the bombardment was nil. The human losses were not as high as might have been expected after such a murderous exchange: 1,500 on the French side, 260 on the British and, according to Totleben, 6,000 on the Russian side. On balance, the Russians had fought well and had maintained their newly built outposts.

After the failure of the second artillery duel, the Allies tried a new stratagem. The admirals of both navies, Admiral Lyons and Admiral Bruat, had for weeks urged on the Commanders-in-Chief an expedition to Kertch, on the eastern tip of the Crimean peninsula, and to the Sea of Azov in order to cut one of the Russian lines of communication along the Don river through the Sea of Azov to the Crimea, and to destroy supplies in the various ports of that sea. Another reason was to allow the two navies, which had hitherto been reduced to a mere ancillary role to the armies, to perform some feats of their own and satisfy public opinion at home, especially in Britain. Raglan was taken by the idea, but Canrobert hesitated as he regarded such an expedition as a dissipation of forces. Influenced by the failure of the recent bombardment, he finally gave in. Thus on the evening of 3 May 1855, a flotilla of fifty-six ships, with over 7,000 French and 2,500 British troops on board, weighed anchor and proceeded north-east towards Theodosia and Kertch.

The expedition soon ended in a fiasco due to a new technical invention which had just been introduced in the Allied armies in the Crimea – the telegraph. On 25 April a telegraph line had been opened between Varna and Balaklava, thus linking the theatre of war directly with Paris and London. Napoleon had just returned from his state visit to London and Windsor, where, as described earlier, a general plan of campaign had been concocted, which aimed at breaking the deadlock before Sevastopol by sending two armies to Simferopol reinforced by fresh troops from the camp at Constantinople. He wired the outlines of the plan to Canrobert. Raglan, however, received no official communication, and was only informed by private letter.[19]

In the early hours of the morning of 4 May, Canrobert received another telegram. Its wording was peremptory:

The moment has come to get out of the situation in which you find yourself. It is absolutely necessary to take the offensive. As soon as the corps of reserve [from Constantinople] has joined you, muster up all your troops and do not lose a single day [ne perdez pas un jour]. I regret not being able to come in person to the Crimea.[20]

Together with the earlier message to collect all available ships and bring reinforcements over from Constantinople, Canrobert thought he had received unequivocal orders. He immediately sent a despatch boat to the flotilla which had almost reached its destination, telling the French commander to return at once. The British commander had no choice but to do likewise. The anger and disgust on the British side knew no bounds. Relations between the two sides, already very strained, almost reached breaking point. Raglan, usually suave in his manners, refused point-blank to prepare the diversionary movement to Simferopol as he had received no orders.

Relations between the two Allies improved, however, as soon as Canrobert, tired of the strain that the burden as Commander-in-Chief of the French forces exerted upon him, asked the Emperor to relieve him of his post. Pélissier took over command on 17 May. The latter had quite different notions of obedience, and, since Raglan had still received no definite orders to execute the new plan of campaign, he went on with the siege and, in order to placate his British counterpart, agreed to send a new expedition to Kertch.

The details were agreed upon at an Allied council of war in which Omer Pasha took part. The flotilla and the landing party were strengthened because it was felt possible that the Russians were now expecting a fresh expedition. In fact, the Russians at that time had about 9,000 troops stationed in the east of the Crimea between Theodosia and Kertch, but they had not been reinforced. The Allied troops were made up of 7,000 French, 3,000 British and 5,000 Turks. They embarked on sixty ships and put to sea on 22 May. Two days later, Kertch and Yenikaleh at the entrance to the Sea of Azov were taken without resistance, the Russian troops fleeing from their positions after having destroyed them. Over the following days, Allied vessels entered the Sea of Azov, gave chase to Russian ships and bombarded several places along the coast like Taganrog and Yeisk. Besides destroying ships, government storehouses and port installations, the Allies set fire to many civilian buildings. As on the Finnish coast the previous year, the captains of British ships especially were not particularly fussy about distinguishing between military and non-military objects. Admiral Lyons was proud to claim the destruction of 250 vessels in the ports, along with vast quantities of grain, flour and fodder.[21]

To describe the result of the expedition to Kertch as a huge success, as British historians invariably do to this day, is unwarranted. Andrew Lambert's claim in 1990, that 'as military operations, the capture of Kertch and the subsequent control of the Sea of Azov rank among the finest achievements of the war', is certainly an exaggeration. His further judgement, that 'it was the decisive blow of 1855, leading to ... the fall of Sevastopol', is even wider of the mark.[22]

The French naval historian Claude Farrère put things in perspective when he wrote in 1934 that the expedition was 'a marginal affair'. This tallies with the judgement of Totleben, who must have had more accurate information about the supply situation of the troops in Sevastopol, and who concluded that 'the entry of the enemy fleet into the Sea of Azov did not impose on our Crimean army any shortages in the supply of food'. On the other hand the psychological effect of the Kertch expedition was certainly of some importance: it boosted the morale of the Allied troops before Sevastopol and especially of the public and the government in Britain.

Some of the ships of the Allied flotilla were dispatched to the Circassian coast of the Black Sea in order to cope with the Russian strongholds there, Sudjuk Kaleh and Anapa. They found the places deserted. The expedition was over by 15 June. Yenikaleh was left in the hands of the Turkish division, with a regiment each of British and French attached to it. Nothing of importance happened in the area for the rest of the war.

The siege of Sevastopol – the last stage, June–August 1855

At the same time as the Kertch expedition set out, the Allies scored two other minor successes in front of Sevastopol. French troops from the corps of observation attacked Russian outposts at the village of Tchorgun. The Russians had by then evacuated the Fedukhin heights and the Turkish redoubts which they had taken in October 1854 during the Battle of Balaklava. French cavalry now occupied the heights, while the newly arrived Sardinian troops were deployed on their right, with Gasfort Hill as their main stronghold.

The new French Commander-in-Chief, General Pélissier, had infused his officers and troops with a fresh spirit of determination. He was also on good terms with Lord Raglan. Ignoring positive orders from Paris to invest the city of Sevastopol completely and to get moving to Simferopol, he doggedly stood to his plan that the siege in its present circumference was to be kept up, but with redoubled vigour. He had by now enough human resources at his disposal: with reinforcements from Constantinople, the Sardinians (17,000) arriving from 8 May, the bulk of Omer Pasha's troops (55,000, including units left at Eupatoria and Yenikaleh) now stationed around Sevastopol, and with the British strength having been brought up to 32,000, the Allies now totalled 224,000 men, of whom 120,000 were French. In the sector of the 'old siege', on the French left, the Russians had dug out and occupied counter-approaches in front of the Quarantine and Central bastions. Pélissier had them attacked on 22 and 23 May. In spite of fierce Russian resistance, the trenches were taken by the French, who thus tightened the ring around the Russians in that sector. The losses on both sides – 3,000 Russians, 1,500 French – are an indication of the tenacity and ferocity which characterized the following three months.

Pélissier's main objective, however, lay in the sector of the 'new siege', with the Malakhov bastion the central point. First, the outposts in front of it and on its left flank, newly built and fortified by the Russians (the two

FIGURE 14 *The Valley of the Shadow of Death. Photo by Roger Fenton.*

redoubts and the lunette on the *Mamelon vert*), had to be taken. Lord Raglan, himself eager to finish with the siege and likewise averse to the French Emperor's strategic ideas, readily fell in with Pélissier's plan and assumed responsibility for a British attack on the 'Quarries', a Russian outpost in front of the Great Redan.

The opening of a new all-out bombardment – the third – was scheduled for 6 June. When, on 5 June, Pélissier received an order from Paris, enjoining him not to persist in the siege 'before having invested the place' and to consult with Lord Raglan and Omer Pasha 'in order to take the offensive, be it by the Tchernaya or against Simferopol',[23] he simply put it in his pocket and feigned the deficiency of the telegraph when answering it three days later. Thus, unperturbed by the possible wrath of his Emperor, Pélissier had the bombardment started on 6 June in the afternoon. The aim was a limited one: to destroy the three outposts and occupy the *Mamelon vert*. Along the sector of the 'new siege' and well into the sector of the 'old siege', the artillery fire was kept up without respite for at least twenty-four hours, until the afternoon of 7 June. The Russians did not show their habitual dexterity in repairing the damage overnight this time. At six o'clock in the evening the two redoubts on the Russian left wing were completely reduced to ruins. The Kamchatka lunette was in similar shape, and the outworks of the Quarries had been demolished by the British gunners.

At this moment the signal for an assault was given. Those attacking the two redoubts had about 500 metres to cross, those attacking the lunette a little less. Both groups managed, despite heavy losses, to reach the outworks and get a footing in them. On the *Mamelon vert*, the French Turcos and Zouaves defied their orders and pursued the Russians fleeing towards the Malakhov. There they came under the fire of the Russian garrison, and many of them having jumped into the moat, two metres deep, in front of the bastion, were helplessly trapped for want of ladders. The French panicked and were driven back by the Russians, who even managed briefly to regain Kamchatka lunette until it was retaken by French reinforcements.

The French were now masters of the two redoubts as well as of the *Mamelon vert*. The British likewise were successful in occupying the Quarries. The Allies had thus gained valuable positions from which to launch their assault on the strongholds of the Malakhov and the Great Redan. The captured works were soon converted into batteries against the Russian defences. The losses, though, were appalling: 5,500 dead and wounded on the French side, 700 on the British, and over 6,000 on the Russian side. Yet the end of the carnage was not in sight.

The Allies had, in front of the Korabelnaya suburb, wrung from the Russians some ground which brought them nearer to the enemy glacis. Pélissier wanted to top this preliminary success with a final one – the assault on the Malakhov. At an Allied council on 16 June he fixed the following day for a fresh bombardment and the day after that – 18 June – for an assault on the Malakhov, the adjacent bastions and the Great Redan. Lord Raglan,

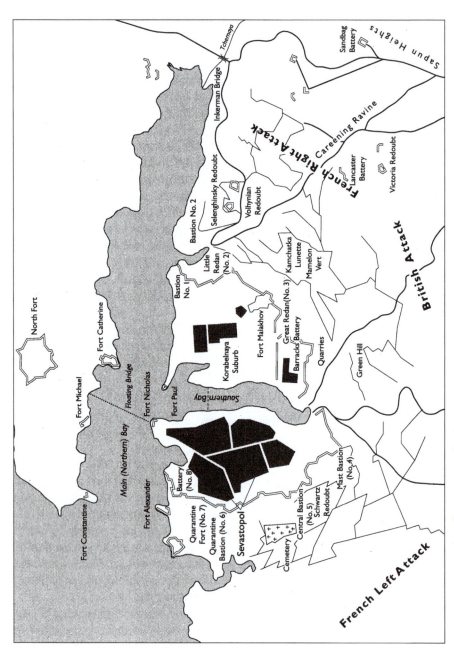

MAP 7 *Sevastopol in the summer of 1855.*

who was by now a dying man and therefore had no stomach to remonstrate, agreed.

The assault ended in a complete failure, the only one for the Allies. Nearly everything went wrong on their side, but Pélissier himself committed several blunders. There is, first of all, the haste and impatience with which he prepared the next stroke after his relative success of the third bombardment. He deliberately chose 18 June for the assault as it was the 40th anniversary of the Battle of Waterloo, for which he wanted to take revenge. He may have secretly hoped that victory would bring him the baton of a Field Marshal.

At the council of 16 June several officers tried to dissuade him from the attack because the distance the assault troops had to cover still seemed too great. Pélissier would not hear of it. He committed a more serious blunder by transferring General Bosquet, who was one of the officers warning him of the uncertain prospect of the assault, to the corps of observation at the Tchernaya. Bosquet knew almost every inch of the ground on which the attack was to be launched, whereas his replacement, General Auguste M. E. Regnault de Saint-Jean d'Angély, had only recently arrived in the Crimea at the head of the Imperial Guard. Of the topography of the assault sector he knew nothing. Perhaps Pélissier wanted to curry favour with the Emperor by letting the general of the Imperial Guard share in the honour of the expected success. Whatever the reason, Bosquet, an independent character who was popular with his soldiers and who had reaped success after success – at the Alma, at Inkerman and at the recent bombardment – was taken from the front line.

A final flaw in the preparation of the assault was that the preliminary bombardment was to stop in the evening of the first day and not recommence until the very beginning of the assault, which was fixed for 3 am on 18 June. Pélissier should have known his counterpart, Totleben, well enough to realize that he would leave no stone unturned to repair the damage done to his bastions and batteries post-haste. Instead, an almost complete lull of several hours was given to the Russians to do what they had always done so ingeniously – put up new defence walls, replace the guns put out of action by new ones, and so on. After the bombardment the Russians expected an assault and they had ample time to prepare themselves for it. They had always been clever enough not to mass too many troops in the exposed bastions so as not to incur excessive casualties from a bombardment. They kept their reinforcements at a short, but safe, distance. They had also concentrated plenty of field guns which could be easily moved to danger-points. These could fire at wider angles than the siege guns in their embrasures, and they were especially effective in showering assault columns with case-shot. Another precautionary measure by the Russians was the completion of a second bridge across the Southern Bay over which quick reinforcements could be moved from the town centre to the suburb.

A final blunder committed by Pélissier was that the reserve – the Imperial Guard – was placed too far away from the scene of action: 1,700 metres.

As arranged, the bombardment – the fourth – began at dawn on 17 June along the whole line of circumvallation. The Russians replied at once with their guns, but were slowly silenced one by one due to the superiority of the Allies. Pélissier was ebullient and thought he could go ahead with the assault.

The plan was that three French divisions should rush forward at a signal given personally by Pélissier at 3 o'clock in the morning. The division on the right had the Point Battery and the Little Redan (Nos 1 and 2 according to the Russian counting) as their objectives and had to cover a distance of some 750 metres. The soldiers of the centre division had to leap only 300 metres across open ground and then overrun the outworks on the left hand (as seen from the Russian side) of the Malakhov and climb up the bastion. The division on the left had to tackle the right flank of the Malakhov and also occupy the Gervais battery on the right of the *kurgan* (hill). Further to their left the British were to advance towards the Great Redan (300 metres ahead of their outer trenches), but only after the French had captured the Malakhov and planted the tricolour on it.

The assault started in confusion, developed in confusion and ended in a complete defeat. First of all, the Russians were everywhere on the alert, and there was no element of surprise. Things on the Allied side went wrong from the start for reasons similar to those that afflicted the Russian deployment at the Battle of Inkerman. The French division on the right began its assault about a quarter of an hour before 3 am because its commander mistook the firing of a rocket for Pélissier's signal. No sooner had the soldiers covered 200 or 300 metres than they received a shower of Russian fire in which the warships riding at anchor in the Careening Bay joined. The division immediately retired in disorder. The centre division fared no better. According to eyewitnesses, Pélissier gave his signal late, but even then the division was not ready to press ahead, as it had lost its way during the night and had not reached its forward trenches in time. When it belatedly moved to its target it was hit by the fire of the Russians who were awaiting it. The division to its right was somewhat more successful. The Gervais battery was taken and some French even reached the Malakhov; however, the Russian commanding general there had ordered reserves in time and repelled the attackers. The survivors fled back to their trenches. Raglan's troops, too, joined the fray in confusion, and, although they came near the Great Redan, they were driven back. At 8.30 in the morning, Pélissier at last sounded the general retreat.

The losses of the Allies had never been so heavy as on this occasion. The French lost about 3,600 men, 1,600 of them killed; the figure does not seem very reliable, as this would leave 2,000 men wounded, a very low figure compared with the number of dead. The British had 1,500 out of action. Totleben puts the losses of the Russians at 1,500 on 18 June and 4,000 men dead and wounded during the preceding bombardment.

It seems that Napoleon had been right when he telegraphed Pélissier, in a tardy reaction to the bombardment of 6 June, 'that a ranged battle which might have decided the fate of the Crimea would not have cost me more'.

And he added, 'I persist therefore in my order that you make every effort to take the field resolutely.'[24] After hearing the details of the failure of 18 June, he was disgusted and ordered Vaillant, his Minister of War, to have Pélissier replaced by Niel. Vaillant, knowing that his master's wrath would soon die down, had the order sent by ordinary mail instead of by telegraph, and then intercepted it when the Emperor had calmed down. Pélissier did not shoulder responsibility for the debacle, but placed the blame on General Mayran, commander of the division on the right wing, and on General Jean L. A. Brunet in the centre – both of whom had died in action.

Although the Russians had, on 18 June, successfully braved the onslaught of the Allies, their forces in terms of men and material were beginning to wear thin. On the day of the bombardment in which the Allies hurled 72,000 rounds into the Russian positions, the Russians could reply with only 19,000 rounds, that is, a ratio of almost 4:1 in favour of the Allies. Also, the daily losses in men during those summer months were clearly to the disadvantage of the Russians: the French were losing 200 men, the Russians 300 to 400 per day during May and June, and, beginning with the bombardment of 17 August, 1,000 – an appalling rate which the world would only get used to fifty years later in the trenches of the Great War. On both sides there was also a loss in leadership: on 28 June, Lord Raglan died from an attack of cholera, which had made its reappearance in the Allied camps; on 10 July, Admiral Nakhimov, the heroic organizer of the defence of Sevastopol, was hit by a bullet while inspecting the Malakhov and succumbed that same day.

The haemorrhage was more than made up by the reinforcements that both sides were pouring into the Crimea. Since the month of June the French had been receiving new recruits at a rate of 2,000 per day. Late in July, two Russian divisions, the 4th and 5th, arrived in the Crimea, although worn out by the long march, adding another 22,000 men to Gorchakov's army, and 13,000 militia arrived a few days later.

The simultaneous arrival of a special officer, Baron Pavel Alexandrovich Vrevsky, from St Petersburg at Gorchakov's headquarters was of particular significance. Vrevsky was Adjutant General to the Tsar and, like General Niel in the case of Emperor Napoleon, was the mouthpiece of the sovereign's will and intentions. The new Tsar, Alexander II, was goading his Commander-in-Chief into taking the offensive against the enemy, just as Nicholas had done before and as Napoleon was doing towards Pélissier. Alexander, in his letters and through Baron Vrevsky, did not peremptorily order Gorchakov to begin a battle, but he made it clear to him that he was expecting just that of him. Thus, in his letter of 1 August, he urged on Gorchakov 'the necessity to do something decisive in order to bring this frightful massacre to a close'.[25] To relieve his conscience, and to place responsibility on several shoulders, the Tsar concluded that Gorchakov should convene a military council.

On receipt of that letter, Gorchakov acted as his master had recommended, and, after informing his generals, the military council met on 10 August. Vrevsky was present. The majority was in favour of an offensive, but

General Osten-Sacken, with three other generals, voted against it. He deployed telling figures in favour of his position: between the beginning of the siege and 1 December 1854 the Russian army had lost 5,000 men, and from that day to 28 July 1855 another 48,023, plus 12,000 casualties at the Battle of Inkerman. Losses due to illness were not included in these figures. Osten-Sacken concluded that the south side of Sevastopol should be evacuated.[26]

Although Gorchakov was relieved that the decision for an attack was taken collectively, he regarded it with great misgiving. He knew that the Russians at Sevastopol were now, in contrast to November 1854 before the Battle of Inkerman, outnumbered by the Allies. The decision was really a frivolous one, taken first and foremost in order to satisfy the Tsar and not to reach a specific military target such as the annihilation of the British camp at Balaklava or the expulsion of the Allies from the Crimea.

The offensive was to be launched against the Fedukhin heights, which the Russians had occupied during the Battle of Balaklava, but given up in May 1855, and which were now held by French units amounting to 18,000 men, and against Gasfort Hill, where 9,000 Sardinians had entrenched themselves. Against these 27,000 men, who could, however, be strengthened by other parts of the Allied army of observation, Gorchakov concentrated an army consisting of two wings of almost equal strength: the right wing was formed of the 7th and 12th Infantry Divisions (15,000 men) under the command of General Nikolai A. Read; the left wing of the 17th and 6th Infantry Divisions (also 15,000 men) under General Pavel P. Liprandi. Behind them, two reserve divisions (the 5th and the 4th, 20,000 men altogether) were posted. Read's men were to cross the Tchernaya river, and a water canal running parallel to it, and then storm the French positions. Liprandi's troops were to clear Telegraph Hill and Gasfort Hill of the Sardinians. The plan also envisaged, though imprecisely, a sortie of 20,000 men from Sevastopol against the French at Kamiesh and possibly also actions against Balaklava.

These strategic dispositions looked sound on paper, but their tactical execution was marred by incompetence, lack of coordination and obscure orders. Gorchakov had reserved to himself the decision, to be made after the opening of the battle, as to where to concentrate the main effort – whether against the Fedukhin heights or Gasfort Hill. His generals were told to approach the Tchernaya, overrun the first Allied positions there, that is, the Traktir bridge across the river and Telegraph Hill in front of Gasfort Hill, and then halt and await his express orders. Halting the troops and waiting for new orders was an extremely dangerous tactic, as it was certain that the enemy would not stay idle while the Russians pondered their next move.

During the night of 15–16 August the Russian troops came down from the Mackenzie heights, and took up their positions along the Tchernaya and in front of Telegraph Hill and the village of Tchorgun. At dawn their guns opened fire on the French and Sardinian positions. Both the French and the Sardinians had been well aware of the Russian movements and had therefore taken precautionary measures. Liprandi's troops easily took Telegraph Hill, and therefore Gorchakov, who was with Liprandi, decided to concentrate his main thrust towards the Sardinian sector. He sent an aide to Read with the curious order 'to begin the thing' (*načinat' delo*).[27] Read interpreted this not as meaning that he should intensify his cannonade, but that he should begin the attack. The aide, asked whether he – Read – was right in doing so, could not clarify 'the thing' as he did not know himself what the order really meant.

The execution of this order – a typical expression of the Russian officers' blind obedience and inability to decide the right thing on the spot – was bound to court disaster. The preliminary firing of the Russian guns had achieved almost nothing because the distance was too great. The only sensible thing would have been to draw the guns closer to the enemy lines and begin an effective cannonade. Instead, Read sent part of his 12th Division across the river and ordered them to climb up the Fedukhin heights, where they came under fire from the French and suffered heavy losses. The 7th Division further to the right, ordered by Read 'to begin the thing' (Read had automatically passed on Gorchakov's ambiguous order), also moved across the river without adequate artillery support and likewise came under well-aimed fire from the French positions.

Liprandi, on hearing the musketry fire on his right wing, decided to change his original disposition and sent part of the 17th Division along the Tchernaya to help in taking the Fedukhin heights. On their march to the right they were an easy target for the French guns up the hill. While both of Read's divisions had to retreat, he was given the 5th Reserve Division in order to renew the senseless assault. Instead of waiting until it could be used in full strength, he sent one battalion after another into what was certain destruction. Although there was some hand-to-hand fighting with the French, the Russians on their right wing, where Gorchakov had by now concentrated his main effort, were in full retreat recrossing the river. General Read was killed, as was Baron Vrevsky who had been one of the most ardent supporters of the offensive. Gorchakov regrouped the remnants of his divisions across the river. Seeing that the Allies took no measures for a pursuit, he ordered a general retreat to the Mackenzie heights.

The Battle of the Tchernaya was almost a repetition of the Battle of Inkerman, the main difference being that this time the Allies had a clear superiority in numbers and far better fortified positions. In both cases it was the Tsar in faraway St Petersburg who pressed his Commander-in-Chief 'to do something' in terms of an offensive. In both cases the Commander-in-Chief went into battle against his own will. In both cases the strategic dispositions were good, but their actual execution was extraordinarily ill managed, leading to appalling casualties. The official Russian losses are given as 8,010 men and 260 officers, a horrible figure, especially if one considers the short duration of the actual fighting – no more than three hours. The French lost about 1,500, the Sardinians 250.

The actual losses of the Russians may well be rated above 10,000. At least this is the figure given by Field Marshal Paskevich, who received the news of the lost battle on his deathbed. In September 1855 he dictated a letter addressed to Gorchakov, but in fact never sent it to him. It is, though, a telling document, indicative of the spirit of the Russian military leadership, of the utter prostration of the leading Russian generals towards their master in St Petersburg, their careerism and their lack of independence in taking decisions. In his letter, Paskevich writes that he would not believe that the 'master' had ordered Gorchakov to invite certain defeat, knowing as he did that the fortifications on the Fedukhin heights were stronger than those at Sevastopol. Strangely for a Russian general of the nineteenth century, he went on to appeal to conscience. Conscience should have told Gorchakov, he wrote, that, even had a strict order to attack been given, the obvious impossibility of executing it should have prompted him to disobey and ask to be relieved. 'Then the blood of ten thousand men would not lie on your soul ... because you did not dare to state your opinion frankly.'[28] Never during his career, or for that matter in 1853 when Paskevich crossed the Danube against his own will, had the Field Marshal listened to his conscience. The letter is as much a self-indictment as it is an indictment of Prince Gorchakov.

The fall of Sevastopol and its consequences

After the unsuccessful bombardment of 18 June, Pélissier, flouting the Emperor's orders, still kept to his doctrine of continuing and stepping up the siege, until the human losses of the enemy would be so great and the destruction of his fortifications so vast that a new assault would bring about the desired end. The Allies now had more than 800 guns at their disposal. This meant that along one kilometre of the front 150 pieces were lined up so that they could pound their deadly charges on the city and suburb of Sevastopol. Never before in history had such massive firepower been concentrated in front of an enemy. The Allies could fire up to 75,000 rounds per day, and more, into the Russian defences.

Confronted by this enormous arsenal, the Russians had to economize. In August 1855 they could reply with only one round for every five or six of the Allies. The destruction wrought by the Allied guns was of course great. The Russians were hardly in a position, as they had been hitherto, to rebuild overnight the defence works that had been battered down during the day.

After the Battle of the Tchernaya, Pélissier did not grant a respite to the Russians. On 17 August the Allies opened a bombardment which lasted unabated, day and night, until 27 August. This extensive artillery preparation was one of the lessons he had learnt from the unsuccessful assault of 18 June. Another was that the trenches had to be pushed nearer the Russian bastions so that the distance the infantry had to cover on leaving the trenches could be decisively shortened. In the first days of September the French trenches had approached the Central Bastion and the Mast Bastion in the city by 70 and 50 metres respectively. In front of the Korabelnaya the distances were even shorter: 40 metres in front of the Little Redan and 25 metres in front of the Malakhov.

The Russians, too, made efforts to improve their defences. Underneath the Malakhov and elsewhere they were digging tunnels which were filled with explosives, so that in case of being overrun they could be ignited and the bastions blown up. On 27 August a floating bridge across the main bay to the northern side was finished. It was built of timber hauled in from southern Russia a feat testifying to the logistical and engineering capabilities of the Russians. Its main purpose was not to enable more supplies and reinforcements to enter the fortress, but to allow Gorchakov to order a sudden evacuation rather than surrender.

At an Allied war council on 3 September it was decided to renew the bombardment (the sixth) on 5 September, and maintain it unabated for three days and nights, and then, on 8 September, launch the final assault. The bombardment should take place along the whole circumference of the siege line, with the assault launched on both sectors of the 'old' and 'new siege'. The Malakhov should be stormed first, and, after the tricolour was planted there, the other bastions should be stormed, the Great Redan again being the only one reserved for the British. Bosquet, who had been allowed to return to the siege, was to be in charge of the assault on the Korabelnaya. The division of General Marie MacMahon, who had recently arrived from Algeria, was singled out for taking the Malakhov.

The bombardment was, according to the testimony of Gorchakov himself, 'infernal'. The Allied tactics were to stop it every now and then for a short time in order to lure the Russians out of their shelters, since a lull in the firing would make them expect an immediate assault which they would have to repel. The bombardment would then be reopened, causing heavy casualties among the Russian ranks. This proved successful, the Russians losing more than 7,500 men during these three days alone. The degree of destruction which the Allied bombardments effected is proved by Russian sources, which say that, out of the 2,000 houses of Sevastopol, only fourteen were intact at the beginning of September 1855.

The assault on the Malakhov on 8 September was fixed for midday. This was a clever move, as this was the time when the Russians least expected an attack (attacks were usually launched at dawn or at dusk) and when the gun crews in the bastions were exchanged or sent to draw their rations. Another means of surprise were the frequent false alarms caused by the ceasing of the Allied bombardment which the Russians were no longer taking seriously. This is what actually happened on the morning of 8 September. The Allied fire was stepped down decisively for several hours but ignored by the Russians, who, on the Malakhov, retired for their meals.

At noon the Zouaves of MacMahon's division jumped from their trenches and within seconds covered the short distance to the ditch in front of the Malakhov, climbed up the parapet and reached the embrasures. Most of the Russian gunners there were stabbed to death and the soldiers in their shelters and dugouts taken by surprise. The tricolour was soon hoisted, giving the signal for the assaults against the other bastions. Inside the Malakhov the French soldiers, being instantly reinforced, were able to hold their own in the outer part of the bastion. The Russians, however, were able to reorganize themselves behind the first traverse (barricade).

It was in this difficult situation that General MacMahon was asked by a British liaison officer whether he would be able to hold fast to his position. He is reputed to have given the reply that has since become famous: 'Tell your general that I am here and that I shall stay here' (que j'y suis, et que j'y reste).[29] As already noted, the possession of the Malakhov was of decisive importance, as it dominated the Korabelnaya and part of the main bay, and as the neighbouring bastions – the Great Redan and the Little Redan – could be taken from the rear.

The Allied assaults on these bastions and all the others in the new and old siege sectors – a dozen altogether – proved unsuccessful. The British, whose force numbered about 11,000 men, tried three attacks against the Great Redan which was defended by 7,500 Russians, but were three times repulsed. The same happened to the French: as soon as they were inside any of the other bastions they were dislodged by the Russians.

There are probably several reasons why the Malakhov remained in the hands of the French. First, the surprise of the very first assault was complete; in all other bastions the Russians had time to rally their forces. Second, the Malakhov, in contrast to the other bastions, had several barricades inside which were of course supposed to act as additional obstacles to the attackers once they had managed to enter the bastion; but they could also act as a defensive wall for the intruders. Third, the bastion had been constructed in a closed form, so that it was difficult to reconquer and reinforce once it was in the hands of the enemy.

Thus, although several fierce counter-attacks were made by the Russians, the French occupiers were able to hold their own. They were, however, greatly agitated by rumours that the bastion would be blown up by igniting the powder in the mines beneath. When they found out that 260 Russians were still working in the mines they managed to take them all prisoner and found out that the powder had not yet been put in place.

General Gorchakov, who was on the north side when the assault had begun, had gone over in the afternoon to inspect the situation of the Malakhov. Judging a counter-attack useless, he issued, after 5 pm, the order for a general retreat from the Korabelnaya and the south side. The movement was carried out mostly across the floating bridge. It lasted all night and was completed the following morning. Sappers were the last to leave; they set fire to the many powder magazines, of which at least thirty-five were blown up at intervals. On 9 September the town was burning on all sides and the Allies dared not enter it for fear of explosions. Only on 12 September did they officially take possession of the ruins of Sevastopol.

The assault of 8 September took a heavy toll in human lives for both sides. According to Totleben, the Russians lost 12,913 men, the vast majority in the Korabelnaya. Allied casualties amounted to 10,040, three-quarters of them French, one-quarter British.

In Paris, where the news of the conquest of the south side of Sevastopol arrived on 9 September, Napoleon's first reaction was to renew his urgent recommendations to Pélissier to move into the interior of Crimea and make the Russians evacuate the whole peninsula. The General, however, thought himself to be the best judge of the state in which his army found itself. He dared not even make a move to the north side of Sevastopol in order to dislodge Gorchakov's army; thus during the following weeks nothing of importance happened in that theatre of war. Napoleon was conscious that the honour of the French nation was satisfied by the conquest of Sevastopol. Public opinion in France was averse to a continuation of the war on a grand scale in that remote corner of Europe. Prince Albert was right when he summed up the general feeling in France at the end of October 1855: 'Si la France doit continuer la guerre à grands sacrifices, il lui faut des objets plus nationaux, plus Francçais: Poland, Italy, the left bank of the Rhine, etc.'[30] When Napoleon sounded out the British government soon after the fall of Sevastopol as to whether they were ready to work with him at the future peace congress for the re-establishment of the kingdom of Poland, London replied on 22 September that it was not. Napoleon then lost all interest in any future campaign in the Crimea.[31]

The state of mind in Britain regarding the continuation of the war against Russia was quite different from that in France. *The Times*, which at the time was as good a barometer of public opinion as one can think of, called the conquest of Sevastopol 'a preliminary operation'.[32] Palmerston emphasized that 'Russia was not yet half beaten "enough".' The generals on the spot and the War Office in London were eager to obliterate the memory of the mismanagement of the war in the preceding winter and demonstrate that they were quite up to the task of waging a new winter campaign and a campaign in 1856. Efforts to recruit foreign legions were in full swing and the dockyards were bustling with activity building a formidable new armada for operations in the Baltic – against Kronstadt, the 'Sevastopol of the North' – in 1856. The Queen gave vent to the general feeling in Britain when she exclaimed that 'she cannot bear the thought that "the failure on the Redan" should be our last *fait d'Armes*'.[33]

In France, the yearning for peace was so widespread after the French *fait d'armes* at the Malakhov that Napoleon, in view of the increasing divergence of peace aims between London and Paris, could not but take heed of it. In a letter he sent to Queen Victoria on 22 November 1855 he laid before her some sober facts and figures:

> Your Majesty has in the East, I think, 50,000 men and 10,000 horses. As to myself I have 200,000 men and 34,000 horses. Your Majesty has an immense fleet in the Black Sea as well as in the Baltic; I, too, have an imposing one, though of smaller size. Well then, in spite of this formidable war machinery it is evident to everybody that although we can cause her much harm we cannot tame her with our forces alone.[34]

Palmerston, for whose consumption just as much as for the Queen's this letter was meant, might very well fly into a rage about this undisguised announcement that France was backing out of the war; he might threaten the Emperor that Britain would go it alone rather than make a bad peace – but he could not ignore facts. There followed many angry exchanges between London and Paris. France was working out an ultimatum with Austria, which the latter was prepared to present to St Petersburg, with the threat of entering the war unless it was accepted unconditionally. Palmerston could rave as much as he liked at this new development, but his threat of Britain carrying on the war on her own was obviously a hollow one. Cowley, the British ambassador in Paris, who had to deliver all these angry despatches from his government, hit upon the idea of convening a military council in Paris where the question of what should be done about preparing a campaign for 1856 should be discussed. This move reduced the tension between London and Paris. It will be dealt with in Chapter 16.

There were two military events after the fall of Sevastopol that were of some importance for the rest of the war: the seizure of the fortress of Kinburn by the Allies on 17 October; and the capture of the fortress of Kars on 26 November 1855. As the latter will be dealt with in the chapter on the Caucasus, it is only necessary to say a few words about the former event.

The plan to bombard Kinburn was of French, not British, origin, although it was mainly an amphibious undertaking on the lines of the former expedition to Kertch and the Sea of Azov. Kinburn was a fort on a long narrow sand spit at the mouth of the Dnieper Liman (gulf) which is the common estuary of the rivers Dnieper and Bug. Farther upstream on the Dnieper is the important town and harbour of Kherson, and upstream on the Bug is Nikolaev, where most of the Black Sea fleet was then built. Kinburn and Ochakov, lying opposite the estuary, were forts, partly stone-built, which were to protect the entrance to the gulf.

The choice of Kinburn as a target for a bombardment goes back to Admiral Bruat, who imagined that its seizure might offer the Allies either a suitable base for an operation in 1856 against Nikolaev or alternatively a pawn for the future peace negotiations. As a work of fortification, Kinburn was of mediocre dimensions and strength, and its garrison was far smaller than that of Kertch before its capture by the Allies in May. Napoleon was in favour of Bruat's idea because it at least offered a way out of the military inactivity in which his army in the Crimea found itself in September 1855. On the 26th, after the British government had fallen in with the idea, an order was telegraphed to Pélissier, who had by then been nominated Marshal of France, to occupy Kinburn.

At Sevastopol the Allies formed an expeditionary corps consisting of 4,000 French and 4,000 British soldiers, plus a 950-man naval brigade. As the expedition to Kertch had been under British command, the Kinburn force was to be under the command of the French General, Achille Bazaine. The combined fleet consisted of ten ships of the line (four of them French), seventeen frigates (six of them French) and a number of corvettes, mortar boats and other ancillary vessels. The force was to be joined en route by the three French ironclad ships, the 'floating batteries' which had just arrived at Sevastopol from France and were originally intended for the bombardment of that city.

On 14 October the armada assembled off Odessa and moved on towards Kinburn. On the following day the troops landed on the sand spit some 4–5 kilometres to the south-east of the fort, in order to cut it off from the interior. They then approached the fort and dug themselves in some 400 metres opposite the enemy ramparts. Meanwhile the ships had taken up their positions around the sand spit, so that the fort and the two batteries in front of it were literally encircled. The three floating batteries anchored nearest to the fort, some 800 to 1,000 metres away. Firing began on 17 October at 9 am.

The use of the ironclads proved a resounding success; together they hurled over 3,000 projectiles into the fort and in return received some seventy rounds. Those that hit the iron plates produced insignificant dents. Together with the fire from the other ships, the ironclads soon reduced the fort and its two batteries. In the afternoon they surrendered, and 1,400 men and forty officers were taken prisoner. The Russian losses were comparatively slight: forty-five dead and 130 wounded. The Allies lost two dead and thirty-two wounded. Fort Ochakov opposite the estuary, fearing the same fate as Fort Kinburn, was blown up by the Russians on the following day. Thus the two inland ports of Kherson and Nikolaev were now cut off from the Black Sea, just as the Sea of Azov had been five months earlier. The Allied troops remained in possession of Kinburn for the rest of the war.

Although British admirals of the time and later British historians thought the praise of the three French ironclads was exaggerated, they fully deserved it. They had clearly proved their invulnerability against enemy projectiles as far as their armoured parts were concerned. In any case, the British were so impressed that they hastened the construction of ironclads of their own, which were to be used in the campaign of 1856 against Kronstadt. In the following years there was sharp competition between Britain and France in perfecting this new weapon. The 17th of October 1855 was the birthday of the modern armoured ship.

Annotated bibliography

The Battle of the Alma

The Allied landing at Eupatoria and the Battle of the Alma are recounted in many books. The Alma takes a particularly prominent place in British historiography. Here is a selection: Tarle, *Krymskaja vojna*, vol. 2, pp. 95–119; Bestužev, *Krymskaja vojna*, pp. 84–93; Seaton, *Crimean War*, pp. 61–103; Rousset, *Guerre de Crimée*, vol. 1, pp. 179–231; Guillemin, *Guerre de Crimée*, pp. 53–62; Gouttman, *Guerre de Crimée*, pp. 277–302; Barker, *Vainglorious War*, pp. 48–115; Hibbert, *Raglan*, pp. 78–118; Peter Gibbs, *The Battle of the Alma* (Philadelphia and New York, 1963); Figes, *Crimea*, pp. 200–25; Fletcher and Ishchenko, *Crimean War*, pp. 71–93.

The siege of Sevastopol – the beginning

The classical account of the siege of Sevastopol is that by the chief Russian engineer, Eduard I. Totleben, *Opisanie oborony goroda Sevastopolja*, 2 vols in 3 parts (St Petersburg, 1863–74); vol. 1 has 2 parts, vol. 3 has 3 parts in 2 vols; the French translation is Eduard I. Totleben, *Défense de Sébastopol*, 2 vols in 3 parts (St Petersburg, 1863–74); the German translation is Eduard I. Totleben, *Die Vertheidigung von Sebastopol ...* 2 vols in 4 parts (Berlin 1864–72). On the scant intelligence information, cf. Stephen M. Harris, *British Military Intelligence in the Crimean War, 1854–1856* (Portland, OR, 1998). For the march of the Allied armies south to Sevastopol, their entrenchment, the Russian defence works and the first bombardment of the place on 17 October 1853, see Tarle, *Krymskaja vojna*, vol. 2, pp. 120–55; Bestužev, *Krymskaja vojna*, pp. 93–103; Seaton, *Crimean War*, pp. 104–37; Rousset, *Guerre de Crimée*, vol. 1, pp. 62–76; Guillemin, *Guerre de Crimée*, pp. 62–76; Gouttman, *Guerre de Crimée*, pp. 302–23; Barker, *Vainglorious War*, pp. 116–49; Figes, *Crimea*, pp. 222–40. The most recent account of the siege is by Anthony Dawson, *The Siege of Sevastopol 1854–1855* (Haverton, 2017).

The Battle of Balaklava

Apart from contemporary accounts and books of the nineteenth century, the fullest treatment of Balaklava, with an analysis of the characters of Lords Lucan and Cardigan, is by Cecil Woodham-Smith, *The Reason Why* (London, 1953). See also John Selby, *Balaclava: Gentlemen's Battle* (New York, 1970), pp. 107–73; Barker, *Vainglorious War*, pp. 150–74; Rousset, *Guerre de Crimée*, vol. 1, pp. 323–43; Gouttman, *Guerre de Crimée*, pp. 327–43; Tarle, *Krymskaja vojna*, vol. 2, pp. 156–64; Seaton, *Crimean War*, pp. 138–56; Vladimir Šavšin, *Balaklava* (Simferopol, 1994), pp. 66–86. The newest accounts are by Ian Fletcher and Natalia Ishchenko, *The Battle of the Alma 1854: First Blood to the Allies in the Crimea* (Barnsley, 2008); Čennyk, *Krymskaja kampanija*, book 4 (also on the Battle of Inkerman; see above, Chapter 6). Inge and Dieter Wernet, two specialists on the history of fortifications, have produced a great book on the siege of Sevastopol, printed on glossy paper, with 450 superbly reproduced illustrations and plans: *Die Belagerung von Sevastopol 1854–1855* (Aix-la-Chapelle, 2017). For the Battle of Balaklava, cf. Inge and Dieter Wernet, *Belagerung*, pp. 126–35.

The Battle of Inkerman

Apart from numerous eyewitness and nineteenth-century accounts, there is no modern study of the battle. One has therefore to rely on the general studies of the war. See, for the Russian side, Tarle, *Krymskaja vojna*, vol. 2, pp. 165–92; Seaton, *Crimean War*, pp. 157–78; Curtiss, *Russia's Crimean War*, pp. 322–35. For the British side, see Barker, *Vainglorious War*, pp. 175–93; Patrick Mercer, *'Give Them a Volley and Charge!' The Battle of Inkermann [!]* (Staplehurst, 1998). For the French, see Rousset, *Guerre de Crimée*, vol. 1, pp. 344–92; Gouttman, *Guerre de Crimée*, pp. 343–53; Inge and Dieter Wernet, *Belagerung*, pp. 145–64; Figes, *Crimea*, pp. 254–72.

The November storm of 1854 and the Crimean winter of 1854–5

On the havoc the November hurricane wreaked on the Allies and on the rigours of the winter, see Barker, *Vainglorious War*, pp. 194–211, 225–6; Stanmore, *Sidney Herbert*, vol. 1., pp. 270–330 (gives the view from above and from London); Gouttman, *Guerre de Crimée*, pp. 362–74 (quotes from eyewitnesses); Guillemin, *Guerre de Crimée*, pp. 98–106 (concentrates on the French fleet). In general there is a spate of letters, eyewitness accounts and memoirs of officers, and sometimes also of privates, from all armies in the Crimea which would provide ample material for writing a history of the war as seen 'from below', but it has still to be produced. Cf. now Inge and Dieter Wernet, *Belagerung*, pp. 185–192.

On the supply problems for the British army, see Sweetman, *War and Administration*, pp. 41–76; John Sweetman, 'Military Transport in the Crimean War, 1854–1856', *English Historical Review* 88 (1973): 81–91; John Sweetman, 'Ad Hoc Support Services during the Crimean War, 1854–6: Temporary, Ill-Planned and Largely Unsuccessful', *Military Affairs* 52 (1988): 135–40; G. F. Chadwick, 'The Army Works Corps in the Crimea', *Journal of Transport History* 6 (1964): 129–41; Brian Cooke, *The Grand*

Crimean Central Railway: The Story of the Railway Built by the British at Balaklava during the Crimean War of 1854–56 (London, 1990, 2nd edn 1997).

On Roger Fenton, the first war photographer, there are a number of books, e.g. John Hannavy, *Roger Fenton of Crimble Hall* (London, 1975); *Roger Fenton: Photographer of the 1850s* (London, 1988) (this is a catalogue of a London exhibition in 1988); Lawrence James, *1854–56, Crimea: The War with Russia from Contemporary Photographs* (New York, 1981) (featuring photographs by Fenton, James Robertson and others). Taken from the extensive holding of Fenton's photographs in the Royal Collection, Sophie Gordon reproduces 250 photographs of the Crimean War (mostly portraying British officers), taken between March and June 1855: *Shadows of War: Roger Fenton's Photographs of the Crimea, 1855* (London, 2017). A new study of the pictorial history of the Crimean War, which not only includes photographs, but also artistic sketches, engravings, newspaper illustrations, is Ulrich Keller's *Ultimate Spectacle: A Visual History of the Crimean War* (Amsterdam, 2001). For a collection of essays about the Crimean War in literature, pictorial media and music, see Georg Maag, Wolfram Pyta and Martin Windisch (eds), *Der Krimkrieg als erster europäischer Medienkrieg* (Berlin, 2010). There are two monographs on the same subject: C. Dereli, *A War Culture in Action: A Study of the Crimean War Period* (Bern, 2003); Stefanie Markovits, *The Crimean War in the British Imagination* (Cambridge, 2009).

The articles of *The Times* war correspondent, William Howard Russell, were published under the title *The War*, 2 vols (London 1855–6). A later selection is provided by Nicolas Bentley (ed.), *Russell's Despatches from the Crimea, 1854–1856* (London, 1966). A new selection of *The Times* articles including some by unnamed correspondents from the Baltic, is provided by Andrew Lambert and Stephen Badsey, *The War Correspondents: The Crimean War* (London, 1994). The effect of the Crimean winter on British domestic policy is fully discussed in Conacher, *Aberdeen Coalition*. Olive Anderson has written a number of articles illuminating various domestic aspects of the war in Britain; they are collected in *A Liberal State at War: English Politics and Economics during the Crimean War* (London, 1967, repr. Aldershot, 1994).

There is no modern full-length study on the supply system of the French *Armee d'Orient*. One has to rely on the nineteenth-century literature and on scant remarks, e.g. in Gouttman, *Guerre de Crimée*, pp. 362–7; Guillemin, *Guerre de Crimée*, pp. 115–16, 119–24, 153–63. The same observation applies to the Russian supply system, although there is considerable information in Totleben, *Opisanie*. Cf. the remarks in Bestužev, *Krymskaja vojna*, pp. 11–12, 138, 160–3; Curtiss, *Russia's Crimean War*, pp. 337–41. There is a moving eyewitness account about everyday life in Sevastopol by Leo Tolstoy, *The Sebastopol Sketches*, transl. in English (Harmondsworth and New York, 1986).

The siege of Sevastopol – the second stage, February–May 1855

On the Battle of Eupatoria of 17 February 1855 and its consequences, see Tarle, *Krymskaja vojna*, vol. 2, pp. 305–14; Seaton, *Crimean War*, pp. 183–8; Rousset, *Guerre de Crimée*, vol. 2, pp. 47–53; Inge and Dieter Wernet, *Belagerung*, pp. 243–51. The siege war before Sevastopol in the early months of 1855, the fighting about the Mamelon vert and the second bombardment of 9 April 1855 are dealt with in Tarle, *Krymskaja vojna*, vol. 2, pp. 338–52; Rousset, *Guerre de Crimée*, vol. 2, pp. 55–86, 111–47; Barker, *Vainglorious War*, pp. 224–33; Inge and Dieter Wernet, *Belagerung*, pp. 251–89. The expedition to Kertch in May 1855 is passed over by Tarle, *Krymskaja vojna*, vol. 2. Bestužev, *Krymskaja vojna*, pp. 127–8, deals lightly with it. For the British side there is documentary evidence in Alfred C. Dewar (ed.), *Russian War, 1855. Black Sea: Official Correspondence* (London, 1945); cf. also Lambert, *Crimean War*, pp. 223–35; Rousset, *Guerre de Crimée*, vol. 2, pp. 156–65, 203–7; Treue, *Krimkrieg*, pp. 67–73; Battesti, *La marine*, vol. 1, pp. 139–43; Inge and Dieter Wernet, *Belagerung*, pp. 289–92, 295–301.

The siege of Sevastopol – the last stage, June–August 1855

The situation before Sevastopol from mid-May 1855 to the fourth bombardment on 17–18 June 1855 is dealt with by Tarle, *Krymskaja vojna*, pp. 345–403; Rousset, *Guerre de Crimée*, vol. 2, pp. 183–299; Gouttman, *Guerre de Crimée*, pp. 391–417; Barker, *Vainglorious War*, pp. 240–56; Inge and Dieter Wernet, *Belagerung*, pp. 302–15, 318–20, 330–55. For the battle on the Tchernaya on 16 August 1855, see Tarle, *Krymskaja vojna*, vol. 2, pp. 429–47; Seaton, *Crimean War*, pp. 194–208; Rousset, *Guerre de Crimée*, vol. 2, pp. 334–57; Inge and Dieter Wernet, *Belagerung*, pp. 320–30. The battle on the Tchernaya is passed over cursorily in English books.

The fall of Sevastopol and its consequences

The final bombardment and the capture of Sevastopol are discussed in Tarle, *Krymskaja vojna*, vol. 2, pp. 448–74; Seaton, *Crimean War*, pp. 208–18; Curtiss, *Russia's Crimean War*, pp. 445–59; Rousset, *Guerre de Crimée*, vol. 2, pp. 358–402; Gouttman, *Guerre de Crimée*, pp. 429–42; Guillemin, *Guerre de Crimée*, pp. 191–202; Barker, *Vainglorious War*, pp. 262–8; Figes, *Crimea*, pp. 373–97; Inge and Dieter Wernet, *Belagerung*, pp. 356–65.

The search for peace after the fall of Sevastopol is fully discussed in Baumgart, *Peace*. The German original is Winfried Baumgart, *Der Friede von Paris. Studien zum Verhältnis von Kriegführung, Politik und Friedensbewahrung* (Munich and Vienna, 1972).

The expedition to Kinburn is not mentioned in Russian historiography (Tarle, *Krymskaja vojna*; Bestužev, *Krymskaja vojna*). Curtiss, *Russia's Crimean War*, and Seaton, *Crimean War*, pass it over in silence since they obviously could not fall back on Russian literature. Even Rousset, *Guerre de Crimée*, vol. 2, pays scant attention to it (pp. 414–16). See Guillemin, *Guerre de Crimée*, pp. 203–9; Battesti, *La marine*, vol. 1, pp. 145–52; Lambert, *Crimean War*, pp. 255–62; Inge and Dieter Wernet, *Belagerung*, pp. 368–85. On the ironclads, see Treue, *Krimkrieg*, pp. 125–31; Basil Greenhall and Ann Giffard, *The British Assault on Finland, 1854–1855: A Forgotten Naval War* (London, 1988), pp. 301–6; G. A. Osbon, 'The First of the Ironclads: The Armoured Batteries of the 1850's', *Mariner's Mirror* 50 (1964): 189–98. Cf. also G. A. Osbon, 'The Crimean Gunboats', *Mariner's Mirror* 51 (1965): 103–16, 211–20; Inge and Dieter Wernet, *Belagerung*, pp. 371–4.

13

The campaigns in the Baltic, 1854 and 1855

Strictly speaking, calling the war of 1853–6 the Crimean War is a misnomer: there were a number of other theatres of war besides the Crimea where the belligerents met each other. The war on the Danube in 1853–4 has already been dealt with. Another area where the two Western powers came to grips with Russia was the Baltic in 1854 and 1855. It clearly shows that the Crimean War was not only related to the Eastern Question, but was also a contest between Britain and Russia about whether Russia was to be allowed to grow in power and press on her neighbours – Turkey in the south and south-east, Austria, Prussia and Germany in the south-west and west, and Sweden in the north-west. It was a typical contest of modern European history, between Britain trying to uphold a balance of power on the European continent and one of the European great powers trying to obtain a dominating position in Europe and, in the case of Russia, also in Asia. France's entry into the war had little or nothing to do with this general struggle for the European balance or for dominion in Europe; it went back to Napoleon's personal desire to establish himself in France after becoming Emperor and regain for France a position in Europe that had been damaged by the Eastern crisis of 1840–1 and the revolution of 1848.

In the eyes of both Britain and France, then, Russian power was to be curtailed in all areas where possible. Palmerston's words in the already cited memorandum of September 1855, that Britain's 'real object of the War' was 'to curb the aggressive ambition of Russia', were therefore one of the best descriptions of that war – at least from a British perspective. Palmerston went on, referring to Russia's threatening position in northern as well as in southern Europe:

> We went to war, not so much to keep the Sultan and his Mussulmen in Turkey, as to keep the Russians out of Turkey; but we have a strong interest also in keeping the Russians out of Norway and Sweden.

He regarded Sweden's entry into the coalition of the West as 'a part of a long line of circumvallation' around Russia.[1]

This attitude applies to the whole duration of the war. Weeks before the declaration of war, at the end of February 1854, a new squadron was hastily formed to meet Russia's diplomatic and military pressure in northern Europe. Strategic planning in that area in those months was vague and unfinished, since, obviously, attention was fixed on south-eastern Europe, the Turkish Straits and the Danube. Britain took the lead in sending a fleet to the Baltic; France acted in her wake. The sending of an expeditionary force was not under consideration at the outbreak of the war, since Britain had none and France was expediting the movement of her divisions to Turkey and then to the Crimea. France, however, had at her disposal a huge military camp at Boulogne where the French 'army of the north' had its headquarters. The camp provided a reservoir of forces which could, if need be, be quickly transferred to the Baltic.

What were the forces which Russia could muster in the north and in the Baltic? Ground forces in the St Petersburg military district totalled 80,000 men; the Sveaborg district, that is, the Finnish coastal areas, had the same number; and in the Dvina district, that is, in the Baltic provinces, another 40,000 men were stationed. Together with the forces of the garrisons, this was an army of 270,000 men.[2] Although the Western powers did not know the exact number, a landing on a grand scale was deemed out of the question. Efforts were therefore undertaken to lure Prussia and Sweden into the Western diplomatic and military front, but, as has been noted, Prussia under Frederick William IV remained staunchly neutral with a pro-Russian bias, and King Oscar of Sweden put his demands and guarantees so high – subsidies, support by Western troops, retrocession of Finland under Western guarantees, Austria's entry into the war – that these two powers, vital for a ground war against Russia, could not be counted upon during 1854.

Russia's sea forces, too, were formidable on paper, as discussed in Chapter 6. The Baltic fleet totalled 196 vessels, including twenty-five ships of the line, but there was not a single steamship among them. The training of the crews – as a meeting of Russian naval experts just before the war had revealed – was nil, although their number, 40,000, was high. Manoeuvring the ships in units was therefore impossible: the only sensible thing for the Baltic fleet to do on the approach of a Western squadron was to hide in its harbours. The best-protected ports were Kronstadt and Sveaborg, among the lesser ones were Reval, Åbo and Hangö. Apart from fortifications, these ports made use of another defensive instrument which was new at the time – sea mines. The Russian engineer, Boris S. Jakobi, had constructed them and hundreds were laid in the waters around Kronstadt and in the approaches to Sveaborg. They were of some nuisance value, but whenever a British vessel hit one of them it did not cause much damage.

On 11 March 1854 the first part of a British naval expedition left Spithead under the command of Vice-Admiral Sir Charles Napier. Another unit soon followed, so that the British squadron amounted to forty-four vessels with about 2,000 guns and a combined strength of 21,800 men. The remarkable thing about this armada was that, in contrast to the British Black Sea fleet, it consisted almost exclusively of screw- and paddle-driven steamers. Its mobility was therefore high. It soon became apparent – and Napier continually emphasized – that it had three basic weaknesses: the crews were badly or not at all trained; there were no good pilots to guide the ships through the dangerous waters of the Baltic; and the fleet lacked small craft with low draught, especially gunboats, which alone could enter the shallow coastal waters.

The first task of the British squadron was to make sure that no Russian ships would pass the Danish Sound in order to molest the British coast. This sort of fear is typical of moments such as the outbreak of war, when hysterical feelings have the upper hand over sober thinking. In view of the poor state of the Russian fleet, its entering the North Sea should have seemed impossible. On 20 March the British squadron anchored south of Copenhagen, surely a warning to Denmark not to pursue her pro-Russian bias. After the declaration of war, Napier, on the orders of Sir James Graham, declared a blockade of the Russian coasts. He was further instructed to reconnoitre the fortified places on the Russian coasts, especially to ascertain the condition of the fortress of Bomarsund on the Åland Islands and 'on no account to attack defenceless places and open towns'.[3]

During March and June 1854, units of the British squadron visited several fortified places: they bombarded Hangö twice, penetrated into the Gulf of Riga, occupied Libau on the coast of Courland and towed away two ships from the harbour of Reval. Along the Finnish coast in the Gulf of Bothnia, several coastal places were raided and shipyards and warehouses destroyed and burnt down. The reports of Rear-Admiral James Plumridge, in charge of the squadron that raided the Finnish coast, reveal that the instruction not to attack defenceless places was not taken very literally. Thus the town of Brahestad (Raahe) went up in flames on 30 May, and two days later it was the turn of Uleåborg (Oulu). Captain George Giffard, in charge of the raid on Uleåborg, recorded with some pride, 'Sent the armed boats of the squadron . . . to take, burn, or destroy . . . The fire from the immense quantities of pitch, tar and timber, could be seen for many miles around.'[4]

These raids were counter-productive in a number of ways. In very many cases, the goods destroyed were not contraband of war or war matériel, but goods bought by British merchants who up to the outbreak of the war were the main foreign traders in these regions. Moreover, these brutal bombardments produced a widespread anti-British feeling among the local Finnish population. There were also unfavourable comments in the neutral press in Prussia, Sweden and Denmark. Even *The Times* condemned the raids and thereby laid the ground for the angry feelings with which the fleet was received in Britain when it returned home at the end of 1854.

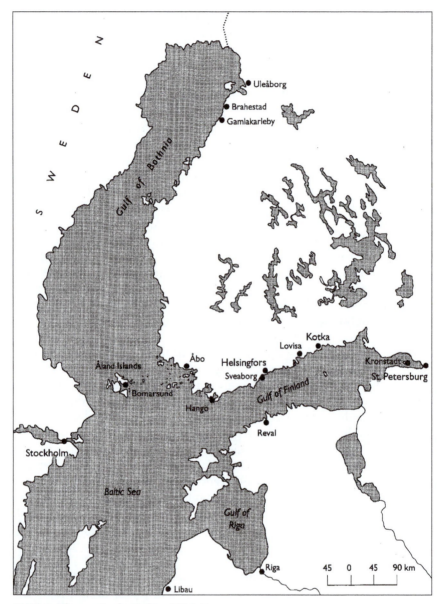

MAP 8 *The war in the Baltic, 1854–5.*

At the port of Gamlakarleby (Kokkola), Plumridge's men for once met a fate which they deserved. On entering the port on 7 June the two British boats were received with heavy fire and grapeshot from Russian infantry and Finnish militia. They were lucky to lose only fifty-two men; killed, wounded or missing. The conduct of the raids in the Gulf of Bothnia was an infamous episode in the history of the Royal Navy.

The effect of the blockade of the Russian Baltic coast in the campaign of 1854 was slight and unimportant. Unfortunately there are no statistics available. There was much blockade-running in which several neutral shipping companies and firms took part: American, Prussian, Belgian, Dutch and from the Hanse towns. Even British firms were involved. American and especially Belgian arms and ammunition and other contraband of war found their way through the Baltic to Russia, mostly by way of a thriving coastal trade which, because of the shallow waters, was out of reach of the heavy British ships.

There was, however, one operation of the Allies which met with success. More than a month after the British squadron had left for the Baltic, a French fleet, put together at Brest, departed for the same destination where it was to cooperate with the British. It consisted of twenty-six vessels, most of them sailing ships, with 2,500 men on board, and was under the command of Vice-Admiral Alexandre Ferdinand Parseval-Deschênes. On 12 June 1854 it joined the British fleet at Baresund at the entrance to the Gulf of Finland. Ten days later a combined fleet moved up to Kronstadt in order to inspect the place. The approach from the north was inaccessible because of shallow water. The southern approach was possible through a narrow and tortuous channel, but the huge complex was protected by at least eight forts with at least 1,000 guns. As no charts were available, the two admirals decided that the fortress was impregnable. After almost a month of cruising, charting and sounding, both fleets received orders from their governments to proceed to the Åland Islands and attack and occupy the fortress of Bomarsund there. A French expeditionary corps of 12,800 men under General Count Achille Baraguey d'Hilliers (the former ambassador to Constantinople) was on its way from Calais to assist in the operation.

The Åland Islands had been ceded to Russia by Sweden in 1809. On the main island in the north, the Russians began in 1829 to build a fortress at Bomarsund. It was obviously meant to exert pressure on Sweden and its capital Stockholm. By 1854 only one fifth of the fortifications were finished; of the fourteen planned defensive towers, only three had been built. The complex was garrisoned by 2,175 men commanded by Major-General Jakov A. Bodisko. By the time the British fleet appeared, the Åland Islands had already been cut off from assistance from the Russian mainland and on 8 August the French troops began to disembark at three different points, without meeting resistance. In comparison with the French force of some 11,000 men, the participation of a British detachment of 900 men was no more than symbolic. On 14 and 15 August the two outposts in the north of the main fortress surrendered, bringing the French siege troops and batteries within 800 metres of the citadel. On 15 August, thirteen ships of the line and frigates took up their positions along the coast so that Bomarsund was completely invested. There was no need for an assault: it was sufficient to rely on the effect of the gunfire. After a heavy bombardment the main fortress and the third fort surrendered.

Once Bomarsund was taken, the question of what to do with it arose. It was no use keeping it, as the sea between the islands and the Finnish mainland would freeze during the winter, allowing a Russian force, even with heavy guns, to cross it. A fresh attempt was therefore made to offer it to King Oscar of Sweden in order to lure him into the war against Russia,

THE RETURN FROM THE BALTIC!!

British Lion. "OH YES, I'LL COME BACK—BUT I MUST JUST LEAVE A CARD AT CRONSTADT FIRST!!!"

FIGURE 15 *Admiral Lord Napier returning home from the Baltic, November 1854. Punch 27 (1854), p. 117. University Library of Heidelberg, CC-BY-SA 3.0.*

but his other demands could not be met and he declined. The three forts and the citadel were completely destroyed by 2 September 1854, and the French expeditionary corps returned home as the winter season was approaching. After the Allied fleets had left the Baltic in September and October, the Russian flag was again hoisted on the ruins of Bomarsund.

The strategic value of the destruction of Bomarsund was small or nil, although it had some political value in the struggle for Sweden's participation in the war. With the approach of the winter season, this struggle ceased. In Britain, Admiral Napier was made a scapegoat for the meagre results of the Baltic campaign of 1854. Rear-Admiral Maurice Berkeley, Lord Commissioner in the Admiralty, had warned him as early as 5 September, writing, 'John Bull is getting uproarious because nobody is killed and wounded. Meetings are being called to condemn the Government, because Kronstadt and Sebastopol have not been captured.'[5] The storm soon broke and the Board of Admiralty directed it at Napier's head. As he was a quarrelsome man, he spent the rest of his life – he died in 1860 – conducting a campaign of self-vindication in the press, in books and in Parliament.

The Allies learnt the lesson of the failure of the 1854 Baltic campaign and in 1855 their fleets set out much better equipped. First, all the vessels, including the French ones, were steamships, so that their mobility was enhanced. Some of them had been detached from the Black Sea squadrons, as no major amphibious operation was planned there. Second, a great number of light vessels which could operate in shallow waters was incorporated in both fleets. The total number of British ships was 105, including eleven battleships, thirty cruisers and some fifty gunboats and mortar vessels. The fleet was commanded by Rear-Admiral Sir Richard Saunders Dundas, who turned out to be as cautious and uninspiring as Lord Napier, whom he replaced. The French fleet was much smaller in size and was under the command of Rear-Admiral André Édouard Penaud, who had been second in command in the Baltic in the preceding year and therefore already had some valuable experience in the area.

No major operation was planned by the Allies besides the enforcement of the blockade and no expeditionary force was attached to the fleets, as all efforts were concentrated on the Crimea, the major object of war in 1855. In his instructions, the French admiral was told to let his ships cruise along different sections of the Russian coast in order to keep the enemy in suspense and make him disperse his forces. If possible, he was to undertake, in conjunction with the British squadron, raids on Sveaborg and Reval.[6] Kronstadt was as hard a nut to crack as Sevastopol, and was therefore not a target in 1855. The bombardment of Sveaborg or Reval was principally meant for home consumption.

The Russians, for their part, had not been idle in stepping up their defences. Their army of the north was brought up to a strength of 303,000 men stationed mainly in Finland (69,000), Estonia (20,000), Courland (40,000), Dunaburg (7,000) and St Petersburg (12,000). Some 90,000 men served as a mobile force and 20,000 as a reserve corps.[7] The production and laying of mines was accelerated; thus Kronstadt was protected by 300 of these 'infernal machines'. Others were laid around Sveaborg. In terms of the material damage they actually produced, they again proved relatively innocuous. The British were quick to respond to the danger and developed a system of minesweeping – the first operation of this kind in history. They hauled up about fifty of them and took a keen interest in the way they were constructed and worked. Admiral Dundas was himself wounded in the face when one of them was dismantled on board.

The main body of the British fleet left home waters at the beginning of April 1855. In the following weeks the blockade of various areas of the Baltic was declared, depending on when the British ships arrived. The small French squadron left Brest on 26 April and joined the British fleet on 1 June. The blockade of the Russian coasts was now enforced much more effectively than in 1854 due to the presence of many light-draught vessels. Many coastal places were visited and bombarded, especially in the Gulf of Finland. Lovisa and Kotka, for example, were almost completely burnt down. Kronstadt was inspected several times and was found to be even better protected than in 1854. In addition to the minefields, which proved their nuisance value to the Allied ships, the admirals were surprised to discover quite a number of screw-propelled Russian gunboats that had not been sighted the year before. Any large-scale assault on the fortress was therefore out of the question.

Discarding Reval as a possible target for bombardment, the two admirals singled out Sveaborg (Suomenlinna) as the next choice. They realized that its destruction in itself was of no great value, but 'the wish to do something', as they acknowledged, was the prime mover of the plan and its execution.[8]

Sveaborg, five kilometres south of Helsingfors which it covers, had been built by the Swedes as a fortress in 1749. It consists of seven rocky islands where the Russians had built various military and naval installations, besides a number of batteries. Access to the islands had been made impossible by the Russians in the same way as to the main bay of Sevastopol: by scuttling several of their own ships. The two admirals decided that the main attack should not be carried out by the heavy ships, as the experience of 17 October 1854 in front of Sevastopol had proved that the firepower of solidly built forts on land was clearly superior to that of wooden ships, even though they disposed of more guns. Thus the main thrust of the bombardment was to be carried out by the small gunboats and mortar ships. The heavy ships were to form a protective cordon behind the line of the small vessels.

After the waters at Sveaborg had been carefully charted and the last four French gunboats had arrived from France, the bombardment was finally scheduled to begin on 9 August at 7 am. During the nights of 7–9 August, the French erected a battery on the small island of Abraham, which the Russians had left unfortified. Altogether sixteen gunboats and sixteen mortar boats (with five each from France) were posted in front of Sveaborg at a distance of 2.5–3 kilometres from the centre of the fortress.

The bombardment was kept up, with interruptions, from 9 to 11 August. Altogether 6,000 shells were fired and a number of installations on the islands went up in flames. On the first day the Russian gunfire was already slackening but the Allies, too, had unexpected trouble. On a number of British mortars the barrels of the guns became defective prematurely, and eight of them burst. It was later established that these were newly-built guns whereas the older ones – one dating back to 1813 – had stood the stress of firing much better. Poor construction methods on the part of the firm that had built them was the cause. The news was not published at the time, but insiders were ashamed that the first industrial nation in the world produced such slipshod weapons while those of France remained serviceable. The Allied vessels waited throughout 12 August to see whether the Russians were still able to return fire. The population of Helsingfors expected a landing after the fire had ceased and fled from the city, but nothing of the sort happened. On the following day the ships steamed away and were not seen again.

The offical Allied announcements of the bombardment of Sveaborg were devoid of truth. The poor performance of the new guns was passed over in silence. It was claimed that the fortress of Sveaborg was completely razed – which it was not; that eighteen Russian ships had been sunk – the majority had been scuttled by the Russians themselves; that the number of dead on the Russian side was probably 2,000. As to the real Russian casualties, the figures range from sixty-two killed and 199 wounded (M. Borodkin) to forty-four killed and 147 wounded (E. V. Tarle). On the Allied side there was one person killed and ten were wounded.

The strategic result of the bombardment of Sveaborg was negligible. In contrast to the Bomarsund affair a year before, the Allies did not go ashore in order to destroy the forts properly because they had no landing parties. Even so, the Russians could not repair the fortress quickly enough to hold up an Allied assault on Kronstadt in 1856. In St Petersburg the impression the Allied bombardment produced on the government and the population was less than that of Bomarsund in 1854.

After Sveaborg, Admiral Penaud wanted to follow up the Allied 'success' by a similar assault on Reval, as his instructions had originally envisaged. He even received some reinforcements for this purpose, but the British mortar boats were in bad shape and the plan had to be abandoned. Nothing of importance was done during the rest of the good weather. Between the middle of September and 23 October 1855 the Allied squadrons left for their home ports. The prospects for a return in 1856 looked much better, due to the huge naval construction programme which the British government launched, and to Sweden's diplomatic alignment with the Western powers through the treaty of 21 November 1855 which was to be the prelude to Sweden's entry into the war.

Annotated bibliography

Although it is often claimed that the Baltic theatre of war is neglected in historical literature on the Crimean War, this is not correct. For the British side there are, apart from nineteenth-century letters, diaries and biographies of participants, two volumes of documents: David Bonner-Smith and Alfred C. Dewar (eds), *The Russian War, 1854. Baltic and Black Sea. Official Correspondence* (London, 1943); David Bonner-Smith (ed.), *The Russian War, 1855. Baltic. Official Correspondence* (London, 1944). There are four modern monographs: Lambert, *Crimean War*; Duckers, *Crimean War at Sea* (both have several chapters on the Baltic and offer details on the naval aspects of the war); Greenhill and Giffard, *Assault on Finland*; Rath, *The Crimean War* (devotes most of his book to the north). For the 1854 campaign, see C. I. Hamilton, 'Sir James Graham, the Baltic Campaign and War-Planning at the Admiralty in 1854', *Historical Journal* 19 (1976): 89–112. The Swedish side is covered by the books mentioned in Chapter 5 by Cullberg, *Roi Oscar*, and Hallendorff, *Konung Oscar*. For public opinion in Sweden, see also Sven Eriksson, *Svensk diplomati och tidningspress under Krimkriget* (Stockholm, 1939). The Finnish side and the question of the Åland islands is covered by Mikhail M. Borodkin, *Kriget vid Finlands kuster, 1854–1855* (Helsingfors, 1905) (the book was also published in Russian: *Vojna 1854–55 gg. na Finskom poberež'e*, St. Petersburg, 1903; rev. and enlarged edn 1904); Carl Michael Runeberg, *Finland under Orientaliska kriget* (Helsingfors, 1962) (the latter also deals with political and diplomatic aspects). The Russian side is covered by Tarle, *Krymskaja vojna*, vol. 2, pp. 42–94, 417–28 (the bibliography is on pp. 587–8). For the French side, cf. Guillemin, *Guerre de Crimée*, pp. 217–52; Battesti, *La marine*, vol. 1, pp. 89–101, 126–33. Cf. also Treue, *Krimkrieg*, pp. 92–113. On Denmark's role, cf. Emanuel Halicz, *Danish Neutrality during the Crimean War (1853–1856): Denmark between the Hammer and the Anvil* (Odense, 1977).

14

The Caucasian battlefield, 1853–5

The Caucasus region was the traditional second theatre of war in all Russo-Turkish conflicts of the nineteenth century, the Danube region being the more important one. In the eighteenth century, some of the areas of the Caucasus had been loosely connected with the Sultan of Constantinople. Russia's push into this area had begun under Peter the Great but by the time of the Crimean War, 150 years later, the conquest was not yet complete. In the west, the Circassians remained unruly, in the east the mountaineers in parts of Daghestan had successfully resisted Russian attempts at domination for decades. They rallied under their leader (or imam) Shamil, who since the 1820s had several times eluded capture by the Russians.

Since the Napoleonic Wars, Britain viewed Russia's piecemeal conquest of northern Caucasia and of Transcaucasia with mounting alarm. In a wider sense the area was part and parcel of the Eastern Question, that is, Turkey's retreat from the northern dominions of her vast empire which Russia conquered from her. In another, but related, sense the Caucasus region was an important element in the so-called 'Great Game for Asia', the struggle between Britain and Russia for predominance in Central Asia. Britain regarded Russia's conquest of the Caucasus and her gaining a foothold beyond the Caspian Sea as a threat to the safety of her Indian empire.

This anxiety was not at the centre of British strategic planning during the Crimean War, but it lurked in the minds of Foreign Office officials, diplomats and political writers. Thus Sir George Hamilton Seymour wrote, while he was still envoy in St Petersburg, in December 1853, 'That a fire might be lighted up in those regions which half the military power of Russia might be unable to extinguish is I think to be inferred.'[1] But it was only in the spring of 1855 that Clarendon acted upon this suggestion and sent consul Longworth on a fact-finding mission to the Caucasus, as discussed in Chapter 3. Longworth's reports were not very encouraging, as he discovered that the internecine strife between the peoples and the innumerable tribes of the Caucasus did not predispose them to be a serious partner in the war against Russia.

Even Shamil, the soul of the resistance of the Caucasian mountaineers against Russia, made no serious efforts to establish a link with Britain, or, for that matter, with Turkey. He seems, however, to have requested and received arms and ammunitions through the British and French embassies at Constantinople. Thus, Marshal Vaillant announced to Saint-Arnaud on 16 May 1854 that 10,000 flintlocks and 300,000 rounds of ammunition were to be sent to Shamil via Constantinople.[2] Whether they reached their destination cannot be verified from the documents. Perhaps they came into the hands of the Circassians, because Captain Hippolyte H. Manduit was sent to their country in the summer of 1854 to ascertain the possibility of furnishing arms to the tribes there. As far as is known the French were more active in the Caucasus at the beginning of the war than the British, whereas their interest slackened towards the end of the war after the fall of Sevastopol, while that of the British was now reaching a high pitch.

Shamil, however, seriously tested Russia's military resilience twice during the Crimean War, in 1853 and in 1854. When war was at the point of breaking out between Russia and Turkey in the middle of 1853, the Russians had to reinforce their garrisons along the Turkish frontier because the Turkish Anatolian army was being furnished with supplies from the Turkish fleet and was obviously planning a movement towards Tiflis. This was Shamil's moment to strike. He wanted to exploit the fair season of the year and did not wait for the Turkish army to begin its invasion, but concentrated a band of 15,000 of his warriors and tried to break through the Russian lines at the village of Zakataly, some 150 kilometres east of Tiflis. Shamil's men were, however, repulsed and retreated to the mountains. They now turned north, and, after a long march, invested the Russian military outpost of Meseldereg, 80 kilometres north of Tiflis. Only when reinforcements reached the place could the Russians drive them off. Thus any hope of linking up with the Turkish Anatolian army now vanished, so much the more as the destruction of the Turkish fleet at Sinope on 30 November 1853 made the supply problem more difficult than ever.

A second and similar opportunity presented itself to Shamil in the fair season of the following year. In the middle of July 1854 he moved again with a horde of 16,000 of his tribesmen towards Tiflis. His advance guard was beaten on 15 July at the village of Shilda, 80 kilometres north-east of the Georgian capital, but the main body of his men forced the Russians to retreat to Tsinandali, 60 kilometres north-east of Tiflis. He was on the point of breaking through the Russian lines when he was halted by a rising of the indigenous population, the Kakhetians, who as part of the Georgian people were loyal to the Russians. For three days Shamil's men fought against the Kakhetians. When Russian reinforcements arrived they had to turn back and flee to Daghestan. The threat which Shamil's mountaineers posed to the Russian army was now over for the rest of the Crimean War.

The fighting with Shamil's bands in 1853 and 1854 was a nuisance to the Russians; it was not, however, of any strategic importance. The beginning of

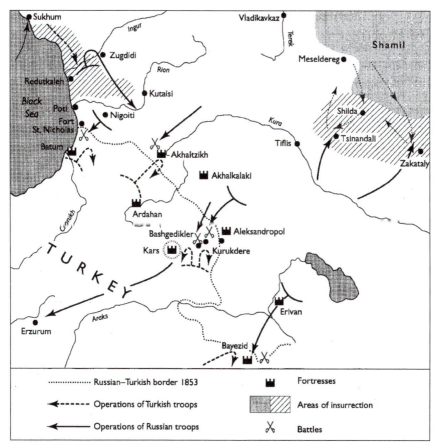

MAP 9 *The war in the Caucasus, 1853–5.*

the Russo-Turkish war in October 1853 forced the Russians to concentrate their efforts on the frontier with Turkey. In the Caucasus region the Russians had one great advantage: whereas Shamil's Muridist forces were clearly hostile to the Russians and sympathetic to the Turks, the Circassians on the north-eastern coast of the Black Sea were sitting on the fence, and in the end they favoured neither of the two sides. Furthermore, the Russians could rely on the sympathies, and even on the aid in terms of men and supplies, of the Christian Georgians, the Kakhetians and the Armenians. On no account did these peoples wish to fall again under the domination of the Turks. The rising of the Kakhetians against Shamil was the surest sign of their anti-Turkish and pro-Russian attitude. Another sign is that many Georgians and Armenians served in the Russian army or cooperated with them with their militia units. Many of their officers held high commands in the Russian army, including Prince Ivan M. Andronikov, Prince Grigorij D. Orbeliani and Prince Ivan K. Bagration.

With regard to the offensive capability and strength of both armies on the Caucasus front, the facts and statistics seemed to favour the Turks, but in reality the Russians, although weak at the beginning, held their positions and were soon able to extend them to the detriment of the Turks.

The Turks had strong fortresses at Trebizond, Erzurum, Batum and, especially, Kars. The latter had been transformed into a fortified camp along modern lines under the supervision of a British colonel, William Fenwick Williams. The fortresses of Ardahan and Bayezid were, however, of inferior quality. In the summer of 1853 the Turkish Anatolian army had its headquarters at Erzurum under Müşir Abdi Pasha. There were 16,000 regular soldiers there, but two-thirds of them were moved to the frontier. At Kars there were originally 5,000 troops, although they were quickly strengthened to 8,000. Ardahan was the point best situated for various reasons (proximity to the frontier, facilities for uniting a major force, sympathies of the local population) for an invasion across the frontier. It also held 20,000 men. A third camp existed at Bayezid with approximately 10,000 men. At the fortified port of Batum there were another 4,000 to 5,000 troops.

At the beginning of the new campaign of 1854, the Turks were able to bring their strength on the Caucasian frontier to 120,000 men, but after losses during the campaign of that year, epidemics in the following winter and the high rate of desertion (which is typical of the Anatolian front), the Anatolian army fell to less than 70,000 men.

Originally the Turkish war plans were offensive and were geared to an invasion of the Transcaucasian regions, with Tiflis, the Georgian capital, being the main target. The Turkish military leadership, however, was incapable of sustaining an offensive after an initial success. It was untrained for such a task, the Turkish general being more interested in satsifying his personal greed by amassing a fortune through all kinds of embezzlement. Although the Turkish leadership counted among its members a number of able European officers from the Hungarian and Polish revolutionary armies of 1848–9, such as Richard Guyon and George Kmety, or from Britain, like Williams, jealousy between them and their Turkish counterparts prevented any fruitful cooperation for the benefit of the country.

At the beginning of the war the Russian army's position in the Caucasus did not look any brighter than that of the Turkish Anatolian army. Prince Michael Semenovich Voroncov, the Governor-General and supreme commander of the Caucasus, was pessimistic about the prospects of the coming war, especially after an Anglo-French fleet had entered the Black Sea. The greatest difficulty for him was the fact that his own Caucasian army was scattered over a vast area and that only a fraction of it could be concentrated in the south-west on the frontier with Turkey. In his reports to the Tsar and to Paskevich he put the strength of the Russian troops to be deployed on the Turkish frontier at four battalions. This was probably a gross understatement in order to underpin his demand for sixteen additional battalions. Paskevich, who knew the Caucasus region from his own experience, was prepared to send him even more than the required reinforcements: four battalions for the Black Sea port of Poti, two for the garrison of Erivan and another twenty for an investment of, or an attack on, the central fortress of Kars.[3] With such a force, or even a lesser one, Paskevich was confident that the Russians could proceed offensively in Transcaucasia, that is, not only take Kars and Ardahan and thus prevent any surprise attacks from the mountain tribes along the Black Sea coast, but also conquer Bayezid as the most important point of communication between Turkey and Persia and as the place through which the whole British trade to northern and central Persia passed.

At the end of September 1853, Voroncov's army received as reinforcements the 13th Division, which disembarked at the port of Anaklia. In the spring of 1854 the Russian army of the Caucasus consisted of 160,000 men, of whom half were stationed along the Turkish frontier.[4] Although such a force should have been enough not only for the defence of Transcaucasia but also for an invasion across the Turkish frontier, Voroncov asked for his recall. He was temporarily replaced by General Read (who later lost his life at the Battle of the Tchernaya). Read was even more despondent than Voroncov, as he feared an Allied landing on the eastern shores of the Black Sea and a Persian attack. When he advocated the evacuation of practically all of Transcaucasia, he was soon replaced by General Nikolai Nikolaevich Muraviev, who became Governor-General of the Caucasus and supreme commander of the Caucasian army. Muraviev was able to instil an offensive spirit into his army and was to become the hero of Kars.

There were several military engagements in 1853 and 1854 in Transcaucasia, often with heavy losses, especially on the Turkish side, but none was decisive. On the night of 27–28 October 1853, a Turkish unit from Batum overran the Russian post of Fort St Nicholas just across the border, thus forcing the Russians to evacuate the garrison of Redutkaleh and cutting the sea links with the Crimea. On 13 November there was an engagement between Turkish and Russian troops west of Akhaltzikh, where the Russians carried the day.

Three days earlier, however, the Russians had been beaten south of Aleksandropol, losing 20 per cent of their force. The Turkish high command was unable to follow up this success. When the Russians received reinforcements, the Turks withdrew to the village of Bashgedikler (Bash-Kadyklar), halfway between Kars and Aleksandropol. There on 1 December 1853 the two sides met again in a bloody encounter. The Turkish army, amounting to 36,000 men, was routed and retreated to Kars. Some 15,000 are said to have deserted. The losses in dead and wounded were at least 6,000, on the Russian side the figure was 1,500. This time the Russian commander did not follow up his victory and did not pursue the Turks, who thus obtained a valuable breathing space.

In the campaign of 1854 the first notable encounter between the two sides was on 15 July along the frontier river Cholok. Both sides suffered heavy casualties, the Turks 4,000, the Russians 1,500. This Russian success on their right flank was soon complemented by one on their left flank. It was Bashgedikler all over again. Not far from this village, at Kurukdere (Kjurjuk-Dar), the two armies clashed on 5 August. The encounter left 8,000 Turks on the field dead, wounded or taken prisoner, and another 10,000, mostly irregulars, deserted. This time the Russian losses were also quite high: 3,000 dead and wounded. As both armies retreated to their fortresses – the Turks to Kars and the Russians to Aleksandropol – the whole affair was mere bloodletting and had no strategic consequences. The rest of the year and the winter of 1854–5 saw no action of importance.

The prospects for 1855 looked bleak for the Turks. Their army had dwindled to about 54,000 men, of whom 16,500 were stationed along the eastern shores of the Black Sea and near Erzurum, some 11,000 on the upper Euphrates, 12,000 at Bayezid and 14,500 at Kars. Because of the fundamental importance of the latter, its garrison was strengthened to almost 20,000 and Bayezid was correspondingly weakened. Omer Pasha and the government at Constantinople were well aware of the danger in eastern Anatolia. Throughout the summer, Omer Pasha was pressing his Allied counterparts to have the bulk of the Turkish troops in the Crimea transferred to the Caucasus. Both Pélissier and Simpson were adamant in refusing the Turkish request as they wanted to concentrate all their efforts on Sevastopol. The opposition of the British government to this diversion was withdrawn in August 1855, so at the beginning of September the Turkish forces began their embarkation for Batum.

Muraviev's plan in the summer of 1855 was to concentrate his efforts on the blockade of Kars and to cut its links with Erzurum, its supply base. In view of the small garrison of Erzurum (1,500 men), he could easily have captured the place and thus have hastened the investment of Kars, but fear of dividing his forces led him to decide otherwise. When he heard that the first of Omer's troops had landed at Batum, he changed his plans to starve out Kars, since he feared that Omer Pasha might move to Kutaisi and on to Tiflis, thus isolating him in the south. He decided instead to storm the fortress.

The defences of Kars had, however, been vastly strengthened in 1855. A ring of eight forts and a system of trenches and redoubts had been built around the citadel, which commanded the heights surrounding the fortress.

Muraviev failed to prepare his attack properly by carefully reconnoitring the strong and weak points of the fortress, by letting his troops familiarize themselves with the terrain and by bringing enough artillery into position. For the assault on 29 September 1855 he had 25,000 men at his disposal. But it miscarried in several respects. Instead of beginning at night, the assault opened in broad daylight. One of the units had lost its way in the darkness and began its attack in a section not assigned to it. Orders were not always clear. As in the Crimea, the Russians went into action in their old assault columns, thus offering a good target to the defenders, many of whom had modern rifles. At 11 am the attack was called off and the Russians retreated.

About 7,500 of their men were killed or wounded, whereas the Turks had again, as at Silistria on the Danube, shown their capacity for stubbornly defending a fortified place.

The Turks did not follow up their resounding success. They hoped that, with the approach of winter, there would be no prospect of the Russians resuming the siege, which is exactly what Muraviev did. Not far from Kars he built a fortified camp and within a short time closed the blockade ring round Kars again. Hunger was the best weapon for the Russians. One hundred Turks were dying daily in the fortress, with no chance of getting supplies. General Williams signed a document of capitulation and on 26 November 1855 the fortress surrendered. Ten generals and over 18,000 officers and men handed over their arms to the Russians. The capture of Kars was a great boon to the Russians after the fall of Sevastopol. It effectually paved the way to sounding out prospects for peace and finally to peace negotiations.

Obviously Omer Pasha's arrival on the eastern shores of the Black Sea had been too late. He had planned to transport troops from Bulgaria and the Crimea to Batum, where together with the garrison they would form an army of 45,000 men. By the end of September he had some 30,000–35,000 troops at his disposal. His target was the capture of Kutaisi, and ultimately of Tiflis, in order to isolate the Russian army along the Turkish frontier and at Kars. He chose Sukhum instead of Redutkaleh as his base of operations, although the distance from the latter to Kutaisi was shorter, because he thus avoided a movement through marshy terrain. From Sukhum, his troops marched south and south-east to reach the River Ingur, where Omer expected to meet the Russian army under Prince Bagration. The latter stationed his troops in isolated detachments along the Ingur river.

On 1 November the two armies came into contact with each other. They were about equal in numbers (some 20,000 Turks as against 18,500 Russians). On 7 November, Omer Pasha attacked. There was confused fighting in the woods, until Bagration, although not really beaten, ordered a general retreat south-east to Kheta and Zugdidi. Omer Pasha did not pursue him, but later moved his army in a leisurely fashion to Zugdidi, which Bagration had abandoned. Slowly moving south, Omer Pasha was caught by the autumnal rains and ordered a withdrawal to the coast. This promenade through Mingrelia was not a distinguished episode in Omer's career. Had the peace negotiations not been opened, Muraviev would have begun the new campaign in 1856 with a march on Erzurum, which would have had all prospects of success.

Annotated bibliography

Britain's interest in the Caucasus in 1853–6 is discussed in two articles: Norman Luxenburg, 'England and the Caucasus during the Crimean War',

Jahrbücher für Geschichte Osteuropas 16 (1968): 499–504; Garry J. Alder, 'India and the Crimean War', *Journal of Commonwealth History* 2 (1973–4): 15–37. Accounts of the military history of the Caucasus in 1853–6 suffer from an imbalance of the sources; there is much from the Russian and little from the Turkish side. Candan, *Ottoman Crimean War*, has some chapters, pp. 190–256; so has Reid, *Crisis of the Ottoman Empire*, pp. 278–306. A number of Russian documents for 1853–4 are in Zaiončkovskij, *Priloženija*, vol. 2. A thorough treatment is found in Chadži Murat Ibragimbejli, *Kavkaz v Krymskoj vojne 1853–1856 gg. i meždunarodnie otnošenija* (Moscow, 1971). The author covers Shamil's struggle as well as the military campaigns in 1853, 1854 and 1855 and also Omer Pasha's operations in Mingrelia. Cf. the relevant chapters in Tarle, *Krymskaja vojna*, vol. 1, pp. 280–7; vol. 2, 448–74 (the bibliography in vol. 1, pp. 539–40, vol. 2, pp. 606–7 includes accounts by British officers with the Turkish army). For an English summary, see W. D. Allen and Paul Muratoff, *Caucasian Battlefields: A History of the Wars on the Turco-Caucasian Border, 1828–1921* (Cambridge, 1953), pp. 57–102. The newest Russian book on 'the Caucasus and the Great Powers' is by Vladimir Vladimirovič Degoev, *Kavkaz i velikie deržavy* (Moscow, 2009), pp. 169–360. The author devotes more than a third of his book to the Crimean War period, making extensive use of the relevant literature, especially the AGKK edition.

15

The minor theatres of war: the White Sea and the Pacific

Besides the four major theatres of war during the Crimean War – the Danube, the Crimea, the Baltic and the Caucasus – there were two minor ones: the White Sea and the Barents Sea in northern Europe, and Petropavlovsk on the Kamchatka Peninsula in the Far East. The dimensions of the actions that took place there, especially in the White Sea, were small indeed; compared to the stubborn trench warfare at Sevastopol involving tens of thousands of victims, they were perhaps infinitesimal. However, the mere fact that they existed points to the important consideration that the 'Crimean' War contained the germs of a worldwide contest which would have developed into an outright world war in 1856, with the two German great powers, the secondary powers of Europe and the United States being directly involved. The First World War would then have taken place sixty years earlier. That it was prevented raises the interesting question why and by what mechanism this was done? The answer will be briefly discussed in the next chapter.

The sea route to the White Sea had been discovered in the sixteenth century during an English polar expedition. Shortly afterwards the English erected a small fort, called Archangel, at the mouth of the Dvina river. It became their main port of call in this region for their trade with Russia. Thus, in the middle of the nineteenth century, there was already a lively trade to and from Archangel, and after the outbreak of the Crimean War it was natural for the Board of Admiralty in London to stop that trade, although part of it affected British interests. The major part of the trade with Archangel, however, took place with the population of Finmark, the northernmost part of Norway. For them this coastal trade – 'cabotage' – was vital. The Swedish government therefore asked the French and British governments after the outbreak of war not to stop this cabotage. Due to climatic conditions, the sea route was open each year by the middle of April at the earliest and closed by the middle of October at the latest.

In the spring of 1854 the British fitted out a small squadron of three ships – a sailing frigate and two corvettes (sailing ships with auxiliary steam propulsion) under Captain Erasmus Ommaney. The French contributed two ships, one sailing frigate and one corvette, under Captain Pierre É. Guilbert. Both the British and French squadrons set out rather late for the White Sea. They established a base at the Swedish (Norwegian) port of Hammerfest for coaling and revictualling en route. By the decision of both governments, the blockade of the White Sea was declared effective as of 23 July. The French ships entered the White Sea on 8 August, where they joined the British squadron which had arrived ahead of them.

The British had already committed their first act of hostility. It was rather a silly one, devoid of any strategic importance and very much on the lines of the raids of Admiral Plumridge's ships on the Finnish coast. On 18 July two of the British ships approached the Solovetskie Islands at the entrance to the bay of Onega. On the main island stood – and still stands today – a monastery that had been founded in the fifteenth century as a hermitage and later developed as an important place of pilgrimage. Besides its religious and cultural importance (it possessed valuable collections of icons and vestments), it was also the centre for the economic development of this part of northern Russia. As the Swedes had besieged the place several times at the end of the sixteenth century, the monastery was protected by walls, towers and a number of guns. This martial appearance was obviously the excuse for Captain Ommaney to open, without warning, a bombardment against the monastery. What else could he have done in that remote corner of Russia? Archangel itself was a strongpoint which he dared not attack by sea or by land, as he estimated the garrison to comprise 6,000 men. Thus a bombardment of the 'fortress' of Solovetskie would make good reading in the English papers and satisfy John Bull. Having silenced the Russian battery on 18 July, Ommaney demanded, on the following day, the unconditional surrender of the place. This was refused. Thereupon a new bombardment opened and did some damage to various buildings of the monastery. On 20 July the two British ships sailed away. Besides the senseless material damage, the Russians suffered no casualties, whereas the British were left to rue one dead and five wounded.

A month later the British White Sea squadron performed a second feat. It was as ridiculous as the first, and barbaric, but made good news in the British press. The French were already present but were not asked to take part. On 22 August one of the British ships steamed into the mouth of the River Kola, destroyed a Russian battery barring its route and then stopped in front of the village of Kola, not far away from the later city of Murmansk, built during the First World War and completely destroyed by the Germans in the Second World War. Kola was then a fishing village and of no strategic importance whatever. The British ship started a cannonade at 3 o'clock in the morning of 23 August which continued with few interruptions until the morning of 24 August. The place was set on fire and almost completely razed. Of the 128 wooden houses, 110 were destroyed.[1] The French captain did not hide his disgust at this inglorious act of war from his British colleague. The Scandinavian press, obviously furnished with appropriate details by the Russians, was full of anti-British comment.

Apart from these two acts of war, the Allied White Sea squadrons tried to ensure the blockade of the Russian coast. They started their journey home at the end of September.

The campaign of 1855 in the White Sea was uneventful compared with the preceding year – there were no 'exploits' like those of 1854. The British set out again with three vessels, under Captain Thomas Baillie. The French this time had three ships commanded by Captain Guilbert. On 11 and 14 June the British and French commanders respectively declared the blockade of the White Sea in force. Unlike the summer of 1854, the Allied commanders did not allow the cabotage to Finmark by Russian vessels and seized some sixty of these small coastal ships. As they could not be towed as prizes to Britain or France, they were set on fire or sunk, the crews being dumped near a coastal village. On 9 October both squadrons left for home.

The balance sheet of the two campaigns in the White Sea was poor. One could argue that the five or six Allied ships might have been better employed on the Mediterranean and Black Sea route, where every single ship was urgently needed. But the mere fact of their appearance in northern Russia immobilized several thousand Russian soldiers there (although they would have been stationed there anyway). More important was the fact that no Russian privateers could leave the White Sea and harass British shipping in the North Sea, or at least – as there were actually no vessels at Archangel capable of playing such a role – no American merchantman could enter the White Sea, be fitted out as a privateer at Archangel and then roam the North Sea.

War activities in the Far East in 1854 were of far greater dimensions than those in the White Sea. Despite a distinct superiority in firepower and men, they ended in ignominious failure for the Allies. They must be set in the wider framework of the conflict of interests between Britain and Russia emerging in that region in those years. Britain had gained a firm foothold in China with the occupation of Hong Kong in 1842 after the First Opium War. France and the United States followed suit, and set in motion a great power struggle about opening up China and Japan in the following years and decades. Russia joined in at the end of the 1840s. The driving force behind Russia's activities was Count Nikolai Nikolaevich Muraviev-Amurskij (not to be confused with the general of the same name, commander of the Russian forces in the Caucasus), Governor-General of Eastern Siberia from 1847. In 1854 he headed an expedition along the Amur river to its mouth, in order to wrest the area north of that river from weaker China. He was aided by Rear-Admiral Efim Putiatin, who headed a mission to Japan in 1852 to establish Russia's influence there, and who succeeded in signing a treaty of commerce, peace and friendship with Japan on 7 February 1855; that is, in the midst of the Crimean War.

The British government was conscious of these Russian activities in the Far East and seized the opportunity of the outbreak of war in March 1854 to counter them and cripple Russia's newly gained influence in that area as far as possible. The opportunity was really a golden one. Britain's China and Pacific squadrons together with France's naval forces there enjoyed a clear superiority over Russia's maritime forces (twenty-five as against six men-of-war) and over her coastal defences along the Sea of Okhotsk and the Kamchatka Peninsula. As for Russian America, the Hudson Bay Company, Britain's oldest trading company in North America which held sway over huge tracts of land in what is today Canada, and its Russian counterpart, the Russian-American Company that controlled Alaska at that time, made a deal early in 1854, before the outbreak of the war, not to extend hostilities to their dominions. Both the British and the Russian governments endorsed this deal, so that a clash of the belligerents was specifically excluded from this area. This is remarkable given the relentless ideological struggle and the fierce war efforts of the two sides elsewhere.

In the Far East, Muraviev sensed the danger which Anglo-French superiority posed to Russia and realistically appraised the importance of the Amur river as a line of communication to the Sea of Okhotsk and Kamchatka. He had troop reinforcements ferried to Mariinsk and Nikolaevsk on the lower stretches of the Amur, to Ayan on the coast and to Petropavlovsk on the south-eastern shore of Kamchatka. The danger to these fortified places did not come from the British China squadron, but from the combined Pacific squadrons of the Allies.

The flagships and other units of these squadrons, with the Commanders-in-Chief Rear-Admiral David Price and Rear-Admiral Auguste Fébvrier-Despointes, were lying at anchor in Callao harbour, Peru, in April 1854, alongside a Russian frigate, neither side yet cognizant of the outbreak of war. The frigate had been sent from Kronstadt to the Pacific well before the war, to reinforce Admiral Putiatin's squadron in Japanese waters. It left Callao on 26 April. On 7 May the news of the outbreak of war at last arrived at Callao. After a pause of another ten days, the Allied squadrons set sail in order to pursue the frigate and mop up other Russian men-of-war encountered in the Pacific. They made a detour to the Marquesas Islands, where they were joined by other Allied ships and then headed for Honolulu on Hawaii (Sandwich Islands), where they arrived on 17 July. Here they learned that the Russian frigate had left that location a month earlier for Petropavlovsk. They stayed at Honolulu for another eight days, Admiral Price poking his nose into the relations between King Kamehameha III and the American mission to Hawaii. When the Allied squadrons finally left Honolulu on 25 July, heading north-west, they numbered nine vessels.

On 28 August the Allied armada arrived at the entrance of Avacha Bay, Kamchatka, and after reconnoitring it decided to move on to Petropavlovsk, which lies 12 kilometres inland. There they found the Russian frigate and another Russian armed transport blocking the entrance of the harbour, with their broadsides facing outwards. The Russians had unloaded half the guns and distributed them to the six batteries overlooking the harbour. The

Russian garrison had received reinforcements sent by Muraviev on 5 August, and it now numbered 1,013 men. The defensive works had been thoroughly overhauled. The governor of Petropavlovsk was the Russian admiral, Vasilij Stepanovich Zavoiko. The Allies had about 2,000 men at their disposal; that is, a force about double the size of the Russian one. On 29 August there was a first exchange of fire, but it did not last long and was inconclusive. The Allies decided to launch a major attack on the following day in order to silence, first of all, at least four of the batteries.

The bombardment was opened on 30 August in the morning. After a couple of hours, something unexpected happened: Admiral Price retired to his cabin and shot himself. He was obviously unable to stand the strain of the cannonade and may have convinced himself that Petropavlovsk was too well defended and could not be conquered. He may have been struck by the contrast between his own Nelsonian grandiloquence when addressing his crew while still at Callao ('Great Britain has a right to expect from it [the Pacific squadron] a proper account of the Russian Frigates that are known to be on the Station'[2]) and the reality now confronting him. The French admiral took command of the Allied squadrons and decided to stop the bombardment and attempt a landing on the following day.

On 31 August a party of sailors and marines landed and took one of the batteries; they were repulsed by a Russian counter-attack and re-embarked. It was decided to renew the raid, but after more thorough preparation. Fighting was reopened on 4 September and it ended in an unmitigated disaster on the Allied side. The Allies landed a party of 700 men, 400 French and 300 British, the two groups acting independently of each other. They were able to climb a hill, but were ambushed by Russian sharpshooters and thrown back. Reports of the number of casualties for both sides differ widely, although the Petropavlovsk engagement is one of the best documented of the Crimean War. According to the most reliable Russian source – Miliutin's diary (Dmitrij Alekseevich Miliutin was then an official in the Russian war ministry, later Russian war minister) – the Russians suffered 115 dead and wounded, if the days of 29–31 August, 1 and 4 September are taken together, and fifty for 4 September only.[3] Estimates of the Allied casualties for that day range from sixty to 350. One source states 209 were killed and most of the rest wounded. At any rate, this was sufficient for Despointes to call off the siege and leave for the open Pacific. The French made their way to San Francisco, while the British wintered at Vancouver.

On the Allied side it was determined that the two squadrons should make their reappearance at Petropavlovsk at the beginning of the summer season of 1855. The armada was brought up to sixteen ships: six French under Rear-Admiral Martin Fourichon and ten British under Rear-Admiral Henry William Bruce. They arrived in batches on the Kamchatka coast at the end of May and the beginning of June, but to their great amazement Petropavlovsk was deserted and partly destroyed – a typical Russian reaction. The Allies burnt the rest of the town and razed what was left of the embrasures.

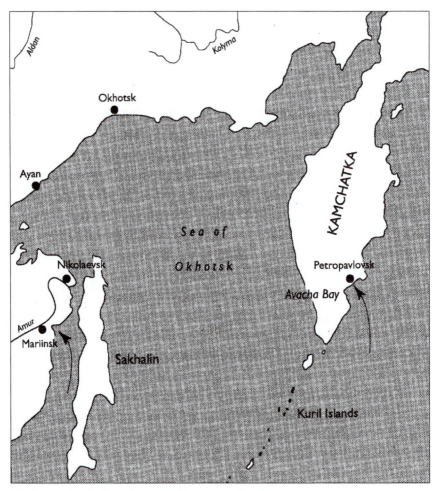

MAP 10 *The theatre of war in the Far East, 1854–5.*

Expecting the Allies to return with a larger force, Muraviev had ordered
the evacuation of Petropavlovsk as early as December 1854, the evacuation
itself taking place in mid-April 1855. The inhabitants and the stocks were
brought to Nikolaevsk at the mouth of the Amur river, to strengthen the
defences there. Some of Bruce's ships, and also a few more from the French
and British China stations, were sent out to find the whereabouts of the
evacuees and their ships. The Russians made a fool of them once more. They
knew sea passages for which the Allies had no charts, so there was no
encounter and no shot fired. The Allied ships returned to their stations
without having achieved anything. *The Times* in London was right in
commenting on 10 September 1855, shortly before it could print the news
of the fall of Sevastopol, 'In the course of the preceding operations no

brilliant success has been achieved, but the Seas of Kamchatka, Japan, and Okhotsk have been traversed in almost every direction.'

The campaign of 1854 in the Far East had ended in a resounding victory for the Russians; that of 1855 had a completely sterile outcome for the Allies: 1854 taught them that it is difficult to attack and conquer a well fortified place by sea without proper preparations. For the Russians the lesson was the high value of possessing the lower Amur, and Muraviev took great pains in the following years to wrest the whole Amur region from the Chinese. He succeeded in 1858 with the Treaty of Aigun. The action at Petropavlovsk in 1854, the non-action there in 1855 and Muraviev's activity on the Amur heightened the tension which had been building up between Britain and Russia in the Near, Middle and Far East.

Annotated bibliography

Surprisingly there are no older accounts in English historiography on the operations in the White Sea. Only very recently have historians paid attention to the subject: Andrew Lambert, 'The Royal Navy's White Sea Campagin of 1854', in *Naval Power and Expeditionary Wars: Peripheral Campaigns and New Theatres of Naval Warfare*, ed. Bruce Elleman and S.C.M. Paine (New York, 2011), pp. 29–44. Rath, *Crimean War*, deals with it in two chapters: pp. 15–32 and 93–109. Duckers devotes one chapter to it in *The Crimean War*. For the Russian side there is a booklet: *Russkij sever i Rossija v gody Krymskoj vojny, 1853–1856 gg.* (Vologda, 1979), but it is not very revealing. Tarle has a brief chapter in *Krymskaja vojna*, vol. 2, pp. 193–9. Valuable remarks are found in Guillemin, *Guerre de Crimée*, pp. 255–71.

In contrast to the White Sea, the operations at Kamchatka are extraordinarily well documented and researched. There are numerous eyewitness accounts from the three participating sides, commemorative articles and even a number of (Russian) books. There are two useful English language articles (with bibliographies): John J. Stephan, 'The Crimean War in the Far East', *Modern Asian Studies* 3 (1969): 257–77; Barry M. Gough, 'The Crimean War in the Pacific: British Strategy and Naval Operations', *Military Affairs* 37 (1973): 130–6. There is also a new book, thoroughly researched: Rath, *The Crimean War*. The author, however, overrates the importance of that distant theatre of war. Somewhat less controversial is John D. Grainger, *The First Pacific War: Britain and Russia, 1854–1856* (Rochester, NY, 2008).

16

Allied war preparations for 1856 and the war council in Paris, January 1856

There were no major war operations in the Crimea after the fall of Sevastopol on 8 September 1855, although Napoleon was continually pressing his Commander-in-Chief to follow up his success. The only operation of some importance was the amphibious one, already discussed, against Kinburn on 17 October, in which the French ironclads showed their value as a new weapon.

The reasons why the French and British armies in the Crimea did not use their victory to expel the Russians from the peninsula are obvious:

1 The Russians had not left their stronghold Sevastopol entirely; they were still entrenched on the north side of the city. Because of the estimated Russian strength, the two Allied commanders were not prepared to attack the Russians there and on the Mackenzie heights frontally.

2 Psychologically speaking, the Allied troops were tired and worn out after almost a year of exacting siege war.

3 They were still labouring under the shock of the preceding winter. In September 1855 they had to face a second such winter and naturally wanted to prepare for this.

4 The British Commander-in-Chief, General Simpson, not a daring commander, was made the scapegoat in London for the failure on the Redan; his replacement on 22 October 1855 by General Sir William John Codrington did not produce any immediate forward strategy.

Much more important than the state of the Allied army at Sevastopol were the divergent strategical aims of the governments in London and Paris. The British government wanted to concentrate the military effort in 1856 on an all-out attack against Kronstadt and St Petersburg. This could only be accomplished by the cooperation of a large French army and the British navy. A second attack was to be launched against the Russians in the Caucasus by a British army with a few French troops attached to it. While Emperor Napoleon was in favour of a combined attack against Kronstadt, he was firmly opposed to a diversion in the Caucasus as this would obviously serve British interests only.

Napoleon's strategic objectives immediately after Sevastopol were the eviction of the Russians from the north side of the town and from the Mackenzie heights, and ultimately the occupation of Simferopol. But Pélissier would not budge. As we have already seen, the decisive moment passed when Napoleon's thirst for continuing the war was quenched by the British refusal, delivered on 22 September 1855, to open up the Polish question, create a new front in Central or Eastern Europe and thereby change the whole character of the war. With his generals in the Crimea immovable and his grand political design for a remapping of Europe nipped in the bud, Napoleon quickly lost interest in continuing the war; he tried to open up channels for peace with St Petersburg and started withdrawing troops from the Crimea. Anglo-French relations were fast deteriorating and reached their nadir when London learned in October that the French and Austrian governments were hatching the terms of an ultimatum to be delivered by Austria to St Petersburg, a step in which London had not been asked to participate.

It was at this moment that Napoleon, fearing that his relations with the British government might soon reach a breaking point, wrote a letter to Queen Victoria (on 22 November 1855) in which he pointed out three ways to continue the war:

1   Restrict military activities to a waiting game by simply blockading the Black Sea and the Baltic and by waiting for Russia to use up her forces and sue for peace.

2   Direct an appeal to all nationalities, proclaiming the resurrection of Poland and the independence of Finland, Hungary, Italy and Circassia.

3   Seek the alliance of Austria, which would force the rest of Germany in her wake, thus compelling Russia to propose conditions of peace.

At the end of his letter, Napoleon confirmed his preference for the third option, but he let it be clearly understood that a redrawing of the map of Europe would be a policy worthy of fresh sacrifices.[1]

Although in London the Prime Minister, Palmerston, was personally in favour of the war developing into a war of nationalities, the rest of the Cabinet and the Queen were conscious of the incalculable dangers of such a hazardous policy and opted for trying out the effect of an Austrian ultimatum. In her reply to Napoleon, Queen Victoria suggested that the

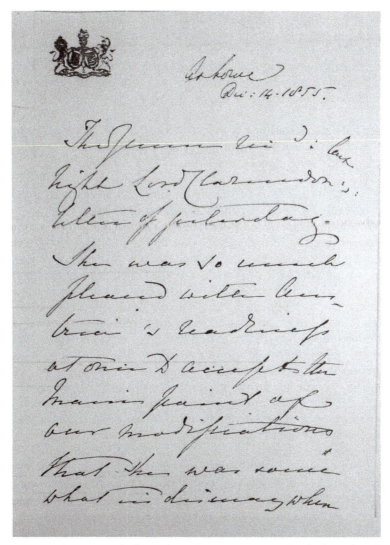

FIGURE 16 *First page of a letter from Queen Victoria to Lord Clarendon. AGKK III/4, pp. 489–90.*

military aspects of the ultimatum – preparing for a possible Russian refusal by working out a plan of campaign for 1856 – should be discussed at an Allied council of war.

The idea of such a council of war had already been raised by Napoleon immediately after the fall of Sevastopol,[2] but it slumbered for some weeks until the British ambassador to Paris, Cowley, reawakened it when inter-allied relations began to deteriorate due to the French withdrawing troops from the Crimea.

Why not a month or six weeks hence, when all military operations . . . must be necessarily suspended invite them [the Commanders-in-Chief] and the Admirals to come home for a week or two. Let then a great Council of War be held . . . – let it be thoroughly explained to them . . . that something must be done in the Spring. What this something is to be should then be maturely deliberated.

The idea fell on fertile ground both in London and Paris. Both governments saw it as a convenient means of extracting themselves from the impasse into which they had manoeuvred themselves. It took more than the six weeks which Cowley had expected for the council to convene. Finally, on 10 January 1856, after the Austrian ultimatum had already been delivered at St Petersburg, the council opened its discussions in Paris.

By common consent the terms of reference of the council were restricted to military matters. The political decision on the plan of campaign to be finally adopted was specifically reserved to the two governments. The council was presided over by Napoleon himself. The two Commanders-in-Chief in the Crimea had not been called to take part, but were represented by the two chiefs of the general staffs, with a number of other generals and admirals in attendance. Lord Cowley took part as the political representative of his government, but the Duke of Cambridge officially led the British delegation.

The council of war met four times between 10 and 18 January 1856. Its proceedings were firmly in the hands of Napoleon. He opened the first session by reading a list of fourteen questions with reference to the situation in the Crimea (e.g., can Eupatoria be made a base for a large operation?) and another five questions relating to the Baltic.[3] Two sub-committees were formed, one for the Crimea and one for the Baltic. Each member had to give his response to the questions in writing and hand it in at the subsequent meeting. For the fourth session, which took place on 18 January, each member had to work out a plan of campaign. On the basis of these proposals, Napoleon hammered out a plan of his own which was ready by 20 January. This plan, together with all the documents of the preceding sessions, was then sent to London.

It became clear during the military discussions that the highest priority was given to continuing operations in the Crimea. The Russian army of the Crimea, which was estimated at 130,000–150,000 men (the estimate was correct), was to be attacked in a pincer movement. An Allied army of 100,000 men operating from Eupatoria under a French commander was to threaten the Russian army in the rear and force it to retreat. A smaller army of 70,000 men or more, based at Sevastopol and Balaklava, would push the Russian army north into the arms of the Eupatoria army. In view of this priority, the British proposal for a simultaneous operation in the Caucasus was dropped, and in the Baltic no major campaign was planned.

Napoleon's own plan of operations was drafted along these lines with minor modifications. In the Baltic, operations would be restricted to the destruction of Kronstadt. The pincer movement to Simferopol was complemented – this was Napoleon's old hobby horse – by a third diversionary attack from Alushta, on the eastern coast, against Simferopol with 16,000 Allied troops.

In London, Napoleon's plan of campaign was accepted with a few minor modifications and one major one.[4] The Eupatoria army was to be reduced in favour of an expedition to the Caucasus. This was to be British-led, consist of 40,000 to 50,000 men and be carried out simultaneously with operations against Simferopol. Apart from strategic considerations, this operation was to be launched for political reasons – to make good the fall of the fortress of Kars and forestall the setting up of a select committee of Parliament to investigate the disaster.

In his reply to the British government of 4 February 1856, Napoleon made it clear that the forces available would not permit such a simultaneous operation. The British government gave in and on 10 and 11 February 1856 orders were sent to the two Commanders-in-Chief in the Crimea telling them to prepare for the operations in the Crimea, which were to start in April 1856.[5] The army of Eupatoria was to consist of 79,500 French, 25,500 British and 15,000 Sardinian troops (120,000 altogether) and be under French command; the army of Sevastopol was to be composed of 48,500 British and 16,500 French troops (65,000 in all) led by the British Commander-in-Chief. Each of the two armies was to incorporate 5,000 men from the German and Swiss foreign legions. The 15,000 Turkish troops were to remain stationed at Kertch. A diversionary movement from Alushta was not mentioned. General Codrington was told that the expedition to the Caucasus would not take place for the time being, but as the Crimean operation would be finished in a month's time, he should lose no time 'in turning the British arms in that direction. You will therefore take this contingency into your consideration, and make such previous arrangements as you are enabled to do for its accomplishment.'

As is known, there was no further campaign in 1856 and the military council in Paris in January 1856 must be regarded as a mock battle. But it nonetheless fulfilled a number of functions: it smoothed the political and strategic differences between the two Allied governments; it served Napoleon as a smokescreen behind which he could conceal his decision not to continue the war in 1856; it applied pressure on Russia to accept the Austrian ultimatum because the fact that the council took place was released to the European press; and it fulfilled the duty of the military and political leadership in both countries to prepare for war so long as a peace treaty was not yet signed.

It was an irony of history that, in the very days that the military council took place in Paris, Tsar Alexander in St Petersburg convened a council of his political and military experts to advise him whether to accept the

Austrian ultimatum or not. This ultimatum consisted of the Four Points, over which the Vienna peace conference had broken down in the spring of 1855, with the essential third point now being given more precision (the Black Sea was to be neutralized; there were to be no ships of war in it; all naval ports and arsenals were to be scrapped) and a fifth point added at the instigation of the British government (the Allied governments would reserve to themselves the right to add new demands to the Four Points at the future peace conference, a vague point which later came to mean the demilitarization of the Åland Islands; the admittance of Allied consuls in Russia's Black Sea ports; and the consideration of the political situation of the Circassians). At a first crown council which met on 1 January 1856 the Tsar accepted this ultimatum, with the important modification that Russia accepted the peace conditions without the fifth point and without the cession of Bessarabian territory, a new demand now contained in point one.[6] As Austria insisted on an unconditional acceptance, since it would otherwise break off diplomatic relations, the Tsar convened a second council, which met at the Winter Palace on 15 January 1856, at the same time as the Allied military council was sitting in Paris.

The vast majority of the members of this council were in favour of accepting the Austrian ultimatum without further ado. The reasons adduced were indicative of Russia's desperate situation. Nesselrode pointed to the deterioration of Russia's international standing: Austria's attitude was now becoming more hostile than ever; she would probably join the war in the new campaign. Nesselrode expressly mentioned the war council in Paris, stating that it had decided to occupy the whole Crimea and allow French troops to move along the Danube to Bessarabia (the latter point had been discussed in Paris, but no such decision had in fact been taken). The war would thereby be transferred to Austria's border, and Austria would become quickly involved in it; Prussia and the German Confederation would then no longer be able to withstand the pressure to join in on the Allied side. He also pointed to the rising hostility of Sweden; her treaty with the Western powers of 21 November 1855 had just become known in St Petersburg and created a deep impression. The prospect of almost the whole of Europe lining up against Russia in 1856 must have been a nightmare for the Tsar.

Other members of the council raised other reasons for accepting the Austrian ultimatum. Voroncov, erstwhile governor of the Caucasus, stressed the dire prospect of losing the Crimea, the Caucasus, Finland and Poland if the war continued. From this it is evident that the Russian leadership was seriously expecting a revolt and the secession of these non-Russian border provinces – a development which Napoleon III and Palmerston were in fact seriously entertaining and trying to encourage.

Peter Meyendorff, the former ambassador to Vienna, painted a bleak picture of Russia's financial and economic situation. Continuing the war, he argued, was bound to lead to bankruptcy of the Russian state. A look at the statistics underlines the cogency of this prophecy. The deficit of the state for

1856 would be eleven times as high as the average deficit of the years 1851–3. Foreign trade between 1853 and 1855 had dwindled by four-fifths and the blockade of Russia's coasts was beginning to tell.

Of special interest for the purposes of this book is the memorandum of Major-General Miliutin, which was probably circulated to the members of the conference before it met. The basic thrust of the memorandum was the conviction that Russia, whose economy was based on the existence of serfdom, could not continue a war with the prospect of success against two great European powers who were so industrially developed. Miliutin presented the following details to support his case:

1   The human reservoir for recruiting young men from among the serfs would soon be exhausted. The mass of the 800,000 men drafted since the beginning of the war lacked proper military training and there were not enough officers for this purpose. The economy could not bear a further drain of young men.

2   The supplies of arms and ammunition were nearly exhausted. Of the 1 million rifles that were stored in the arsenals at the beginning of the war, only 90,000 were left. Of the 1,656 field guns, only 253 were still in the depots. Russia's primitive arms industry could not supply the quantities needed, while clandestine imports provided no more than a trickle of supplies.

3   Worse still were the low stocks of gunpowder and projectiles. The production of gunpowder in 1855 had only satisfied the consumption at Sevastopol without counting the needs of other fronts. The raw materials for the production of gunpowder – saltpetre and sulphur – were not available in sufficient quantities.

4   The supply of food for 1856 would not fulfil the needs of the army.

5   The transport situation would not allow any major movement of supplies and troops. The lack of railways doomed Russia's war machinery to come to a virtual standstill.

The essence of Miliutin's memorandum was self-evident. Russia did not have the human reserves and the war matériel necessary to successfully continue the war. Tsar Alexander drew from this desperate situation the only possible rational conclusion: to accept the Austrian ultimatum and thus open the door for the re-establishment of peace.

Annotated bibliography

The search for peace after the fall of Sevastopol is discussed in Baumgart, *Peace of Paris*, pp. 1–99. On the war council in Paris, January 1856, cf. Baumgart, 'Ein Kriegsrat Napoleons III. Englisch-französische Feldzugspläne gegen Rußland 1855/56', in *Festschrift für Eberhard Kessel zum 75. Geburtstag*, ed. Heinz Duchhardt and Manfred Schlenke (Munich, 1982), pp. 212–35; Martin Senner, 'La guerre de 1856 n'aura pas lieu. Ein "Scheinkriegsrat" Napoleons III.', *Militärgeschichtliche Mitteilungen* 54 (1995): 31–59. On the two crown councils in St. Petersburg early in January 1856, cf. Baumgart, *Peace of Paris*, pp. 68–80; Igor V. Bestužev, 'Krymskaja vojna i revoljucionnaja situacija', in *Revoljucionnaja situacija v Rossii v 1859–1861 gg.* (Moscow, 1963), pp. 189–213.

PART FIVE

The End of
the War

17

The Paris peace congress, February–April 1856

Russia's acceptance of the Austrian ultimatum on 16 January 1856 was the decisive step for the opening of peace negotiations. On 1 February a protocol was signed in Vienna between Buol and the diplomatic representatives of the four belligerent powers (excluding Sardinia), stating that preliminaries of peace, an armistice and a definitive peace treaty should be signed, and that plenipotentiaries of these five powers should meet within three weeks. The Five Points were annexed to the protocol.

Contrary to the diplomatic usage of the time, the preliminaries of peace were not in fact negotiated and signed. Instead, the Vienna protocol was annexed to the first protocol of the peace negotiations, which opened in Paris on 25 February 1856. This procedure was due to Napoleon's wish for a speedy conclusion of peace. As mentioned earlier, diseases like scurvy and typhoid fever were raging in the French army and immobilizing it. At the end of February, of 150,000 soldiers, 22,000 were reported sick. This figure jumped to 42,000 at the beginning of April.[1]

Hostilities were declared ended on 29 February. A formal armistice was concluded on the Traktir bridge on the Tchernaya on 14 March. It was to be valid on land only. The British government had feared that an extension to the sea would lead to the lifting of the blockade, thereby giving Russia free communications by water. The Allied naval commanders were, however, instructed not to commit hostile acts against enemy coasts.

Peace negotiations opened in Paris on 25 February and the peace treaty was signed on 30 March. After that date the peace congress held five more sessions in which matters outside the Eastern Question were discussed, but no resolutions were taken. The choice of Paris for the congress instead of Vienna, which had been the *centre d'entente* during the war, was a clear indication of the new international standing of France in Europe. It was also the apex of Napoleon's personal reputation in Europe. His dream of converting the Paris peace congress into an international meeting, where a general redrawing of the map of Europe – Napoleon's grand design – would take place, did come to fruition. The peace congress was, according to

international usage, presided over by the host country so that Count
Walewski took the chair. The Russian delegation was led by Count Orlov,
adjutant general to the Tsar. Count Buol represented Austria, while Lord
Clarendon had come from London. The Sultan had sent his Grand Vizir, Ali
Pasha. Sardinia had been admitted as a belligerent power, mainly due to
British pressure, and was represented by Count Cavour. Prussia, as one of
the five great powers, was admitted belatedly, on 18 March, after the main
questions had been dealt with.

   Three territorial matters were discussed and resolved. The trickiest one
was the cession of part of Bessarabia. This cession was of Austrian origin
and was incorporated in Point One on the Danubian Principalities. Britain
had supported the demand, whereas Napoleon was unwilling to force it on
the Russians. It was supposed to remove Russia from the left bank of the
Danube and enable the Principalities (and the suzerain power, Turkey, and
the neighbouring power, Austria) to build a line of fortifications from the
fortress of Chotyn in the north, south beyond the Pruth river, and south-east
beyond the Danube to Lake Sasyk, north of the mouth of the Danube.
During the discussions the Russian delegation managed by open demands
and foul play (by producing an inaccurate map) to reduce the extent of the
territorial cession. They tried to bring the possession of Kars into the deal
and offer its retrocession for a reduction of the slip of Bessarabian territory.
Despite this maneuvre, the main reason for Russia succeeding in her demand
was the support given her by France. This points to the remarkable
realignment of powers which brought France and Russia, which had been
waging war against each other, closer together before the opening of the
congress. The new boundary line in Bessarabia that was finally agreed gave
several advantages to Russia compared to the territory she had in principle
ceded through her acceptance of the Austrian ultimatum:

1   The area she had to give up was much smaller.
2   Russia kept the important fortress of Chotyn and did not directly
    border on the Bukovina.
3   Russia retained the village of Bolgrad, the centre of her Bulgarian
    colony in Bessarabia. As she did not reveal that there were two
    villages of the same name close to each other, she regained direct
    access to the Yalpukh Sea and thereby to the Danube.

In another territorial question, Russia scored a similar success. This time
Britain was the dupe. The Fifth Point had, indirectly, provided for 'the
consideration of the territories on the east coast of the Black Sea'. When
Clarendon was asked what the British meant by this vague demand, he
revealed that the line of the Kuban river should henceforth be the border
between Russia and the Ottoman Empire. When he was confronted with
treaty documents (the Treaty of Adrianople of 1829 and the Petersburg
convention of 1834) stating that Russia enjoyed the rightful possession 'of

the territories on the east coast of the Black Sea', he had to give in and drop his demand. The meagre point gained was the setting-up of an international commission that had to delineate the frontier line unequivocally.[2]

Russia ceded the fortress of Kars and the adjoining territories after she had been assured of the reduction of her Bessarabian cession.

Another territorial question which was hidden behind the Fifth Point was the future of the Åland Islands. The fortress of Bomarsund had been razed by the French and British navies in the summer of 1854. Sweden, with the sympathy of Britain, was trying hard in January 1856 to obtain the cession of the Åland Islands. But it was too late. She had to content herself with the reduction of her demand to the demilitarization of the islands. This Count Orlov readily conceded in the peace negotiations, adding with some irony that Russia no longer attached any value to the fortifications as their construction had been faulty from the start.

It is quite remarkable that the solution of the Third Point posed few difficulties during the peace negotiations. Russia had accepted the principle of neutralization, that is, demilitarization, of the Black Sea. The Third Point had been the heart of Britain's war aims. Originally it was worded as the 'revision' of the Straits convention of 1841 'in the interest of the European balance of power'. During the Vienna peace negotiations in the spring of 1855 it was clarified and now meant the 'cessation of Russia's preponderance in the Black Sea'. The peace conference foundered on Austria's and Russia's resistance to this formula. The French Foreign Minister, Drouyn, had tried in vain to save the conference by bringing under consideration the 'neutralization' of the Black Sea. The idea was now resurrected and accepted by Russia. The blood spilt at Sevastopol had made this possible. During the Paris peace congress only one or two side issues that emanated from the principle were discussed. One point of contention was the number and size of the police vessels that were to be granted to Russia and Turkey. According to the British documents it was Palmerston who was pettifogging in this matter, because he feared such police vessels could form the nucleus of a future Russian Black Sea fleet. In the end, Russia was granted six steamships with a weight of up to 800 tons each, and four light steam or sailing ships of up to 200 tons each. Another point which the British treated with pettiness was whether the Sea of Azov and the inland ports of Kherson and Nikolaev fell within the scope of the principle of demilitarization. Here Orlov gracefully conceded the point and the British delegates carried the day.

According to the First Point, Russia had to give up her exclusive protectorate over the two Danubian Principalities, Wallachia and Moldavia. This she had done by accepting the Austrian ultimatum. During the peace negotiations the Russian delegates could lean back and let the others hammer out an alternative arrangement. The Austrian documents now published clearly show that it is wrong to state, as older books on the Crimean War often do, that Austria was trying hard to use her occupation of the Principalities to keep them for good. Some of the generals – like Hess and Coronini – certainly had this idea in mind, but the documents show that Emperor Francis Joseph and Buol never considered such a solution, even though Napoleon every now and then threw out a bait in this direction. They wanted a European solution to the status of the Principalities.[3]

In Paris it was again Napoleon who was the troublemaker. On 8 March he threw the gauntlet into the ring of the negotiations by making Walewski announce his intention to unite the two provinces. This proposal, supported lukewarmly by Clarendon (after the conclusion of peace, Britain was against it), militated against the interests both of Turkey and of Austria. The unification of the Principalities would loosen the bonds between the suzerain and his provinces and finally lead to independence. Such an independent medium-sized power on the flank of the Habsburg Empire would become a focus of territorial ambition for the Rumanians living in the Austrian crown land of Transylvania. It might also form an instrument of aggression in the hands of Russia, the other neighbouring power.

Why did Napoleon pose this dangerous principle, the principle of nationality, which had, up to that time, not been invoked in international relations? He had two objectives in view. By calling upon this new-fangled maxim, Napoleon hoped to create a precedent which he might invoke in other instances more directly advantageous to France – on the left bank of the Rhine, in Belgium or Savoy, for example. Another function that the principle would serve was, in a tortuous – typically Napoleonic – way, to raise the power of Sardinia and make that country dependent on him: the Duke of Modena in northern Italy was to be deposed and made king of the united Principalities. The Duchy of Parma would then be transferred to Modena and the latter be apportioned to Sardinia.[4]

Due to Austrian and Turkish resistance, the proposal was rejected. In the final peace treaty the status of the Principalities was paraphrased in negative terms: there was to be no more Russian protectorate; there was to be no further Russian interference in the internal affairs of the provinces, and so on. The positive side was shrouded in vagueness: the Principalities were to enjoy autonomy from the Porte; a mixed European commission was to be set up to inquire into the actual state of the provinces and then propose the basis for their future organization. It is obvious that these stipulations simply postponed the final decision and contained the germs for a future power struggle in this corner of Europe.

The Second Point demanded the freedom of navigation of the Danube, which had been impeded by Russia in the past. The peacemakers in Paris wanted to apply the principle of internationalizing rivers that flow through several countries to the Danube. The principle had been proclaimed by the Congress of Vienna and later on had been applied to the Rhine and the Elbe rivers. As regards the Danube, Austria wanted to restrict the principle to the delta and the lower Danube, but this was a weak position in view of the precedents that existed. In order to implement the principle the congress set up two commissions. One was the European Commission which had the task of dredging the river from Isacchea down to the delta region within two years. Its delegates would represent France, Austria, Britain, Prussia, Russia and Sardinia. The other commission was the Permanent Riverain Commission consisting of delegates from Austria, Bavaria, Württemberg, Turkey and the three Danubian Principalities (i.e. including Serbia). Its mandate was to work out a statute for the navigation and policing of the Danube and ultimately assume the role performed by the European Commission when the latter had been wound up.

The Fourth Point of the ultimatum concerned the immunity of the non-Muslim subjects of the Sultan. As noted earlier in relation to the Menshikov mission, the right assumed by Russia in a piecemeal fashion since the Treaty of Kutchuk-Kainardji (1774) to act as the protector of the Orthodox Christians within the Ottoman Empire had originally given rise to the occupation by Russian troops of the Danubian Principalities and to the outbreak of the Russo-Turkish war in 1853. Just before the opening of the Paris peace negotiations, on 18 February 1856, the Sultan published the *hat-i humayun*, an edict in which the equality of all cults and races within his empire was solemnly proclaimed. This was a revolutionary break with the old Ottoman principle that the subjects of the Sultan consisted of two classes: the Muslims, the dominant class; and the non-Muslims, the subject class. The proclamation of equality meant that Muslims would now be free to change their religion – an act which, according to the Koran, was punishable by death. Another consequence of the *hat* was that Christian missions would now be allowed to operate in the empire free from fear of persecution or molestation. Christian subjects of the Sultan would also be admitted to all public offices and there would be mixed courts for judicial matters concerning Christians and Muslims alike.

The Sultan proclaimed the *hat* of his own accord, but with the intention of forestalling any discussion at the peace congress that might infringe upon his dignity as an independent sovereign. In this calculation he was right. The powers found an innocuous formula in the peace treaty which acknowledged 'the high value' of the communication of the *hat* to the peace congress.

The congress finished its work in nineteen sessions within five weeks and signed the peace treaty on 30 March 1856. This speedy conclusion was due to efficient management by Napoleon, who behind the scenes gave audiences to the delegates when they found themselves at an impasse and wanted to appeal to him as an arbiter. It was also due to the negative experience of the Vienna peace conference a year earlier and to the general exhaustion of the belligerent powers in the theatres of war.

The delegates stayed in Paris beyond 30 March and held another five sessions. They discussed matters loosely or even wholly unconnected with the Eastern Question. The former included the Allied blockade, the evacuation of the occupied territories and the setting up of the international commissions provided for by the treaty. In the famous session of 8 April 1856, Walewski as president of the congress placed the Italian Question on the agenda. This

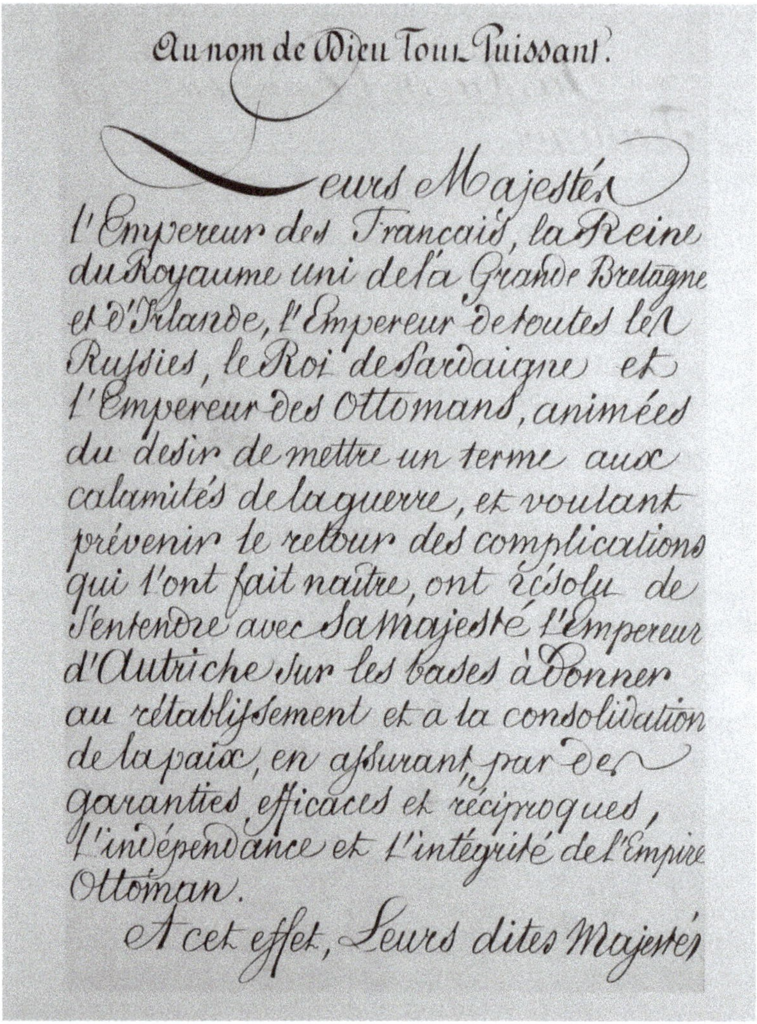
Au nom de Dieu Tout Puissant.

Leurs Majestés
l'Empereur des Français, la Reine
du Royaume uni de la Grande Bretagne
et d'Irlande, l'Empereur de toutes les
Russies, le Roi de Sardaigne et
l'Empereur des Ottomans, animées
du desir de mettre un terme aux
calamités de la guerre, et voulant
prévenir le retour des complications
qui l'ont fait naître, ont résolu de
s'entendre avec Sa Majesté l'Empereur
d'Autriche sur les bases à donner
au rétablissement et a la consolidation
de la paix, en assurant, par des
garanties efficaces et réciproques,
l'indépendance et l'intégrité de l'Empire
Ottoman.
A cet effet, Leurs dites Majestés

FIGURE 17 *The first page of the Treaty of Paris of 30 March 1856. Courtesy of Le Ministère des Affaires étrangères, Paris.*

was of course due to the untiring machinations of Cavour behind the scenes and to the wish of Napoleon 'to do something for Italy'. Napoleon had originally wanted to let the congress glide into a general discussion of all international questions currently unsolved or likely to produce contention in the future, ranging across Poland and the question of Cracow, the Italian Question, the situation of the press in Belgium, political refugees in Switzerland, the issue of Neuchâtel in Switzerland, the Danish Sound dues and many others. Such discussions would offer the opportunity to revise the whole treaty structure of the Vienna Congress and begin a general '*remaniement de la carte de l'Europe*', but after many exchanges behind the scenes, Napoleon was dissuaded from opening this Pandora's box.

The Italian Question was the only one which Britain – besides Cavour, of course – wanted to put on the agenda. It was to be expected that Buol would jump up and tell the congress that it had no mandate to discuss matters outside the framework of the Eastern Question. This is what actually happened. There were angry recriminations and counter-recriminations – the Russian delegates relishing the scene as the enemy powers cut each other up mercilessly. The upshot of it all was the meaningless 'wish' expressed by the congress to see a speedy evacuation of the Papal States by foreign troops (among them French troops!). Nobody was satisfied and everybody was angry. 'We have made bad work of it today with the Italian question,' Clarendon wrote to Palmerston. Cavour was in despair and described the declarations of 8 April as 'sterile wishes'.[5] The Italian Question was later solved not because of the Paris congress but in spite of it.

Another 'sterile wish' was placed on record in the session of 14 April. There Clarendon rose and asked the congress to give a general extension to the principle laid down in article 8 of the peace treaty that in case of future dissension between Turkey and one of the European great powers the disputants should, before using force, ask the powers not concerned to offer their mediation. This principle should be applied to all future international conflicts. After some desultory discussion, the proposal for a resolution was watered down to the expression of a 'wish' that the powers in conflict with each other should, before having recourse to arms, appeal to 'the good offices' of a friendly power.

From the documents now published it emerges that Clarendon's source of inspiration for his proposal was the London 'Peace Society', which had asked the Foreign Secretary to introduce into the peace treaty an article about arbitration in international conflicts.[6] This idea was one of the core features of the international peace movement of the nineteenth century. In contrast to the wish expressed by the Paris congress on 14 April to appeal to the 'good offices' of a third power by two states at loggerheads with each other, the Peace Society had asked for 'arbitration' to be provided for in the peace treaty. 'Arbitration' supposed the existence of a court or some such institution which would arbitrate and confront the conflicting powers with a decision they had to accept. The appeal to the 'good offices' was a completely non-obligatory affair.

Greater binding force was given to another proposal on international law that was brought forward in the session of 8 April 1856, again by Lord Clarendon. The congress, this time with unanimity, subscribed to the following principles of maritime law:

1 Abolition of privateering.
2 No seizure of enemy goods under neutral flags (except contraband of war).

3   No seizure of neutral goods under enemy flags (except contraband).
4   Effectiveness of blockades.

These proposals, which the British and French governments had worked out, were an outgrowth of the practice of both powers during the Crimean War. The right of privateering had in fact fallen into disuse since the end of the Napoleonic Wars. The European powers had issued no more letters of marque (government licences to capture a vessel of an enemy state) since 1815. Point 1 of the declaration is therefore only the formal renunciation of a practice in naval warfare that had lost its importance. Points 2 and 3 were in favour of neutral trade in times of war. Any ships carrying goods not contraband of war were now no longer subject to being halted, boarded and captured. The fourth principle underlined the necessity that for a blockade to be valid it had to be applied by force of arms, not simply by a paper declaration. Britain was now quite ready to subscribe to a more liberal approach to ships' cargoes than in former times of war because by the middle of the nineteenth century she was more dependent on the free flow of goods than ever before. On the other hand, she could now more easily cripple the war effort of an enemy country by virtue of her naval superiority, which would permit an effective blockade of enemy coasts.

With its declaration on maritime law the Paris peace congress closed its work after the actual signing of the peace treaty, not with a 'sterile wish', but with a resolution that marked an important advance in international law.

18

The consequences of the war
for international relations

In assessing the results of the Crimean War, two different, but complementary perspectives may be chosen: (i) the significance of the Treaty of Paris within the narrower framework of Russo-Turkish relations; and (ii) the repercussions of the Crimean War for international relations.

The Crimean War gave a chance of survival to the Ottoman Empire. Had Tsar Nicholas had his will in 1853 and had the Menshikov mission succeeded, this huge but decrepit empire would have fallen under the sway of Russia. The integrity of Turkey was, however, ensured by the war effort of Britain and France. Turkey was received as an equal member into the Concert of Europe and was put under the collective guarantee of the European great powers. This did not save Turkey from outside interference – in fact, it now became much more frequent and marked than in the period before 1853. However, this constant meddling in the internal affairs of Turkey by each of the great powers naturally led to competition, which in turn neutralized their influence. In the event, this was a major reason for the long survival of the Ottoman Empire until the First World War. Another reason was the will of the new Turkish leaders, Reshid, Ali and Fuad Pasha, to introduce and implement reforms to the structure of the empire.

The effect of these reforms was not only impaired by the interference of the European powers, but also by the poison of nationalism. It led to the disintegration of the empire, starting on its periphery – the Balkans, Syria, Palestine, Egypt and Crete. In the Balkans the first peoples to emancipate themselves from Turkish dominion and suzerainty were the Serbs, the Rumanians and the Montenegrins. Turkey as the suzerain power and Austria as the immediate neighbour were the champions of the status quo of 1856 in the Balkans. This was vague enough. France on the other hand supported the process of emancipation in these regions. To a certain extent she was joined by Russia, which wanted to take revenge for the defeat of 1856. Britain vacillated. The leading circles in Rumania and Serbia took political matters into their own hands, sure of French support, and exploited every European crisis after 1856 – the wars of 1859, 1864, 1866 and 1870–71 – in order to free themselves from the Turkish yoke. Step by step Serbia, Rumania and

Montenegro obtained autonomy until their independence was sanctioned by Europe in 1878 at the Congress of Berlin.

The stipulations of the Treaty of Paris that were most vexatious to Russia were the neutralization of the Black Sea and the cession of parts of Bessarabia. Neutralization meant the restriction of Russia's sovereignty over her Black Sea coast. Her foreign policy after 1856 was geared to regaining that sovereignty. On the other hand, each of the European powers, except Britain, offered Russia concealed help to undo that stipulation. After 1858, hardly a year elapsed in which Russia was not told by France, Prussia or Austria that they would support her in scrapping the article for a quid pro quo. In the summer of 1866 – during the Austro-Prussian war – Alexander M. Gorchakov, Russia's Foreign Minister after the end of the war, prepared a circular for Russia's diplomatic representatives abroad announcing the neutralization of the Black Sea to be null and void. But the war of 1866 was over too soon for Gorchakov's pronouncement to be opportune. Four years later, after the outbreak of the Franco-Prussian war, the moment seemed once again propitious. On 31 October 1870, Gorchakov took the circular from the drawer and announced to Europe that Russia no longer felt herself bound by the relevant articles of the Paris peace treaty. Although there was a general outcry over the unilateral way in which Russia handled the question, all the signatory powers, Britain now included, did not raise material objections. In a European conference, which took place in London between January and March 1871, Russia's action was sanctioned *post festum*.

The article of the Treaty of Paris that dealt with the cession of part of Bessarabia remained in force only a few years longer. After Russia's next war against Turkey in 1877–8, which this time did not lead to a general European war, one of Russia's demands was the retrocession of Bessarabia. The relevant article in the Treaty of San Stefano of 3 March 1878 was given European sanction by the Berlin Congress of that year. Thus Russia had undone two of the most humiliating clauses of the Paris peace treaty within a relatively short time.

The repercussions of the Crimean War for the policy of the European great powers and their mutual relations were far reaching. Together with the revolution years of 1848–9, the Crimean War marks a turning-point in European history. The Concert of Europe, which had been formed after the Napoleonic Wars in order to subdue revolutionary movements and settle international conflicts through international conferences, had to a large extent broken down. Power politics that had been softened up to that time by the principle of solidarity were now pursued in a more naked, brutal and unilateral form. The age of *realpolitik* began and was pursued by a new generation of statesmen – of whom Schwarzenberg in Austria, Napoleon III in France, Gorchakov in Russia and Bismarck in Prussia are the most conspicuous representatives.

For Russia, the Crimean War marked a radical change in her foreign policy. The war had revealed the basic weaknesses in the fabric of her

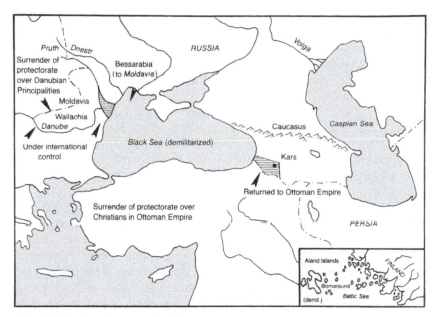

MAP 11 *Russian losses under the Treaty of Paris, 1856.*

power: her autocratic government system, her sterile social structure, her army system based on serfdom, the backwardness of her economy. Defeat in war had taught the new Tsar that reforms had to be introduced, but reforms that would not undermine his autocratic power. Thus the abolition of serfdom was prepared and implemented as a necessary prerequisite for reform of the army. Foreign capital was attracted in order to build a railway network that would develop industry and make the army, the most important pillar of the autocratic system, more mobile. Russian policy after 1856 was therefore focused on development of the social and economic resources of the country.

Foreign policy now played second fiddle to domestic policy. Russia relinquished her role as the 'gendarme of Europe', a role she had played for decades under Alexander I and Nicholas I. In one of his first diplomatic circulars to Europe, the new Foreign Minister announced, 'People say that Russia is sulky. Russia is not sulky, she is collecting her strength.'[1] Russia would also abstain from intervention in foreign countries in order to defend general principles, like solidarity among the great powers and the legitimacy of sovereigns. Russia would now go about her own business, and this meant first and foremost revising the Paris peace treaty of 1856.

To facilitate such a policy Russia was open to a rapprochement with France. This had been initiated before and during the Paris peace congress. Napoleon had by then dropped Austria as a partner because she was such a

dyed-in-the-wool conservative power that any revision or any redrawing of
the map of Europe seemed impossible. Why should not two revisionist
powers come together? Napoleon dreamt of bringing Britain into such an
alliance, but he misinterpreted the deep-rooted antagonism of that power
towards Russia. So he had to content himself with a rapprochement with
Russia. Yet it never reached the intimacy of a proper alliance. It bore fruit
when France together with Sardinia waged war on Austria over northern
Italy in 1859, when Russia repaid Austria in kind by concentrating an army
of observation on the Galician frontier. It showed its first cracks when Tsar
Alexander II realized that France's intervention in the process of Italian
unity was openly revolutionary. It broke down when Napoleon supported
the Polish uprising of 1863.

Austria was the country that suffered the most serious consequences
from the Crimean War. She may be accused of having vacillated between an
alliance with Russia, which Nicholas had offered her, and a war alliance
with the two Western powers, but, as already noted, there was no alternative
to this policy. Any participation in the war on either side would have meant
a general European convulsion which would in turn have led to a second
edition of the revolution of 1848–9 and the break-up of her multinational
empire. Such prospects were clearly before Buol's and Francis Joseph's eyes,
and they therefore chose the lesser evil of staying out of the war and running
the risk of isolating Austria in the midst of the other great powers. Their
search for a firm alliance with Britain and France was unsuccessful because
the conditions for such an alliance, in terms of the inner structure of the
three powers, were missing. Austria had thus to cope with the forces of
nationalism by falling back on her own resources. She succumbed to them
in two wars: in 1859 when Italian nationalism allied itself with France; and
in 1866 when Prussia, allied to the new Italy, solved the perennial problem
of German dualism in her favour.

Prussia had managed to withstand the temptations from East and West
during the Crimean War. She was the power that profited more than any
other country from the disintegration of the Concert of Europe. She profited
from Austria's weakness and from the passiveness of Russia's foreign policy
after 1856. This was not due to the dynastic ties that existed between the
houses of Hohenzollern and the Romanovs, or any sense of gratitude that
the Tsar might have felt for Prussia's neutrality during the Crimean War, but
rather the immobility of her two neighbours that she exploited under
Bismarck and which paved the way to German unification. In three short
wars she brought about the *kleindeutsch* solution of the German question
without having to fear the intervention of Russia or any other power.

Napoleon III found himself in 1856 at the zenith of his power. He had
managed to strike the death blow to the Holy Alliance, the guardian of the
system of 1815. He had allied himself to Britain and together with her had
brought Russia to her knees. For a short while he was the arbiter of Europe,
but as he made the principle of nationality the focal point of his foreign

policy he barred the way to a lasting alliance with one of the great powers. Although his alliance with Britain survived the Crimean War, both partners drifted apart and their interests soon collided over Italy and over countless details of the Eastern Question. France lost Russia over the Polish uprising. Napoleon flirted again with Austria, but in the German Question he was no match for the craftiness of Bismarck. He finally discredited himself through his Mexican adventure. He had come to power through revolution and finally perished through war.

For Britain, the Crimean War ended too soon. Great exertions had been made to continue the war in 1856, with hundreds of gunboats built specifically for a grand naval campaign in the Baltic. In February 1856 the British army in the Crimea for the first time surpassed the French army in numbers. The humiliation of the failure before the Redan was not yet avenged. Napoleon's yearning for peace after Sevastopol and Austria's ultimatum cheated Britain out of a resounding success in the campaign of 1856. Therefore the general feeling in the country, both in terms of public opinion and within the government, was one of despair and exasperation. Much blood had been spilt and much money had been spent. And the result? Russia's power was not reduced substantially, but had received only a scratch on the surface. The antagonism between the two countries remained as strong as ever; it was now merely transferred from the Near to the Middle and the Far East. The result of Britain's disappointment over the meagre results of the Crimean War was that she turned her back on the affairs of the European continent and concentrated her efforts on reforms at home and on the consolidation of her empire overseas. Sir Robert Morier later described the Crimean War as 'the only perfectly useless modern war that has been waged'.[2] In a somewhat softer tone, Disraeli, who was Leader of the Opposition during the Crimean conflict, referring to the many problems it had left unsolved and the new ones it had created, called the struggle 'a just but unnecessary war'.[3] Indeed, it was as unnecessary as every war is, but it was rich in consequences.

Annotated bibliography
(for chapters 17 and 18)

The Paris peace congress of 1856 is discussed in Baumgart, *Peace of Paris*. All the issues mentioned here are discussed at length in this book. There are two collections of essays commemorating the 150th anniversary of the peace congress: George-Henri Soutou (ed.), *Napoléon et l'Europe. 1856, le congrès de Paris* (Versailles, 2006); Gilbert Ameil (ed.), *Le congrès de Paris (1856). Un événement fondateur* (Brussels, 2009). How the results of the war related to the execution of the peace treaty is dealt with by Werner E. Mosse, *The Rise and Fall of the Crimean System, 1855–71: The Story of a*

Peace Settlement (London, 1963). For a general discussion on the context of international relations, cf. the corresponding chapters in Winfried Baumgart, *Europäisches Konzert und nationale Bewegung. Internationale Beziehungen 1830–1878* (Paderborn, 1999, 2nd edn 2007). A new study on Austria after the war is provided by Katharina Weigand, *Österreich, die Westmächte und das europäische Staatensystem nach dem Krimkrieg (1856–1859)* (Husum, 1997).

19

The medical services

As to human losses in the wars in modern European history up to the Crimean War,[1] the general statement is correct that death from actual fighting plays a far lesser role than death from disease, first of all from infectious disease. Most of the time soldiers do not fight, but sit or lie in cramped space in the most uncomfortable conditions of life. Such masses of men are an ideal hotbed for infectious diseases – and these affect the health of armies either marching or camping. When in the summer of 1829, during the Russo-Turkish War, Russian troops arrived at Adrianople, the capture of Constantinople seemed just a matter of days away. But then dysentery spread among the army to such a degree (more than one-third of the Russians in the city of Adrianople were affected) that the Russian commander-in-chief preferred to conclude peace with the Turks as quickly as possible.[2]

Twenty-five years later, at the time of the Crimean War, medical science had progressed compared with 1829; but the decisive breakthrough in combating infectious disease had not yet succeeded. The causes of such diseases – bacteria – were not yet discovered and therefore could not be controlled, but instead rage freely. A handful of researchers at the time adhered to the theory of 'contagium vivum', that is, that the focus of infectious diseases could only be found within the living organism; but the majority adhered to the 'miasma theory', that is, that (infectious) diseases arise solely outside the human body. The actual dissemination could not be described. It was only when Robert Koch and Louis Pasteur made their discoveries in the second half of the nineteenth century that the causes became clearer. In 1882, Koch discovered the tubercle bacillus and a year later the cholera bacillus so that from now on preventive countermeasures (vaccination) could be taken.

The Crimean War with its many epidemics that raged among the soldiers was the occasion for an acrimonious debate between 'miasmatics' and 'contagionists' (who thought that the centres of contagion were to be sought within the human body). Thus in July–August 1854, when cholera spread among the Allied troops assembled at Varna, the surgeon general of the British Army of the East, Dr John Hall, advocated the opinion that by

taking the troops from the unhealthy town of Varna with its heaps of
garbage and swampy surroundings and transporting them across the Black
Sea to the Crimea, the health of the soldiers would improve considerably. In
reality, the cholera travelled with them on board the ships to Eupatoria.[3]
Hall's French colleague, Dr Auguste Marroin, was quite right when he
wrote:

> The convalescents coming from the hospital at Gallipoli brought the
> infection with them on our ships and then to the hospitals at Varna ...
> On the day of the departure of the ships [on 1 September 1854], the
> cholera struck the vessels with an extraordinary intensity ... This fact
> seems to furnish arguments to the contagionists.[4]

Diseases: cholera, typhoid, hospital gangrene, scurvy

Cholera

In contrast to typhoid or scurvy, cholera was a fairly new disease for
Europeans. It had invaded the continent thirty years earlier, when it was
transported from the Ganges region of India to Eastern Europe in the mid-
1820s, whence it trickled across the Russian frontiers to Central and Western
Europe. In the course of the nineteenth century it caused millions of deaths
in Europe and the United States. The epidemic of 1832 – the second of its
kind in Europe – caused, in France alone, the death of 103,000 people. The
Crimean War occurred during a third epidemic visiting Europe from 1847
to 1857. In 1854 the cholera wave reached the British Isles. It wrought
havoc in London especially: in the three summer months of June to August,
the death rate there amounted to 11,777.[5] At the same time it hit the Allied
expeditionary corps in Varna.

The starting-point of this cholera epidemic was not in Varna itself, but in
southern France. Even at the time, its progress could be clearly traced.[6] On
26 June 1854, the French steamer *Alexandre* had left Marseilles with troops
on board. The soldiers were taken ill immediately on departure. The first
casualty was disembarked at Messina, the second at Piraeus. The soldiers
had previously marched through Avignon where the cholera was already
raging; Marseilles was affected, too. In the course of further shipments, the
cholera spread among the French expeditionary corps. Instead of isolating
the infected vessels at Gallipoli or Constantinople, the French Commander-
in-Chief, Marshal Saint-Arnaud, ordered them to proceed to Varna and
thereby gave free reign to the disease. On 21 July, ninety-four cases were
registered there, thirty-seven of which ended fatally. The men died within a
few hours.

Saint-Arnaud made matters worse by ordering three of his divisions away from the crowded situation in Varna to march to the Dobrudja in order to expel Russian troops there. The expedition very quickly ended in utter desaster. In the hot and humid climate the soldiers dropped dead like flies. Within a few days, 6,000 died, having hardly seen any Russians. Thus without engaging with the enemy, all three divisions were decimated.

In the same period there were also many cholera victims in the English camp at Varna. The disease spread among the two fleets.[7] The Allied commanders, spurred on by orders from London, hit upon the idea of evacuating the troops to the Crimea as quickly as possible. But this proved of no avail. Throughout the war, cholera remained a constant companion of the Allied troops in the Crimea. In the winter of 1854–5 it did not spread significantly, but with the onset of warmer weather in 1855, the disease in both armies developed again into an epidemic. In the British camp at Balaklava the death toll rose to 1,600 within a few months.[8]

Prominent victims of the cholera included Marshal Saint-Arnaud, on 29 September 1854, and Lord Raglan, the British Commander-in-Chief, on 28 June 1855. Admiral Bruat, the Commander-in-Chief of the French fleet in the Mediterranean and the Black Sea, followed suit on 19 November 1855. Nonetheless, cholera caused fewer deaths among officers than among the ranks. This phenomenon was attributed to better living conditions and observation of the basic rules of hygiene among officers.[9] Although the opinion was still widespread that bad air on the ships, in the tents and barracks was the main cause of the disease spreading, it was noticeable that officers who helped themselves to much wine and avoided water were hardly affected by cholera. It was only in the second half of the nineteenth century that the opinion gained ground that the main cause of cholera was polluted water.

In total, cholera was responsible for 11,000 deaths in the French *Armée d'Orient* and 4,500 deaths in the British Army of the East.[10] The death rate among cholera cases in both armies reached 60 per cent. It is remarkable that cholera in the Russian garrison in Sevastopol never grew to the dimension of an epidemic as it did with the French and British.[11] This may be due to the fact that the Russians, who were quartered in fortified garrisons, had a far more regular supply of drinking water than the Allied soldiers. One of the Russian staff physicians, Anton Hubbenet, pointed out that each soldier was questioned by his officer twice a day about stomach and intestinal complaints, proof that precautions against the spread of disease were applied in a systematic fashion by the Russians. According to Hubbenet, there were few cholera cases in 1854, whereas for the year 1855 he mentions the figure of 3,500 deaths.[12]

In November 1855 the German Legion, comprising 10,000 men, arrived at Skutari (Constantinople) and was immediately struck by cholera. Some 200 cases were registered,[13] but there are no figures for the death rate.

Typhoid

In British books on the Crimean War and in British national identity, the 'Crimean winter' of 1854–5, with its thousands of victims from diverse diseases, has been raised to a myth, especially due to by the articles by *The Times* correspondent William Howard Russell. In addition to cholera, diarrhoea and scurvy, frostbite is also at the top of Russell's list. But he does not mention the causes of death. These reflected the poor supply of clothes and food. Yet, Russell does not mention a disease that was well known and widespread at the time – typhoid. It was never an epidemic in the British army, but judging from French research, the picture for the French *Armée d'Orient* was quite different. Although the death rate due to typhoid among French soldiers was almost the same in both winters (1854–5 and 1855–6) – that is, 11,000[14] – it was the second winter that stood out, not because of the statistics – 20,000 soldiers suffering from typhoid, 10,000 of whom died – but because there was hardly any fighting in this period.[15] In the same winter, the British Army of the East lost only sixteen soldiers due to typhoid.

The first cases of typhoid appeared in the French army in spring 1855, but the number was at first limited. In January 1856 the number of infected men rose dramatically and reached its climax in March when in one day alone, 257 new cases were recorded.[16] The French physicians knew very well what the causes really were. Because typhoid is infectious, the situation was exacerbated due to 'the impossibility to isolate the infected men and the overcrowding of hospitals'.[17] From the beginning of the war, those who were sick but could be moved were evacuated from the Crimea to Constantinople, while the convalescents who were no longer fit for military service were reshipped to France. In this way the highly infectious disease spread widely. The inspector of the French medical service, Lucien Baudens, demanded two precautionary measures to check the disease: 'First to send no more sick to France and secondly to keep all typhoid cases in the Crimea and isolate them from the sick bound for Constantinople.'[18] Tragically, Baudens himself fell ill with typhus and died in Paris in 1857.

The really nasty thing about the epidemic was that because of the high risk of infection the medical staff themselves succumbed. In the winter months of 1855–6, forty-six doctors died from typhoid (eighty-two during the whole war) as did twenty-four 'Sisters of Mercy' (thirty-one in all).[19] Only when the evacuation of the *Armée d'Orient* was completed, in August 1856, did the epidemic die down.

Hospital gangrene

Like cholera, hospital gangrene was widespread in all three (four, if the Turks are included) Crimean armies. It was one of the most dreaded diseases in the overcrowded military hospitals at that time. Baudens called it 'the most terrible enemy the Army of the East had to fight with'.[20] Gangrene develops in fresh or healing wounds and makes them grow deeper and larger. The tissue involved decays: it 'necrotizes'. There was no treatment for this problem at the time: the affected limbs, mostly feet or hands, had to be amputated. A few years later, in the 1860s, the English surgeon Joseph Lister promoted the idea of sterile surgery, that is, he disinfected the wounds and protected them with sterile dressings so that they could no longer get into contact with putrefactive agents. In the Crimean War, all wounded soldiers were liable to hospital gangrene either due to an injury or to its surgical treatment.

There are no statistics about the number of those who died from gangrene. The official statistics generally carry the designation 'killed and wounded'. Sometimes the categories are separated, but there are no details about the wounded who survived or died sooner or later. In any event, it is hardly possible to extract the number of gangrene-dead from the general number of casualties. Many wounded soldiers developed several diseases that ended in death, so that the statistician is at a loss to determine who died from which disease. At any rate, contemporary data permit us to establish the ratio between those who were wounded and died and those who were discharged and cured. It varies between 1:3 and 1:5, so that a rough average of 1:4 should be realistic. In individual cases, however, one must differentiate. Thus, on the battlefield of the Alma, there were about 1,800 Russians killed and 3,900 wounded. Nobody counted the latter. The Russian army had to evacuate the field after having lost the battle and had not been able to recover these men. The Allies' first priority was their own dead and wounded, and only two or three days later did they attend to the Russians, many of whom had by then succumbed to their wounds. To a much higher degree, this also applies to the Battle of Inkerman of 4 November 1854.

Scurvy

Scurvy exemplifies the phenomenon that Crimean soldiers often suffered from several diseases which exacerbated their physical weakness. It was a disease well known long before the Crimean War and was widespread among ships' crews, in besieged fortresses and among expeditionary groups. It was already known that it was a nutritional disorder, which led to spontaneous bleeding, pain in the limbs, and so on, and that it could be combated by vitamin C. The absence of vitamin C from a diet for two to four months causes tooth bleeding or even the loss of teeth, which makes chewing very painful or even impossible, bleeding from the nose and the intestines and also ulceration, which may lead to gangrene.

In the Crimean War the British fleet and army were much less affected by scurvy than their French allies. This was possibly due to the experience of the British as a seafaring nation who knew how to deal with the disease much better than the French. Since the 1760s, ships of the Royal Navy had been obliged to carry lemons as part of their food supplies as a preventive measure.

The first cases of scurvy in the French Crimean navy appeared as early as August 1853. In the second half of 1854, scurvy developed to epidemic proportions in both the navy and the army. The cause was the uniform food which mostly consisted of salted meat and dried vegetables. The countermeasures were obvious. The symptoms could be subdued by introducing fresh meat and fresh vegetables. The nutritional situation was normally good at Constantinople, where there were many military hospitals and where the necessary food could be procured in the bazaars. Shipping traffic between Constantinople and Kamiesh (the French supply depot in the Crimea) and Balaklava developed curious practices: in winter, half pigs and cows were hung up in the open air; in summer, live animals were put on board which could be slaughtered on the spot.

In spite of these preventive measures, the death rate among soldiers suffering from scurvy was appallingly high. However, the available records differ widely and point to a problem which is inherent in all statistics relating to the Crimean War: their unreliability, which at times is incredible. Baudens mentions 26,000 cases of scurvy in the French army for the period of April 1855 to August 1856. Of these, 3,634 died.[21] The surgeon general of the *Armée d'Orient*, Jean Charles Chenu, writes of 16,000 scurvy cases for the longer period of October 1854 to March 1856, of whom 1,109 died.[22] He lists 1,935 scurvy cases and 165 dead for the British army in the same period. The latter figure at least shows that scurvy did not assume epidemic dimensions in the British Army of the East. In Russian statistics, scurvy does not show up at all because, obviously, their supply sitution was much more favourable as the hinterland was open to them.

The medical service: surgeons and nursing staff

In comparison with the Napoleonic Wars, the medical and nursing situation during the Crimean War was relatively good on both sides. This is due to the fact that the war of 1854–6 was a trench war which enabled a stable infrastructure for the medical service; the Napoleonic Wars, in contrast, were mobile wars which did not permit of a mobile medical service. And after all, forty to fifty years had elapsed since the Napoleonic Wars, during which medical treatment had made some progress. Of course, the Crimean War years cannot be compared with the two world wars of the twentieth century in terms of medical advances.

Surgeons

The French medical service, which dates back to the beginning of the eithteenth century, suffered, under Napoleon, from a basic problem which Chenu in 1870 formulated thus:

> Les médecins de l'armée française ne sont . . . que des agents d'exécution, sans autorité, sans initiative et sans responsabilité. Ils ne dirigent rien, et il leur est même interdit de s'immiscer dans les détails du service administratif.

> [The doctors of the French army are . . . only executive organs having neither authority nor initiative nor responsibility. They have . . . no right whatsoever to interfere in the details of the administrative service.][23]

In the Crimean War the subordination of the medical service to the commissariat meant that the doctors did not develop initiatives in questions vital to the medical service: in the construction and the equipment of military hospitals or tents, in the supply of food and medical material, in the ambulance service from the front line to the various hospitals at Kamiesh and Constantinople, and so on. Besides, the rank of surgeon carried no military status unlike later on (and today), so that at the barrack gates, curious scenes might be played out: for example, the medical inspector (who possessed the highest rank in the medical hierarchy) would not be saluted by the guard, whereas an accompanying officer, whatever his rank, would be.[24]

The training of surgeons in the French army was better organized than in the British army. They had gone through the normal training in the medical faculties and then specialized in the military hospital of Val-de-Grâce in Paris. The surgeons who were on duty in the Crimea and at Constantinople came from this hospital or from the army in Algeria where they had gained useful experience.[25]

The medical service in the French *Armée d'Orient* was inspected by two prominent military surgeons: Michel Lévy and Lucien Baudens. Lévy was one of the great hygienists of the nineteenth century. In his book of 1845, *Traité d'hygiène*, he underlined the importance of public hygiene, which he termed 'social medicine'. When he inspected the hospitals in Constantinople and the Crimea, he waged a futile battle against the routine and apathy of the commissariat. The members of this service did not know what prevention or hygiene really was. Thus, in the hospital in Constantinople they had cholera cases and wounded soldiers in proximity. Six months after Lévy had departed from the Levant, Baudens took over the duty of inspection in September 1855. He fought the same futile battle against the indolence of the commissariat officers. His recommendations regarding hygiene were either ignored or put into practice too late.

The 550 French surgeons on duty in the East suffered a high death toll: eighty-three died while on duty, only one of them from a war wound: fifty-eight from typhoid, eighteen from cholera and six from other diseases.[26]

The death toll in the British medical service was somewhat lower because there was no typhoid epidemic in the British army. In contrast to France, there was no special training centre for military surgeons in Britain, but they were supposed to have obtained a commission at one of the royal surgical institutions and practical experience in a hospital. When the war started in the East, it was not easy to establish a medical corps in sufficient numbers. During the first Crimean winter, when everything went wrong in the British army, quite a number of surgeons made use of their right to quit the service and return to Britain. It was simply nerve-racking to grapple each day with the red tape instead of helping the sick and wounded as conscience demanded. At the political top in London there were not only two state secretaries for war (one Secretary at War and one Secretary for War and the Colonies), but also three different organizations overseeing the medical and hospital services of the British army: the Commissariat and the Purveyor's Department, both of which came under the authority of the Treasury, and the Medical Department, which was answerable to the Secretary at War (Sidney Herbert until February 1855, Lord Panmure thereafter).[27] The spheres of authority of the first two organizations overlapped inextricably, so that a surgeon who ordered some medical equipment was sent back and forth with the result that a sick man on the spot would come to a wretched end over the interminable red tape.

The immovability of these institutions was so scandalous that, together with the deadlock in the fighting at Sevastopol, it provoked a change of government in January 1855. During the course of the war, no fewer than four committees of inquiry investigated this bureaucratic quagmire. The result, though, was quite remarkable. The supply of the British army and of the medical service worked much better in the second Crimean winter. The service was now up to its task and the mortality rate among soldiers dropped significantly, ultimately reversing the situation that had prevailed in the first Crimean winter in comparison to the condition of the French army. Now the British were doing well whereas the French lost thousands and thousands of sick, so that Napoleon III began to seriously consider withdrawing his army from the East in the spring of 1856.

A typical British expedient in the second half of the Crimean War was to recruit civilian doctors from across Britain and even institute two hospitals managed entirely by civilian doctors: at Smyrna and at Renköy (Renkioi) on the Dardanelles.[28]

Of the 720 British doctors who served in the East, fifty died of sickness and two from war wounds.[29] The ratio between survivors and dead looks much better than on the French side.

Civilian doctors not only served in the British medical service of the East but also, in greater numbers, in its Russian counterpart – 118 altogether.[30] A special feature of the Russian side was the presence of 114 German and American doctors in the Russian medical corps. Their salary was higher than that of the Russian doctors, which produced much envy of the foreign personnel. The communication problems created additional complications.

A high percentage of Russian military surgeons in the Crimea were young and inexperienced, many of whom had not even finished their training. Anton von Hubbenet specifies their number as 1,231, working alongside more experienced colleagues who numbered 1,608.[31] Compared with the French and British surgeons, the figure is enormous, the more so when one adds the 'auxiliary surgeons', which brought the total to 3,759.

However, this figure must be seen in relation to the size of the Russian army in the Crimea. In the garrison of Sevastopol alone there were 170,000 soldiers during the whole siege period;[32] in addition there were approximately 230,000 men stationed in other garrisons of the Crimea. Hubbenet's casualty list (dead, wounded and sick) for Sevastopol amounts to the appallingly high number of 139,000, which means that only about 31,000 survived the war without injury or sickness.[33] The total number of Russian army personnel in the Crimea who were treated medically up to 13 November 1855 is about 325,000. In light of these figures, the number of military surgeons is by no means high so that the complaint in the sources of a want of medical personnel – which one reads in the French and British Armies of the East as well – is very justified.

There is another fact peculiar to the Russian side which should be mentioned. Although no clear difference is made in Russian statistics between wounded and sick, the number of wounded, in comparison with the corresponding Allied figures, is incomparably higher. The number of Russian casualties in the battles of the Alma, Balaklava, Inkerman, Evpatoria and the Tchernaya (over 26,000 dead and wounded)[34] was enormous. And the rate of wounded and dead in the twelve months' siege is even higher. This can be illustrated by just a few statistics: the two days of the Allied bombardment of 17–18 June 1855 cost the Russians about 5,500 dead and wounded; the continuous bombardment in August produced 1,000 dead and wounded per day. The list of dead and wounded from October 1854 to 8 September 1855 amounted to 100,000.[35] These figures clearly show that Russian surgeons had to look after many more wounded than did the Allies.

The most prominent Russian surgeons to serve in the Crimean army were Nikolay Ivanovich Pirogov and Anton Christian von Hübbenet (Hubbeneth). Pirogov was professor at the Medical-Surgical Academy in St Petersburg; Hubbeneth was professor of medicine at the Saint Vladimir University in Kiev. Pirogov was the most renowned Russian surgeon of the time, who made a name for himself in the field of 'war surgery'. When he went to the Crimea he took with him several surgeons he had trained in St Petersburg. He arrived there in November 1854, and in the course of the following months he performed numerous operations and amputations. His letters from Sevastopol, written in the form of a diary from November 1854 to December 1855, are published[36] and give a graphic description of his work in the Crimea. Hubbeneth brought with him four of his best disciples from

Kiev. A comprehensive report of his stay in the Crimea was published in 1870. It is Hubbeneth to whom we are in debt for the wealth of statistics about the self-sacrifice of Russian surgeons in the Crimea.[37] Of the 2,839 surgeons, 354, or one-eighth, died, only five of them from war wounds. Of the 3,759 auxiliary surgeons, 1,664 died (or were unfit for service) during the years 1853 to 1856.

Nursing staff

There are practically no sources available regarding non-medical auxiliary staff. Suffice to say that this group – medical orderlies, stretcher-bearers, dressers, and so on – performed the lower services and consisted of older, convalescent or punished soldiers who were mostly drunk and difficult to manage.

In contrast to this male group of auxiliary personnel, we are well informed about the female nursing staff. Their activity on both sides of the Crimean War is a novel thing in the history of war and of the medical service. Up to that time, the employment of women in the rough and brutal circumstances of war was inconceivable. In comparison with the medical service – trained and untrained – their number is small indeed. It may have been 500 altogether in all three armies. From the viewpoint of the surgeons – and this is well documented in the British case – their presence was unwelcome. The relationship gradually changed, but tensions remained until the end of the war. Between the most prominent nurse, Florence Nightingale, and the surgeon general of the British Army of the East, Dr John Hall, there developed a deep-seated animosity which almost resulted in a parliamentary committee of inquiry. Pirogov, on the other side, seems to have gladly taken the Russian sisters with him; at least he is full of praise for them during his stay at Sevastopol.[38]

The British nurses

Among the nurses of the Crimean War, Florence Nightingale is the most prominent and the best known. She has become a legend and the books on her are her legacy. Through the classical biography of Cecil Woodham-Smith[39] and her letters from the Crimean War published by Sue M. Goldie,[40] Nightingale has emerged as a figure of some substance. Most of the surgeons in Constantinople and in the Crimea met her with dislike or even hostility because she ruled over the hospitals with an iron fist and regularly subverted the procedures of the hospital service. In contrast to the surgeons, she had the immeasurable advantage that public opinion in Britain was unanimously on her side and praised her to the skies, while the Secretary at War, Sidney Herbert,[41] supported her with enthusiasm and the Queen was her mighty protectress.

Nightingale was the symbol of a mighty reform movement in Britain which wanted to improve the lot of the industrial workers, slum dwellers, the privates in the army, the child workers, the slaves in the British colonies and the whole milieu of the underclass. Her activity in the East therefore caused a sensational response in her mother country. Nightingale was absolutely convinced of her misson. On the one hand her letters reveal a boundless conceit, on the other a morbid distrust of almost everybody she had to deal with at Skutari (Constantinople) and Balaklava: the military surgeons, the officers of the army and of the commissariat, the ambassador in Constantinople (Lord Redcliffe), the chief surgeon of the hospitals in Constantinople (Dr Duncan Menzies) and the principal medical officer of the Army of the East (Dr John Hall). She even developed reservations about the nurses she had brought with her from England because they did not sacrifice themselves for the sick with the same selfless devotion that she did. She hated red tape which, in the special situation of the war, clung to routine and produced immobility. She hated the surgeons because they did not care two hoots about the wellbeing of the soldiers, whom they and the officers regarded as 'the scum of the earth'. She did not trust anybody an inch because she feared rivalry. Like someone possessed, she was wrapped up in her work. At heart she revelled in the feeling of riding a wave of popularity in Britain, but she also feared the prospect of falling from this pinnacle if she should fail in her superhuman effort to save thousands of wounded and sick from death.

When the war correspondent William Howard Russell published his moving reports in *The Times* about the suffering of the British army in the Crimea, on 9, 12 and 13 Ocotber 1854, the moment had come for Florence Nightingale to leave England for the East. On 9 October, Russell had said of the Battle of the Alma, 'The number of lives which have been sacrificed by the want of proper arrangements and neglect must be considerable.'[42] And on 13 October, he wrote about the conditions in the Skutari hospital:

The manner in which the sick and wounded are treated is worthy only of the savages of Dahomey . . . The worn-out pensioners who were brought as an ambulance corps are totally useless, and not only are surgeons not to be had, but there are no dressers or nurses to carry out the surgeon's directions . . . Here the French are greatly our superiors. Their arrangements are extremely good, their surgeons who have accompanied the expedition in incredible numbers. These devoted women are excellent nurses.

On 24 October 1854, Florence Nightingale set out with a group of thirty-eight nurses for Constantinople, where she arrived on 5 November. The group, which had been pulled together in a great hurry, consisted of fourteen professional nurses from English hospitals and ten Catholic and Anglican Sisters of Mercy. The surgeons at Skutari received them with coolness, even hostility. Nightingale therefore went to work with caution. But when the hospital organization broke down with the arrival of the many wounded from the Crimea, the contribution of the nurses was accepted with gratitude.

Nightingale's activity has been described in many books and articles so that it is only necessary to point to its beneficial results. Step by step she introduced a basic standard of cleanliness and order into what had been the chaotic and unhygienic conditions of the hospitals. With the support of *The Times*, she had a sum of money at her own disposal, which had been gathered in Britain. This meant she could circumvent the army bureaucracy. But she soon groaned under the red tape which, in many ways, she was forced to produce herself. The result was that she did not have much time for her personal work at the sickbed. The image of the 'Lady with the lamp', therefore, is far from accurate. Rations for the sick were raised to a level worthy of human beings and diet kitchens were introduced. After months of indefatigable activity, even mental and emotional care was introduced by setting up recreation and reading rooms and even singing hours and theatre performances.

At the same time, Nightingale kept a keen eye on the Catholic nurses lest they should proselytize among the convalescents. In this respect, there was an oversensitivity about Nightingale that strikes one as odd today. When on 15 December 1854, at the instigation of Sidney Herbert, a second group of forty-six sisters arrived at Skutari from Britain, Nightingale was on the verge of a nervous breakdown. She behaved in the same manner as the doctors had when she had arrived some weeks before. She cut dead the leader of the group, Mary Stanley,[43] with whom she had been friends, and did not admit her to the two hospitals at Skutari. She got ready to leave Constantinople because Herbert had sent the group without her knowledge. On top of this, she dreaded the predominance of the Catholic element as fifteen of the women were of that denomination. She wrote angry letters to Herbert, but in the end came to terms with Stanley and the other new arrivals and tacitly allowed them to work in the new hospital being established at Kuleli (north of Skutari) at the end of January 1855.

However, when some of Stanley's sisters moved to the hospitals at Balaklava in the Crimea, relations darkened again between Nightingale and her former friend because Nightingale had strictly forbidden the newcomers to work in a hospital at the front line. Nonetheless, Nightingale paid several visits to the Crimea in order to reform and improve nursing in the hospitals there. On her first visit in May 1855 she fell ill herself, suffering from the 'Crimean fever' (probably typhoid symptoms). For several days she hovered between life and death, yet such was the animosity between her and Dr Hall that he put Nightingale, not yet fully recovered, on board a steamer bound for England without an intermediate stop at Constantinople. When Nightingale got wind of the plan during the journey, she took ashore on the Bosphorus. She returned twice to the Crimea (in October 1855 and March

1856) and was nominated 'General Superintendent of the Female Nursing Establishment of the military hospitals of the Army', thus gaining a triumph over Hall[44] who denounced her activity in the Crimea as illegal because up to that time she had borne the title 'Superintendent of the Female Nursing Establishment of the English Hospitals in Turkey'.

In spite of her personal weaknesses – a domineering nature, a craving for popularity – one must admit that Florence Nightingale was thoroughly committed to her mission to improve the lot of the British army's rank and file. While on board a steamer to Balaklava on 5 May 1855, she wrote to her family:

> What the horrors of war are, no one can imagine, they are not wounds & blood & fever, spotted & low, & dysentery chronic & acute, cold & heat & famine. They are intoxication, drunken brutality, demoralization & disorder on the part of the inferior – jealousies, meanness, indifference, selfish brutality on the part of the superior.[45]

Cecil Woodham-Smith's judgement still holds true: Florence Nightingale 'set herself a new and gigantic task – she determined to reform the treatment of the British private soldier'.[46]

The Sisters of Mercy in the French and Russian armies

Civil nurses and Sisters of Mercy served not only in the British army but also in the French *Armée d'Orient* and the Russian Crimean Army. In the Sardinian expeditionary corps, too, there were sixty 'sisters'.[47] The term 'Sister of Mercy' or 'Sister of Charity' denotes a religious affiliation in both Catholic and Protestant orders (here they were called deaconesses) and in the Russian Orthodox Church of those who worked in nursing and other activities. In the French version they were known as Vincentians.

There was a French hospital in Constantinople as early as the end of the seventeenth century, which cared for sick seamen. In 1846 it was handed over to the Sisters of the Congregation of St Vincent de Paul. In the course of the Crimean War, 255 Sisters of Charity served on the French side. Of these Vincentians, twenty-three died while on duty at Constantinople, Varna and in the Crimea.[48]

In Russia the 'Order of the Exaltation of the Cross' was founded shortly after the Battle of the Alma by Grand Duchess Helena,[49] a member of the royal house of Württemberg and wife of the Grand Duke Michael Pavlovich. She was also the person who moved the famous surgeon Pirogov to go the Crimea. Thanks to Pirogov's intercession and authority, the Russian sisters did not face the obstacles that confronted Florence Nightingale. The first sisters, sixty-eight in total, arrived in Simferopol between 12 December 1854 and 10 April 1855. In the course of the war months their number rose to 161. Pirogov assigned them various tasks: together with priests, one group had to look after the fatally ill and mortally wounded; another group assisted in emergency surgery in the Assembly Hall of the Nobility, the main hospital in Sevastopol; the less seriously wounded were prepared for later operations in other quarters; the minor casualites were tended immediately and then handed over to their regiments. Of the Russian sisters, seventeen died during the war months.

Before the arrival of the first group, some local women had already rendered a great service in helping the wounded. In his letters, Pirogov mentions Darja, an orphan and daughter of a Black Sea sailor, and Marfa, who helped in a field-dressing station and in a hospital of the city.

A third category of sisters who arrived in the theatre of war at the end of 1854 were the Widows of Charity, a small group of sisters who were recruited by the Tsarina Alexandra Fedorovna from the dower houses of St Petersburg and Moscow. Their number cannot be ascertained, but twelve of them lost their lives while on duty. The Order of the Exaltation of the Cross was still active after the Crimean War until 1894, when it merged with the Russian Red Cross.

The treament of the sick

As already noted, certain sections of the medical art had gone through a period of upheaval during the Crimean War. The antiseptic and aseptic treatment of wounds was not yet invented, so that gangrene often ended fatally. But in the area of anaesthetics, medicine had made a breakthrough just before the war.

In 1839 the famous French surgeon Alfred Velpeau had written, 'Avoiding pain in operations is a chimera which is impossible to pursue.'[50] Eight years later he admitted that the use of ether, which had been applied in the United States in operations for the first time (in 1844), would drastically change surgery and beyond it physiology and psychology, too. In the same year, 1847, the great benefit of chloroform was first recognized, but a long debate would now ensue about its advantages and disadvantages. During the subsequent decades, the deaths caused by both forms of anaesthetic were more or less equal on a low level.

In the First Schleswig War (1848–9), chloroform was used sporadically, but in the Crimean War it was used extensively. In the French army, 20,000 operations were carried out using chloroform in the Crimea[51] and it was also applied by Russian surgeons. Its use in the British Army of the East was controversial. Although in England Queen Victoria had given birth to her eighth child in 1853 under chloroform, she had been rebuked for doing so by the Archbishop of Canterbury, citing the Bible, while the conservative John Hall expressed his opposition to its use with the oft-quoted line, 'However barbarous it may appear, the smart use of the knife is a powerful stimulant, and it is much better to hear a man bawl lustily than to see him sink silently into the grave.'[52] Young British surgeons did not agree and made ample use of chloroform.

Most surgical operations in the Crimean armies involved the extraction of bullets, resections (the cutting out of organ parts) and amputations. While the round (or spherical) bullet which got stuck in the body often caused only flesh wounds because if it hit a bone it was simply deflected, the new pointed (cylindro-conical) bullets fired by the Minié and Enfield guns had a much greater striking force, which could easily smash a bone. The death rate after amputations in all three armies – depending on the gravity of the wound and on the amputated part of the body – was between 70 and 100 per cent (but less in the case of dissevered fingers), that is, 80 per cent on average. In his report, the Russian surgeon Hubbeneth, who had carried out hundreds of amputations, posed the not unreasonable question why, in view of the slim chance of success, so many amputations were carried out. The simple answer Hubbeneth offered was that the severely wounded soldier would suffer even greater pain without an amputation: 'The slightest movement causes the most cruel pains! He cannot help screaming after an amputation; without it he would imagine to die soon.'[53]

All the armies in the Crimea used a remarkable range of drugs, although to varying effect, for example opium for soothing and pain relief and also against diarrhaea; digitalis for heart trouble; quinine and antimony for reducing fever. Brandy, red wine and beef tea were administered for strengthening the body, while arrowroot and salep (root) were used as sedatives.

Hospitals

The Crimean War produced hundreds of thousands of casualties on both sides who had to be cared for in hospitals. An adequate infrastructure did not exist at the beginning of the war and had to be constructed in piecemeal fashion as the conflict progressed. The supply of beds always lagged behind the requirements.

The Russian army was able to adapt the billets that existed in Sevastopol, on the northern side of the city, and behind the lines in the Crimea as well as many civil hospitals beyond the Crimean peninsula. The Allies had to establish their main hospitals in the very cramped area at Kamiesh and Balaklava. According to the regulations of the medical service, each regiment and each division had to provide field-dressing stations and ambulances behind their lines. The severely sick and wounded were supposed to be transferred to buildings and barrack camps away from the front line. The Turks assisted their Allies in this task by offering various forms of accomodation on the Bosphorus for the sick and convalescent. The great disadvantage here was that the sick had to undertake an excruciating voyage of more than 310 miles, lasting two or three days, which many did not survive. Nonetheless, most of the French and English sick had to endure this ordeal. The French were mostly put up in Turkish military compounds (hospitals, barracks, hut camps, drill grounds, palaces of the Sultan) on the European side of the Bosphorus, while the English were located on the Asiatic side.

The French hospitals

The first French hospital to come into operation was the sailors' hospital of the Vincentians in Constantinople, referred to earlier. When the first French troops arrived, a hospital was established for them at Gallipoli (on the Dardanelles). In Constantinople itself, they were soon given the Turkish military hospital at Matepe, followed by other hospitals at Dolmabakche and Pera (on the banks of the Bosphorus), in the Turkish barracks of Ramichiflik and Daoud Pasha (both of them together with Maltepe situated on a plateau which made the transport of the sick difficult) and at Gulhane (on the Bosphorus). A big barrack encampment was also established on a plateau in Maslak. The hospital of Canlidshe (Kamlica) was exceptional: it was a holiday retreat of the Egyptian Viceroy on the Asiatic side and was reserved for the French officers who later on moved to the Russian embassy building at Galata. Baudens writes of a total of nineteen French hospitals in Constantinople,[54] a figure that probably includes the hospital at Gallipoli and another hospital on Princes' Island, which used the local naval training school.

One other hospital worth noting was the one at Varna on the western shores of the Black Sea. It was used by both the French and the British during the war, the sick and wounded sent there from the Crimea, especially from Eupatoria. In Sevastopol itself, the French had a hospital at Kamiesh, their main storage depot. More than twenty French hospitals were in operation during the Crimean War, in addition to a small number of hospital ships stationed in the bay of Kamiesh or on the Bosphorus. These vessels could of course accomodate only a limited number of patients.

The British hospitals

The two biggest British hospitals were established at Skutari on the Asiatic side of the Bosphorus in September 1854. The General Hospital was originally a military hospital and could accommodate 1,000 patients. One kilometre to the north, the Barrack Hospital, originally a run-down Turkish barracks (Selim Barracks), had a similar capacity. It was here that Florence Nightingale installed her headquarters. It still exists today (its cleanliness can compete with every five-star hotel) and has a small room dedicated to Britain's most famous nurse. In addition to the two main hospitals, there were two other smaller facilities in the vicinity: an emergency hospital, called the Stables, and at Haydar-Pasha a hospital for officers.

TURKISH BARRACK AT SCUTARI, USED BY THE ENGLISH ARMY AS THEIR GENERAL DEPOT HOSPITAL.

FIGURE 18 *The General Hospital at Skutari on the Asian side of the Bosphorus. Courtesy of Inge and Dieter Wernet.*

At the end of January 1855, at the height of the Crimean winter, there were 4,500 sick and wounded accommodated at Skutari.[55] Another thousand were waiting for disembarkation from transport ships.

The death rate of the dysentery patients in those weeks was 60 per cent: forty-five people died every week. Because of the critical situation, a Turkish barracks at Kuleli, five miles north of Skutari, was converted into a British hospital. Florence Nightingale, who supervised the sisters there for a few weeks only, placed obstacles in the path of the newly arrived group around Mary Stanley – this was by no means a sign of human greatness.

At the same time, a hospital for convalescents was finished at Abydos in the Dardanelles, but there were no nurses yet stationed there. Accommodation for convalescents existed also in Corfu and Malta. The British and French also sent many sick and wounded back to their home countries where they were received by the public with great warmth.

In the Crimea itself, due to the restricted size of the two Allied encampments and the lack of infrastructure, there was only a limited hospital capacity. At Balaklava, the first general hospital set up could house only 100 patients; it was overcrowded at all times. To relieve the congestion a second hospital was built – Castle Hospital – on top of a hill overlooking the sea and near the ruins of an ancient Genoese fortress. Even today one can easily identify its outline in the form of rectangular excavations. Later on, another small hospital was added in the precincts of St George's monastery on the southern coast. Like the French at Kamiesh and on the Bosphorus, the British, too, had various ships lying at anchor at Balaklava and on the Bosphorus which served as emergency hospitals.

A distinct feature of the British hospital organization was the fact that in 1855 a civil hospital was opened for soldiers at Smyrna on the western coast of Turkey and another one at Renköy on the Dardanelles in October.[56] They served as relief institutions for the light and convalescent cases. The hospital at Smyrna was established in a large Turkish barracks and soon had 1,000 patients. Apart from the civilian doctors, eighteen sisters from England had arrived, whose services Florence Nightingale had refused at Skutari. The hospital at Renköy was a testimonial to British engineering and architecture of the time, employing the services of none other than Isambard Brunel. Within a short time, he had erected a complex with prefabricated parts furnished with the most modern sanitary facilities. It could accommodate up to 1,000 patients, but in fact only 500 beds were installed, which were occupied by 1,300 patients until February 1856. Florence Nightingale made no contribution to this development.

The Russian hospitals

Although the hinterland with its numerous hospitals for the sick and wounded was open to the garrison of Sevastopol, the situation of these soldiers was more miserable than that of their Allied counterparts. The hospital capacity of Sevastopol and also that of Simferopol fifty miles away was soon exhausted and the sick had to be transported over ever longer distances. Railways did not yet exist in the Crimea. In summer, transportation through the treeless steppe was mere torture, while at other times of the year the roads were sunken in mud and hardly passable. The bullock carts and wagons requisitioned from the farmers were unsprung and open-top with the result that many sick and wounded never made it to their destination. On 29 October 1854, a convoy of wounded, many still with bullets in their bodies due to lack of treatment by the surgeons, began a journey from Simferopol to the German colony of Melitopol, beyond the Crimea. The convoy reached its destination on 7 November, but it wasn't until the end of the month that the survivors could be operated on, after the hospital had scraped together the necessary instruments and medicine.[57]

At the beginning of the Crimean War, the Russians had a hospital capacity of 2,000 beds and emergency accommodation for 1,000 further cases. The Battle of the Alma brought almost 6,000 casualties, many of the wounded leaving the battlefield and making their own way to Sevastopol. After the Battle of Inkerman, the Russian hospital system in Sevastopol broke down. In the crisis situation, Simferopol was chosen as the general hospital and several auxiliary hospitals were established. In addition, hospitals at Bakhchisaraj, Karazubazar (today Belogorsk), Feodosia and Perekop could receive a limited number of patients. Soon the transport radius had to be widened: to Melitopol (as mentioned), Kremenchug, Nikolaev, Kherson and Berislav. In 1855 the Crimean army had at its disposal some 57,000 hospital beds.[58]

As already noted, the main hospital at Sevastopol was set up in the Assembly Hall of the Nobility. However, as it faced increasing bombardment from the Allies, its operation had to be dispersed to several buildings in Artillery Bay. Another hospital was also opened in Korabelnaya suburb. As this, too, came under fire, it had to be evacuated to the north side, but for many this was but the first stage of a longer journey into the interior, a journey that not everyone completed.

The Sardinian and Turkish medical services

The Sardinian army, coming directly from Genoa, arrived in Balaklava at the end of May and beginning of June 1855 and comprised 15,000 men. They were stationed on the Tchernaya on the observation front opposite the Russians. In the course of the following months the Sardinians increased to a total of 21,000 men. When the soldiers arrived the situation they encountered was not particularly promising: 'The harbour [of Balaklava] looked like a sewer. The water was covered with rubbish of all sorts and from it rose a repulsive stench.'[59] On their march to the front line they regularly found dead animals which had not been buried. No wonder that the soldiers were immediately struck by the cholera. At the beginning of June there were already 869 sick, 387 of whom died.

Yet the Sardinians were not badly equipped in terms of medical services. They were accompanied by 150 surgeons, 286 dressers and forty or sixty Sisters of Charity. Facing a war, they had, naturally, prepared for tending the wounded rather than the sick. Their only combat mission was during the Battle of the Tchernaya on 5 August 1855, which claimed 30 to 34 dead and 156 wounded. In Sardinian and Italian national consciousness, the battle has been celebrated as an Italian victory. But people have forgotten the number of soldiers who died of disease. Their number soon reached the appalling figure of 2,257. No other army came close to this ratio of 98.5 per cent of dead due to sickness and only 1.5 per cent due to wounds.

Only one source could be traced for the Turkish medical service in the Crimean War, namely the report of the inspector of the French Medical Service, Baudens.[60] The new book by the Turkish historian C. Badem sheds no light on the matter. Baudens' report must not be generalized. He offers no data for the situation at the front line, but only for the four hospitals which the Turks had reserved for themselves in Constantinople. For the situation here, Baudens is full of praise, describing the 'organization of the Ottoman medical service' as 'very satisfactory'. But it should be borne in mind that he only arrived in Constantinople in September 1855, when the medical service in the city was in much better shape than a year earlier. The population of the city had also been spared the typhoid epidemic that had struck the French army. Baudens placed particular focus on the cleanliness of the Turkish hospitals: 'The fumigation of rooms with chlorine and especially with aromatic herbs, repeated several times per day, draws off the disgusting miasmas that emanate from the sick; a usage which I would like to introduce into our hospitals in France.' He also envied the wash-houses and described the food provided for the sick as 'healthy and very simple'. Of course, we need more sources to truly determine the accuracy of this very positive picture.

The death toll of the war

At the end of a military history of the Crimean War it is appropriate to say something about the impact of the conflict in terms of human victims. However, assembling the necessary statistics is a Sisyphean task, as the data drawn from various sources reveals one contradiction after another. One general point can be made at the outset about the two major Allied armies: that for each soldier killed in action or who shortly succumbed to his wounds, there are at least four who died of sickness. This figure does not apply to the Sardinian army, as noted above, or to the Russian army, as will be shown shortly.

One must set aside the numbers published daily and monthly by the bulletins of all armies because they do not differentiate between soldiers killed in action, those who died of their wounds soon afterwards or those who died of sickness. Such statistics cannot be taken at face value. The official French figures were often dressed up or were simply wrong. The *Moniteur* observed in February 1855 that 'If these statistics are wrong, they mislead public opinion; if they are correct, they are even more objectionable; they give away to the enemy something of the plans and means of attack which the commanders-in-chief work out in the deepest secret.' The French commander-in-chief Canrobert reported tersely: 'The sanitary state of the army, the weather and the morale of the troops are excellent.'[61] A man who equates the medical state of the army with the state of the weather, describing both as 'excellent', cannot be taken seriously.

In Britain the press could not be as easily muzzled as in France. However, what Russell published in *The Times* was general impressions and experiences, not precise figures, which the military authorities, of course, were not likely to make available. And what do the actual numbers held in the archives tell a researcher? Florence Nightingale lamented in a letter of 9 June 1856, 'The Medical Statistics of the L[and]T[ransport]C[orps] [which was responsible for the transportation of the wounded and sick] are in a state of great confusion, so that it is hardly possible to obtain correct results.' She was very much interested in statistics and regretted the absence of reliable figures. In contrast, she admired the French achievement in that respect: 'Their Medical Statistics should make us envious. How they keep any is a physical problem.'[62]

In sum, the statistics put together at the time of the Crimean War are far from reliable. One has therefore no choice but to resort to accounts, from both sides, compiled in the months and years after the war for internal purposes. They must, of course, be questioned as well, but broadly speaking they are not misleading.

The total number of French troops that served in the Crimea is, according to Baudens, who refers to the *Moniteur de l'Armée* of 27 November 1857, 309,270 men.[63] Whether this includes soldiers sent to the Baltic in 1854 and 1855 is uncertain, but unlikely. To this figure, one must relate the total number of soldiers sent to hospital. The surgeon general of the French *Armée d'Orient*, Gaspard-Léonard Scrive, gives the relevant figure for the period from 1 April 1854 to 1 May 1856 as 192,091.[64] Included in this number are about 40,000 wounded, a very imprecise figure. The number he gives for those who died of sickness is 62,000. The *Moniteur* of 23 October 1856 assessed a death toll of 69,299 for all categories.[65] Comparison of these statistics suggests that those provided by the *Moniteur* – published at the express wish of the Emperor – were fabricated. The figures published by Baudens in 1862 and 1864 are nearer the truth:[66]

FIGURE 19 *The Dragon (of war) devouring the soldiers.* Kladderadatsch 12, 11 March 1855, p. 48.

Killed in action	8,750
Died of sickness and wounds in the Crimea	31,000
Died in hospitals at Constantinople of sickness and wounds	32,000
Died on the expedition to the Dobrudja	6,000
Died en route from the Crimea to Constantinople	7,500
Died in the hospitals of Gallipoli, Varna and elsewhere	3,000
Died during the evacuation of the Crimea and the Turkish Straits	5,000

This adds up to a total of 93,250 deaths. If one includes the dead of the two expeditions to the Baltic in 1854 and 1855 and those who died of their wounds after returning to France (their exact number cannot be established) one arrives at a figure of at least 100,000 French deaths.

The figures for British casualties vary widely in the relevant sources. The principal medical officer of the British Army of the East, John Hall, gives the total number of British soldiers who arrived in the Crimea as 97,934 up to April 1856.[67] The total number of deaths for the Crimea, for Bulgaria (Varna) and for the inmates of the hospitals are, according to him, 21,412. However, the figure is not broken down into men killed in action or dead of wounds and sickness. But as a whole it is very similar to the information provided to the House of Commons by Lord Panmure, Secretary of War, on 8 May 1856.[68] When the deaths in the Baltic[69] are added, one reaches a total figure of 22,000 British deaths.

The number of casualties suffered by the Russians differs widely in the older literature. But Hubbenet, who offers many (in part inconsistent) statistics in his book, is the most trustworthy. He determines that there were 85,000 Russians who died in the Crimea;[70] with the inclusion of the Danube front and southern Russia in general, the total is 110,000.[71] But Hubbeneth points out that the figure may be too low in view of the high rate of sickness in 1856 in the army in southern Russia. Not included in his figures are the casualties in the Caucasus. According to more recent research, the figures are as follows:[72] by the end of 1853, the number of the Russian field army totalled 1,123,583 men. During the war, another 878,000 men were called up. This means a total of 2,001,583 men under arms. The effective force of the Russian army by the end of 1855 was 1,527,748. The difference yields the total number of dead (those killed in action as well as those dead from sickness) as 473,835. If from this figure the 'normal' death rate of the Russian army is subtracted, which is 35 per thousand per year (double the rate of Western armies), that is, about 100,000, the sum total of dead amounts to roughly 364,000 men.[73] The most recent study of the matter revises the figures yet again: about 105,000 deaths (from all causes) in the

Crimea and about 60,000 on the Danube, with the number of dead for the whole Russian army for 1853–6 totalling about 406,000.[74]

If one adds to the number of dead of these three armies (486,000), 2,300 Sardinians and an estimated 45,000 in the Turkish army, the total number of dead for the war is about 533,300. The British diplomat Sir Robert Morier's judgement that the Crimean War was 'perfectly useless' seems a gross understatement in view of such a figure.

Annotated bibliography

There is no comprehensive account of the medical aspect of the war, covering all its features and all its participants (France, Britain, Russia, Turkey and Sardinia). General books about the conflict devote a few pages, if any, to the matter, but there is much specialized research, mainly from a national perspective. An early book on the French medical service, which also touches on the services of the other participants, is Lucien Baudens, *La guerre de Crimée. Les campements, les abris, les ambulances, les hôpitaux etc. etc* (Paris, 1858, 2nd edn 1858, repr. 2011). We owe much statistical data on the French side of this matter to the zoologist and surgeon Jean Charles Chenu, *De la mortalité et des moyens d'économiser la vie humaine: extraits des statistiques médico-chirurgicales des campagnes de Crimée en 1854–1856 et d'Italie en 1859* (Paris, 1870). The British medical history is well covered by John Shepherd, *The Crimean Doctors: A History of the British Medical Service in the Crimean War* (Liverpool, 1991). For the Russian medical service, we have a good though dated account by Anton Hubbeneth, *Service sanitaire des hôpitaux russes pendant la guerre de Crimée, dans les années 1851–1856* (St Petersburg, 1870). A more recent study, based on archival research, is provided by Julija A. Naumova, *Ranenie, bolezn' i smert'. Russkaja medicinskaja služba v Krymskoj vojnu 1853–1856 gg* (Moscow, 2010). A new study, based on archival sources, that examines the toll of the war on the Russian population, on the animals and on the environment is that by Mara Kozelsky, *Crimea in War and Transformation* (New York, 2019).

Diseases during the war are covered in many articles. Notable is the book on cholera by Frank Spahr, *Die Ausbreitung der Cholera in der britischen Flotte im Schwarzen Meer während des Krieges im August 1854. Eine Auswertung von Schiffsarztjournalen der Royal Navy* (Frankfurt, 1989). A comprehensive survey of diseases and epidemics in European history is provided by Stefan Winkle, *Geißeln der Menschheit. Kulturgeschichte der Seuchen* (Düsseldorf, 1997, 3rd edn 2005, repr. 2014).

There are few biographies of the major surgeons of the Crimean War. There is an old life-and-letters biography of Sir John Hall, Inspector General of Hospitals. He had intended writing a book on the medical history of the war, but nothing came of it. The Crimean letters of Nikolaj I. Pirogov, the great Russian medical pioneer, are now edited (in Russian only): *Sevastopol'skie pis'ma i vospominanija* (Moscow, 1950; re-edited in his *Collected Works* (in Russian) as vol. 5, 1961). Regarding medical staff in the war, the best known is of course Florence Nightingale. Her collected works are now published in twelve volumes between 2001 and 2012. Volume 14, edited by Lynn McDonald, covers the Crimean War. Nightingale's correspondence with Sidney Herbert form the core of that volume. An older collection of letters from the war is handled by Sue M. Goldie (ed.), *'I have done my duty.' Florence Nightingale in the Crimean War 1854–56* (Manchester, 1987). The classic biography is by Cecil Woodham-Smith, *Florence Nightingale, 1820–1910* (New York, 1951). A good modern biography is that by Mark Bostridge, *Florence Nightingale: The Woman and her Legend* (London, 2008). For the Russian Sisters of Mercy, see John Shelton Curtiss, 'Russian Sisters of Mercy in the Crimea, 1854–1855', *Slavic Review* 25 (1966): 84–100. For the plight of women on all sides of the war, see Helen Rappaport, *No Place for Ladies: The Untold Story of Women in the Crimean War* (London, 2007, new edn Brighton, 2013).

Epilogue

As noted in the first chapter, the Crimean War contained all the elements for a world war. If the conflict had continued in 1856, Prussia and Sweden would have declared war on Russia and engulfed all Europe in the fray; the United States would have joined the Russian side because of the tension in her relations with Britain. It was the statesmanship of Tsar Alexander II and his advisers that made Russia stop before crossing the Rubicon.

In the subsequent fifty-eight years, Europe witnessed only a few short wars. In the age of imperialism, when nationalism and Darwinism wielded great influence on policymaking, the traditional principle of the balance of power was gradually weakened. It became a dead letter in the July crisis of 1914. In that summer, a hundred years after Napoleon I, the European powers found themselves in the Great War. It led to the dissolution of the old empires in Europe and the rise of new ones across the world. The Crimea featured only briefly at the end of that war – in 1918. With the collapse of the Tsarist Empire, German troops occupied the peninsula and used it as a springboard for an occupation of the Caucasus which, according to the German Supreme Command, was to function as a stepping stone for an advance on Afghanistan and India.

The same idea was revived by Hitler in the Second World War, yet also ended in failure. In the plans of the Nazis, the Crimea was to serve as the riviera for the Thousand-Year Reich. The Russian reconquest of the peninsula in 1944 featured prominently in subsequent Stalinist propaganda and in Russian nationalism. Added to the dozens of monuments commemorating the Russian heroism of 1854–6, hundreds of further monuments were erected in memory of the great feats of the Red Army. The Crimea again became a symbol of the suffering and resistance of the Russian people. Khrushchev's decision in 1954 to assign the Crimea to the Ukraine, then part of the Soviet Union, was done simply for economic and administrative purposes. The peninsula by now was the home of big holiday resorts for millions of Russian holidaymakers.

With the collapse of the Soviet Union after 1989, the Crimea remained part of the new independent Ukraine. But the Russian Black Sea Fleet remained there – in Sevastopol and Balaklava – in accordance with treaties signed by the two states. With Putin's rise to power, a new Russian nationalism was fostered which today dreams of the bygone greatness of the Tsarist and Soviet empires. Like Hitler's Germany, which wanted to undo the Treaty of Versailles and recover the territories lost in 1919, Putin wanted to restore the greatness of the Soviet past and recover those territories lost in 1989 which contained large numbers of ethnic Russians. Thus parts of the Dniestr region and Georgia were reoccupied by Russian troops, with only token condemnation by the international community. In 2014, Putin annexed the Crimea to Russia in a night-time raid, which this time was met with more outspoken criticism and with sanctions by the Western world. Putin burnt his fingers even further with his undisguised intervention in the Ukrainian Donbass region.

Just as Nicholas I had wanted, in 1853, to use the Crimea to invade Constantinople and the Turkish Straits and thus enhance Russian power, but was met with resistance from the other great European powers, so Putin's occupation of the Crimea in 2014 brought instability to international relations. The immediate consequence has been the rearmament of Western Europe and the United States and the beginning of a new Cold War.

APPENDIX: CHRONOLOGY

1852

9 Feb.	*Firman* of the Sultan (ends monks' dispute in Holy Places)
2 Dec.	Napoleon III proclaims himself Emperor
27 Dec.	New Cabinet formed in London by Lord Aberdeen

1853

9 Jan.	Beginning of secret conversations between Tsar Nicholas and British envoy Sir George Hamilton Seymour
28 Feb.	Prince Menshikov arrives at Constantinople
19 Mar.	Council of Ministers at Paris decide to send fleet to Bay of Salamis
5 May	Prince Menshikov presents ultimatum to the Porte
10 May	Porte rejects Menshikov's ultimatum
21 May	Menshikov leaves Constantinople
2 June	Admiral Dundas ordered to sail to Besika Bay
13–14 June	Anglo-French fleets enter Besika Bay outside the Dardanelles
2 July	Russian army starts occupying the Danubian Principalities
31 July	Vienna Note (mediates between Russian and Turkish demands)
19 Aug.	Turkey demands three modifications of Vienna Note
4 Oct.	Turkey declares war on Russia
27–28 Oct.	Turkish unit overruns Russian fort St Nicholas (near Batum)
28–30 Oct.	Turkish troops cross Danube at Vidin and occupy Kalafat
4 Nov.	Encounter between Turkish and Russian troops at Oltenitsa (Danube)
13 Nov.	Anglo-French fleets arrive at Beicos Bay
30 Nov.	Destruction of Turkish fleet at Sinope
1 Dec.	Battle of Bashgedikler between Turks and Russians (Caucasus)
5 Dec.	Protocol of Vienna signed
20 Dec.	Sweden and Denmark declare their neutrality
31 Dec.	Battle of Cetate on Danube between Turkish and Russian forces

1854

3–4 Jan.	Anglo-French fleets enter Black Sea
6 Jan.	(Second) Battle of Cetate (Danube)
29 Jan.	Count Orlov in Vienna fails to woo Austria to Russian side
13 Feb.	General Gorchakov ordered to besiege Silistria (Danube) (siege given up on 24 June)
27 Feb.	Prussia declares her neutrality
11 Mar.	British fleet (under Admiral Napier) sets out for the Baltic
12 Mar.	Treaty signed at Constantinople between Turkey, Britain and France
19 Mar.	First French troops depart from Toulon for Gallipoli
27 Mar.	Britain declares war on Russia, followed by France on 28 March
5 April	British troops arrive in Turkish Straits
10 April	France and Britain sign treaty of alliance with Turkey in London
20 April	Defensive and offensive treaty between Prussia and Austria signed in Berlin
22 April	Allied fleets bombard Odessa
19 May	Allied war council at Varna
25 May	French troops occupy Piraeus (Athens)
25 May	Bamberg conference of German middle states (closes on 30 May)
3 June	Austria demands that Russia evacuate Danubian Principalities
12 June	French fleet under Admiral Parseval-Deschênes joins British fleet at Bomarsund
14 June	Austro-Turkish convention on Principalities (at Boyadji-Köi)
25 June	French and British fleets arrive near Kronstadt
9 July	Cholera spreads at Varna
10 July	50,000 French and 20,000 British troops assembled at Varna
18 July	Allied war council at Varna: decision to attack Sevastopol; British ships bombard Solovetskie Islands in White Sea
21 July	French expedition to the Dobrudja
24 July	Tsar Nicholas orders total evacuation of Principalities (afterwards occupied by Austrian troops)
5 Aug.	Battle of Kurukdere (Caucasus)
8 Aug.	Austria and Western powers exchange notes on 'Four Points' (war aims)
16 Aug.	Allied troops occupy Bomarsund on Åland Islands
20 Aug.	Austrian troops begin to enter Principalities
23–24 Aug.	British squadron destroys Kola (near Murmansk)

26 Aug.	Russia rejects Four Points
29–31 Aug.	British squadron bombards Petropavlovsk (Kamchatka) (landing party leaves on 4 Sept.)
1–2 Sept.	Allied troops ordered to sail to Eupatoria
14 Sept.	Allied troops disembark at Eupatoria
19 Sept.	Allied troops march south towards Sevastopol
20 Sept.	Battle of the Alma
29 Sept.	St Arnaud dies; Canrobert takes over command of French troops
9 Oct.	Allied trenches built outside Sevastopol
17 Oct.	First bombardment of Sevastopol
25 Oct.	Battle of Balaklava
4 Nov.	Florence Nightingale arrives at Skutari
5 Nov.	Battle of Inkerman
14 Nov.	Hurricane destroys and damages Allied ships on Crimean coast
28 Nov.	Gorchakov in Vienna announces Russian acceptance of Four Points
2 Dec.	Alliance between Austria and Western Powers signed in Vienna
19 Dec.	First article in *The Times* (by W. H. Russell) on situation of British army in the Crimea
28 Dec.	Russian government expresses desire in Vienna to begin peace talks

1855

7 Jan.	Russia accepts Four Points as basis for negotiations
10 Jan.	Sardinia signs political convention with Western powers (to enter war against Russia)
23 Jan.	In House of Commons, Roebuck demands inquiry into conduct of war (leading to fall of Aberdeen government)
26 Jan.	Sardinia concludes military alliance with Western powers
5 Feb.	Palmerston forms new government in London
26 Feb.	Napoleon III informs Palmerston of his intention to go to the Crimea
2 Mar.	Tsar Nicholas dies; Alexander II succeeds
15 Mar.	Vienna conference (Austria, Western powers, Russia) begins peace talks
9 April	Second bombardment of Sevastopol (until April 18)
16 April	Napoleon III and Eugénie arrive on official visit to Britain
26 April	Vienna conference ends without result
8 May	Walewski nominated French Foreign Minister; Sardinian troops land at Balaklava
15 May	World exhibition opens in Paris
16 May	General Canrobert resigns; replaced by General Pelissier

22 May	Allied expedition to Kertch (returns 15 June)
4 June	Official closing of Vienna conference
6 June	Third bombardment of Sevastopol begins (until 7 June)
June 17	Fourth bombardment of Sevastopol (ends in failure on 18 June)
28 June	Lord Raglan dies of cholera; General Simpson takes over
9–11 Aug.	Allied Baltic fleets bombard Sveaborg (near Helsingfors)
16 Aug.	Battle of the Tchernaya
17 Aug.	Fifth bombardment of Sevastopol (until 27 Aug.)
5 Sept.	Sixth bombardment of Sevastopol
8 Sept.	French troops occupy Malakhov bastion; British troops fail to take the Redan; Russian troops retreat to northern side of Sevastopol
29 Sept.	Russian attack on Turkish fortress of Kars fails
17 Oct.	Fortress of Kinburn occupied by combined French and British expedition
15 Nov.	World exhibition in Paris closes
21 Nov.	Treaty of alliance between Sweden and Western powers
26 Nov.	Russian troops storm fortress at Kars
16 Dec.	Austrian ultimatum signed (includes fifth point)
28 Dec.	Austria delivers ultimatum to Russia

1856

5 Jan.	Russian counterproposals rejected by Allies
10 Jan.	Anglo-French council of war opens in Paris (closes 20 Jan.)
15 Jan.	Tsar convenes council in St Petersburg
16 Jan.	Russia accepts Austrian ultimatum
1 Feb.	Protocol signed in Vienna stating that peace negotiations should begin
18 Feb.	Sultan publishes *Hat-ı şerif* in favour of Christians of his empire
25 Feb.	Congress of Paris opened
18 Mar.	Prussian delegation takes part in peace negotiations in Paris
30 Mar.	Treaty of Paris signed
8 April	Italian Question on the agenda of Paris congress; Declaration of Paris on maritime law
16 April	Congress of Paris closes
21 April	Allied troops (230,000) start evacuating the Crimea
5 July	Completion of evacuation of the Crimea

NOTES

2 Diplomacy during the war, 1853–6

1 *The History of the Times*, pp. 191–2.
2 *Hansard's Parliamentary Debates*, Third Series, vol. 130. London, 1854, col. 568.
3 Winfried Baumgart (ed.), *Akten zur Geschichte des Krimkriegs* (henceforth *AGKK*), II/1, p. 422 (see the introduction to this volume, pp. 36–7).
4 The text of the Four Points is, *inter alia*, in *British and Foreign State Papers*, vol. 44, pp. 88–90.
5 *AGKK* III/3, pp. 42–4 (with the references cited there).
6 *AGKK* III/3, pp. 619–21, 631–8.

3 The war aims of the belligerents

1 The text is reproduced in Schiemann, *Geschichte Rußlands*, vol. 4, pp. 281–2.
2 Printed in Zaiončkovskij, *Vostočnaja vojna*, vol. 1, pp. 582–3.
3 Zaiončkovskij, *Vostočnaja vojna*, vol. 1, pp. 385–6.
4 Zaiončkovskij, *Vostočnaja vojna*, vol. 1, pp. 437–8; Zaiončkovskij, *Priloženija*, vol. 2, pp. 43–4, 243–4.
5 *AGKK* I/1, pp. 262–4, 321–2.
6 Zaiončkovskij, *Priloženija*, vol. 2, p. 109. For the following remark, cf. Zaiončkovskij, *Priloženija*, vol. 2, pp. 322–4.
7 Zaiončkovskij, *Priloženija*, vol. 2, pp. 402–3.
8 *AGKK* I/1, p. 551.
9 The text is in Gooch (ed.), *Later Correspondence of Lord John Russell*, vol. 2, pp. 160–1.
10 *AGKK* III/4, pp. 140–2.
11 Baumgart, *Peace of Paris*, p. 14.
12 See Clarendon's own account in *AGKKK* III/4, pp. 819–20.
13 Cf., e.g., *AGKK* III/2, pp. 267, 427–8, 761; III/4, pp. 194, 202, 244, 261, 987; IV/3, p. 57, n. 215.

14 Ernst II., *Aus meinem Leben*, vol. 2, p. 141.

15 Pottinger Saab, *Origins of the Crimean Alliance*, pp. 81–5; Badem, *The Ottoman Crimean War*, pp. 91–8.

16 Di Nolfo, *Europa e Italia*, p. 445.

4 The non-belligerent German powers: Austria and Prussia

1 *AGKK* I/1–3.

2 *AGKK* I/1, p. 463.

3 For a closer examination of the relevant documentary evidence, see Baumgart, 'Die Aktenedition zur Geschichte des Krimkriegs', pp. 217–36 (especially pp. 220 and 223). Also Baumgart, 'Österreich und Preußen im Krimkrieg', pp. 45–70 (especially pp. 54–7).

4 They are now in three collections: *AGKK* II,1–2; Poschinger (ed.), *Preußens auswärtige Politik*; Baumgart, *Der König und sein Beichtvater*.

5 *AGKK* II/1, p. 608.

6 *AGKK* II/1, p. 422.

7 Strachey and Fulford (eds), *The Greville Memoirs*, vol. 7, p. 186.

8 *AGKK* III/4, p. 559; Cf. also *AGKK* III/4, pp. 583–4.

9 *AGKK* II/2, p. 757.

10 As to the following statistics, cf. A. S. Nifontov, 'Vnešnjaja torgovlja Rossii vo vremja vostočnoj vojny 1853–156 gg.', in *Problemy social'no-ėkonomičeskoj istorii Rossii. Sbornik statej* (Moscow, 1971), pp. 69–90.

11 Cf., e.g., *AGKK* II/2, pp. 844–7.

5 The neutral powers

1 The documentary evidence from the Swedish side is printed in Hallendorff, *Konung Oscar I's politik*, pp. 37–53; for the French side, see *AGKK* IV/2, pp. 174–5, 184, 210–11, 219–20, 228–9, 296, 353–5, 389–90, 397–400, 402–5, 412–15, 447–8; for the British side, see *AGKK* III/2, pp. 214–15, 264–5, 318–19, 325–6, 340–3, 351–2, 364–6, 367–8, 381–2, 498–9, 533–4, 555–7, 591–3, 613–14, 681–3.

2 Cf. *AGKK* III/3, pp. 686–7. For the following despatches, see *AGKK* III/3, p. 724.

3 Cf. *AGKK* III/4, pp. 140–2.

4 Cf. *AGKK* III/4, pp. 591–2, 639–41.

5 Otero, 'España ante la guerra di Crimea'. Cf. *AGKK* III/4, pp. 410–46 (especially p. 426).

6 *AGKK* III/3, pp. 772–3, 777, 780, 807–8, 828–30, 834, 852; IV/3, pp. 397–9, 452–3, 499–511.

7 Mariñas Otero, 'España ante la guerra di Crimea', p. 441; Becker, *Historia de las Relaciones Exteriores de España*, vol. 2, pp. 228–9. As to the following remarks, cf. the relative documents in *AGKK* III/4.

8 Cited in Saul, *Distant Friends*, p. 201.

9 Cited in Van Alstyne, 'Anglo-American Relations', p. 497.

10 Cf. Van Alstyne, 'Great Britain, the United States, and Hawaiian Independence', pp. 15–24.

11 It was soon published by the American government: *The House of Representatives*, pp. 127–32. For the following quotation, see *The House of Representatives*, p. 131.

12 Eastern Papers, p. 10.

13 The relevant documents are in *AGKK* I/2, pp. 74–5, 128–9. For the following remark, cf. Ritter, *Frankreichs Griechenlandpolitik*, pp. 205–6; *AGKK* I/2, p. 129, n. 6, pp. 131–2.

14 *AGKK* I/2, p. 498.

15 *AGKK* I/1, p. 603.

16 Cited in Baumgart, 'Die deutschen Mittelstaaten und der Krimkrieg', p. 374. On Bavaria, on the basis of new documents, see Baumgart, 'Bayern und die Europäischen Großmächte im Krimkrieg', pp. 285–303.

17 *AGKK* I/2, p. 224. For the two quotations in the following paragraph, see *AGKK* I/2, pp. 214–15; Simon, *Die Außenpolitik Hessen-Darmstadts während des Krimkrieges*, pp. 88–9.

18 Cited in Baumgart, 'Die deutschen Mittelstaaten und der Krimkrieg', p. 388.

6 Russia

1 These figures are in Zaiončkovskij, *Priloženija*, vol. 1, p. 476. Cf. Zaiončkovskij, *Priloženija*, vol. 2, p. 403. The figures are discussed in Bestužev, *Krymskaja vojna*, pp. 19–22; in pp. 23–9, Bestužev discusses other aspects of Russia's army system.

2 Much of the correspondence between Paskevich and the Tsar up to the summer of 1854 is printed in Zaiončkovskij, *Priloženija*, especially in vol. 2. Tarle, *Krymskaja vojna*, vols 1–2, also quotes from the unpublished correspondence.

3 Figures for the Russian navy are given in Beskrovny, 'The Russian Army and Fleet', pp. 300–1. Cf. also Treue, *Der Krimkrieg*, pp. 36, 38–9.

4 Zaiončkovskij, *Priloženija*, vol. 1, pp. 582–3.

5 Petrow, *Der russische Donaufeldzug*, pp. 36–7.

6 Cf. Nicholas's Memorandum of November 1853 in Zaiončkovksij, *Priloženija*, vol. 2, pp. 274–6.

7 France

1 Figures for the French army are taken from various sources: Guillemin, *La guerre de Crimée*, pp. 27, 31, 32; Treue, *Der Krimkrieg*, p. 84; Clodfelter, *Warfare and Armed Conflicts*, p. 300; Gouttman, *La guerre de Crimée*, pp. 195–201.

2 Quatrelles L'Épine, *Saint-Arnaud*, vol. 2, p. 300, n. 1.

3 Hess's memoranda are printed in Rauchensteiner (ed.), *Feldmarschall Heinrich Freiherr von Hess*, pp. 243–5, 247–53. Cf. the relative documents in *AGKK* I/2, pp. 279–30, 850–1, 790–1. On Crenneville's mission to Paris cf. also Koch, *Generaladjutant Graf Crenneville*, pp. 30–63. As to Napoleon's reaction mentioned in the following paragraph, cf. *AGKK* IV/2, pp. 850–1.

4 On Napoleon's idea to go in person the the Crimea and on his visit to Britain and the plan of campaign agreed there on 20 April, cf. the documents in *AGKK* III/3, pp. 364–6, 375–6, 397, 449, 581, 602; *AGKK* IV/2, pp. 689, n. 1, 870–1, 874, 879–80, 881–2, 883–4, 896; *AGKK* IV/3, pp. 80–1, 95–7, 103–4, 124–5, 137, 218–19, 226–7, 229. See also, *inter alia*, Martin, *The Life of His Royal Highness the Prince Consort*, vol. 3, pp. 233–59; Brison D. Gooch, *The New Bonapartist Generals*, pp. 181–7.

8 Great Britain

1 Martin, *The Life of His Royal Highness the Prince Consort*, vol. 3, pp. 188–9.

2 *AGKK* III/3, p. 231.

3 The figures are taken from various sources: Strachan, *Wellington's Legacy*, pp. 182, 220; Guillemin, *Guerre de Crimée*, p. 51; Stanmore, *Sidney Herbert*, vol. 1, p. 310; Gooch, *The New Bonapartist Generals*, p. 206; *AGKK* III/4, p. 1017.

4 *AGKK* III/3, pp. 271–3; *AGKK* IV/2, p. 829.

5 *AGKK* IV/4, pp. 738–40.

6 Cited in *AGKK* III/2, p. 255; also in Lambert, *The Crimean War*, p. 84.

7 More details and the necessary references are in Chapter 16.

9 Turkey

1 These figures are from *Augsburger Allgemeine Zeitung*, no. 10, 10 January 1856. Cf. now Badem, *The Ottoman Crimean War*, pp. 284–5. His sources give a total of 235,568 men in October 1855.

2 For other details of the two units, see the preceding chapter.

3 For more details, cf. now the relevant documents in *AGKK* III/3 and 4 (cf. the index of both volumes under the heads 'Türkisches Kontingent', 'Kosakenregiment', 'Baschi-Bosuk', 'Vivian', 'Czartoryski', 'Zamoyski'); Badem,

The Ottoman Crimean War, esp. pp. 257–68; Reid, Crisis of the Ottoman Empire, pp. 105–74.

10 Sardinia

1   Curato (ed.), Le relazione diplomatiche, vol. 2, p. 307.

2   Cavour, Carteggi, vol. 7, p. 400.

3   Di Nolfo, Europa e Italia, p. 445.

11 The Danube front, 1853–4

1   Schiemann, Geschichte Rußlands, vol. 4, p. 292.

2   Zaiončkovskij, Priloženija, vol. 2, p. 6.

3   Zaiončkovskij, Priloženija, vol. 2, pp. 120–1.

4   Goldfrank, The Origins of the Crimean War, pp. 226–8.

5   Zaiončkovskij, Priloženija, vol. 2, pp. 312–17. On the Russian occupation of the Danubian Principalities, cf. Tarle, Krymskaja vojna I, pp. 236–79; Petrow, Donaufeldzug, pp. 39–110.

6   AGKK I/1, pp. 637–40.

7   Zaiončkovskij, Priloženija, vol. 2, pp. 402–3.

8   As to the campaign on the Danube front in 1854, cf. Petrow, Donaufeldzug, pp. 111–350; Tarle, Krymskaja vojna, vol. 1, pp. 425–500. Many documents are in Zaiončkovskij, Priloženija, vol. 2.

9   Cf. Quatrelles L'Épine, Saint-Arnaud, pp. 315–18; Rousset, Histoire de la guerre de Crimée, vol. 1, pp. 103–14.

10   Cited in Tarle, Krymskaja vojna, vol. 1, p. 485.

11   Cited by Petrow, Donaufeldzug, vol. 1, p. 215.

12   The more important documents for Austria's decision to occupy the Danubian Principalities are in AGKK I/1, pp. 195, n. 1, 241–2, 258–60, 542–3, 550. Cf. also Antić, Neutrality as Independence, pp. 115–23.

13   AGKK I/1, pp. 551–4, 610, 625–7.

14   Cf. Friedjung, Krimkrieg, pp. 59–60; AGKK I/2, pp. 128–9, 147, 178–82, 184, 192–7, 232–3, 236–7.

15   Friedjung, Krimkrieg, p. 99; AGKK I/2, p. 383.

16   AGKK I/2, pp. 184, 263–4, 272, 312–14, 326–30, 344–5, 349, 358–60, 390, 398; Quatrelles L'Épine, Saint-Arnaud, pp. 349–50; Rousset, Guerre de Crimée, vol. 1, p. 136; Zaiončkovksij, Priloženija, vol. 2, pp. 431–2.

17   AGKK I/2, pp. 372–6; Friedjung, Krimkrieg, pp. 70, 98.

18   AGKK I/2, pp. 253–4, 258, n. 2, 261–2; Wimpffen, Erinnerungen aus der Walachei, pp. 102–23.

19 Wimpffen, *Erinnerungen aus der Walachei*, pp. 136–46; *AGKK* I/2, pp. 448–9, 458–61, 480–2.

20 Wimpffen, *Erinnerungen aus der Walachei*, pp. 146–65.

21 *AGKK* I/2, pp. 572, n. 6, 954–5; Friedjung, *Krimkrieg*, pp. 96, 116.

22 Nistor (ed.), *Corespondenţa lui Coronini*, pp. 414, 688–9, 709.

23 Nistor, *Corespondenţa lui Coronini*, pp. 728–9, 904–7; *AGKK* I/3, pp. 576–8 (also pp. 32–8).

24 Lambert, *Crimean War*, pp. 83–5.

25 Gouttman, *Guerre de Crimée*, p. 203; Quatrelles L'Épine, *Saint-Arnaud*, p. 313.

26 Tarle, *Krymskaja vojna*, vol. 2, pp. 7–11; Bestužev, *Krymskaja vojna*, pp. 67–8; Petrow, *Donaufeldzug*, pp. 176–80; Rousset, *Guerre de Crimée*, vol. 1, pp. 96–7; Gouttman, *Guerre de Crimée*, pp. 213–14; Lambert, *Crimean War*, pp. 101–3.

27 Zaiončkovskij, *Priloženija*, vol. 2, pp. 385–95; Gouttman, *Guerre de Crimée*, pp. 219–21; Rousset, *Guerre de Crimée*, vol. 1, pp. 105–14.

28 Rousset, *Guerre de Crimée*, vol. 1, p. 131; Benson and Esher (eds), *The Letters of Queen Victoria*, vol. 3, pp. 35–6.

29 Rousset, *Guerre de Crimée*, vol. 1, pp. 133–44; Gouttman, *Guerre de Crimée*, pp. 239–41.

30 Spahr, *Die Ausbreitung der Cholera*. More details are below in Chapter 19.

31 Gouttman, *Guerre de Crimée*, pp. 242–54; Rousset, *Guerre de Crimée*, vol. 1, pp. 142–58; Gooch, *The New Bonapartist Generals*, pp. 98–104.

32 Cf. for a general discussion of British military thinking about the expedition, see Strachan, 'Soldiers, Strategy and Sevastopol', pp. 312–24.

33 *AGKK* IV/2, p. 283 (no. 120), n. 1. As to Vaillant's ideas, cf. *AGKK* IV/2, pp. 311–4. For the technical preparations, cf. Guillemin, *Guerre de Crimée*, pp. 50–9; Figes, *Crimea*, pp. 197–9.

12 The Black Sea theatre

1 Seaton, *The Crimean War*, pp. 50–9, 104–10.

2 Barker, *Vainglorious War*, pp. 35–56; Figes, *Crimea*, pp. 200–3.

3 Bestužev, *Krymskaja vojna*, p. 90; Tarle, *Krymskaja vojna*, vol. 2, p. 107; Gouttman, *Guerre de Crimée*, p. 289; Figes, *Crimea*, p. 206.

4 Cited by Tarle, *Krymskaja vojna*, vol. 2, p. 113. As to the losses mentioned in the following paragraph, cf., e.g., Seaton, *Crimean War*, pp. 101–2; Gouttman, *Guerre de Crimée*, pp. 300–1; Barker, *Vainglorious War*, pp. 113–14; Figes, *Crimea*, p. 218.

5 Cited by Tarle, *Krymskaja vojna*, vol. 2, p. 125. The following quotation, Tarle, *Krymskaja vojna*, vol. 2, p. 125.

6   Cited by Barker, *Vainglorious War*, pp. 163–4. The quotation in the following
    paragraph, Barker, *Vainglorious War*, p. 165.

7   Barker, *Vainglorious War*, p. 174.

8   The figures are given by Tarle, *Krymskaja vojna*, vol. 2, pp. 166–7.

9   Cf. Tarle, *Krymskaja vojna*, vol. 2, p. 168. Seaton, *Crimean War*, pp. 174–5.

10 Rousset, *Guerre de Crimée*, vol. 1, p. 384.

11 Differing figures are in Tarle, *Krymskaja vojna*, vol. 2, p. 183; Gouttman,
    Guerre de Crimée, p. 348; Rousset, *Guerre de Crimée*, vol. 1, p. 388; Barker,
    Vainglorious War, p. 192; Figes, *Crimea*, p. 268.

12 Stanmore, *Sidney Herbert*, vol. 1, p. 278.

13 For the figures, see Stanmore, *Sidney Herbert*, vol. 1, pp. 291, 310.

14 Stanmore, *Sidney Herbert*, vol. 1, p. 296.

15 Calthorpe, *Letters from Head-Quarters*, vol. 1, p. 441.

16 Curtiss, *Russia's Crimean War*, p. 337; Seaton, *Crimean War*, p. 56.

17 For more details about this aspect of the war, cf. Chapter 19 below (which is
    new in the second edition of this book).

18 This important letter is cited at length in Tarle, *Krymskaja vojna*, vol. 2,
    pp. 314–16.

19 Douglas and Dalhousie Ramsay (eds), *The Panmure Papers*, vol. 1,
    pp. 156–9.

20 Rousset, *Guerre de Crimée*, vol. 2, p. 159.

21 Dewar (ed.), *Russian War*, p. 175.

22 Lambert, *Crimean War*, p. 233. Cf. the sober account by Figes, *Crimea*,
    pp. 244–5. The following quotations are in Farrère, *Histoire de la marine
    française*, p. 349; Totleben, *Die Vertheidigung von Sewastopol*, vol. 2, pp. 1,
    293.

23 Rousset, *Guerre de Crimée*, vol. 2, p. 232.

24 Rousset, *Guerre de Crimée*, vol. 2, p. 256.

25 Tarle, *Krymskaja vojna*, vol. 2, p. 431.

26 Tarle, *Krymskaja vojna*, vol. 2, p. 435.

27 Tarle, *Krymskaja vojna*, vol. 2, p. 438.

28 Tarle, *Krymskaja vojna*, vol. 2, p. 446.

29 Gouttman, *Guerre de Crimée*, 436.

30 Martin, Life of the Prince Consort, vol. 3, p. 385.

31 Baumgart, *Peace of Paris*, pp. 27–8.

32 Baumgart, *Peace of Paris*, p. 31. The following quotation, Baumgart, *Peace of
    Paris*, p. 14.

33 Benson and Esher, *Queen Victoria*, vol. 3, p. 163.

34 Martin, *Life of the Prince Consort*, vol. 3, pp. 525–6.

13 The campaigns in the Baltic, 1854 and 1855

1 *AGKK* III/4, p. 141.
2 The figures are in Tarle, *Krymskaja vojna*, vol. 2, pp. 42–3.
3 Greenhill and Giffard, *The British Assault on Finland*, p. 137.
4 Greenhill and Giffard, *The British Assault on Finland*, p. 178.
5 Cited in Greenhill and Giffard, *The British Assault on Finland*, pp. 273–4.
6 Cited in Guillemin, *Guerre de Crimée*, p. 238.
7 Tarle, *Krymskaja vojna*, vol. 1, p. 421.
8 Lambert, *Crimean War*, p. 282; Rath, *Crimean War*, pp. 14, 24, 44.

14 The Caucasian battlefield, 1853–5

1 Cited in Alder 'India and the Crimean War', p. 29.
2 *AGKK* IV/2, p. 292, n. 2.
3 Zaiončkovskij, *Priloženija*, vol. 2, pp. 105–7; cf. Zaiončkovskij, *Priloženija*, vol. 2, pp. 110–11.
4 Zaiončkovskij, *Priloženija*, vol. 2, pp. 163, 445–52.

15 The minor theatres of war: the White Sea and the Pacific

1 Tarle, *Krymskaja vojna*, vol. 2, p. 197. For more details, cf. the new account by Rath, *The Crimean War*, pp. 98–9.
2 Cited in Gough, 'The Crimean War in the Pacific', p. 131.
3 Tarle, *Krymskaja vojna*, vol. 2, p. 210.

16 Allied war preparations for 1856 and the war council in Paris, January 1856

1 Martin, *Life of the Prince Consort*, vol. 3, pp. 524–6. Queen Victoria's reply, mentioned in the following paragraph, is printed in Martin, *Life of the Prince Consort*, vol. 3, pp. 526–31.
2 *AGKK* III/4, p. 90. For the following quotation, see *AGKK* III/4, p. 289.
3 *AGKK* III/4, pp. 581–3. On the follwing sessions, cf. *AGKK* III/4, pp. 598–600, 610, 629–30, 643–4.

4   *AGKK* III/4, pp. 712–22, 738–40.

5   *AGKK* III/4, pp. 749–54. The following quotation is in Baumgart, 'Ein Kronrat Napoleons III', pp. 212–35 (230). The documentary evidence is in *AGKK* III/4 and in IV/3.

6   For further details, cf. Baumgart, *Peace of Paris*, pp. 68–80.

17 The Paris peace congress, February–April 1856

1   Cf. Baumgart, *Peace of Paris*, p. 106.

2   *AGKK* III/4, pp. 789, 816, 818–19, 846–7.

3   *AGKK* I/3, pp. 30–8.

4   On this point, cf. Senner, *Die Donaufürstentümer als Tauschobjekt*, pp. 118–38.

5   Baumgart, *Peace of Paris*, pp. 151–2.

6   *AGKK* III/4, pp. 956, 958, 969–71. Cf. also Henderson, 'The Pacifists of the Fifties', pp. 123–52.

18 The consequences of the war for international relations

1   Baumgart, *Peace of Paris*, p. 201.

2   Wemyss, *Memoirs and Letters of Sir Robert Morier*, vol. 2, p. 213.

3   This quotation, often found in the relevant books and sometimes wrongly attributed to other British politicians besides Disraeli, goes back to a remark Disraeli made in a leading article of 9 December 1854 in his weekly, *The Press*.

19 The medical services

1   This new chapter of the second edition of this work is a revised version of the author's article, 'Der Sanitätsdienst im Krimkrieg'. Regarding the following remarks, cf. Clodfelter, *Warfare and Armed Conflicts*.

2   Curtiss, *Russian Army*, p. 73.

3   Cf. Mitra, *Life and Letters of Sir John Hall*.

4   Marroin, *Histoire médicale de la flotte française dans la mer Noire*, pp. 11 and 15–17. A finding aid to the reports of ship's doctors of the French navy, which are kept in the French National Archives and which concern every ship from the time of the Crimean War, is provided by Brisou, *Catalogue raisonné*.

5 *AGKK* III/3, p. 206, n. 19.

6 Pennanéac'h, 'Un centenaire', pp. 182–4.

7 See above pp. 119–120 for more details.

8 Cf. Spahr, *Die Ausbreitung der Cholera*.

9 Kaufman, *Surgeons at War*, p. 163.

10 Kaufman, *Surgeons at War*, p. 130; Poirier, 'Questions sanitaires', p. 251.

11 Pennanéac'h, 'Un centenaire', p. 178; Kaufman, *Surgeons at War*, p. 172.

12 Hubbeneth, *Service sanitaire*.

13 Hubbeneth, *Service sanitaire*, p. 92.

14 Hubbeneth, *Service sanitaire*, p. 198.

15 Cadier-Rey, 'Les aspects sanitaires', p. 195.

16 Chenu, *De la mortalité*, p. 131. Pennanéac'h, 'Un Centenaire', p. 200, gives lower figures. In cases where varying figures are given, one has to ask whether only the French Black Sea fleet is considered or whether the Baltic See fleet is included as well.

17 Baudens, *Der Krimmkrieg*, p. 117; for the following quotation, see Baudens, *Der Krimmkrieg*, p. 132.

18 Baudens, *Der Krimmkrieg*, p. 150.

19 Baudens, *Der Krimmkrieg*, pp. 148–9.

20 Baudens, *Der Krimmkrieg*, p. 73.

21 Baudens, *Der Krimmkrieg*, p. 213.

22 Chenu, *De la mortalité*, p. 131. Differing figures are presented by Pennanéac'h, 'Un Centenaire', p. 178.

23 Chenu, *De la mortalité*, p. 133.

24 Lemaire, 'Service de santé militaire,' p. 1196.

25 Roche, 'L'assistance médicale française à Constantinople,' p. 634.

26 Cadier-Rey, 'Aspects sanitaires,' p. 189. Different figures are given by Pennanéac'h, 'Un Centenaire', p. 200. Pennanéac'h obviously includes navy surgeons and pharmacists and therefore arrives at a higher figure. Nevertheless, the figures of both are inconsistent.

27 Sweetman, *War and Administration*, pp. 41–59.

28 Kaufman, *Surgeons at War*, pp. 164–7.

29 Cadier-Rey, 'Aspects sanitaires', p. 183.

30 Hubbeneth, *Service sanitaire*, p. 20. For the following remarks, see Hubbeneth, *Service sanitaire*, pp. 20–1; also Parry, 'American Doctors', pp. 478–490.

31 Hubbeneth, *Service sanitaire*, p. 22. For the following remarks, see Hubbeneth, *Service sanitaire*, p. 23.

32 Hubbeneth, *Service sanitaire*, p. 24.

33 Hubbeneth, *Service sanitaire*, p. 169. For the following remarks, see Hubbeneth, *Service sanitaire*, p. 8.

34 Hubbeneth, *Service sanitaire*, p. 169.

35 Hubbeneth, *Service sanitaire*, pp. 128, 150, 166.

36 Pirogov, *Sevastopol'skie pis'ma*.

37 Hubbeneth, *Service sanitaire*, pp. 22–23.

38 Pirogov, *Sevastopol'skie pis'ma*, pp. 196–209.

39 Woodham-Smith, *Nightingale*. For a recent biography, see Bostridge, *Nightingale*. For an older biography, see Cook, *The Life of Florence Nightingale*. Her collected works are edited by McDonald (ed.), *The Collected Works*, vols 1–16. Vol. 14, *The Crimean War*, was published in 2010.

40 Goldie (ed.), *'I have done my Duty'*.

41 The letters between him and Nightingale in 1854–5 are published in his biography: Stanmore, *Sidney Herbert*, pp. 331–421; now also in vol. 14 of her published works (see above, n. 39).

42 *The Times*, 9 October 1854; 13 October 1854. Cf. also Shepherd, *The Crimean Doctors*, vol. 1, pp. 145–50.

43 As to Stanley's group, cf. Bolster, *The Sisters of Mercy*; Luddy (ed.), *The Crimean Journals of the Sisters of Mercy*; J. J. W. Murphy, 'An Irish Sister of Mercy'; D. Murphy, *Ireland and the Crimean War*. For the following remarks, cf. Woodham-Smith, *Nightingale*, pp. 181–95; Shepherd, *Crimean Doctors*, pp. 270–6.

44 Shepherd, *Crimean Doctors*, p. 250; Goldie, *'I have done my Duty'*, p. 229.

45 Goldie, *'I have done my Duty'*, p. 126.

46 Woodham-Smith, *Nightingale*, p. 238.

47 According to information from the Archives of the Vincentians, Paris, which Miss Patricia Mowbray, Kew (Richmond), former head of the Florence Nightingale Museum at St Thomas' Hospital, London, kindly placed at the author's disposal.

48 Gilbrin, *L'hôpital français à Constantinople*, p. 143; *Monsieur Vincent vit encore*, pp. 70–1.

49 Curtiss, 'Russian Sisters of Mercy', pp. 84–100; Sorokina, 'Nursing in the Crimean War', pp. 57–63.

50 Cf. Lemaire, 'Anesthésie', p. 62.

51 Baudens, *Krimmkrieg*, p. 82.

52 Quoted by Bonham-Carter (ed.), *Surgeon in the Crimea*, p. 13. Cf. Shepherd, *Crimean Doctors*, vol. 1, pp. 57–61.

53 Hubbeneth, *Service sanitaire*, pp. 75–6.

54 Baudens, *Krimmkrieg*, p. 105; cf. also Roche, 'L'assistance médicale', pp. 631–3.

55 Kaufman, *Crimean War*, pp. 194–5. As to the 'Crimean winter', cf. Shepherd, *Crimean Doctors*, vol. 1, pp. 287–339.

56 Shepherd, 'The Civil Hospitals in the Crimea', pp. 199–204; Shepherd, *Crimean Doctors*, vol. 2, pp. 412–51.

57 Hubbeneth, *Service sanitaire*, pp. 27–8.

58 Hubbeneth, *Service sanitaire*, p. 117.

59 Heyris, 'Les problèmes de santé du corps expéditionnaire piémontais', p. 58.

60 Baudens, *Krimmkrieg*, pp. 164–7. Cf. Shepherd, *Crimean Doctors*, vol. 2, pp. 562–71 (the remarks refer to the 'Turkish Contingent', an auxiliary unit attached to the British Army of the East).

61 Quoted by Cadier-Rey, 'Aspects sanitaires', p. 184.

62 Goldie, *'I have done my Duty'*, p. 272. For the following quotation, see Goldie, *'I have done my Duty'*, p. 273.

63 Baudens, *Krimmkrieg*, p. 214.

64 *AGKK*, III/4, p. 1015.

65 Kaufman, *Surgeons at War*, p. 173.

66 Kaufman, *Surgeons at War*, p. 174.

67 *AGKK* III/4, p. 1017. In the House of Commons, on 8 May 1856, Secretary of State for War, Panmure, quantified the total number of soldiers sent to the Levant (including Foreign Legion and Transport Corps of the Army) as 149,764. Cf. *Hansard's Parliamentary Reports*, Third Series, vol. 142 (London, 1856), pp. 183–4. Cf. also Shepherd, *Crimean Doctors*, vol. 2, p. 591.

68 Shepherd, *Crimean Doctors*, vol. 2, p. 187. His number is higher by more than 1,000: 22,457.

69 Kaufman, *Surgeons at War*, p. 169.

70 Hubbeneth, *Service sanitaire*, p. 170.

71 Hubbeneth, *Service sanitaire*, p. 9.

72 Baumgart, *Peace of Paris*, p. 76.

73 Curtiss comes to a total of 450,000: Curtiss, *Russia's Crimean War*, pp. 470–1.

74 Naumova, *Ranenie*, p. 297.

BIBLIOGRAPHY

Abbenhuis, Maarthe M. *An Age of Neutrals: Great Power Politics, 1815–1914*. Cambridge: Cambridge University Press, 2014.

Alder, Garry J. 'India and the Crimean War'. *Journal of Commonwealth History* 2 (1973/74): 15–37.

Allen, W. D. and Paul Muratoff. *Caucasian Battlefields: A History of the Wars on the Turco-Caucasian Border, 1828–1921*. Cambridge: Cambridge University Press, 1953.

Ameil, Gilbert, ed. *Le congrès de Paris (1856). Un événement fondateur*. Brussels: Lang, 2009.

Ancel, Jacques. *Manuel historique de la question d'Orient, 1792–1923*. Paris: Delagrave, 1923; 3rd edn 1927.

Anderson, Edgar. 'The Role of the Crimean War in Northern Europe'. *Jahrbücher für Geschichte Osteuropas* 20 (1972): 42–59.

Anderson, Matthew S. *The Eastern Question, 1774–1923: A Study in International Relations*. London: Macmillan, 1966; repr. Basingstoke 1991.

Anderson, Olive. *A Liberal State at War: English Politics and Economics during the Crimean War*. London: Macmillian, 1967; repr. Aldershot: Gregg Revivals, 1994.

Angelow, Jürgen. *Von Wien bis Königgrätz. Die Sicherheitspolitik des Deutschen Bundes im europäischen Gleichgewicht (1815–1866)*. Munich: Oldenbourg Verlag, 1966.

Antić, Čedomir. *Neutrality as Independence: Great Britain, Serbia and the Crimean War*. Belgrade: Serbian Academy of Sciences and Arts, 2007.

Badem, Candan. *The Ottoman Crimean War (1853–1856)*. Leiden: Brill, 2010.

Bailey, Frank E. *British Policy and the Turkish Reform Movement: A Study in Anglo-Turkish Relations, 1826–1853*. Cambridge, MA: Harvard University Press, 1942; repr. New York: Fertig, 1970.

Bapst, Germain. *Le Maréchal Canrobert. Souvenirs d'un siècle*, vols 2–3. Paris: Plon, 1902–4.

Barker, A. J. *The Vainglorious War 1854–56*. London, Weidenfeld and Nicolson, 1970.

Battesti, Michèle. *La marine de Napoléon III. Une politique navale*, vols 1–2. Vincennes: Service Historique de la Marine, 1997.

Baudens, Lucien. *La guerre de Crimée. Les campements, les abris, les ambulances, les hôpitaux etc. etc.* Paris: Lévy, 1858; 2nd edn 1858; repr. 2011. German trans.: *Der Krimkrieg. Die Lager, die Unterkunft, die Ambulanzen, die Spitäler*. Kiel: Homann, 1864. English trans.: *On Military and Camp Hospitals, and the Health of the Troops in the Field, being the Results of a Commission to Inspect the Sanitary Arrangements of the French Army, and Incidentally of Other Armies in the Crimean War*. London: Baillière Brothers, 1862.

Baumgart, Winfried. 'Probleme der Krimkriegsforschung. Eine Studie über die
    Literatur des letzten Jahrzehnts (1961–1970)'. *Jahrbücher für osteuropäische
    Geschichte* 19 (1971): 49–109, 243–64, 371–400.
Baumgart, Winfried. *Der Friede von Paris. Studien zum Verhältnis von
    Kriegführung, Politik und Friedensbewahrung*. Munich and Vienna:
    Oldenbourg, 1972.
Baumgart, Winfried. 'Die Aktenedition zur Geschichte des Krimkriegs. Eine
    Zwischenbilanz auf Grund der österreichischen Akten'. In Ostmitteleuropa.
    Berichte und Forschungen, edited by Ulrich Haustein et al., 217–36. Stuttgart:
    Klett-Cotta, 1981.
Baumgart, Winfried. *The Peace of Paris: Studies in War, Diplomacy, and
    Peacemaking*. Santa Barbara, CA: ABC Clio, 1981.
Baumgart, Winfried. 'Ein Kriegsrat Napoleons III. Englisch-Französische
    Feldzugspläne gegen Rußland 1855/56'. In *Festschrift für Eberhard Kessel zum
    75. Geburtstag*, edited by Heinz Duchhardt and Manfred Schlenke, 212–35.
    Munich: Wilhelm Fink Verlag, 1982.
Baumgart, Winfried. 'Neue Forschungsergebnisse aufgrund der österreichischen
    Akten'. In *Vorträge und Studien zur preußisch-deutschen Geschichte*, 45–70.
    Cologne and Vienna: Böhlau, 1983.
Baumgart, Winfried. 'Die deutschen Mittelstaaten und der Krimkrieg 1853–1856'.
    In Landesgeschichte und Reichsgeschichte. Festschrift für Alois Gerlich zum 70.
    Geburtstag, edited by Winfried Dotzauer, 357–89. Stuttgart: Franz Steiner
    Verlag, 1995.
Baumgart, Winfried. *Europäisches Konzert und nationale Bewegung. Internationale
    Beziehungen 1830–1878*. Paderborn. Schöningh, 1999; 2nd edn 2007.
Baumgart, Winfried. 'Bayern und die Europäischen Großmächte im Krimkrieg
    1853–1856'. In *Bayern und Europa. Festschrift für Peter Claus Hartmann zum
    65. Geburtstag*, edited by Konrad Amann et al., 285–303. Frankfurt: Lang,
    2005.
Baumgart, Winfried. 'Der Sanitätsdienst im Krimkrieg (1854–1856). Ein
    internationaler Vergleich'. In *Religiöse Prägung und politische Ordnung in der
    Neuzeit. Festschrift für Winfried Becker zum 65. Geburtstag*, edited by Bernhard
    Löffler and Karsten Ruppert, 221–56. Cologne: Böhlau Verlaug, 2006.
Baumgart, Winfried, ed. *Akten zur Geschichte des Krimkriegs [AGKK]*. Series I.
    Österreichische Akten zur Geschichte des Krimkriegs, vols 1–3. Munich:
    Oldenbourg, 1979–80. Series II: *Preußische Akten zur Geschichte des
    Krimkriegs*, vols 1–2. Munich: Oldenbourg, 1990–1. Series III: *Englische Akten
    zur Geschichte des Krimkriegs*, vols 1–4. Munich: Oldenbourg, 1988–2006.
    Series IV: *Französische Akten zur Geschichte des Krimkriegs*, vols 1–3. Munich:
    Oldenbourg, 1999–2003.
Baumgart, Winfried, ed. *Der König und sein Beichtvater. Friedrich Wilhelm IV. und
    Carl Wilhelm Saegert. Briefwechsel 1848 bis 1856*. Berlin: Duncker & Humblot,
    2016.
Bayley, C. C. *Mercenaries for the Crimea: The German, Swiss, and Italian Legions
    in British Service, 1854–1856*. Montreal: MacGill-Queen's University Press,
    1977.
Bazancourt, César L. de. *L'expédition de Crimée jusq'à la prise de Sébastopol.
    Chroniques de la guerre d'Orient*, vols 1–2. Paris: Amyot, 1856, 5th edn 1857.
    Editions after the fifth have the title *L'expédition de Crimée. La marine française*

dans la mer Noire et la Baltique. Chronique . . ., vols 1–2. Paris 1858. English trans., vols 1–2. London: Sampson, Low & Co., 1856; German trans., vols 1–2. Pest: Hartleben, 1856.

Becker, Jerónimo. *Historia de las Relaciones Exteriores de España en el sigo XIX*, vol. 2. Madrid: Ratés, 1924.

Beer, Adolf. *Die orientalische Politik Österreichs seit 1774.* Prague: Tempsky, 1883.

Ben-Arieh, Yehoshua. *The Rediscovery of the Holy Land in the Nineteenth Century.* Jerusalem: Magnes Press, 1979; repr. 2007.

Benson, Arthur C. and Viscount Esher, eds. *The Letters of Queen Victoria: A Selection from Her Majesty's Correspondence*, vol. 3. London: John Murray, 1908.

Bentley, Nicolas, ed. *Russell's Despatches from the Crimea, 1854–1856.* London: Deutsch, 1966; repr. Annapolis, MD: Naval Institute Press, 2007.

Beskrovny, L. G. *The Russian Army and Fleet in the Nineteenth Century: A Handbook of Armaments, Personnel and Policy.* Gulf Breeze, FL: Academic International Press, 1996.

Bestužev, Igor V. *Krymskaja vojna 1853–1856 gg.* Moscow: Izdatel'stvo Akademii Nauk SSSR, 1956.

Bogdanovič, Modest I. *Vostočnaja vojna 1853–1856 gg.*, vols 1–4. St Petersburg: M. Stasjulevič, 1876.

Boicu, Leonid. *Austria şi Principatele Române în vremea războiulu Crimeii (1853–1856).* Bucharest: Ed. Academiei Republicii Socialiste Romăniă, 1972.

Bolster, Evelyn. *The Sisters of Mercy in the Crimean War.* Cork: Mercier Press, 1964.

Bonham-Carter, Victor, ed. *Surgeon in the Crimea: The Experiences of George Lawson, Recorded in Letters to his Family 1854–1855.* London: Constable, 1968.

Bonner-Smith, David, ed. *The Russian War, 1855. Baltic. Official Correspondence.* London: Navy Records Society, 1944.

Bonner-Smith, David and Alfred C. Dewar, eds. *The Russian War, 1854. Baltic and Black Sea. Official Correspondence.* London: Navy Records Society, 1943.

Borodkin, Mikhail M. *Kriget vid Finlands kuster, 1854–1855.* Helsinki: Söderström, 1905. Russian version: *Vojna 1854–55 gg. na Finskom poberež'e.* St. Petersburg: Tip. Glavnago Upravlenija Udelov, 1903; rev. edn St. Petersburg: Galilei Vil'berg, 1904.

Borries, Kurt. *Preußen im Krimkrieg (1853–1856).* Stuttgart: Kohlhammer, 1930.

Bostridge, Mark. *Florence Nightingale: The Woman and her Legend.* London: Viking, 2008.

Brisou, Bernard. *Catalogue raisonné des rapports médicaux annuels ou de fin de campagne des médecins et chirurgiens de la maraine d'État 1790–1914.* Vincennes: Service Historique de la Marine, 2004.

British and Foreign State Papers, vol. 44 (1853–4); vol. 45 (1854–5); vol. 46 (1855–6). London: Her Majesty's Stationery Office, 1865.

Cadier-Rey, Gabrielle. 'Les aspects sanitaires de la Guerre de Crimée dans les armées française et britannique'. In *Les entreprises et leurs réseaux. Hommes, capitaux, technique et pouvoirs, XIXᵉ–XXᵉ siècles. Mélanges en l'honneur de François Caron*, edited by Michèle Merger and Dominique Barjot, 181–97. Paris: Presse de l'Université de Paris Sorbonne, 1998.

Calthorpe, S. J. G. *Letters from Head-Quarters; or, the Realities of the War in the Crimea. By an Officer on the Staff*, vol. 1. London: Murray, 1857.

Carmel, Alex. *Christen als Pioniere im Heiligen Land. Ein Beitrag zur Geschichte der Pilgermission und des Wiederaufbaus Palästinas im 19. Jahrhundert*. Basel: F. Reinhardt, 1981.

Cavour, Camillo. *Carteggi*, vol. 7: *Cavour e L'Inghilterra. Carteggio con V.E. d'Azeglio*; vol. 1: *Il Congresso di Parigi*. Bologna: Zanichelli, 1961.

Čennyk, Sergej Viktorovič. *Krymskaja kampanija 1854–1856 gg. vostočnoj vojny 1853–1856 gg. Voenno-istoričeskij očerk*, vols 1–5. Sevastopol: Gala, 2010–14.

Chadwick, G. F. 'The Army Works Corps in the Crimea'. *Journal of Transport History* 6 (1964): 129–41.

Chenu, Jean Charles. *De la mortalité dans l'armée et des moyens d'économiser la vie humaine; extraits des statistiques médico-chirurgicales des campagnes de Crimée en 1854–1856 et d'Italie en 1859*. Paris: Hachette, 1870.

Clayton, Gerald D. *Britain and the Eastern Question: Missolonghi to Gallipoli*. London: University of London Press, 1971.

Clodfelter, Michael. *War and Armed Conflicts: A Statistical Reference to Casualty and Other Figures, 1618–1991*, vols 1–2. Jefferson, NC., and London: McFarland, 1992.

Conacher, James B. *The Aberdeen Coalition, 1852–1855: A Study in Mid-Nineteenth-Century Party Politics*. London: Cambridge University Press, 1968.

Conacher, James B. *Britain and the Crimea, 1855–56: Problems of War and Peace*. London: Macmillan, 1987.

Cook, Edward. *The Life of Florence Nightingale*, vol. 1 (1820–61). London: Macmillan, 1913.

Cooke, Brian. *The Grand Crimean Central Railway: The Story of the Railway Built by the British at Balaklava during the Crimean War of 1854–56*. Knutsford: Cavalier House, 1990; 2nd edn 1997.

Cullberg, Albin. *La politique du Roi Oscar I pendant la Guerre de Crimé. Études diplomatiques sur les négociations secrètes entre les cabinets de Stockholm, Paris, St. Pétersbourg et Londres les années 1853–1856*, vols 1–2. Stockholm: Författarens Förl., 1912 and 1926.

Curato, Federico, ed. *Le relazioni diplomatiche fra la Gran Bretagna e il Regno di Sardegna*, III series: 1848–60, vols 4–5. Rome: Istituto Storico Italiano per l'età moderna e contemporanea, 1868–9.

Curato, Federico, ed. *Le relazioni tra la Gran Bretagna e il Regno di Sardegna dal 1852 al 1856. Il carteggio diplomatico di Sir James Hudson*, vol. 2. Turin: Istituto Storico Italiano per l'età moderna e contemporanea, 1956.

Curtiss, John Shelton. *The Russian Army under Nicholas I, 1825–1855*. Durham, NC: Duke University Press, 1965.

Curtiss, John Shelton. 'Russian Sisters of Mercy in the Crimea, 1854–55'. *Slavic Review* 25 (1966): 84–100.

Curtiss, John Shelton. *Russia's Crimean War*. Durham, NC: Duke University Press, 1979.

Davis, John R. 'The Bamberg Conference of 1854: A Re-Evaluation'. *European History Quarterly* 28 (1998): 81–107.

Davison, Roderic H. *Reform in the Ottoman Empire, 1856–1876*. Princeton, NJ: Princeton University Press, 1963; repr. 1973.

Davison, Roderic H. *Turkey*. Englewood Cliffs, NJ: Prentice-Hall, Inc., 1968; 3rd edn Huntingdon: Eastern Press, 1998.

Dawson, Anthony. *The Siege of Sevastopol 1854–1855*. Barnsley: Frontline Books, 2018.

Degoev, Vladimir Vladimirovič. *Kavkaz i velikie deržavy 1829–1864 gg. Politika, vojna, diplomatija*. Moscow: n.p., 2009.

Dereli, C. A. *War Culture in Action: A Study of the Literature of the Crimean War*. Paris and Bern: Peter Lang, 2003.

Derrécagaix, Victor B. *Le Maréchal Pélissier, Duc de Malakoff*. Paris: Chapelot, 1911.

Dewar, Alfred C., ed. *Russian War, 1855. Black Sea. Official Correspondence*. London: Navy Records Society, 1945.

Di Nolfo, Ennio. *Europa e Italia nel 1855–1856*. Rome: Istituto per la storia del Risorgimento italiano, 1967.

Douglas, Sir George and Sir George Dalhousie Ramsay, eds. *The Panmure Papers: Being a Selection from the Correspondence of Fox Maule, Second Baron Panmure, afterwards Earl of Dalhousie*, vols 1 2. London: Hodder and Stoughton, 1908.

Dowty, Alan. *The Limits of American Isolation: The United States and the Crimean War*. New York: New York University Press, 1971.

Duckers, Peter. *The Crimean War at Sea: The Naval Campaigns against Russia, 1854–1856*. Barnsley: Pen & Sword Maritime, 2011.

Eastern Papers. Part V: Communications Respecting Turkey Made to Her Majesty's Government by the Emperor of Russia . . . January to April 1853. London: Harrison and Son, 1854.

Eckhart, Franz. *Die deutsche Frage und der Krimkrieg*. Berlin: Osteuropa Verlag, 1931.

Eriksson, Sven. *Svensk diplomati och tidningspress under Krimkriget*. Stockholm: P.A. Norstedt och söners förlag, 1939.

Ernst II., Herzog von Sachsen-Coburg-Gotha. *Aus meinem Leben und aus meiner Zeit*, vol. 2. Berlin: Verlag Wilhelm Hertz, 1888.

Ettinger, Amos A. *The Mission to Spain of Pierre Soulé 1853–1856: A Study in the Cuban Diplomacy of the United States*. New Haven, CT: Yale University Press, 1932.

Fairey, Jack. 'Russia's Quest for the Holy Grail: Relics, Liturgies, and Great Power Politics in the Ottoman Empire'. In *Russian–Ottoman Borderlands: The Eastern Question Reconsidered*, edited by Lucien J. Frary and Mara Kozelsky, 131–64. Madison: University of Wisconsin Press, 2014.

Fairey, Jack. *The Great Powers and Orthodox Christendom: The Crisis over the Eastern Church in the Era of the Crimean War*. Basingstoke: Palgrave Macmillan, 2015.

Farrère, Claude. *Histoire de la marine française*. Paris: Flammarion, 1934; repr. 1962.

ffrench Blake, R. L. V. *The Crimean War*. London: Cooper, 1971; repr. 1993.

Figes, Orlando. *The Crimean War: The Last Crusade*. London: Allen Lane, 2010.

Fletcher, Ian and Natalia Ishchenko. *The Crimean War: A Clash of Empires*. Staplehurst: Spellmount, 2004.

Fletcher, Ian and Natalia Ishchenko. *The Battle of the Alma 1954: First Blood to the Allies in the Crimea*. Barnsley: Pen & Sword Military, 2008.

Friedjung, Heinrich. *Der Krimkrieg und die österreichische Politik*. Stuttgart: Cotta, 1907; 2nd edn 1911.

Geffcken, F. Heinrich. *Zur Geschichte des Orientalischen Krieges 1853–1856*. Berlin: Gebrüder Paetel, 1881.

Gibbs, Peter. *The Battle of the Alma*. Philadelphia: Lippincott, 1963.

Gildbrin, Émile. 'L'hôpital français de Constantinople'. *Histoire des sciences médicales* 11 (1977): 141–51.

Gleason, John H. *The Genesis of Russophobia in Great Britain: A Study of the Interaction of Policy and Opinion*. Cambridge, MA: Harvard University Press, 1950.

Goldfrank, David. *The Origins of the Crimean War*. London: Longman, 1994.

Goldie, Sue, M., ed. *'I have done my duty': Florence Nightingale in the Crimean War 1854–56*. Manchester: Manchester University Press, 1987.

Gooch, Brison D. *The New Bonapartist Generals in the Crimean War*. The Hague: Nijhoff, 1959.

Gooch, Brison D. 'A Century of Historiography on the Origins of the Crimean War'. *American Historical Review* 62 (1965–6): 33–58.

Gooch, George P., ed. *The Later Correspondence of Lord John Russell, 1840–1878*, vol. 2. London: Longmans, Green, 1925.

Gorce, Pierre de la. *Histoire du Second Empire*, vol. 1. Paris: Librairie Plon, 1894.

Gordon, A. H., Baron Stanmore. *Sidney Herbert, Lord Herbert of Lea*, vols 1–2. London: John Murray, 1906.

Gordon, Sophie and Louise Pearson, eds. *Shadows of War: Roger Fenton's Photographs of the Crimea, 1855*. London: Royal Collection Trust, 2017.

Gough, Barry M. 'The Crimean War in the Pacific: British Strategy and Naval Operations'. *Military Affairs* 37 (1973): 130–6.

Gouttman, Alain. *La guerre de Crimée 1853–1856*. Paris, SPM, 1995; 2nd edn Paris: Perrin, 2006.

Grainger, John D. *The First Pacific War: Britain and Russia, 1854–1856*. Woodbridge: Boydell Press, 2008.

Greenhill, Basil and Ann Giffard. *The British Assault on Finland, 1854–1855: A Forgotten Naval War*. London, Conway, 1988.

Gugolz, Peter. *Die Schweiz und der Krimkrieg 1853–1856*. Basel: Helbing & Lichtenhahn, 1965.

Guichen, Eugène vicomte de. *La guerre de Crimée (1854–1856) et l'attitude des puissances européennes*. Paris: Pedone, 1936.

Guillemin, René. *La guerre de Crimée. Le Tsar de toutes les Russies face à l'Europe*. Paris: Ed. France-Empire, 1981.

Halicz, Emmanuel. *Danish Neutrality during the Crimean War (1853–1856): Denmark between the Hammer and the Anvil*. Odense: Odense University Press, 1977.

Hallendorff, Carl. *Oscar I, Napoleon och Nikolaus. Ur diplomaternas privatbrev under Krimkriget*. Stockholm: Geber, 1918.

Hallendorff, Carl. *Konung Oscar I's politik under Krimkriget*. Stockholm: Akad. Förl., 1930.

Hamilton, C. I. 'Sir James Graham, the Baltic Campaign and War-Planning at the Admiralty in 1854'. *Historical Journal* 19 (1976): 89–112.

Hannavy, John. *Roger Fenton of Crimble Hall*. London: Fraser, 1975.

Harris, Stephen M. *British Military Intelligence in the Crimean War, 1854–1856*. London: Frank Cass, 1999; repr. London: Routledge, 2014.

Hearder, Harry. 'Clarendon, Cavour, and the Intervention of Sardinia in the Crimean War'. *International History Review* 18 (1996): 819–36.

Henderson, Gavin B. 'The Pacifists of the Fifties'. In *Gavin B. Henderson, Crimean War Diplomacy and other Historical Essays*, 123–52. Glasgow: Jackson, 1975.

Heyries, Hubert. 'Les problèmes de santé du corps expéditionnaire piémontais pendant la guerre de Crimée'. *Revue historique des armées* 26, no. 1 (1999): 55–64.

Hibbert, Christopher. *The Destruction of Lord Raglan*. London: Longman, 1961.

The History of the Times: The Tradition Established: 1841–1884. London: The Times, 1939.

Hopwood, Derek. *The Russian Presence in Syria and Palestine, 1843–1914: Church and Politics in the Near East*. Oxford: Clarendon Press, 1969.

Hösch, Edgar. 'Neuere Literatur (1940–1960) über den Krimkrieg'. *Jahrbücher für Geschichte Osteuropas* 9 (1961): 399–434.

Hoskins, Halford I. *British Routes to India*. London: Longmans, Green, 1928, repr. New York: Octagon Books, 1966.

The House of Representatives (US). *Executive Documents*, 33rd Congress, 2nd Session, no. 93. Washington, 1855.

Hubbeneth, Anton. *Service sanitaire des hôpitaux russes pendant la guerre de Crimée, dans les années 1854–1856*. St Petersburg: Nékludow, 1870.

Husen, Werner. *Hannovers Politik während des Krimkrieges*. Emsdetten: Lechte, 1936.

Ibragimbejli, Chadži Murat. *Kavkaz v Krymskoj vojne 1853–1856 gg. i meždunarodnie otnošenija*. Moscow: Izd. Nauka, 1971.

James, Lawrence. *Crimea 1854–56: The War with Russia from Contemporary Photographs*. New York: Van Nostrand Reinhold Company, 1981.

Jasmund, Julius von, ed. *Aktenstücke zur orientalischen Frage. Nebst chronologischer Uebersicht*, vols 1–2. Berlin: F. Schneider, 1855–6.

Jelavich, Barbara. *Russia's Balkan Entanglements, 1806–1914*. Cambridge: Cambridge University Press, 1991; repr. 1993.

Jomini, Alexandre. *Étude diplomatique sur la guerre de Crimée (1852 à 1856)*, vols 1–2. St Petersburg: Librairie H. Schmitzdorff, 1878.

Jonasson, Axel J. 'The Crimean War, the Beginning of Strict Swedish Neutrality, and the Myth of Swedish Intervention in the Baltic'. *Journal of Baltic Studies* 4 (1973): 244–53.

Kaufman, Matthew H. *Surgeons at War: Medical Arrangements for the Treatment of the Sick and Wounded in the British Army during the Late 18th and 19th Centuries*. Westport, CT, and London: Greenwood Press, 2001.

Keller, Ulrich. *The Ultimate Spectacle: A Visual History of the Crimean War*. Amsterdam: Gordon and Breach, 2001; repr. London: Routledge, 2013.

Kinglake, Arthur William. *The Invasion of the Crimea, and an Account of its Progress down to the Death of Lord Raglan*, vols 1–8. Edinburgh and London: Blackwood, 1863–7; 6th edn in 9 vols, Edinburgh: Blackwood, 1877–8.

Kinjapina, Nina S. et al. *Vostočnyj vopros vo vnešnej politike Rossii konec XVIII–načalo XX v*. Moscow: Nauka, 1978.

Klemensberger, Peter. *Die Westmächte und Sardinien während des Krimkrieges. Der Beitrag des Königreichs Sardinien zur britisch-französischen Allianz im Rahmen der europäischen Politik*. Zürich: Juris Druck + Verlag, 1972.

Koch, Klaus. *Generaladjutant Graf Crenneville. Politik und Militär zwischen Krimkrieg und Königgrätz*. Vienna: Österreichischer Bundesverlag, 1984.

Kofas, Jon F. *International and Domestic Politics in Greece during the Crimean War*. New York: Columbia University Press, 1980.

Kozelsky, Mara. *Crimea in War and Transformation*. New York: Oxford University Press, 2019.

Krautheim, Hans-Jobst. *Öffentliche Meinung und imperiale Politik. Das britische Rußlandbild 1815–1854*. Berlin: Duncker & Humblot, 1977.

Krusemarck, Götz. *Württemberg und der Krimkrieg*. Halle (Saale): Max Niemeyer Verlag, 1932.

Lambert, Andrew. *The Crimean War: British Grand Strategy, 1853–56*. Manchester: Manchester University Press, 1990; 2nd edn Farnham: Ashgate, 2011.

Lambert, Andrew. 'The Royal Navy's White Sea Campaign of 1854'. In *Naval Power and Expeditionary Wars: Peripheral Campaigns and New Theatres of Naval Warfare*, edited by Bruce Elleman and S. C. M. Paine, 29–44. New York: Routledge, 2011.

Lambert, Andrew and Stephen Badsey. *The Crimean War: The War Correspondents*. Stroud: Alan Sutton, 1994.

Laws, M. E. S. 'Beatson's Bashi Bazooks'. *Army Quarterly and Defense Journal* 71(1955): 80–5.

Lemaire, Jean-François. 'Anestésie'. In *Dictionnaire du Second Empire*, 62. Paris: Fayard, 1995.

Lemaire, Jean-François. 'Service de santé militaire'. In *Dictionnaire du Second Empire*, 1195–6. Paris, Fayard, 1995.

Lewis, Bernard. *The Emergence of Modern Turkey*. London: Oxford University Press, 1961; 3rd edn 2002.

Luddy, Maria, ed. *The Crimean Journals of the Sisters of Mercy 1854–56*. Dublin: Four Courts Press, 2004.

Luxenburg, Norman. 'England and the Caucasus during the Crimean War'. *Jahrbücher für Geschichte Osteuropas* 16 (1968): 499–504.

Maag, Georg, Wolfram Pyta and Martin Windisch, eds. *Der Krimkrieg als erster europäischer Medienkrieg*. Berlin: Lit Verlag, 2010.

Manfredi, Cristoforo. *La spedizione sarda in Crimea nel 1855–56*. Rome: E. Vojhera, 1896; repr. Rome: Regionale, 1956.

Mange, Alyce Edith. *The Near Eastern Policy of the Emperor Napoleon III*. Urbana: University of Illinois Press, 1940; repr. Westport, CT: Greenwood Press, 1975.

Markovits, Stefanie. *The Crimean War in the British Imagination*. Cambridge: Cambridge University Press, 2009.

Marriott, John. *The Eastern Question: An Historical Study in European Diplomacy*. Oxford: Oxford University Press, 1917; 4th edn 1940; repr. 1969.

Marroin, Auguste. *Histoire médicale de la flotte française dans la mer Noire, pendant la guerre de Crimée*. Paris: J.-B. Baillière et fils, 1861.

Martin, Kingsley. *The Triumph of Lord Palmerston: A Study of Public Opinion in England before the Crimean War*. London: Allen & Unwin, 1924; repr. London: Hutchinson, 1963.

Martin, Thedore. *The Life of His Royal Highness the Prince Consort*, vol. 3. London: Smith, Elder, & Co., 1878.

McDonald, Lynn, ed. *The Collected Works of Florence Nightingale*, vol. 14, *The Crimean War*. Waterloo, Ontario: Wilfrid Laurier University Press, 2010.

Meiboom, Siegmund. *Studien zur deutschen Politik Bayerns in den Jahren 1851–1859*. Munich: Kommission für Bayer. Landesgesch., 1931; repr. Aalen: Scientia-Verlag, 1974.

Mel'nikova, Ljubov' V. *Russkaja Pravoslavnaja cerkov' i Krymskaja vojna 1853–1856 gg*. Moscow: Kučkovo pole, 2012.

Mercer, Patrick. *'Give them a Volley and Charge!' The Battle of Inkermann 1854*. Staplehurst: Spellmount, 1998.

Mismer, Charles. *Souvenirs d'un Dragon de l'Armée de Crimée*. Paris: Librairie Hachette, 1887.

Mitra, S[iddha] M[ohana]. *The Life and Letters of Sir John Hall*. London: Longmans, Green and Co., 1911.

Monier, Luc. *Étude sur la guerre de Crimée*. Geneva: Librairie Droz, 1977.

Monsieur Vincent [de Paul] vit encore . . . Sa survie par ses Filles de la Charité au long des siècles. Paris: Les Filles de la Charité, 1960.

Mosse, Werner E. *The Rise and Fall of the Crimean System, 1855–71: The Story of a Peace Settlement*. London: Macmillan, 1963.

Murphy, David. *Ireland in the Crimean War*. Dublin: Four Courts Press, 2002.

Murphy, J. J. W. 'An Irish Sister of Mercy in the Crimean War'. *Irish Sword 5* (1962): 251–61.

Naumova, Julija, A. *Ranenie, bolezn' i smert'. Russkaja medicinskaja služba v Krymskuju vojnu 1853–1856 gg*. Moscow: Regnum, 2010.

Nifontov, A. S. 'Vnešnjaja torgovlja Rossii vo vremja vostočnoj vojny 1853–1856 gg.'. In *Problemy social'no-ėkonomičeskoj istorii Rossii. Sbornik statej*, 69–90. Moscow: Akademija nauk SSSR, Institut istorii, 1971.

Nightingale, Florence. *Collected Works*, vol. 14: *The Crimean War*, edited by Lynn Mcdonald. Waterloo, Ontario: Wilfrid Laurier University Press, 2010.

Nistor, Ion. I. 'Die Polenlegion im Krimkriege'. *Codrul Cosminului 9* (1935): 69–102.

Nistor, Ion. I., ed. *Corespondenţa lui Coronini din Principate. Acte şi Rapoarte din Iunie 1854–Martie 1857*. Czernowitz: Glasul Bucoviniei, 1938.

Nomikos, Eugenia Voyiatzis. *The International Position of Greece during the Crimean War*. PhD thesis, Stanford University, CA, 1962.

Osbon, G. A. 'The First of the Ironclads: The Armoured Batteries of the 1850s'. *Mariner's Mirror 50* (1964): 189–98.

Osbon, G. A. 'The Crimean Gunboats'. *Marriner's Mirror 51* (1965): 103–16.

Otero, Luis Mariñas. 'España ante la guerra di Crimea'. *Hispania. Revista española de historia 26* (1966): 410–46.

Pamuk, Şevket. *The Ottoman Empire and European Capitalism, 1820–1913: Trade, Investment, and Production*. Cambridge: Cambridge University Press, 1987.

Parry, A. 'American Doctors in the Crimean War'. *South Atlantic Quarterly 54* (1955): 478–90.

Pawlicowa, Marja. 'O formacjach Kozackich w czasie wojny krymskiej'. *Kwartalnik Historyczny 60* (1936): 3–50, 622–55.

Pemberton, W. Baring. *Battles of the Crimean War*. London: Batsford, 1962.

Pennanéac'h, J. 'Un centenaire: le choléra nautique de la mer Noire (1854–1856). Étude épidemiologique'. *Revue de la médicine navale 11* (1856): 177–201.

Petrosjan, J. A., ed. *Vnešneėkonomičeskie svjazi Osmanskoj imperii vo novoe vremja (konec XVIII – načalo XX v)*. Moscow: Nauka, 1989.

Petrow, A. N. *Der Russische Donaufeldzug im Jahre 1853/54*. Berlin: Mittler, 1891.

Pirogov, Nikolaj I. *Sevastopol'skie pis'ma i vospominanija*. Moscow: Izd. Akademija nauk SSSR, 1950.

Pischedda, Carlo, ed. *Camillo Cavour. Epistolario*, vols 10–13. Florence: Olschki, 1985–92.

Poirier, J. L. 'Questions sanitaires pendant la guerre de Crimée'. In *Les empires en guerre et paix 1793–1860. Journées franco-anglaises d'histoire de la Marine. Portsmouth, 23–26 mars 1988*. Actes recueillis et présentés par Edward Freeman, 245–65. Vincennes: Service Historique de la Marine, 1990.

Ponting, Clive. *The Crimean War: The Truth behind the Myth*. London: Chatto & Windus, 2004.

Poschinger, Heinrich von, ed. *Preußens auswärtige Politik 1850 bis 1858. Unveröffentlichte Dokumente aus dem Nachlasse des Ministerpräsidenten Otto Frhrn. v. Manteuffel*, vols 2–3. Berlin: Mittler und Sohn, 1902.

Pottinger Saab, Ann. *The Origins of the Crimean Alliance*. Charlottesville: University Press of Virginia, 1977.

Puryear, Vernon J. *England, Russia, and the Straits Question, 1844–1856*. Berkeley: University of California Press, 1931; repr. Hamden, CT: Archon, 1965.

Puryear, Vernon J. *International Economics and Diplomacy in the Near East: A Study of British Commercial Policy in the Levant,1834–1853*. Stanford, CA: Stanford University Press, 1935; repr. Hamden, CT: Archon, 1965.

Quatrelles L'Épine, Maurice. *Le Maréchal de Saint-Arnaud*, vol. 2. Paris: Plon, 1929.

Rappaport, Helen. *No Place for Ladies: The Untold Story of Women in the Crimean War*. London: Aurum Press, 2007; new edn Brighton: Victorian Secret Ltd, 2013.

Rath, Andrew. *The Crimean War in Imperial Context*. Basingstoke: Palgrave Macmillan, 2015.

Rauchensteiner, Manfried, ed. *Feldmarschall Heinrich Freiherr von Hess. Schriften aus dem militärwissenschaftlichen Nachlaß*. Osnabrück: Biblio Verlag, 1975.

Reid, James J. *Crisis of the Ottoman Empire: Prelude to Collapse, 1839–1878*. Stuttgart: Steiner, 2000.

Ritter, Monika. *Frankreichs Griechenland-Politik während des Krimkrieges. (Im Spiegel der französischen und bayerischen Gesandtschaftsberichte 1853–1857.)*. PhD thesis, Munich, 1967.

Roads, C. H. *The British Soldier's Firearm 1850–1864*. London: Jenkins, 1964.

Roche, M. 'L'assistance médicale française à Constantinople durant la guerre de Crimée'. *Médicine et armées* 8 (1980): 629–34.

Roger Fenton: Photographer of the 1850s. London: South Bank Board, 1988.

Rousset, Camille. *Histoire de la guerre de Crimée*, vols 1–2. Paris: Hachette, 1977; 2nd edn 1978.

Royle, Trevor. *Crimea: The Great Crimean War, 1854–1856*. London: Little, Brown and Company, 1999; repr. London: Abacus, 2010.

Russell, William Howard. *The War*, vols 1–2. N.p.p: n.p., 1855–6. Vol. 1: *From the Landing at Gallipoli to the Death of Lord Raglan, 1855*. Vol. 2: *From the Death of Lord Raglan to the Evacuation of the Crimea, 1856*.

Russkij sever i Rossija v godu Krymskoj vojny, 1853–1856 gg. Vologda: Volog. gosud. pedag. inst., 1979.

Saul, Norman E. *Distant Friends: The United States and Russia, 1763–1867*. Lawrence: University Press of Kansas, 1991.

Šavšin, Vladimir. *Balaklava*. Simferopol: Tavrija, 1994; 3rd edn Simferopol: Biznes-Inform, 2016.

Schiemann, Theodor. *Geschichte Rußlands unter Kaiser Nikolaus I.*, vol. 4. Berlin: Reimer, 1919.

Schroeder, Paul W. *Austria, Great Britain, and the Crimean War: The Destruction of the European Concert*. Ithaca, NY: Cornell University Press, 1972.

Seaton, Albert. *The Crimean War: A Russian Chronicle*. London: Batsford, 1977.

Selby, John. *Balaclava: Gentlemen's Battle*. London: Hamilton, 1970.

Senner, Martin. *Die Donaufürstentümer als Tauschobjekt für die österreichischen Besitzungen in Italien (1853–1866)*. Stuttgart: Steiner, 1988.

Senner, Martin. 'La guerre de 1856 n'aura pas lieu. Ein "Scheinkriegsrat" Napoleons III.'. *Militärgeschichtliche Mitteilungen* 54 (1995): 31–59.

Shaw, Stanford S. and Ezel Kural Shaw. *History of the Ottoman Empire and Modern Turkey*, vol. 2. Cambridge: Cambridge University Press, 1977.

Shepherd, John. 'The Civil Hospitals in the Crimea (1855 1856)'. *Proceedings of the Royal Society of Medicine* 69 (1966): 199–204.

Shepherd, John. *The Crimean Doctors: A History of the British Medical Service in the Crimean War*, vols 1–2. Liverpool: Liverpool University Press, 1991.

Simon, Michael. *Die Außenpolitik Hessen-Darmstadts während des Krimkrieges. Unter besonderer Berücksichtigung der mittelstaatlichen Beziehungen zu England und Frankreich*. Frankfurt: Keip, 1977.

Sinno, Abdel-Raouf. *Deutsche Interessen in Syrien und Palästina 1841–1898. Aktivitäten religiöser Institutionen, wirtschaftliche und politische Einflüsse*. Berlin: Baalbek-Verlag, 1982.

Skrickij, Nikolaj Vladimirovič. *Krymskaja vojna 1853–1856 gody*. Moscow: Veče, 2006.

Slade, Adolphus. *Turkey and the Crimean War*. London: Smith, Elder and Co., 1867.

Small, Hugh. *The Crimean War: Queen Victoria's War with the Russian Tsars*. Stroud: Tempus, 2007; 2nd edn 2019.

Sorokina, T. S. 'Russian Nursing in the Crimean War'. *Journal of The Royal College of Physicians of London* 29 (1995): 57–63.

Soutou, Georges-Henri, ed. *Napoléon III et l'Europe. 1856: le congrès de Paris*. Versailles: Éd. Arthys, 2006.

Spahr, Frank. *Die Ausbreitung der Cholera in der britischen Flotte im Schwarzen Meer während des Krimkrieges im August 1854. Eine Auswertung von Schiffsarztjournalen der Royal Navy*. Frankfurt: Lang, 1989.

Stanmore, Baron (Arthur Hamilton Gordon). *Sidney Herbert, Lord Herbert of Lea: A Memoir*, vol. 1. London: John Murray, 1906.

Stauch, Martin. *Im Schatten der Heiligen Allianz. Frankreichs Preußenpolitik von 1848 bis 1857*. Frankfurt: Lang, 1996.

Stavrianos, Leften S. *The Balkans since 1453*. New York: Rinehart, 1958; repr. New York: New York University Press, 2005.

Stephan, John J. 'The Crimean War in the Far East'. *Modern Asian Studies* 3 (1969): 257–77.

Strachan, Hew. 'Soldiers, Strategy and Sevastopol'. *Historical Journal* 21 (1978): 303–25.

Strachan, Hew. *European Armies and the Conduct of War*. London: Allen & Unwin, 1983.

Strachan, Hew. *Wellington's Legacy: The Reform of the British Army, 1830–54.* Manchester: Manchester University Press, 1984.

Strachan, Hew. *From Waterloo to Balaclava: Tactics, Technology, and the British Army, 1815–1854.* Cambridge: Cambridge University Press, 1985.

Strachey, Lytton and Roger Fulford, eds. *The Greville Memoirs 1814–1860*, vol. 7. London: Macmillan, 1938.

Straube, Harald. *Sachsens Rolle im Krimkrieg.* PhD thesis, Erlangen, 1952.

Sweetman, John. 'Military Transport in the Crimean War, 1854–1856'. *English Historical Review* 88 (1973): 81–91.

Sweetman, John. *War and Administration: The Significance of the Crimean War for the British Army.* Edinburgh: Scottish Academic Press, 1984.

Sweetman, John. 'Ad Hoc Support Services during the Crimean War, 1854–6: Temporary, Ill-Planned and Largely Unsuccessful'. *Military Affairs* 52 (1988): 135–40.

Sweetman, John. *Raglan: From the Peninsula to the Crimea.* London: Arms and Armour Press, 1993; 2nd edn Barnsley: Pen & Sword, Military, 2010.

Tarle, Evgenij V. *Krymskaja vojna*, vols 1–2. Moscow and Leningrad: Izd. Akademii Nauk SSSR, 1941–3; 4th edn Moscow: n.p., 1959; repr. Moscow: Izografus, 2003.

Tate, Trudi. *The Crimean War.* London: I.B. Tauris, 2019.

Temperley, Harold. *England and the Near East: The Crimea.* London: Longmans, Green, 1936; repr. Hamden, CT: Archon, 1964.

Tibawi, Abdul Latif. *British Interests in Palestine, 1800–1901: A Study of Religious and Educational Enterprise.* London: Oxford University Press, 1961.

Todorova, Maria N. 'The Greek Volunteers in the Crimean War'. *Balkan Studies* 25 (1984): 539–63.

Tolstoy, Leo. *The Sebastopol Sketches.* Harmondsworth and New York: Penguin Books, 1986.

Totleben, Èduard I. *Opisanie oborony goroda Sevastopolja*, vols 1–2. St Petersburg: Tip. N. Tiblena i Komp., 1863–74; repr. Moscow: Principium, 2017.

Totleben, Eduard von. *Die Vertheidigung von Sewastopol*, vol. 2. St Petersburg: Thieblin, 1869.

Treue, Wilhelm. *Der Krimkrieg und seine Bedeutung für die Entstehung der modernen Flotten.* Göttingen: Musterschmidt, 1954; 2nd edn Herford: Mittler, 1980.

Unckel, Bernhard. *Österreich und der Krimkrieg. Studien zur Politik der Donaumonarchie in den Jahren 1852–1856.* Lübeck: Matthiesen Verlag, 1959.

Valsecchi, Franco, ed. *Le relazioni diplomatiche fra l'Austria e il Regno di Sardegna*, III series, 1848–1860, vol. 4. Rome: Istituto Storico Italiano per l'età moderna e contemporanea, 1963.

Van Alstyne, Richard W. 'Great Britain, the United States, and Hawaiian Independence, 1850–1855'. *Pacific Historical Review* 4 (1935): 15–24.

Van Alstyne, Richard W. 'Anglo-American Relations, 1853–1857'. *American Historical Review* 42 (1936–7): 491–500.

Weigand, Katharina. *Österreich, die Westmächte und das europäische Staatensystem nach dem Krimkrieg (1856–1859).* Husum: Matthiesen, 1997.

Wemyss, Rosslyn. *Memoirs and Letters of the Right Hon. Sir Robert Morier from 1826 to 1878*, vol. 2. London: Arnold, 1911.

Wentker, Hermann. *Zerstörung der Großmacht Rußland? Die britischen Kriegsziele im Krimkrieg.* Göttingen: Vandenhoeck & Ruprecht, 1993.

Wernet, Inge and Dieter. *Die Belagerung von Sevastopol 1854–1855.* Aix-la-Chapelle: Helios, 2017.

Werth, German. *Der Krimkrieg. Geburtsstunde der Weltmacht Rußland.* Erlangen: Straube, 1989.

Wimpffen, Alfons. *Erinnerungen aus der Walachei während der Besetzung durch die oesterreichischen Truppen in den Jahren 1854–1856.* Vienna: Gerold, 1878.

Winkle, Stefan. *Geißeln der Menschheit. Kulturgeschichte der Seuchen.* Düsseldorf: Artemis and Winkler, 1997; 3rd edn 2005; repr. 2014.

Woodham-Smith, Cecil. *Florence Nightingale, 1820–1910.* New York: McGraw-Hill, 1951.

Woodham-Smith, Cecil. *The Reason Why.* London: Constable, 1953.

Zaiončkovskij, Andrej M. *Vostočnaja vojna 1853–1856 gg. v svjazi s sovremennoj ej političeskoj obstanovkoj*, vols 1–2. St Petersburg: Ėncopedija Zagotovlenija Gosudarstvennych Bumag, 1908–13; repr. St Petersburg: Poligon, 2002.

Zverev, Boris I. *Sinopskoe sraženie.* Moscow: Izd. Znanie, 1953.

GENERAL INDEX